AIRLINE INDUSTRY

Many business sectors have been, and are being, forced to compete with new competitors – disrupters of some sort – who have found new ways to create and deliver new value for customers, often through the use of technology that is coupled with a new underlying production or business model, and/or a broad array of partners, including, in some cases, customers themselves. Think about the disruption created by Apple by the introduction of the iPod and iTunes, and by Netflix within the entertainment sector using partners within the ecosystem; think of Uber that didn't build an app around the taxi business but rather built a mobility business around the app to improve customer experience.

Airline Industry considers whether the airline industry is poised for disruptive innovations from inside or outside of the industry. Although airlines have a long history of continuous improvements and innovation, few of their innovations can be classified as disruptive. The few disruptive innovations that did emerge were facilitated, for example by new technology (jet aircraft) and government policy (deregulation). Now there are new forces in play – customers who expect to receive products that are more personalized and experience-based throughout the entire journey, new customer interfaces (via social media), advanced information systems and analytics, financially powerful airlines based in emerging nations, and the rise of unencumbered entrepreneurs who think differently, as well as platform-focused integrators.

Nawal K. Taneja has over 45 years of experience in the airline industry sector, having worked for and advised major airlines and related businesses worldwide. His experience also includes the presidency of a small airline that provided schedule and charter service with jet aircraft and the presidency of a research organization that provided consulting services to the air transportation community throughout the world.

AIRLINE INDUSTRY

Poised for Disruptive Innovation?

Nawal K. Taneja

Routledge
Taylor & Francis Group

LONDON AND NEW YORK

First published 2017
by Routledge
2 Park Square, Milton Park, Abingdon, Oxon OX14 4RN

and by Routledge
711 Third Avenue, New York, NY 10017

Routledge is an imprint of the Taylor & Francis Group, an informa business

British Library Cataloguing in Publication Data
A catalogue record for this book is available from the British Library

Library of Congress Cataloging in Publication Data
Names: Taneja, Nawal K., author.
Title: Airline industry : poised for disruptive innovation? / Nawal K. Taneja.
Description: Abingdon, Oxon ; New York, NY : Routledge, 2016.
Identifiers: LCCN 2016007982| ISBN 9781472484017 (hardback) |
ISBN 9781315566429 (ebook)
Subjects: LCSH: Airlines. | Disruptive technologies.
Classification: LCC HE9776.T3577 2016 | DDC 338.7068/4–dc23
LC record available at http://lccn.loc.gov/2016007982

ISBN: 978-1-4724-8401-7 (hbk)
ISBN: 978-1-315-56642-9 (ebk)

Typeset in Bembo
by Wearset Ltd, Boldon, Tyne and Wear
Printed and bound by CPI Group (UK) Ltd, Croydon, CR0 4YY

Dedicated to Angela, Matthew, and Sophia.

CONTENTS

FIGURES

TABLES

MORE ABOUT THE BOOK

Disruptive innovation, the creation and delivery of new value to customers, is not a new concept within the global airline industry. In the past it was facilitated, for example, when game-changing aircraft entered the marketplace and when governments changed their policies, enabling low-cost carriers (LCCs) to enter the marketplace. It could happen again, claims Nawal Taneja, given the shift in power from businesses to customers enabled by a much broader array of technologies (both relating to the aircraft and consumers), new distributors, changes in regulations, and dramatically changing behavior of customers (for example, the desire for, and the ability to obtain, choice). It could also happen if the new competitive hybrid airlines develop new value propositions, not to mention external businesses developing compelling value propositions for products and services in the space between airlines and their customers.

The author, an acknowledged airline business strategist, claims that uncertainty within the airline industry relates only to the timing, intensity and pace of disruptive innovation. While most airline leaders do see the need for disruptive innovation to remain viable, only a few think they have the necessary resources (especially the resources required to create a relevant corporate culture) and the risk tolerance to undertake truly innovative initiatives. Nevertheless, there are a few airline leaders committed to creating and leveraging innovation strategies and using a structured approach to achieve a profitable and sustainable growth in the hyper-competitive market in which customers are in control. At the other end, airlines working with a business-as-usual mindset and culture for incremental changes only, believing that barriers to disruptive innovation are too strong (government regulations, the complexity of the airline business, constraints of legacy systems and the power of the labor force) could be disrupted in the long run, lose profit share, or even be acquired by more adaptive airlines, or simply become irrelevant.

In this book, the author:

- interprets the concept of disruptive innovation – basically, a sudden and abrupt change, or shock – based on the thought leadership of globally acclaimed experts, what C-Suites of different businesses are doing about it, what disruptive innovation means to them and how to get there;

- discusses the relevance of disruptive innovation to the global airline industry, and provides an overview of the contemporary disruptive forces and their convergence, as well as a wide range of strategies adopted by airlines and other members in the travel value chain, such as airports and mobility facilitators;
- illustrates how adaptive airlines can pursue disruptive innovation or at least implement some forms of dynamic and transformational changes to create and/or deliver new value by re-defining what is possible to meet the needs of a growing number of customers for simplicity, reliability and affordability, as well as the availability of personalized and experience-based services;
- recognizes and shows examples of how disruptive innovation has either been facilitated or obstructed by government policies and how committed entrepreneurs have worked with and around the government policies to achieve their goals;
- examines how an airline can move away from providing basic transportation from a jet bridge at airport A to one at airport B to become a retailer and provider of customer experience, preempting, in some ways, customers to become "owned" by other businesses than the airlines;
- contemplates how to build a better relationship with customers by providing relevant choice of products and services, by integrating within the digital ecosystem and by providing a balance between the privacy of information and the intimacy of service aspects; and
- points out that a key barrier to the implementation of disruptive innovation is the increasing gap between technological capability and organizational capability – mostly in the context of organizational culture and human skills.

As with the other eight books in this series, the author challenges and encourages C-Suites to think differently, this time about the potential for disruptive innovation, in general, and the potential areas for, and layers of, disruptive innovation, in particular. The author's work is accompanied at the beginning in the Forewords by the perspectives on the theme of the book by numerous senior executives from the airline sector and related businesses and, at the end, by numerous Thought Leadership Pieces contributed by a broad spectrum of practitioners with diverse insights.

Nawal Taneja's career in the global airline industry spans 45 years. As a practitioner, he has worked for and advised major airlines and airline-related businesses worldwide, facilitating their business strategies. His experience also includes the presidency of a small airline that provided schedule and charter services with jet aircraft, and the presidency of a research organization that provided advisory services to the air transportation community worldwide. Within the academic community, he has served as Professor and Chairman of Aerospace Engineering and Aviation Department at the Ohio State University, and an Associate Professor in the Department of Aeronautics and Astronautics of the Massachusetts Institute of Technology. Within the government sector, he has been recognized as an influential thinker and has advised worldwide Departments of Civil Aviation, Finance, Economics, and Tourism on matters relating to the role of governments in facilitating the development of the aviation sector to promote travel and tourism and enhance economic growth.

He has also served on the Boards of both public and private organizations and continues to be invited as a keynote speaker at industry conferences worldwide, and continues to advise senior executives in airlines and related businesses as well as senior government policymakers on managing the:

- changing dynamics of the global aviation industry (evolving consumers, competitors, infrastructure, government policies, and technologies – information and aircraft); and
- evolving airline business models (based on market fragmentation and segmentation, organizational structures, aircraft technology, and new-generation information and enabling technologies, social media, as well as best global business practices).

At the encouragement of and for practitioners in the global airline industry he has authored eight other books:

- *Driving Airline Business Strategies through Emerging Technology* (2002)
- *Airline Survival Kit: Breaking Out of the Zero Profit Game* (2003)
- *Simpli-Flying: Optimizing the Airline Business Model* (2004)
- *Fasten Your Seatbelt: The Passenger is Flying the Plane* (2005)
- *Flying Ahead of the Airplane* (2008)
- *Looking Beyond the Runway: Airlines Innovating with Best Practices while Facing Realities* (2010)
- *The Passenger Has Gone Digital and Mobile: Accessing and Connecting through Information and Technology* (2011)
- *Designing Future-Oriented Airline Businesses* (2014)

All eight books were published by the Ashgate Publishing Company (now part of Routledge) in the UK.

He holds a Bachelor's degree in Aeronautical Engineering (First Class Honors) from the University of London, a Master's degree in Flight Transportation from MIT, a Master's degree in Business Administration from MIT's Sloan School of Management, and a Doctorate in Air Transportation from the University of London.

FOREWORD

Ben Baldanza

Chief Executive Officer
Spirit Airlines

Innovation has been a hallmark of the airline industry. Since the first flying machines became a reality, companies have tried to make money flying passengers and freight on airplanes. Many of these companies have failed, but others have thrived. Those who have innovated, both in their original design and in reaction to changing environments, have proven the most sustainable.

Following the deregulation of pricing and scheduling of the US airline industry in the late 1970s, the US industry has seen a lot of innovation. Southwest Airlines brought a new and simpler form of air travel to millions once they moved from their original in-state (Texas) only network. Southwest didn't serve meals, didn't sell through travel agents, had no first class, and differentiated themselves in other ways too. These things "just weren't what airlines did" back then. But look at Southwest today, and you see the juggernaut that they have become by sticking to their guns, and showing a bold willingness to be different.

MGM Grand tried all-first-class service between New York and Los Angeles, but this was short-lived. Similarly, Legend tried using a loophole in the Wright Amendment to fly premium-only service from Love Field in Dallas. Internationally, EOS flew all business class configured 757s from New York to London. These airlines all failed, but they all clearly tried something that wasn't in vogue at the time.

In the early 2000s, the US airline world seemed to look like big airlines, eight of them in all, plus Alaska Airlines and the new upstart named jetBlue. They changed the standard of what would be considered normal for coach travel by offering TVs in every seat and made JFK something more than an international gateway. In the 1980s, officials in Syracuse, NY asked American Airlines to consider non-stop service to New York. American offered service to JFK, and the Syracuse officials responded "We want service to NY, not JFK." How things have changed!

In the 2000s, Allegiant Travel realized that not only those in big cities needed to travel, and everyone wanted service to places like Las Vegas and Orlando. Using old but reliable airplanes, they have established a new model that has little competition and has been soundly profitable. In the mid-2000s, Spirit Airlines changed from a full-service, low-fare airline (which lost money) into North America's first "Ultra Low Cost Carrier" focusing on only the most price-sensitive travelers. While innovations like a fully unbundled pricing structure, subscription based discounts, and using charges to modify consumer behavior were not all originally embraced by customers and the media, they have proven to be highly resilient and show the power of sticking to a good idea when that idea is based on a fundamental truth. In Spirit's case, that truth is that many people like low fares more than they like fleeting luxuries onboard.

Innovations in the US airline space have occurred in all aspects of the business. How the planes are configured, how they are financed, how the pricing structure works, how tickets are distributed, how technology has both lowered costs and made airplanes safer, how retirees are treated, how mechanics get information about the machines they need to repair, the airports themselves, and many other areas of this complex business have seen significant changes, some of which have stuck and some that died on the vine. This process continues. While no one can predict the future with certainty, it is safe to say that the airlines that continue to innovate, try new things, and push boundaries are more likely to grow and succeed than those that don't.

Nawal Taneja has followed these changes for years and has written many books about the fast-changing landscape of the world airline business. Rather than dismiss the odd idea, he embraces it to see if there is validity in the idea and if this idea could transform the industry in positive ways. This newest book is sure to be thought-provoking, well researched, and written to give anyone with an interest in the airline business a fresh way to think about age-old problems. Bravo!

Fort Lauderdale, USA

FOREWORD

Alex Cruz

Chairman and Chief Executive Officer
British Airways

In aviation, if you are not feeling disrupted, you are not taking your job seriously. And no, I am not talking about fuel price, currency, or supplier costs – they have always "disrupted" us. I am talking about the digital world and the way in which we conduct business with our passengers. Don't take refuge on the fact that there is no real Uber or Airbnb for airplane tickets – our digital disruption is around the corner, being built right now, as you read this book, somewhere around the world, in a garage with limited funding. And your job is to acknowledge it and prepare yourselves for it – or you will not survive (as many others have not survived earlier disruptions!). Nawal's book, illustrative as always, is an excellent first step in your preparation process. It will certainly get you going and thinking about how you and your team can work on your commercial digital anti-disruptors.

London, England

FOREWORD

Pieter J. Th. Elbers

President and Chief Executive Officer
KLM Royal Dutch Airlines

When I read the key question of this book – whether the airline industry is poised for disruptive innovation – I was wondering whether the industry hasn't been influenced and changed by innovation and even mild disruption for years. Especially with the advent of new business models (e.g. low-cost carriers LCCs) and customer interface (social media), disruption has become a fact of our lives and almost "the new normal" we all have to deal with. Therewith, the question is not "will the airline industry be poised for disruption," but what (disruptive) innovations will drive it, how, and by whom.

So who will be driving these disruptive innovations? It can be questioned if a business can intentionally disrupt itself *and* control the outcomes from it. Disruption is often just a resultant; something that happens. It is the consequence of many diverse and often unexpected interactions within a complex system. This makes the outcome of disruptive innovations difficult to plan intentionally. Take for example the creation of the smartphone and the subsequent "addiction" to always being online, or the unexpected changes digitization will bring about in society. So although one can strive for innovations that disrupt existing markets (and hope to profit from it), disruption itself is not really a business model.

Innovation writer Henry Doss recently stated in an article in *Forbes*: "With most debates about strategies (such as disruption) the trouble starts when we focus on the idea or strategy, outside of the context of culture and leadership." I tend to agree with him that the idea of disruption, isolated from a cultural context, is virtually meaningless. The key to understanding disruptive events, and their threat to the status quo, lies in our culture, in ways of thinking and dominant beliefs.

He argues that it is unlikely that organizational leaders can simply call for disruption without at the same time recognizing the enormous cultural aversion against disruption. The analogy Doss uses is that of telling the dinosaurs to disrupt themselves when they don't know anything about asteroids. They might be convinced that their current biological state could be problematic, under certain rather unlikely cosmic conditions; but probably their culture would incline them to see themselves as "top-of-the-food chain creatures, doing very well, thank you."

As in the example, most organizations – including those in the airline industry – will resist disruption because their culture reinforces the belief that in principle things are okay as they are. And even when people are aware of things not being okay, it is difficult to overcome cultural barriers to disruption. As Doss reminds us: "Everyone likes change; no one likes to be changed." The problem is therefore not so much disruption itself, but *culture*.

To answer who will drive disruptive innovations, we should look toward organizations that have successfully created a culture that routinely embraces change and are able to truly question longstanding, often implicit, beliefs. This is a hard-earned, organizational capability that stems from understanding and addressing the barriers to change, rather than a call for a one-time innovation. It is this point that I wanted to highlight, for the complexity of the airline industry has given many a misguided sense of stability and an unwillingness to change.

KLM Royal Dutch Airlines prides itself on a long and successful history of pioneering and adapting to change. We co-created the hub-and-spoke concept, set up groundbreaking joint-ventures, and are at the forefront of social media (where we successfully exploited one of the more recent disruptions in our industry). The speed of change is accelerating and sometimes difficult to catch up with – let alone forestall. Consequently the gap between internal and external rate of change only seems to widen. This is especially true for carriers with legacy systems and labor relations dating back from the time the airline was established.

Hence, will the airline industry be poised for disruption? No doubt! How? New disruption will likely come from both unexpected events as well as from changes such as those currently taking place in distribution and retailing, emerging possibilities for door-to-door travel enabled by digitization or even re-defined aviation business models through partnerships with, for example, robotics or connectivity companies. By whom? Companies who are new to the industry are more likely to disrupt. They lack legacy systems and a longstanding industry culture, and often have the typical out-of-the-box "cowboy-like attitude" spread around their offices. They might fail several times, and have no problem doing that, before they punch us in the face. Even though disruption from within is doubtful, the smarter airlines do address their cultural inhibitors and prepare themselves for disruptions to come by using their tremendous capacity to execute to their advantage. Not only reactively (where older and larger airlines are hampered by their size), but by proactively pursuing options for unforeseen futures. Ultimately, the resilience of the company will determine the extent to which it can exploit new opportunities to its advantage.

So in order to profit from disruption, in the form of disruptive innovations, we as airline leaders should be comfortable challenging our assumptions and taking risks (entrepreneurially not operationally!); maybe regain some of the pioneering spirit that, as Nawal Taneja rightfully points out, is nowadays often more present outside our industry than within it. In order to successfully innovate and change the "rules of the game," we have to be willing to embrace failures and support our staff in becoming more audacious. Perhaps this is where partnerships spanning across and outside the industry will actually yield their highest value; not in disrupting innovations, but in *disrupting beliefs*.

Taneja manages, with this ninth book in the series, to be a thought leader on the ongoing challenges and opportunities facing airlines. The broad spectrum of outlined industry disruptions is highly relevant and maybe even more so the ways to prepare for them. Interesting times are ahead, and to be prepared is half the victory!

Amstelveen, the Netherlands

FOREWORD

Michael Issenberg

Chairman and Chief Executive Officer
AccorHotels Asia Pacific

In the past decade technology has been the biggest disruptor to the hospitality industry and has completely changed the way the industry works, from the birth of online travel agencies to Google Bookings, from the rise of online review sites to the advent of digital check-ins. The industry is currently going through an exciting time of growth and innovation, which is dramatically changing the way travel is booked and how travel companies communicate with their customers. The power is shifting from the service provider to the customer, with consumers now able to research, compare, and choose their travel products in a way that is actually reshaping the industry. The changes are driven by three big technology shifts – mobility, big data, and user experience. And we can see these disruptions as either a challenge or an opportunity.

For the hotel industry, one of the biggest disruptors of recent times is Airbnb. Much has been made about Airbnb as a competitor for hotels. Actually this is like comparing apples to oranges. Airbnb actually has more in common with sites such as Expedia or Priceline than with hotel brands, so it is more of an extension of the disruption wrought by online travel agencies. Unlike a hotel group such as AccorHotels, these sites are not investing in building new hotels, supporting tourism infrastructure, or training the next generation of hoteliers. Rather, they provide a range of accommodation options to choose from in one site.

In the same way that low-cost carriers (LCCs) were once considered a threat to full-service airlines, Airbnb has been considered a threat to traditional hotel accommodation. But what we have seen is that LCCs and legacy airlines can co-exist, with LCCs actually attracting new travelers, such as people who had never flown before, rather than stealing share away from traditional airlines. The advent of LCCs has meant that more people travel, more often, a point that is supported in this book by Nawal Taneja. We could look at Airbnb in a similar way because, in many cities where Airbnb has taken hold, there has not been a huge effect on hotel occupancy and revenue per available room. With rising wealth across the world, there is room for more players in the market and the emergence of new players can help speed up disruptive innovation, which is good for the industry overall.

For now, despite making forays into the business travel market, Airbnb remains – for the most part – a leisure player. There will always be some people for whom a hotel will provide more comfort, security, and assurance and who will never be open to staying in a stranger's home without the protection of staff on call and the security of knowing a building has passed fire safety standards and has proper plans in place for an emergency.

Airbnb, Expedia, and Priceline are actually technology companies rather than travel or hospitality companies, and to compete with them we need to make our technology smarter and better. This is why AccorHotels is investing 225 million euros into a five-year digital plan which aims to consolidate our position in the hospitality value chain and focuses on technology rather than on upgrading the physical features of hotel rooms.

The strategy has been crafted around eight programs and aims at three groups – customers, employees, and partners. Key components of the program include a single mobile application to target the guest journey before, during, and after their stay; better use of business intelligence and analytics to provide a more personalized service for guests; and online training programs and applications to make staff more efficient and effective.

Our industry must increasingly take lessons from digital disruptors in our own and other industries. Travelers are increasingly seeking out unique and more personalized, localized experiences. We must therefore become less standardized and offer a more personalized service to our guests. We have invested significantly in big data to ensure we can target our more than 25 million LeClub AccorHotels loyalty members to launch specific tailored promotions or experiences to them. In fact, loyalty is one of our key strengths against some of the newer disruptors. We have one of the most powerful and most generous loyalty programs in the industry and this enables us to target frequent guests and attract them back to stay with us, because we all know loyalty members stay more often and spend more when they do. Airlines understand better than most the importance of a strong loyalty program and for AccorHotels we are investing significantly in technology that can help us better meet the needs of our most loyal guests. In addition to the 25 million members we have of our own program, we recently signed an alliance with Huazhu Hotels Group in China which will give us access to their 54 million loyalty members and our recent acquisition of FRHI will deliver a further three million loyalty members to our program. Loyalty will become a key sector for digital innovation in coming years and we will see loyal customers gain more power as everyone fights to win their business.

Technology will allow us to target customers with marketing promotions, but more importantly we can use it to learn our customers' habits and preferences so that when they stay with us we can cater to their specific needs. The same could be said of airlines, who can learn much about their customers' flying patterns and preferences onboard to cater to them in a more targeted way.

While hotels used to focus only on what happened between check-in and check-out, now we need to be present at every step of the customer journey, from the idea, to the planning, to preparing for the trip to the stay itself and even afterwards.

And we need to provide better, more useful and more in-depth information to our guests. Thanks to technology, customers have come to expect more detailed information on websites they use to research their travel. Our challenge then becomes to upgrade our website with more imagery and video footage of our hotels because this is what customers have come to expect. Airlines also could certainly do more in this arena.

As more and more travelers go online to research and book their accommodation, it becomes more and more essential to be in the top few sites used to do this. This is why we launched Marketplace in 2015, opening up our digital distribution platform to independent hoteliers. Our aim is to have 10,000 properties listed in more than 320 cities around the world. We are doing this because we know that when you have more products available on your website you attract more customers. However, because we will actually curate the hotels allowed onto the site, guests will have a guarantee of quality. It is quite revolutionary for a hotel group like AccorHotels to allow non-branded properties into our network, but we are doing this to make our site more attractive to the traveling public and to make it easier for travelers to access a large selection of quality accommodation in one place. Above all, it is a customer-facing strategy and a customer-value proposition. With the increasing shift in power to the customer, we all need to ensure the customer is the focus of our business if we are to compete and this is true for both airlines and hotels.

With technology now leading change in our industry, we also need to put innovation at the core of our business. To this end, AccorHotels is looking at acquisitions of technology companies, such as our recent acquisition of French start-up Wipolo, which provides mobile and web itinerary services to help make our customers' journeys better. Including Wipolo technology into the AccorHotels app means our customers can now collect together all the information they need for their trip, including hotel information, flight information, car rental, and other bookings, all in one place for easy access.

With the rise of mobile devices, our aim is to make the AccorHotels app one of the few travel apps that our customers will keep on their phones. The app will offer assistance and services in real time to travelers on the go, while enabling us to generate additional sales and ancillary revenue. Rather than just focusing on what happens at your hotel, it is possible to expand to tourist services, transportation, meals, and activities so that guests who stay with AccorHotels have access to the best experience at any destination. These sectors of the tourism industry are now ripe for digital innovation.

We are also participating in a range of innovation incubators so that we can react to changes in the industry more quickly, or even develop our own disruptors.

What disruptive innovation has taught us is that we need to rebuild our offerings and tailor our services because this is what customers demand today. We need to more deeply understand our customers and offer them targeted services that not only meet their needs but fulfill needs they didn't even know they had. We believe we can go deeper into the guest experience than Airbnb and, as expert hoteliers, we can compete with them by offering our guests more.

Change is coming and we must all embrace this change and become more agile, more flexible, and more innovative. Instead of being afraid of disruption, we should all embrace the opportunity to replace outdated products and services, and overturn traditional business models to better meet the needs of today's travelers. Our industry has always been susceptible to change and disruption – from natural disasters to economic downturns, from airline strikes to contagious diseases – and we have proven that we can continue to grow and succeed. We should all be excited by what technology can still bring to our business and what it can mean for our customers, with digital innovation helping us to build a stronger industry.

Singapore

FOREWORD

Kay Kratky

Chief Executive Officer
Austrian Airlines

Airline business is changing in a very fast way. Years ago the main focus was on selling tickets from A to B, but now this is not enough to be successful. The overall customer experience and travel chain has to be kept in mind while designing new products and innovations.

From my point of view, essential for succeeding in the travel business industry are two major parts. At first it is important to differentiate between various needs and the role of the customer. Strictly speaking, it is mandatory to offer the customers variable ways of booking their travel experiences. Business passengers prefer other ways of booking than leisure passengers do. One key factor in this area is the managing of unmanaged travelers – no matter which segment they belong to.

This is closely linked to personalization and individualization, which are terms on everybody's lips, and this leads to the second important part. Airlines should not just sell tickets, as I mentioned in the beginning of the foreword – they should offer and, even more, sell travel experiences. The customer journey starts long before taking a step on the plane. Experiences start at the earliest stage, before even knowing where to travel – it sounds weird, but will become reality. To gain competitive advantage, it is essential to know more about the customer's wishes and preferences in order to offer tailored experiences. To make a long story short, that means the airline industry has to offer tailored, personalized and customized experiences instead of offering a mass product. The challenge is to remain scalable and to create ways of satisfying the customer's needs. Do not forget: "Over-personalization" in a way that the customer perceives as annoying and in a mis- and over-use of data is completely not what we are heading for. The customer should have the option to choose which degree of personalization and individualization fits perfectly to his or her needs.

Austrian Airlines is part of the Lufthansa Group and in the international context is a small airline-speedboat. Just a second: airline-speedboat? Yes, it is exactly what I am thinking about when I look at the company structure and processes. Our short decision-making processes can be seen as an enormous advantage and the possibility to implement projects without conceptualizing them in every little detail – agility, as referred to by Nawal Taneja in this book – and these are just a few benefits that drive innovations. This enables our approach to be a test market within the Lufthansa Group. Mostly, innovations won't be planned for years, they just happen in short time periods. We at Austrian Airlines try to act in a way like startups do. For sure, a long existing company with thousands of employees cannot completely switch to a "startup mode," but we try to become more flexible and faster. Certainly, it enormously helps to work closely together with startups and to use the brand Austrian Airlines in order to create new innovative products and place/position them on the travel market.

As an example, we recently launched our new voucher solutions. Some of you maybe would say "vouchers have existed for decades," but together with an Austrian startup we re-invented a new way to go. Our voucher solution is also a social media tool and a way to acquire new customers. FlyMeTo offers a solution which is thought of as for group gifting. A digital voucher with a certain amount will be created online and can then be spread via Facebook or e-mail to friends and other people who would like to participate in the gift. After reaching a defined amount of money the voucher will be sent in a digital format, including the names of the participants. It is a combination of friend-crowdfunding and a kind of social media tool which can be used for Christmas, weddings, or other special gifts. It is also possible to personalize the voucher by sending special airline material (e.g. airline gift balloons) and/or a printed voucher in extra-large size. As a second example we will launch a so-called "service agent in motion" program. The agents will be hosts for guests coming to Vienna airport as a first point of contact. An individually tuned service for each customer can be made in order to take individual needs into consideration. The agents are equipped with a mobile device which allows customizing the service individually with special software.

On that note, I would like to explain my point of view regarding the role of big digital and social media players like Facebook and Google in the travel sectors – a subject discussed by Nawal Taneja at some length in Chapter 4. I think it's the wrong approach to try to lock them out of the business. The travel industry is growing every year and the customer travel chain does not only include airline tickets now. One of the core businesses of Google and Facebook is to enable personalization and individualization and that is exactly the knowledge we have to use in the travel sector. I would strongly recommend cooperating in a way that customer needs will be satisfied perfectly. As an example I can mention the cooperation between Lufthansa and Google Flights in order to offer the customer experiences, which leads to another vision: We have to enable seamless customer experiences, no matter on which device.

Vienna, Austria

FOREWORD

Dermot Mannion

Deputy Chairman
Royal Brunei Airlines

Disruption is a term which often strikes terror into the hearts of airline folk; with visions of canceled flights and unhappy passengers. Perhaps that is very good preparation when it comes to dealing with the theme of disruption technology which, in and of itself, can strike very quickly and have a huge and almost immediate impact on any unsuspecting business.

So what is disruptive innovation and why is it important to the progression of our industry?

Disruption is all about changes to a product or service, or indeed a new innovation altogether which causes often abrupt changes to the status quo. In that sense, the airline industry – from its early years – has been a pioneer in disruptive innovation, especially impacting other forms of transportation, such as: intercontinental passenger shipping, railroads, and now even the mass transit bus sector. Airlines acting as "disrupters" themselves have made long-distance travel accessible and affordable to a much wider audience, connecting all corners of the globe at astonishing speed. Fast-forward a few decades, and we have seen the emergence of low-cost airlines acting as super "disrupters" to make short-haul travel much more affordable with a range of low fares and "no frills" service. For the future, the environment gets ever more interesting with the demarcation lines between full service and low cost becoming blurred. Many full-service carriers now have their own subsidiary low-cost carrier (LCC) brands and at the same time, LCCs are beginning to offer flexible business-friendly fares and are now even talking about frequent flyer programs! At the same time, the demarcation lines between long haul and short haul are themselves becoming blurred. Soon, fuel-efficient, next-generation narrow-body aircraft will be flying for up to six hours. This opens up new route possibilities which were previously thought to be too "thin" for wide-body operation.

In recent times, social media has become another very strong catalyst for disruptive innovation. I believe this is particularly good news for the smaller-scale "boutique" carriers.

There is a certain democracy in social media which enables the voices of carriers both large and small to be heard in equal measure. Costs, too, can be constrained to modest levels, making this a very powerful tool for airlines with limited spending capability. My experience has been that a small team of young, talented staffers can do a really effective job in this area.

Recently, RB was delighted to be one of only three airlines worldwide to be recognized as award winners in the inaugural International Travel Media awards for social media. The RB award-winning campaign in the UK was designed to promote Brunei as the gateway to the island of Borneo. A great achievement for an airline in the smaller-scale category, especially so in beating off stiff competition from major international travel brands. It is the perfect example of how the "democracy" of social media works, giving an equal voice to everyone.

More generally, I have also seen that a proactive social media response to service recovery issues can often turn what might otherwise have been a passenger complaint into a compliment.

Passengers understand that flight disruption can occur from time to time, despite the best efforts of all involved. What really defines the quality of the customer experience is what happens next. Did the airline respond promptly? Was I treated with respect? Did the airline take active steps to minimize the disruption and to get me to my destination as quickly as possible?

What passengers dislike most of all is the feeling of being abandoned at a time of disruption or uncertainty. Social media can play a huge role in staying in touch with passengers (and friends and relatives) at all stages of the process, giving frontline personnel some limited breathing space within which to fix the problem. Passengers are reassured to know there is someone out there with whom they can interact.

So in a very positive way social media has become a "disrupter" to flight disruption.

In my career, I have learned it is important to have the foresight to get ahead of the trend on technology. From time to time, small organizations can feel inhibited from tackling a particular challenge because they just simply do not have the expertise internally to do so.

There is always a strong case for putting yourself in the hands of the right technology partner. RB recently identified the need to upgrade our storefront internet selling capability. At the same time, Amadeus was extremely keen to find a partner to launch its latest storefront offering in Asia. The solution was obvious and the Amadeus implementation at RB went on to become a great success.

RB benefited by being "first to market" with the new offering and our customers benefited by having early access to new technology. This highlights the need for carriers to avoid the risk of trying to do too much themselves, possibly even getting in the way of the right solution, which may have been there all along.

Over the years, airline technology has already driven huge innovation in the areas of computer reservation systems, ticketless travel, satellite communications, interline connectivity, self-service check-in, loyalty programs, ancillary bundling, in-flight entertainment – the list goes on. And for customers, the choices just get ever wider: LCCs continue to drive pricing lower, while full-service carriers are offering more and more extras to attract high-yield passengers.

However, there are still areas of activity where there remains much to be done on the technology front. Passengers often still experience air travel as a mass-produced impersonal process, with continuing frustrations at various points in the journey.

So, what can airlines do to address these pressure points and transform air travel into a more personalized and streamlined experience? One essential ingredient is Big Data. Access to insights into how our customers travel – which routes, what class, add-on services, travel frequency; these analytics help build up a true picture of each passenger's profile, their preferences, and potential trip spend. Working with the right technology providers, all airlines can gather this intelligence in order to offer the right product or service, at the right time, through the right channel. Equipped with these necessary tools, airlines can become more effective in driving increased sales through up-sell/cross-sell techniques and higher conversion rates. The potential is enormous. For instance, a recent white paper which examines the evolution of merchandizing and retailing concluded that merchandizing could add as much as $130 billion in additional annual revenues for airlines by 2020.[1]

RB, together with other airlines, has been able to leverage the multiple capabilities of new technology to bring about important changes in how we streamline operations and look after our customers at all touchpoints: from pre-trip search through to check-in and boarding. And the process will not stop there. As merchandizing becomes the "name of the game," RB will continue to look to technology solutions as the focus turns ever more toward total trip personalization.

But what of the future for airports; and what improvements can passengers look forward to?

Already it seems clear that someone reading this book in ten years' time will be unlikely to be dragging their baggage for long distances through departure or arrival lounges. Thanks to the electronic tag, you are more likely to be able to track, on your smartphone, the progress of your baggage as you journey to your destination. You will also be able to determine where and when you will be reunited with your luggage, using your smartphone.

And one may not even have to use the baggage carousel. You could be more likely to be reunited with your baggage at your home or hotel. It may well take time to build confidence to the point where passengers are comfortable to leave the airport without having been reunited with their baggage. However, reliable technology is there already to make this happen.

Another challenge will be to get to the point where the passenger can transfer from curb to boarding with no delays. Airports are already rolling out beacon technology in this area to enable passenger mobile apps to interact with and navigate through the terminals of the future.

By 2020, communications specialist Ericsson[2] predicts there will be more than double the number of smartphones in circulation. More than 70 percent of the world's population will be using smartphone technology, with 90 percent having access to mobile broadband networks. What is called the "internet of things" is growing rapidly, with more devices potentially connected to more systems. And it does not stop there; 90 percent of all children of six years and older will soon be starting down the road of technology with their first handheld device.

At the same time, airlines are addressing how to make the airport experience seamless and stress-free: whether it's cutting down queues or empowering passengers to take more ownership of their journey. Once again, technology is proving to be a key enabler. From self-service kiosks and bag drops, to fast-lane security control and mobile alerts – technology is keeping passengers on the move, through the channel and device of their choice. In other words, technology has put passengers firmly in control of how they book, manage, and customize their trip, leading to a more rewarding experience.

Transformational change in the aviation industry is certainly moving in the right direction thanks to enhanced systems and processes, as well as collaborative partnerships within the airline ecosystem. However, our industry is also characterized by a multiplicity of complex factors which limit the pace of disruptive innovation: regulatory policies, constrained infrastructure, rising costs, aggressive pricing models, tighter security measures; not to mention unpredictable events which impact operational performance, such as extreme weather.

Finding ways to work around these constraints will be critical to the success of our industry as we explore opportunities to create value and enhance our business. Creativity and innovation is what will help us address the evolving demands and high expectations of travelers, to achieve the "holy grail" of a hassle-free seamless journey.

A trouble-free travel experience is precisely what passengers want more than anything else. The passenger of tomorrow will be much more self-sufficient in his/her own information/entertainment needs with smartphones and tablets. For that reason, future passengers will not be as bothered about issues such as airline IFE systems which cause carriers a great deal of cost and headache today. Instead, passenger focus will turn much more to just getting the basics right and this could be good news for airlines of all sizes. For many airlines, being able to divert resources to addressing important operational matters will be very welcome news indeed. This is a good example of where the increasing sophistication of the traveling public can be leveraged to provide airlines with more time and space to resolving problems elsewhere.

In *Airline Industry: Poised for Disruptive Innovation?*, Professor Nawal Taneja in his own very passionate and inimitable style examines the disruptive forces at work in the air travel space (economies, customers, competitors, technologies). Taneja also looks at the kind of adaptation strategy which airlines will need in order to implement constant dynamic and transformational change. Readers will be challenged to consider the impact of disruptive innovators – ultra low-cost carriers, super connectors, virtual reality systems, sophisticated digital marketers – and what these new realities could mean for air travel. What is clear, is that adding value to create more personalized and experience-based services will be fundamental to any successful disruptive innovation.

In my career, which has now spanned three continents with airlines of varying size and challenges, I have seen the pace of technological change accelerate rapidly over the years. The most exciting feature is the way in which "cloud" technology is now accessible to both larger and smaller organizations alike. In these circumstances, the challenge for senior management across the industry is to give the next generation of leaders the training, experience, and confidence necessary to fully exploit the opportunities which technology can provide. Let us encourage an atmosphere of collegiality and openness in our organizations in order to foster a spirit of thought and new ideas.

A random thought today can become tomorrow's great idea. In that context, this latest book by Professor Taneja will be essential reading for the young aviation leaders of the future.

Brunei

Notes

1 Martin Cowen, "The evolution of airline merchandising," commissioned by Amadeus.
2 Ericsson Mobility Report June 2015.

FOREWORD

Mike McGearty

Chief Executive Officer
CarTrawler

Bloomingdale's Don't Let Amazon Run Their Shop Window, So Why Should You?

I believe Google Flights is a bad thing for your airline. It's bad for the long-term control of your brand, and it's bad in the short and medium term for your non-air ancillary revenue. Here's why.

Disruption is a theme that has become particularly prevalent across all industries in recent years. This book, by Nawal Taneja, is an example of the challenges and opportunities for disruptive innovation within the airline industry. As technology continues to evolve and innovation happens before our eyes, the ability for companies to disrupt a traditional industry – and make millions of dollars doing so – is increasing all the time. The likes of Airbnb, WeChat, and Uber are growing proof of that.

The travel industry is no different. There are plenty of travel companies that are grabbing market share with disruptive business models around the globe. However, the fact is that, within the industry, as much as companies are thriving, there are plenty who are missing out.

So who is missing out? In short, it is the airlines. Global distribution systems and search engines have long been taking advantage of airlines' lack of technological know-how by accessing customer data at the point of purchase and making money off it.

Companies like Google and Priceline are getting immediate access to airlines' customer itineraries from the moment they book or search for a flight, giving them a direct insight into what customers want, as well as how and when they want it. These companies have a broader insight into your customers than you can possibly ever have – and are more adept at using that insight for commercial gain.

Google auctions off your customers to myriad bidders via pay-per-click (PPC) and other advertising channels. Furthermore, travel intermediaries such as eDreams and Priceline buy these insights and use them for sales leads. For all intents and purposes, it is the equivalent of retailer Bloomingdale's letting Amazon run their shop window.

Today, intermediaries can even buy advertising space on the itinerary and booking confirmation emails that your companies send to Gmail inboxes without any benefit flowing through to your airline.

Take car rental – a subject close to my own heart – as an example of an ancillary airline product. When you take into account the ancillary car rental market as a whole, just 20 percent of car rental is sold by airlines to their own customers, while the remaining 80 percent is sold by intermediaries.[1]

This is a staggering figure, particularly when you consider the natural advantage that airlines have when it comes to customers. They are at the start of the trip-planning funnel. Whenever customers think about taking a holiday or a trip, the destination – and hence the flight – comes first.

In many cases, the flight comes at least two weeks before car rental. That's a two-week lead airlines have over all of the intermediaries to take advantage and retail non-air ancillaries to their own customers.

Airlines know more about what a customer wants – and earlier – than anybody else. But the sad reality is that, largely, they don't do enough about it. By surrendering their technological right to their own customer data, airlines are making life extremely tough for themselves.

Intermediaries are continuing to get smarter as they wrestle more data away from airlines. Their sophistication is such that in the future it is not unrealistic to imagine advertisers purchasing itinerary searches in real time, and bidding on an ultra-micro level for bookings in the intermediary space in a way that pre-determines customer behavior in the future.

Airline.com will become an increasingly irrelevant sales channel.

So this begs the question, why are airlines missing out? In short, because they lack the digital platform and the supply chain to adequately run an ancillary service like car rental or airport transfers themselves. Hence, they outsource their ancillary offerings to companies such as my own so their relationships and revenues are preserved and enhanced.

Companies like Ryanair, Emirates, and Norwegian Airlines are the barometer to which airlines should aspire. Those airlines are doing more to "Amazon-ize" their relationship with customers than any other airline through ancillary products.

For example, Ryanair have prioritized the creation and growth of a highly skilled digital team, which will propel them toward their goal of completely taking over the customer relationship not just from airport to airport, but from door to door, and beach to office.

The CEO's office should be right in the middle of the company's digital team. Where is yours?

Dublin, Ireland

Note

1 Based on CarTrawler estimates from over 90 international airlines across 174 markets.

FOREWORD

Aleks Popovich

Senior Vice President
Financial and Distribution Services
International Air Transport Association

Industry innovation is central to IATA's vision:

> To be the force for value creation and innovation driving a safe, secure
> and profitable air transport industry that sustainably connects and enriches
> our world.

At the International Air Transport Association (IATA), industry innovation
is supported by regular investment in the development of new products,
services, and standards, which meet industry demand and are supported by
our Board and Industry Committees. Why we innovate is a matter of vision
and relevance. In line with our vision we aim to be the industry force for
value creation and innovation, and we also aim to ensure that our products,
services, and standards stay relevant as industry needs and technologies
evolve.

Two years ago we formed an innovation team to manage our innovation
process. We have always worked closely with our member airlines and with
strategic partners to identify ideas and opportunities. We also have an internal
network to collect ideas from our own colleagues. However, our innovation
process now also ensures that the best ideas find their way through the
required steps of market validation and funding before a business case is
approved.

During regular strategic reviews, both internally and externally with our
members and value chain partners, we welcome disruptive innovation from
two basic perspectives: as the disrupter, and as the disrupted! Indeed, innovation which delivers significant industry value is likely to carry both strategic
opportunity as well as threats for IATA. Let's start by examining one area
where innovation can be a force for IATA being disrupted.

Usually major disruption comes from outsiders. While it may be more difficult for an insider, in a leadership position, to justify any major change that
could jeopardize their own function, an outsider may take a bet in order to
conquer a new market or a new industry.

Startups have disrupted industries such as ground transport or hotels. Internet or IT companies have disrupted traditional media or music companies.

We all know of disruptive examples where part of the value chain (e.g. intermediaries) or the entire chain has been replaced. And we can also speculate on the disruptive impact of future innovation. For example, in aviation the most recent solar-power aircraft or drones are built by startups or internet companies.

Let's consider one of IATA's core businesses, which is industry settlement of funds between travel agents, forwarders, and airlines. This business dates back to 1971 with the first billing and settlement plan (BSP) in Japan. Since then IATA has managed this business on behalf of the industry, sending bills and reconciling payments. But what if payments become digital and efficient to the point that airlines, travel agents, and forwarders no longer need an intermediary? With the development of e-wallets and mobile payment, the financial services market is certainly evolving. Travel agents are evolving as well. Online travel agents, even in the corporate space with booking engines, are leading the digital transformation. Such change can have a dramatic impact on IATA's core business.

Let's consider another core business of IATA, which is developing standards for airlines and IT providers. In the age of agile developments and startups, who needs, or can wait, for standards? Messaging standards were developed at a time when IT development took years and the infrastructure was dictating the content of messages. Fast-forward to today's environment where: IT developments leverage components or objects that can be re-used; IT for airlines does not have to be different from IT in other industries; and the development and production cycles can be much shorter, indeed shorter than the industry standard development cycle. Such speed and agility is a game-changer for IATA's core business.

Now let's consider IATA as the force for innovation, where IATA can lead the disruption.

IATA is developing a global e-wallet solution for air travel. It will be live in 2016 and work with NDC, the new standard for distribution. This simple cost-effective payment method is being adapted to the NDC method for merchandizing and ancillaries. It will benefit customers with seamless experiences, and airlines with a cost-effective option. Combining distribution and payment to enable merchandizing is a game-changer.

IATA is also developing an industry data model and a developer portal. To accelerate the pace of industry standards development, as agreed by all IATA members, new messaging standards will now come in alpha and beta releases. The cycle of standard development starts with expression of need, and ends with the standard globally implemented in production. We aim to transform a traditional ten-year cycle to one of ten months: from the time decisions are made to the time a critical mass of adopters are in place. It sounds impossible today; but when it happens we can speak of disruptive standards!

There are several other examples of disruptions on our radar; for example, the impact of blockchain technology on our financial services, and use of commercial drones.

Finally, let's move from the "what" to considering the "how" of disruptive innovation. Whereas the "what" will change over time, the "how" tends to be constant. IATA's approach to industry innovation has four main drivers:

1 *We champion the global big picture.* We observe local trends and niche applications. However, we will always look at the bigger picture, connecting the dots to assess the potential for global impact. We will focus on major global themes that can make our industry sustainable and healthy.

2 *We build standards through expertise.* When we approach new themes in the form of ideas or trends, we try to bring as much expertise as possible to the table and to assess the need for an industry solution based on a standard. Typically a simple theme, not involving much expertise, or a competitive theme, where each carrier has its own edge, would be out of scope for IATA.

3 *We partner for mutual benefits.* In our strongly connected industry and complex value chain we believe that we can create more value by partnering. We are looking for the right partners who can innovate together. All partners will benefit from an enhanced process and interoperability.

4 *We act with a simple human touch.* We seek to be transparent and accountable for our actions. We focus on the end customer. Innovation will translate into simplicity and lower costs for customers.

In conclusion, I'm looking forward to reading Nawal's new book on disruptive innovation. Nawal is a close colleague and strong supporter of change in our industry. Customers will always look for more service and simplicity, and technology evolution is bringing opportunities to deliver just what customers expect. We need to stay on top of digital changes and transform them into opportunities for aviation. Only time will tell how effective each of us are in dealing with disruptive innovation, both as disrupter and as disrupted!

Geneva, Switzerland

FOREWORD

Craig Richmond

President and Chief Executive Officer
Vancouver Airport Authority

Nawal has kindly asked me to provide a foreword to his book which will discuss the airline industry response to disruptive innovation. Disruptive innovations don't come around very often. In contrast, there are innumerable examples of iterative innovations in this industry, and as with most such incremental changes, they are largely forgotten, as improvement follows improvement. On board the aircraft, books gave way to projected movies, to videos on TVs hanging above every third row, to seat-back screens, and now to extensive in-flight entertainment systems (IFE). On the ground, walking to the aircraft gave way to buses and then loading bridges with heating and cooling and then glass walls, and then twin or triple bridges. All these changes were rational and iterative but they were not disruptive (although they greatly enhanced the flying experience).

The commercial aviation industry of today is itself an incredible disruptive innovation in the course of human affairs – a vastly productive and enjoyable disruption. This remarkable mix of technology and process has enabled the safe and efficient movement of three million passengers each day, all over the world, the stuff of science fiction only a century ago. In fact, air travel has become so routine and so safe, and has woven itself so tightly into the fabric of our entire civilization that it hardly seems innovative at all.

There have been many large disruptors in this industry – the jet engine, the jumbo jet, slot controls and ultra low-cost carriers, to name a few. In any disruption there are always business winners and losers, and there are always unintended side-effects, both small and great. The growth of mega-carriers is an unexpected and significant side-effect of deregulation. Desynchronosis or "jet lag" is a new biological condition that did not exist before the jet engine, the Comet and 707.

We have all watched with trepidation innovative technology, wondering if it would negatively disrupt our industry. A decade ago, we wondered if videoconferencing would decrease the need or desire for air travel, and many predicted that it would. Videoconferencing started in elaborate, specially designed rooms and it worried us, but then it jumped to tablets and smartphones in almost no time. Applications like Skype, FaceTime, ooVoo,

Tango, Camfrog, and Viber became hugely popular overnight – but the growth in air travel has not slowed, it has accelerated.

Airport disruptive innovations have occurred in many areas. One with far-reaching effects was the changed governance structure of airports. Prior to the 1980s most airports were either run by various levels of government or the airlines. Privatized airports came onto the scene in the 1980s and changed the way airports were operated. Some became private companies (heavily regulated), some became public–private partnerships, and others went the not-for-profit authority route (e.g. Canada). Airlines and airports have had to learn how to work with each other in this new paradigm, and stop arguing over who owns the customer.

Sometimes the changes were generally invisible to the passenger but were tremendously effective. An example in this regard would be common-use check-in systems: a novelty, and then a sometimes unwelcome intrusion in the 1990s which became an industry standard by the 2000s. Lately, partially automating customs and immigration process through the use of kiosks is an example of an airport-led disruptive innovation which has been a game-changer for reducing passenger wait times. They have also increased border agency efficiency – processing more passengers with fewer resources – and decreased capital for airports by delaying the need for expanding terminals to accommodate growth. This is also a great example of a public–private partnership helping all stakeholders.

Can a government aviation policy be a disruptive innovation? I would argue that yes, it can be. It can be just disruptive (like many regulations) or it can be a positive change. A great example in our industry was deregulation, which greatly expanded access to air travel. And the recent global trend in Open Skies agreements, border policies like US Preclearance and Intransit Preclearance, and transit without visa policies, has stimulated traffic growth, increased connection opportunities, and greatly improved the travel experience.

I have come to the point in a foreword where I try to explore future disruptive innovations, but with some ground rules. For starters, let's agree that there are some physical constraints to consider when we are talking about the reasonably foreseeable future of airports. Aircraft capable of fast intercontinental travel will probably need runways and strong, connected operating surfaces. Such aircraft will have wings that dictate the size of terminals. People and baggage need to be on- and offloaded. There will be border and security rules that need to be followed. In addition, I will also try to stay away from incremental improvements, as exciting as they may be. (For example, it's not that hard to imagine the next generation IFE incorporating 3D virtual reality headsets.) Finally, I will pose my thoughts on disruption as questions.

As a start, what about slower intercontinental travel? Could there come a day when electrically propelled helium-filled rigid airships travel more lazily between major cities, like flying cruise ships? Incorporating them into our airport plans would be challenging, as they would still need to be processed.

Airports are really just big processors, so I'll start with the inevitability of security processes, which, in my opinion, greatly need disrupting. Can we not design a less intrusive process using new technology which scans passengers arriving at our airport (by bus, train, self-driving cars, or hoverboards)? As they traverse the departure area they would be cleared, without ever dropping their change in a tray, while they are shopping or strolling. This would surely be a disruption cheered by everyone on the planet.

In this idyllic terminal, new lightweight and smart materials could disrupt the current methods of terminal design and construction. Could walls act more like adjustable membranes, adapting themselves to the current conditions and traffic sectors?

For shorter city-to-city shuttles, might they leave when they are full, instead of at a predetermined time? That would certainly disrupt airport scheduling. Would this work on intercontinental flights?

Could our innovative security extend to border processes? It seems odd to me that people are trapped in a tube at 35,000 feet for 12 hours but have to wait to clear the border when they arrive and stand in lineups. I realize that there are smugglers and persons of interest, and there always will be, but the overwhelming majority of travelers are not. Can't we use that fact, and the fact that people are held quite safely and securely in an aircraft for a known period of time?

Let me pose a very bold question: why do I have to wake up to transfer aircraft on a long series of flights? Why can't we move my sleeping pod with me in it? (After all, I will have cleared customs while sleeping).

Adding these process improvements up, I can envision an airport journey where the future passenger never stands in a lineup, hands over paperwork, or has to guess where to go. They would just walk in and through the airport, doing what they fancy, and then walk onto the aircraft, doing the same in reverse upon landing. This would be a disruptive innovation which would, interestingly, bring us back to where we were in the 1920s and 1930s. Imagine that!

Vancouver, Canada

FOREWORD

Pekka Vauramo

President and Chief Executive Officer
Finnair

Disruption in aviation? If we think about operational models of airlines, the underlying structure has remained pretty similar for decades: Network airlines, mostly previous national flag carriers, running their hub-and-spoke systems, transporting passengers through these gateways to their final destination with focus on safety and punctuality. Global airline alliances have now been around for a couple of decades, enlarging respective airlines' global coverage through interline and code-share arrangements.

New aircraft types have increased operational reliability and improved both financial economics, but also had positive impact on environmental burden.

But has this industry really been disrupted yet? Probably not; I strongly feel that many big changes are still in front of us, and this book by Nawal Taneja, gives a number of insights and food-for-thought for all of us.

There has been many excuses for not changing the airline industry. It is a lot easier to continue with the status quo than actually transforming the business model. Low-cost carriers (LCCs) were the first movers into disruption; they started to destroy the status quo. Thanks to LCC growth as well as its "clean-sheet" approach and business model, the airline industry has transformed in almost all continents. We cannot imagine Europe anymore without the likes of Ryanair, easyJet and Wizz. We will see increased blends of business models, and the legacy carriers and LCCs will meet in the middle, as hybrid carriers, with all of the players picking the best of both business models. Thereby the new normal has been created.

At the same time, the Gulf carriers have dramatically disrupted the status quo among European and Asian carriers for key traffic lanes, and the Gulf ability to invest and change the global traffic flows is impressive, and has surely forced us to rethink, to innovate, to become hungry again for growth and competition. LCCs and Gulf carriers have got everybody's attention, and for a reason.

The next "big thing" will surely be in the area of technology. Digital transformation is happening as we speak. The focus is now on data-driven customer intelligence: How can we ensure we get all relevant data on customer behavior, predict consumers' future needs, search patterns, changes in e-commerce and retail? How can we as an airline compete with right, rich content, with relevant personalized offers, with ideally personalized fares, to suit that individual's willingness and ability to pay in the moment of desire to purchase? How can we be present, available, and ready to match consumers' wishes in all parts of the globe, in consumers' desired device, with tailored content?

Finnair is one of those airlines that many thought would not survive the tightened competition. With a small home market on the edge of Europe, prospects of survival were challenging. And yet, we have not only survived but we target growing significantly.

Finnair has been a pioneer in many strategic moves, being the first European airline to fly non-stop to Japan from Europe over the North Pole in the early 1980s, and first airline to benefit from Siberian routes to China, cutting the flight times considerably. Now in 2016, Finnair serves 17 Asian gateways, being one of Europe's largest carriers for Europe–Northeast Asia traffic flows.

How did we achieve that? Continuous focus on building a solid operational platform, utilizing the shorter northern routes, cutting the total travel time, and benefiting from the solid operational reliability of Helsinki airport, with 35 minutes minimum connecting time and 99 percent success rate on transit passenger connectivity reliability; these have been the foundations for Finnair's existence and position. The ability to operate to any Northeast Asian destination with a below 24-hour rotation gives us a solid base to further develop the business. But that's not enough. We want to offer a unique Nordic customer experience to our customers. The customer needs to be the focus of everything we do.

I strongly believe that the future of successful airlines will be driven around solid airline–hub airport joint management, creating powerhouses in their own right, with the ability to create fulfilling customer experiences onboard and at hub airports, giving passengers smooth travel experiences, giving satisfaction to their senses, and creating an environment in which the passengers are more likely to spend more money, enjoy the total travel experience, and commit instantly to the next offer to travel with us. With the new customer intelligence tools available, we need to be integrating cutting-edge technology with the right talents to re-invent airline business models, with strong integration with hub airports, retail, onboard experience with new technologies, like virtual reality and social networking.

We are at the beginning of a new era in the aviation industry. We will be disrupted by technology companies, so let's prepare to be the ones who participate actively in disruption and become tech-driven ourselves, with increasing customer value in the core of our business thinking. Enjoy the latest Nawal Taneja book, and let the innovation evolve!

Helsinki, Finland

FOREWORD

Chris Zweigenthal

Chief Executive
Airlines Association of Southern Africa

It is indeed a great honor and privilege for me to write this foreword to the new book by Nawal Taneja dealing with disruptive innovation. Working on the fascinating and sometimes unpredictable African continent with a focus on Southern Africa, one is often frustrated at the inability of many states and their airlines to see beyond their own specific issues, problems, and challenges and to make decisions and implement political, aviation, and business solutions that are in the best interests of their airlines and states, and indeed Africa as a whole.

Taneja has dealt in depth with examples of disruptive innovation undertaken by forward-thinking entrepreneurs and business people both within and outside the airline industry to make a difference, stretch the boundaries of conventional thinking, and to provide new value-added customer experiences which ultimately lead to the success of their companies. These are in many cases ground-breaking initiatives which have changed the face of the industry in which they operate. Current examples include the emergence and success of Uber, Google, Airbnb, Alibaba, and others. In the airline industry, a specific example of disruptive innovation is the low-cost carrier (LCC) concept pioneered by Southwest Airlines in the USA. Within Africa, however, with a few exceptions, the disruptive innovation in aviation is in fact a catch-up to the current business-as-usual practices in other areas of the world before being able to move on to new groundbreaking initiatives.

A classic example is the one of liberalization of the African skies. The 1988 Yamoussoukro Declaration failed and, subsequently, the 1999 Yamoussoukro Decision (YD) was the hope for African aviation following on the 1978 deregulation of the US skies and the EU liberalization packages of the 1990s. This provided an opportunity for African states to enable their airlines to strengthen their home domestic markets and regional traffic with their neighbors, and thereafter expand into international markets. However, there were a number of barriers to implementation, including the requirement for competition regulations, dispute resolution mechanisms, implementing provisions, the necessity to incorporate the YD into domestic legislation, and delays in setting up the relevant competition authorities and executing agency to manage the implementation of the YD. There is unfortunately also different thinking between individual states, and this initiative has never got traction on a continent-wide basis as intended, with limited states voluntarily agreeing bilaterally on the application of the YD. Disruptive innovation to catch-up with the rest of the world would involve groundbreaking decisions to implement the YD as already agreed by the African heads of state. During 2015, new initiatives have been proposed to achieve a single African aviation market by 2017 through the implementation of the YD.

Taneja makes reference to the Gulf carriers, who are excellent exponents of capitalizing on new opportunities and also exploiting the weaknesses of competitors. The lack of development and growth of African aviation due to the above intransigence has seen the three large Gulf carriers, Turkish Airlines, and several European carriers expand their operations; 30 years ago international airlines carried 40 percent of African international traffic, whereas in 2015 this number is around 82 percent. African airlines are still keen to achieve individual success and survive, but they are playing catch-up to the current strength of the international airlines flying into Africa.

The emergence of LCCs is noted by Taneja as one of the significant examples of disruptive innovation in the history of aviation. Kulula.com was formed in South Africa in 2001 and was the first major launch of a low-cost airline in Africa. This was followed in 2004 by 1time Airlines (ceased operations in 2012), Mango Airlines in 2006, Velvet Sky in 2012 (ceased operations in 2013) and later by FlySafair and Skywise in 2015. Within the rest of Africa, low-cost airlines were established in Kenya (Jambojet), Tanzania (Fly540 and fastjet), and Zimbabwe (Flyafrica). Where Africa is possibly poised to push the boundaries and experience some disruptive innovation is with the establishment of some of the above low-cost airlines which are testing the ownership and control provisions of many African states' regulations. Fastjet and FlyAfrica have the vision of being pan-African airlines with multiple states as home bases, operating multiple networks of domestic and regional services. This will test ownership and control provisions as well as the boundaries of safety oversight, as several states question the jurisdiction of these airlines. The lack of alignment and uniformity in application of ownership and control regulations could provide a challenge to the success of this model in the short to medium term. For it to be successful in Africa, states need to make a significant shift in policy. This will not happen until African airlines have achieved a "critical mass" share able to compete with global carriers, or conversely that states have given up on the priority of having their own flag carrier. They would further need to accept that a foreign airline, or preferably a well-established African airline, can form a sustainable airline operation in their state.

African aviation faces significant additional challenges and each one of these can be considered a candidate for disruptive innovation in their being overcome and preparing for global competitiveness. These challenges include the high costs of airline operations in Africa, high taxes and charges, lower than average load factors, overcoming the poor safety record in Africa on a consistent basis, maintaining aviation security in line with international best practice and skills development and transformation imperatives. An unprecedented level of government understanding and appreciation of the airline's operations and the impact of high costs, taxes and charges imposed on airlines could lead to realistic or comparable cost bases for African airlines compared to international developed and successful airlines. A commitment to the implementation of agreed upon action plans has led to significant progress being made to address the poor African safety record, with 2014 realizing a zero hull loss rate for IATA carriers. In respect of skills development and transformation, the retention of skills in Africa remains a top priority and the funding thereof an even greater challenge as the pressure for cost-effective training and in some quarters even free education gathers momentum.

I believe there are "disruptive entrepreneurs" in Africa. The problem is that the system in which they currently work is constrained by barriers to entry and does not allow them unrestricted freedom to ply their trade. Regulatory control, particularly within the airline industry in Africa, remains in place. I believe there is certainly significant scope for the relaxation of these controls to enable disruptive innovation forces to prevail in Africa. It is clear from the examples presented in this book that those who have disrupted the business and differentiated their product offering by adding value to the customer have prevailed and probably run some of the most successful businesses the world over, such as Apple, Ryanair, easyJet, and the new innovators mentioned previously, namely Uber, Airbnb, Google, etc.

What is the alternative to the airline industry? It is the safest, quickest, most effective way to transport people around the world. However, it needs to transform and find ways to keep itself attractive to its customers. One of the secrets is probably to change the interaction with the customer from a traditional "transactional" disruption (process of buying a ticket) to a "relational" disruption, thereby creating a completely new experience for the customer. Airlines are already achieving this to a limited extent through new self-service, technological, mobile, and customer-friendly offerings, but to achieve a complete disruptive innovation requires implementation of new initiatives through partnerships across the entire value chain to sell experiences instead of selling just travel.

Africa possesses the potential to unleash these disruptive innovators on the world. If they are allowed to operate, there is no saying how successful they would be. Maybe through reading this book, governments and authorities will see the opportunities out there and the real benefits that can be realized and provide the enabling environment so necessary to achieve these goals.

Johannesburg, South Africa

PREFACE

Many business sectors have been, and are being, forced to compete with new competitors – in some cases disrupters – who have found new ways to create and/or deliver new value for customers often through the use of technology that is coupled with a new underlying production or business model. The need to change business models is not new. What is different is the speed at which business models must be changed and the potential to use a much broader array of technologies and partners, including, in some cases, customers themselves. Think about the disruptions created by Apple and Netflix products in the entertainment industry. Think of Uber and Airbnb, which used the platform business models to facilitate the exchange between consumers and producers (travelers and taxi drivers in the case of Uber and travelers and homeowners in the case of Airbnb). As a result, Uber did not build an app around the taxi business but rather built a mobility business around the app to improve the customer experience. Think about Bitcoin and Blockchain – the digital platform for recording and verifying financial transactions with the potential of digital currencies disrupting the financial sector. Think about the HDFC bank in India and its digital and innovative process to approve a category of loans in literally minutes.

This book, the ninth in the series, considers whether the airline industry is poised for disruptive innovations from the inside or the outside of the industry, or both. Although airlines have a long history of continuous improvements and innovation – convenient services in long-haul markets, low-fare services, hub-and-spoke systems, loyalty programs and revenue management systems, just to name five – only a few of their innovations can be classified as disruptive innovations. The few disruptive innovations that did emerge were facilitated by external developments, for example, by new technology (jet aircraft) that led to the availability of faster, more convenient, and more affordable air travel services, and government policy (deregulation) that enabled the introduction of low-cost, low-fare airlines. Now there are new, or at least more powerful, forces in play:

- Customers, in developed markets, who expect to receive products that are more personalized, more digitalized, and more experience-based throughout the entire journey and on a micro-moment basis; customers in emerging markets, who are becoming more affluent and looking for enriching experiences in their travel; and customers in developing markets, who expect services that are reliable, affordable, more frequent and more direct.

- The accelerating pace of change, enabled by technology, has had a profound effect on consumer expectations, making them much more open to more rapid adoption of new and re-defined products and services – a development, in turn, that supports much more rapid scaling for marketplace winners (value creation), as well as greater jeopardy for marketplace losers (value destruction).
- New competitors, not just the financially powerful airlines based in the Persian Gulf, but also the increasingly prevailing hybrid airlines based in the Asia–Pacific region leveraging the new level of connectivity.
- New customer interfaces (via social media), enabling customers to not only engage with sellers on their own terms, but also other customers on a one-to-one as well as one-to-many formats.
- Mobility facilitators, leveraged by advanced information systems and customer analytics, who think differently to enter the non-flying phases through more effective customer engagement methods as well as better management of customer relationships.
- Pressure on governments in developing and emerging regions to liberalize their markets to promote air travel by creating an environment in which entrepreneurs can succeed to create and/or deliver new value for customers and service providers.

These powerful forces and their convergence and intersection, particularly in the "era of cognizance," could easily bring about disruptive innovation leading to the availability of airline services that are even more reliable from an operational point of view, more personalized, more digitalized, and more experience-based for some segments, and simply more affordable and more accessible for other segments, such as for travelers on the lower end of the travel pyramid in developing and emerging markets.

The main audience of this series continues to be senior-level practitioners of differing generations of airlines and related businesses worldwide, as well as senior-level government policymakers. The material presented continues to be at a pragmatic level, not an academic exercise, to lead managements to undertake some critical thinking about the viability and stability of their current business models as well as new business models. Based on the author's own extensive experience gained from his ongoing work in the global airline industry, as well as through a synthesis of leading business practices, both inside and outside of the industry, this book builds upon some concepts contained in previous books in this series – for example, concepts discussed on *business model innovation* as well as new thoughts such as the need to develop *innovation strategies* to improve operational and commercial performance to benefit both customers and airlines.

Based on the input provided by some readers, while continuing to present some thought-provoking concepts and promote non-conventional thinking, the mix of the content in this book has been changed. There are still numerous and lengthy forewords for readers to get the viewpoints of senior executives in airlines and related businesses. And as in the previous book there are a number of value-adding Thought Leadership Pieces contributed by insightful and experienced business analysts. However, this section has been lengthened by including an even broader group of Thought Leadership Pieces. Although these Thought Leadership Pieces cover a broad range of topics, the overall perspective is still on the theme of the book – challenges and opportunities related to disruptive innovation.

ACKNOWLEDGMENTS

I would like to express my appreciation for all those who contributed in different ways, especially my business research analyst, Angela Taneja, Peeter Kivestu (Transportation and Logistics Industry Consultant at Teradata), Dr. Dietmar Kirchner (formerly a SVP at Lufthansa and now a Senior Advisor and Co-Chairman of the International Airline Symposium Planning Committee), and Rob Solomon (formerly an VP and Chief Marketing Officer at Outrigger Enterprises and now Co-Chairman of the International Airline Symposium Planning Committee) for discussions on challenges and opportunities facing the global airline industry and related businesses. In the first group I would also like to thank all the writers of forewords at the beginning of the book and all the writers of Thought Leadership Pieces in Chapter 10.

The second group of individuals that I would like to recognize include: Accenture – Dirk-Jan Koops and Carsten Weisse; Air China – Zhihang Chi; Airlines Association of Southern Africa – Chris Zweigenthal; American Airlines – Richard Elieson; Austrian Airlines – Andrea Pernkopf; Bombardier Aerospace – Nico Buchholz; British Airways – Alun Pryer; CAPA (Centre for Aviation) – Peter Harbison, Derek Sadubin, and Binit Somaia; CarTrawler – Bobby Healy; Cii Holdings – Barry Parsons; Emirates Airline – Rob Broere; Expedia – Ike Anand; Finnair – Juha Järvinen, Jaron Millner, and Piia Karhu; Google – David Pavelko and Rob Torres; Hawaiian Airlines – Mark Dunkerley; HNA Aviation Holdings – David Liu; IATA – Eric Leopold; IBM – Steven Peterson; Inmarsat – Frederik Van Essen and Lida Mantzavinou; Lufthansa Cargo – Monika Wiederhold; MASKargo – Guo Xianqin; OAG – Phil Callow, John Grant, and Caroline Mather; Outrigger Enterprises Group – Dan Wacksman; PricewaterhouseCoopers – Jonathan Kletzel and Bryan Terry; Sabre – Angela Berry, Derek Birdsong, Stan Boyer, Rodolfo Elizondo, Michael Gerra, Ken Goldberg, Janie Hulse, Dana Jones, Paul Pederson, Kamal Qatato, Michael Reyes, Darren Rickey, Jen Sacks, Sergey Shebalov, Sam Shukla, Parminder Singh, Donald NS Unger, and George Whitney; SITA – Jürgen Kölle; United Airlines – Mark Nasr and John Slater; Vancouver Airport Authority – Gerry Bruno; and Volantio – Azim Barodawala.

Third, there are a number of authors whose work and ideas have been referenced throughout this book. They include Jake Bright, Erik Brynjolfsson,

James Canton, Mitch Cohen, Peter Diamandis, Richard Dobbs, Aubrey Hruby, Steven Kotler, James Manyika, Andrew McAfee, Albert Meige, Dayo Olopade, Jacques Schmitt, Doc Searls, John Sviokla, Bill Tancer, Don Tapscott, Ray Wang, and Jonathan Woetzel.

Fourth, there are a number of other people who provided significant help: at the Ohio State University – Jim Oppermann, Delsi Winn, Brad Wendel, and Seth Young; and at Ashgate Publishing Company, now part of Routledge (Guy Loft – Senior Editor, Aviation/Health & Safety; Laura Johnson – Editorial Assistant Economics; and Alaina Christensen – Production Editor) and Hannah Riley at Wearset; and Gary Smith, Copy Editor.

Finally, I would also like to thank my family for their support and patience.

1 PERSPECTIVES ON DISRUPTIVE INNOVATION

What Is Disruptive Innovation?

- It is reported that IKEA introduced the ideas of selling products (a) through a catalog (instead of door-to-door); (b) directly to customers (instead of through distributors); (c) through self-service processes in stores (instead of through sales staff); and (d) with unassembled parts in flat boxes (to the extent possible) to make transportation easier for the customers.
- Aldi started selling basic and long-lasting food products (for example, in cans) at low prices, then added fresh, refrigerated foods, then came up with non-food products at very low prices and deep-frozen food, then introduced some branded products, and thus expanded the product line without losing focus on price and smart processes.
- Zara evolved its strategy that started by selling reasonably priced fashion clothes similar to those from more well-known brands, followed with designing and marketing many shorter-run collections rather than the typical two per year, and then moved the production line closer to home, involving higher costs but reducing the need to discount prices heavily to move inventory.
- Sony produced state-of-the-art radios and televisions in the 1960s and 1970s, and in the 1980s brought to the market camcorders, video recorders, and digital cameras. But it was when Sony introduced the Walkman in 1979 that changed the way people listened to music.[1]
- Within the airline industry, Singapore Airlines decided from the start to (a) develop a business model based on the transportation of sixth freedom traffic; (b) renew its fleets more frequently than did its competitors; (c) offer significantly higher levels of cabin and in-flight service; (d) introduce the world's longest non-stop flight between Newark, New Jersey and Singapore (about 9,500 miles); (e) offer the Singapore Airlines Suites product (separate compartments with walls and doors); (f) introduce private jet connections in the US markets with JetSuite; and (g) offer service with four brands to cover different lengths of haul and different levels of customer service.

- Continuing within the airline industry, Laker Airways and PEOPLEx-press tried to bring air transport "to the masses." They paved the way for what became the low-cost concept.

Which part of the change in business models of these companies can be considered to be represented as an improvement, which part as an innovation, and which part as a disruption? This leads to the question of what is disruptive innovation and why is it important, not just within business sectors, but also within the government, higher education, and healthcare sectors? Is developing a better product or service considered to be disruptive innovation? Is disruptive innovation developing a product or service that meets a market need that was previously unmet? Is disruptive innovation developing a product or service that is not only less expensive, but also easier to use? As businesses improve their products at different paces and at different levels, at what point can an improvement be described as innovative and when can an innovation be described as disruptive?

Improvement represents simple and modest increases in usefulness and functionality, and innovations lead to higher levels of increase in value added to products and services. Innovation can be evolutionary or revolutionary, depending on whether it enhances value or creates new markets, or both. If an innovation is revolutionary, could it be classified as disruption? Paraphrasing one acclaimed expert, Clayton Christensen, there are two basic attributes relating to disruptive innovation, *new-market disruption* and *low-end disruption*. He explains that disruptive innovation takes place when a business transforms a once expensive and/or complicated-to-use product that had a limited number of customers. The innovative disrupter transforms the product into one that is *affordable* and *accessible* for many more buyers.[2] This transformation provides value for a much larger segment of buyers while enhancing value to existing customers. According to Christensen, disruptive innovations come from the "bottom and rise up." One could assume, then, that the mass-produced and low-priced Ford Model T represented disruptive innovation in that it made the automobile affordable to a larger segment of the population and changed the transportation systems within cities as well as the associated layout of the cities themselves in the USA. Within the computer industry, Christensen exemplifies the perspective of disruptive innovation by the progressive transformations from a mainframe to mini to desktop to laptop to smartphone. Disruptive innovation created value by making the product more affordable and easier to use for a larger and different market.

According to another acknowledged business analyst, whereas value was created through mass production and mass consumption until recently, increasingly value is being created through the development, marketing, and delivery of personalized products and services created through partnerships within the ecosystem.[3] The personalized product or service may not be cheaper. Prices could, in fact, be higher as long as customers receive higher values that encompass, for example, brand and quality.

Many business sectors have been and are being forced to compete with new competitors – disrupters of some sort – who have found new ways to create and/or deliver new value for customers often through the use of technology that is coupled with a new underlying production or business model, and/or a broad array of partners, including, in some cases, customers themselves. Increasingly, these changes have been emerging from "outside-in" rather than "bottom-up," making them much harder to anticipate or regard as significant threats in early stages. With massive and nimble technology enablement of consumers, disrupters are placing control in the hands of customers so they can receive the services in the form, at the precise time, and through the channel to suit the convenience of customers. For example, as explained by one former senior airline executive, for years, channels were called "distribution channels" as technology was expensive and cumbersome. Sellers made arrangements with "distribution channels" to connect sellers with buyers. Now, with the power shifting from businesses to customers, customers have "acquisition channels" that can be personalized on a variety of devices that can help buyers find their most appropriate suppliers.

One former senior executive at a hotel chain suggests that traditional intermediaries are under stress to evolve older systems, while new intermediaries have been investing in and renewing technologies on faster cycles, making them inherently more dynamic. Think about the traditional hotel sector that is competing with not only online travel agencies (OTAs) with enormous amounts of information on customers and their behavior, as well as review sites such as TripAdvisor, but also sharing economy players such as Airbnb that connect property owners who want to rent out their facilities to travelers looking for unique places to stay. Although the vacation rental business provided a similar marketplace, and has undergone significant growth and consolidation, Airbnb fundamentally re-defined the business model and achieved phenomenal growth through an end-to-end model based on consumer-controlled digital interactions.

Think about the disruption created by Apple by the introduction of the iPod and iTunes and by Netflix within the entertainment sectors using partners within the ecosystem. Consumers could download, using iTunes (instead of going to a store to purchase CDs), songs they wanted (instead of purchasing CDs with a predetermined list of songs) and listen at their convenience on a mobile device (iPod). And now we have Spotify and other streaming services for which consumers do not even have to "buy" a download, but rather subscribe to unlimited access to a music database. Netflix enabled consumers to stream movies they want to see on devices they want to use and see the movies at times convenient for them. Let us also not forget the disruptive impact Apple's iPhone had on the major player, RIM's BlackBerry, through an improvement in the user interface. The innovation provided by the iPhone's larger screen and the touchscreen capability (making it easier to use) destroyed the sales of BlackBerry phones when, in 2008, it had a market share of more than 50 percent of the smartphone business. Think about Uber. A customer can be in a given city and at any location in that city and simply touch the Uber app. The driver knows the *exact* location of the customer and the customer knows the *exact* location of the vehicle. Uber did not build an app around the taxi business. It built a mobility business around the app to improve customer experience. Although the service may not be cheaper than a standard taxi, it is much more convenient both in ordering a service and in payment handling.

Disruptive innovation is not limited to business sectors. Even within the bureaucracies of public and education sectors and the inefficiencies in the healthcare sector, there are examples of disruption. Singapore's Land Transport Authority is developing an Intelligent Transport System (in a land-scarce country) to maximize safety and the capacity of its road network by monitoring and managing traffic flow to improve user experience. In Helsinki, Finland, a multi-modal transit system is being analyzed to encourage people to reduce the use of cars and subscribe to a system that provides an array of mobility options with services that can be paid for using mobile phones.

Within the high-cost education sector, disruptive innovation could result in more personalized programs in higher education, not to mention more affordable programs. These points fit well with the Khan Academy, which offers "a free, world class education system for anyone, anywhere." Think about the potential ramifications of open online courses and their almost zero marginal costs. There are some who believe it is possible to replace, in some cases, traditional professors in business schools with video games that are carefully designed by academicians who have a lot of practical knowledge and with machines. And, as in acquiring other products and services, experience now plays a role in the learning space too. Students, particularly practitioners, care as to where and how they access the knowledge desired.[4]

Within the healthcare sector, CVS Health, an enormous pharmacy chain in the USA, has established walk-in MinuteClinics (as discussed in a previous book), to care for common family illnesses and soon chronic conditions such as high blood pressure and diabetes. These facilities are staffed with nurse practitioners and physician assistants who are trained to diagnose and treat common health problems. They are also establishing relationships with nearby physicians and hospitals. The idea is to provide the right care to the right patient at the right time, while saving money for both the patient and the system.[5]

Within the banking industry, consider the potential disruption that could result from "Blockchain," the "shared database technology" that reflects crypto-currency Bitcoin. In very simple terms this technology enables consumers and suppliers to make online connections directly by bypassing intermediaries and saving money. Just as iTunes changed the music industry, this technology has the potential to dramatically change some sub-sectors within the financial services sector through an increase in the speed of and a reduction in the costs of certain types of transactions such as security settlements. These changes do not even take into consideration the reduction in margins.[6]

The potential for disruption is causing many business leaders to re-think the markets they serve, re-design their business practices, and re-imagine the depth and intensity of their relationships with their actual and prospective customers and partners. A survey of CEOs conducted by Pricewaterhouse-Coopers (PwC) shows that 97 percent of all CEOs (and 85 percent of airline CEOs) list innovation as a key priority for growth; and 67 percent of all CEOs (and 92 percent of airline CEOs) believe new market entrants will disrupt their industries. Finally, 10 percent of all CEOs (and 18 percent of airline CEOs) see their companies as innovative leaders. While the CEOs, in general or within the airline sector, do see the need for high levels of innovation, there seems to be a gap between the innovation initiatives taken and the results achieved. According to PwC the gap is the result of a lack of *innovation strategy* that can fill the gap between incremental growth and the desired growth (see Figure 1.1).[7]

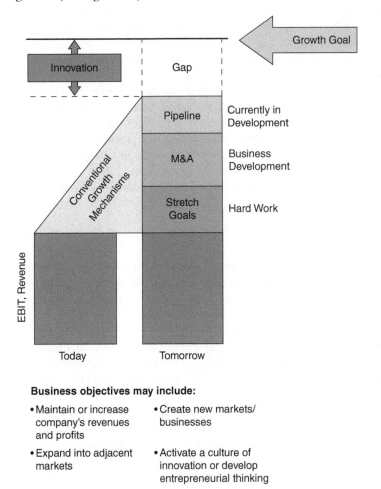

Business objectives may include:

- Maintain or increase company's revenues and profits

- Expand into adjacent markets

- Create new markets/ businesses

- Activate a culture of innovation or develop entrepreneurial thinking

Figure 1.1 Role of Innovation Strategy (source: PricewaterhouseCoopers Survey of CEOs, 2015).

The innovation-focused business leaders are looking beyond the met and unmet needs of customers. They are exploring needs that are unstated and, in some cases, needs that customers may not have even thought about. Did customers ask about having cameras in their mobile phones when the mobile phones became available? It is partly for reasons of unstated needs that traditional automakers have become concerned about the technology-empowered potential disrupters entering the marketplace offering "connected cars." It is reported that there are as many as 100 million lines of code in an average car. In addition to Google with its "self-driving" car, technologists such as those providing the "tabletlike infotainment system(s)" with an open computer browser environment built into cars being developed by Tesla Motors, are leading to cars that are truly mobile friendly. According to IHS Automotive, the economic value of control software in a $94,000 Mercedes-Benz's S550 is $23,000. And Bill Ford Jr., the Chairman of Ford, is quoted about his concern that he does not want his company to become a "handset maker" in the internet-centric world, dominated by software integrators.[8]

However, the PwC strategists caution on the proportion of resources committed to initiatives related to incremental changes versus radically new businesses. Although the innovation mix would depend on such factors as the dynamics of the industry, corporate strategy, and risk profile, they suggest a rule of thumb to be 60 percent for incremental ideas, 30 percent for breakthrough ideas, and 10 percent for radical ideas (see Figure 1.2).

How about improvements, transformations, innovations, and disruptive innovations within the airline industry? This is the content of the book.

Outline of the Book

Whereas this chapter tries to explore what disruptive innovation is, Chapter 2 outlines its relevance to the global airline industry. While there have been numerous and significant improvements throughout the airline industry's history, few can be categorized as disruptive innovations. Even the introduction of the jet aircraft in long-haul markets that led to fast, convenient, and cheaper air travel was a transformational change as opposed to disruptive innovation. It was a long time in coming and over time it was accessible to and deployed across the entire industry. It was a fundamentally superior product with better economics, and if there was any disruption involved, it occurred in other segments of the travel industry rather than the airlines. In contrast, the entry of LCCs represented a different business and operating model that was inherently more difficult for established competitors to adapt to or cope with, hence truly disruptive – and it did disrupt the marketplace. The low-cost, low-fare airline model was first facilitated by the US government policies and later by governments in Europe, as well as regions around the world, to deregulate the airline sector. Consequently, many changes belong more in the category of transformational changes rather than disruptive

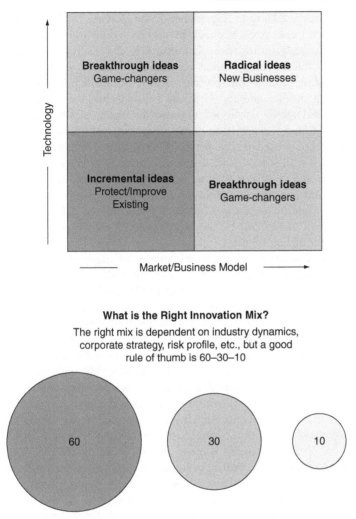

Figure 1.2 Right Mix of Incremental and Radical Ideas (source: PricewaterhouseCoopers Survey of CEOs, 2015).

innovations – the introduction of loyalty programs, revenue management systems, hub-and-spoke systems, global alliances, electronic tickets, self-service kiosks, and mobile boarding passes.

Chapter 3 provides an overview of the disruptive forces and their convergence. These forces relate to the changing nature of economies, customers, competitors, and technologies. With respect to economies, the tidal forces include the impact of new emerging markets, dramatically changing demographics, digital platforms and peer-to-peer characteristics. *Customer expectations* and motivations are changing, for example, with respect to their desire for more personalized and more experience-based services and mobile-enabled capabilities to book, pay for, check-in, and receive boarding passes as well as relevant and timely information. Customers in the emerging markets may have similar or different expectations relating, for example, to the availability of reliable and more convenient services and at affordable prices. Competition is increasing in all segments, from the evolving business models of low-cost, low-fare airlines in developed regions (for example, Ryanair), in emerging markets (IndiGo and Azul), to newer generations of full-service airlines (for example, those based in the Persian Gulf region). As for evolving technologies, the powerful forces relate to the new aircraft (lower unit costs), the internet, mobile, and cloud, facilitating information and communications, computing power and cognitive capability, and reach and access facilitating digital marketing – finding customers, attracting customers, and engaging with customers. It will most likely be the deployment of digital technologies that will transform the airline business.

Chapter 4 provides an overview of the wide range of adaptation strategies by airlines. There are many traditional airlines that are dealing with the traditional challenges of costs and competition (for example, Lufthansa). There are a few aggressive younger-generation airlines that would like to expand not only within their home regions, but also in intercontinental markets (for example, Azul). From the older-generation group, British Airways (now part of the International Airlines Group), having stabilized its financial position and made a decision to focus on the much higher yield O&D traffic to and from London Heathrow and diversified its structure, is now initiating strategies to leverage technology to improve customer service and the personalization of products and services. Delta Air Lines, having stabilized its financial position and expanded its equity partnerships (for example, a substantial equity position in Virgin Atlantic) is now focusing on operational and product improvements and on capturing a higher percentage of the business traveler segment. Also discussed in this chapter are some trends relating to customer management (leveraging real and holistic information as well as smart communication technologies and connectivity) and distribution management (with the entry of powerful outside players). The emerging entrants into the distribution space might include companies whose visions and business models could fit strategically with the travel sector that is big and growing. They could monetize or demonetize information as they see opportunities to create new businesses around existing businesses through the deployment of information and technologies to achieve high capitalization value and high profit margins.

Chapter 5 raises the question of what disruptive innovation means for airlines based in developing markets (Africa) and emerging markets (Asia). How can airlines survive and thrive in a continent, Africa, saddled with ongoing challenges such as a fragmented aviation regulatory environment and the high costs of, as well as the lack of, sufficient infrastructure? The chapter begins with some key characteristics of developing and emerging markets (such as socio-economic related growth and government intervention) followed by a section on the key characteristics of airlines based in these regions (such as state ownership, control, or influence and uncompetitive value propositions in Africa and the expansion of hybrid airlines in Asia). This chapter ends with a comparison of the development of the aviation sectors in two very large markets – India and China – as well as the development of airline services between the two countries that is insignificant at the present time, given the size of the two countries.

Chapter 6 provides an overview of the different strategies adopted by airports. The chapter describes how the forces compelling airlines to re-invent themselves are the same forces that are driving airports to change their business models, why airports are not changing their business models as fast as airlines, and how the goals of airlines and airports are similar in some areas and diametrically opposed in other areas. The chapter describes a spectrum of strategies adopted by airports to meet the needs of low-cost airlines at one end (through the development of low-cost terminals and airports) to enhance customer experience for all customers, and to fulfill the needs of local communities at the other end (by becoming destination airports). The chapter ends with some thought-provoking perspectives on how the business models of airports could be disrupted by emerging technology such as self-driving cars and the emergence of the peer-to-peer economy.

Chapter 7 provides some examples of transformational opportunities for airlines, both at the corporate level as well as at the functional level. At the corporate level there are changes that relate, for example, to designing an organization for agility and scale, and to managing during periods of great uncertainty. The key to "designing" innovation is to integrate the physical hub-and-spoke system with the digital hub-and-spoke system. At the functional level, there are transformational initiatives that would certainly lead to a significant change in products and operations – for example, (1) by optimizing network, fleet, schedules, and operations at the integrated and enterprise level; and (2) by optimizing revenue with considerations of dynamic pricing, dynamic retailing, and revenue optimization based on revenue per customer as opposed to revenue per seat. Just think about the impact on costs, customer experience, and value to customers from the optimization of the day of operations by connecting the airline internally. Some changes could even lead to disruptive innovation – for example, (1) managing revenue based on an optimization at the enterprise level; and (2) moving from the sale of ancillary products and services based on a static menu to embracing retailing at the truly dynamic level.

Chapter 8 provides some perspectives on potential disruptive innovators and scenarios. The chapter begins with a synopsis of the experience with past disruptive initiatives. Commentators have always questioned the airline industry's conventional beliefs about how and where value is created and the associated notions that support such beliefs. The first scenario is about a major global airline such as Emirates becoming a disrupter by innovating in both operational and commercial areas. This airline already has a global network. Not being saddled with legacy technology, legacy processes, or a legacy mindset, it can commit the resources necessary to acquire and implement quickly new technology systems, change processes, and acquire contemporary human skills (internally or working with other multi-disciplinary teams) to become a disruptive innovator. The key component is the digitalization at the enterprise level and the availability of an incredibly powerful Passenger Service System that leverages internal and external data not only within the context of an enterprise level, but also within the ecosystem to design, develop, and deliver products and services (around the airline seat), accompanied by relevant value propositions, through customer engagement (not just customer satisfaction) to capture and maintain profit generated throughout travelers' entire journeys.

A second scenario is presented in which aggressive low-cost airlines such as Ryanair, AirAsia, and Azul expand their operational networks and transform their digital networks. Ryanair could enable comparison shopping, offer to sell a broad spectrum of travel-related products and services that produce much higher profit margins, and offer trans-Atlantic service with narrow-body aircraft. AirAsia could become a low-cost network/hybrid carrier. Azul could become a carrier that provides not only services in regional markets but also in intercontinental markets with its own aircraft as well as through partnerships with carriers based in the USA and Europe. A third scenario is presented in which airlines could develop strategic partnerships with outside businesses (that possess rich information and expertise in technologies, as well as customer relationship management) to offer compelling value propositions.

Chapter 9 provides some closing thoughts on innovating in the air travel space while adapting to the new realities – actual and potential disruption of some industries, an increasingly technology-led world, and the shift in power from airlines to customers, as well as the dramatically changing expectations of customers. Airlines can leverage the exponentially changing technologies to improve operations while bringing themselves closer to their customers and collaborators to create and deliver extraordinary value. This adaptation to the dramatically changing marketplace calls for a change in culture that starts with the acceptance of the assumption that airlines represent the front door to the travel space, and then the need for constant re-invention of the business by developing innovation strategies per se and management with the appropriate skills. The chapter provides five trends that the C-Suite executives can monitor to see how they can be proactive in the disruption space, and raises four fundamental questions for managing and, where possible, de-risking the business.

As with the previous book, Chapter 10 provides 11 Thought Leadership Pieces by practitioners that elaborate upon some points discussed throughout this book.

- The first piece, contributed by Rob Broere, Co-Chairman of the IATA Simplified the Business Steering Group and Think Tank, provides an overview of the technical aspects of processing passengers since the 1960s and what the upcoming changes will achieve for airlines and their customers.

- The second piece, contributed by Nico Buchholz of Bombardier, provides some insights into the role of disruptive innovation in fleet decisions incorporating economies of size and marketplace needs.
- The third piece, contributed by John Grant of OAG, provides an historical perspective of the changes in the airline industry just in the past decade, and some thought-provoking scenarios for the 2025 and the 2035 time frames developed around the structure of the airline industry and the role of aircraft technology, particularly the deployment of long-range narrow-body aircraft.
- The fourth piece, contributed by Peeter Kivestu of Teradata, provides an overview of the past role of the physical hub-and-spoke systems relating to aircraft and now the new emerging role of digital hub-and-spoke systems involving a wide range of sources of information.
- The fifth piece, contributed by Dirk-Jan Koops and Robert Engelen of Accenture, discusses the digital point of view with respect to personalization, physical products, relevancy, and digitalization.
- The sixth piece, contributed by Eric Leopold of IATA, provides an overview of simplifying the air travel business based on more than ten years of research conducted by the group within IATA in terms of three waves: the electronic wave, the digital transformation wave, and the attributes of the next disruptive wave.
- The seventh piece, contributed by Leo Mondale of Inmarsat, discusses the role of in-flight and high-speed internet connections and the value created both for airlines and their customers.
- The eighth piece, contributed by Barry Parsons of Cii Holdings, discusses various aspects of disruption from within and outside the airline industry from both the supply and the demand side.
- The ninth piece, contributed by Rob Solomon, Co-Chairman of the International Airline Symposium Planning Committee, discusses the lessons learned and the issues that linger relating to the role of leadership in bringing about disruption.
- The tenth piece, contributed by Dan Wacksman with the Outrigger Resorts, discusses the changing role of consumer influential distributors in the travel sector through the use of powerful search engines.
- The eleventh piece, contributed by Guo Xianqin with MASKargo, discusses the challenges and opportunities relating to the air cargo sector and insights for the passenger sector from the experience from within the dramatically changed air cargo sector.

These 11 Thought Leadership Pieces, in combination, provide not only good examples of new thinking, but can be catalysts for introducing disruptive change in the airline industry.

Notes

1 Tett, Gillian, *The Silo Effect: The Peril of Expertise and the Promise of Breaking Down Barriers* (New York: Simon & Schuster, 2015), p. 52.
2 The thought leadership of Clayton M. Christensen on disruptive innovation in the public and private sector can be found in his numerous books, including: *The Innovator's Dilemma* (1997), *The Innovator's Solution* (2003), *Seeing What's Next* (2004), *The Innovator's Prescription* (2009), and *The Innovative University* (2011).
3 Zuboff, Shoshana, "Creating value in the age of distributed capitalism," *McKinsey Quarterly*, September 2010. See also her book *In the Age of the Smart Machine: The Future of Work and Power* (1989).
4 "Academic rigour makes room for industry experience," *Financial Times*, Business Education, November 2, 2015, p. 10.
5 Lorenzetti, Laura, "Betting big on health," *Fortune*, May 1, 2015, p. 22.
6 Wild, Jane, Arnold, Martin, and Stafford, Philip, "Chain gang," *Financial Times*, November 2, 2015, p. 6.
7 This information was presented by Bryan Terry with PwC at the International Airline Symposium held in Hong Kong on November 5, 2015.
8 Ramsey, Mike, "Ford, Mercedes-Benz set up shop in Silicon Valley," *Wall Street Journal*, March 27, 2015.

2 RELEVANCE TO THE AIRLINE INDUSTRY

Generally speaking, the word *disruption* in the airline industry has been associated with operations, such as when aircraft operations are disrupted due to severe weather, mechanical problems, or for security-related reasons. This association of disruption relates to irregular operations. The word disruption, as used in this book, relates to disrupting the business in general and managing it differently. Within this context, the airline industry has some experience with disruptive change.

Across the Innovation Spectrum

In its early years, the airline industry disrupted other forms of transportation. Think about what airlines such as Pan American, BOAC, and Qantas did to the intercontinental passenger shipping sector. It was entrepreneurs like Juan Trippe who integrated the ingredients needed to offer services in intercontinental markets. He encouraged airplane makers to manufacture the needed aircraft, worked with governments to develop the needed bilateral agreements, worked with airport operators to develop landing strips, and with electronic companies to develop the essential navigational aids. Think about what airlines such as American, TWA, and United did to the railroad industry in North America. What about the disruptive business of Eastern Airlines' Shuttle within the North East Corridor of the USA – high frequencies, no reservations required, onboard ticket purchasing capability, and no conditions or restrictions? Eastern took out most of the complexity from the user's viewpoint while guaranteeing a seat by changing the way the airline scheduled its aircraft and crews. How about what airlines such as Southwest did to the Greyhound bus business in the USA, and what GOL and Azul did to the bus services within Brazil. These are examples of disruptive innovation by which air transportation services were made *affordable* and *accessible* for travelers in the lower end of the pyramid and, as such, the disrupters also increased the market demand, benefiting both the new and existing airline businesses.

While airlines have a long history of continuous improvements and innovations, few of their innovations can be classified as disruptive innovations. Developments such as the inter-line system (enabling a traveler to fly around the world on one ticket paid for in one currency at one location, charged on one credit card), multi-class cabins and fares to appeal to different segments, ground transportation for passengers traveling in premium cabins, and pick-up and delivery of bags could be classified as continuous improvements. Examples of innovations could include the introduction of the long-range aircraft (the Boeing 707 and the Douglas DC8 with higher speeds and higher capacities) to provide non-stop services, computer reservation systems, air-to-ground and satellite communications, lie-flat seats in intercontinental markets, self-service check-in systems (boarding passes, automated gates, and passengers printing and attaching their own baggage tags), in-flight entertainment and connectivity, and boarding passes on mobile phones.

If we were to classify inter-line systems as improvements and the introduction of long-haul services with jet aircraft as innovations, then one could classify as disruptive innovations the introduction of hub-and-spoke systems by Eastern and Delta in the USA, by Singapore Airlines in Asia, and by KLM in Europe. The hub-and-spoke systems led to the development of other sub-sectors within the industry, such as feeder services by regional airlines. The concept was taken to a new level when Northwest and KLM optimized their networks between three hubs across the Atlantic and the Pacific – Amsterdam, Detroit, and Tokyo (Narita) (see the Thought Leadership Piece by Peeter Kivestu in Chapter 10). COPA Airlines in Panama developed an enormous hub-and-spoke system considering its own size, connecting the Americas with the use of 100 narrow-body aircraft (Figure 2.1). Emirates Airline has developed an enormous hub-and-spoke system in Dubai with the use of wide-body aircraft, especially with the use of exceptionally long-haul aircraft such as the Boeing 777 (see Figure 8.1). Figure 2.2 shows the development by Turkish Airlines of an extensive network serving over 40 cities in Africa from its hub in Istanbul, mostly with narrow-body aircraft. The airline served only about half a dozen destinations in Africa in 2005. In the USA, the airlines took the hub-and-spoke system further by developing a franchise system around the hubs to connect their short-haul markets. Initially the feeder airlines used small turboprop airlines, but disruption became much more prominent when Bombardier introduced a cost-effective jet aircraft, the 50-seat Canadian Regional Jet.

The second innovation could be represented by the introduction of the 747, the first wide-body aircraft with a capacity of up to 550 seats, that changed the way people traveled. It had lower available seat mile costs (due to better fuel consumption) and provided a superior level of comfort in long-distance markets. It could even be categorized as disruptive innovation as it enabled an increase in travel in the low end of the passenger market – mass transportation in intercontinental markets. The penetration of the low end of the market was facilitated by the additional capacity of the aircraft with low seat mile costs and the movement toward the liberalization of international fares that had previously been coordinated through the IATA framework for many years. Some people called it the democratization and globalization of air travel – a new world standard in civil aviation.

Figure 2.1 COPA Airlines Connecting the Two Americas (source: OAG Schedule Analyser and Mapper).

But it was the introduction of low-cost, low-fare services by new airlines (Southwest Airlines in the USA and Laker Airways in the UK, for example) that disrupted the airline business of incumbent airlines. Thus, one disruptive innovation was started by airlines – hub-and-spoke systems – and two were facilitated by outsiders, one by aircraft technology and the second by a change in government regulations. All three disruptive innovations led to the start of mass transportation within the airline industry. These disruptive innovations also led airlines and related businesses to change their business models in other areas. The introduction of the 747 led to significant re-designs at airports, reduced airport congestion at some airports, and changed various aspects of airline operations. The introduction of services by low-cost, low-fare airlines also led a couple of incumbent airlines to transform their business models

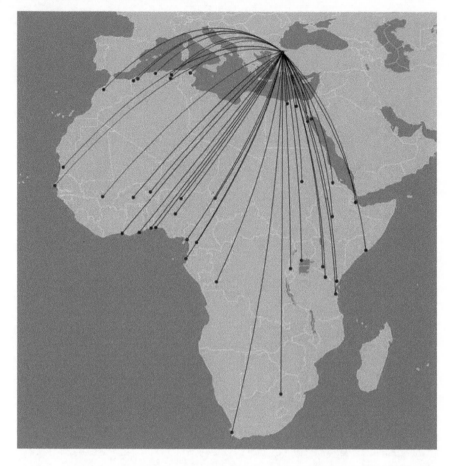

Figure 2.2 Turkish Airlines Connections between Istanbul and Africa (source: OAG Schedule Analyser and Mapper).

(American Airlines and British Airways, for example) in a disruptive manner to respond to the external disrupters by developing and implementing yield management systems, now referred to as revenue management systems.

Low-Cost Carriers

It was the global growth of low-cost carriers (LCCs) that accelerated the fundamental shift in the entire industry for almost three decades. Figure 2.3 shows the proliferation worldwide of low-fare airline services. They not only had low operating costs, but also went directly to customers and had customers book flights via their own websites. This process kept the distribution costs low and built stronger relationships between customers and airlines. In 2014 the market share of LCCs in Europe reached 37.7 percent; in the

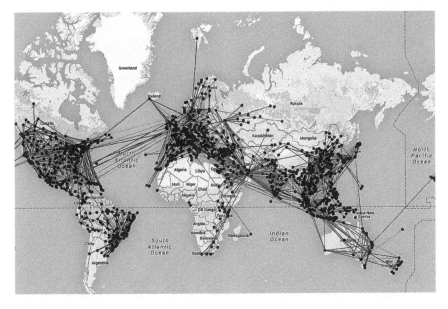

Figure 2.3 Worldwide Proliferation of Low-Fare Airline Services (source: OAG Schedules
Analyser).

Asia-Pacific region 27.3 percent; and in North America 23.6 percent.[1]
However, some carriers in this group no longer have low costs or low fares –
for example, Southwest and jetBlue in the USA. On the other hand, just as it
was the prevalence of high fares, as well as the backdrop of a history of over-
regulation, that attracted lower-fare airlines to enter the marketplace, more
recently, two new trends have been emerging. First, there is the emergence
of ultra low-cost carriers (ULCCs) with even lower fares. According to Spirit
Airlines, the average fare received by Spirit, for the period 12 months ending
September 2014 was $106, compared to $149 for Southwest and $153 for
jetBlue.[2] These fares represent total revenue per passenger, including the
charges for bags and seat options. It is, in part, the existence of low-fare competition that has led to a decline in fares in US domestic markets (Figure 2.4).
Moreover, this sector is continuing the expansion of the low-end segment of
the marketplace. An analysis of five Spirit Airlines' markets shows that it
gained market share more from stimulation than from diversion of passengers
from incumbent airlines (Figure 2.5).

Second, some LCCs are now flying in long-haul markets and with unbundled fares. Norwegian, having succeeded in the introduction of lower fares, as
one example, to and from the high-fare region (Scandinavia) within Europe
is now flying to Bangkok to the east and five destinations in North America
to the west. Norwegian has announced its plans to provide additional transatlantic service between Cork, Ireland and the USA with narrow-body
equipment, the Boeing 737 (see the dotted lines in Figure 2.6). The airline

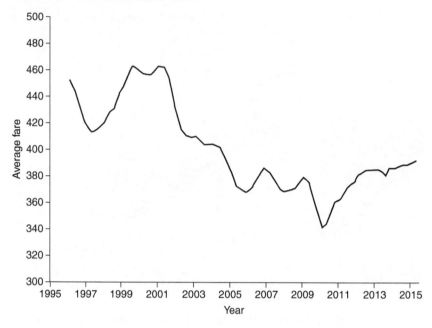

Figure 2.4 Average Fares in US Markets: Four-Quarter Moving Average (source: US Department of Transportation).

Notes
1 Measurement period begins January 2007 through June 2014. System average measures only those markets Spirit has served for at least 12 months.
2 Sample markets do not necessarily reflect system average. Pre-Spirit is the average for the four calendar quarters prior to Spirit's entry; Post-Spirit is the average for the four calendar quarters following Spirit's entry.

even mentioned the possibility of thin routes such as Billund in Denmark (the home of Legoland) to New York using the Boeing 737MAX.[3] Even more recently, Norwegian announced that it would increase its transatlantic services by offering flights between Paris and three cities in the USA. Norwegian has attempted to disrupt the marketplace by capitalizing on three resources – the use of cost-efficient aircraft such as the Boeing 787; the traffic rights between the European Union and the USA by setting up a base at London's Gatwick Airport and an operating organization in Ireland; and labor costs by setting up a base in Thailand. Other carriers offering low costs in intercontinental markets include Australia's Jetstar, Canada's WestJet, Iceland's Icelandair, Malaysia's AirAsia X, the Philippine's Cebu Pacific, and Saudi Arabia's flynas. This list does not include services provided by the low-cost divisions of full-service carriers (FSCs) such as Singapore's Scoot and Air Canada's Rouge.

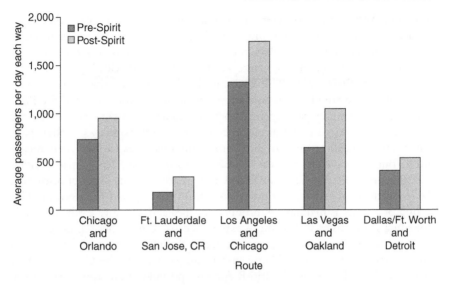

Figure 2.5 Spirit Airlines Stimulates the Market (source: Spirit Airlines Presentation on its Website, 2015).

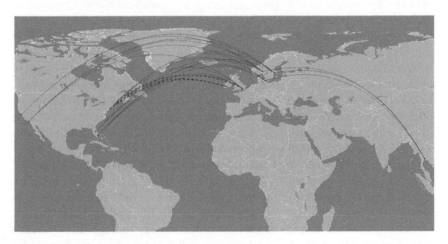

Figure 2.6 Transatlantic Network of Norwegian Air Shuttle (source: OAG Schedule Analyser and Mapper).

Full-Service Carriers

On the FSC side, the financially powerful Persian Gulf-based airlines, facilitated by their governments, have been developing and offering global services through their own mega-hubs (just as KLM and Singapore Airlines did a few decades ago) but with even higher levels of scale and scope; for example, wider price–service options. To succeed within the high end of the market,

Emirates Airline offers shower facilities in First Class in some markets, and Etihad Airways offers private suites with butlers in some markets. In an effort to woo budget-minded travelers, these carriers offer extensive services to segments to and from emerging markets at lower fares and with higher frequencies through their hubs. Think about the low end of the market for a moment. There are places in countries such as India, Indonesia, and the Philippines, where some passengers who save money for years can now make long-haul trips to visit friends and relatives in distant markets. On their part, these airlines need service to and from numerous cities to feed their megahubs. But for travelers, it means direct access to service from smaller cities. Consequently, the Persian Gulf-based airlines are showing signs of disrupting large swaths of the global industry, both from the top and the bottom. This group of airlines is making the product cheaper and/or more easily accessible for some segments as well as more experience-based for other segments.

As an example, consider a specific market within Europe and the Indian subcontinent region – travel between various gateways in the UK and various gateways in India. In 2002, British Airways provided non-stop service from London's Heathrow Airport to four destinations in India (Chennai, Delhi, Kolkata, and Mumbai) and connecting services in 24 markets – for example, between Newcastle and Kolkata and between Manchester and Chennai. In the same year, Emirates served 16 markets with connecting services through Dubai (Birmingham, London's Gatwick and Heathrow, and Manchester in the UK, and Chennai, Delhi, Hyderabad, and Mumbai in India). In 2014, British Airways served five markets with non-stop services from London Heathrow to Bengaluru, Chennai, Delhi, Hyderabad, and Mumbai and provided connecting services in 35 markets. Emirates, on the other hand, served 60 markets with connecting services through Dubai. So, passengers traveling from various gateways in the UK to various gateways in India had access to 44 markets in 2002 and 100 markets in 2014. As for frequency, it increased from about 60 per week to about 160 per week! How about fares? Compiled from the Global Demand Data provided by the Sabre Airline Solutions Group, in 2002 Emirates introduced considerably lower fares, based on the average, between the four airports served in the UK and the four airports served in India, and continued the lower-fare strategy through 2014 when it served six airports in the UK and nine in India. Think about the benefit for passengers in low-density markets. Passengers can now fly from Newcastle in the UK to cities such as Cochin in India, with a single connection in Dubai.

Ongoing Frustrations

However, despite these ongoing improvements, evolutionary innovations, and disruptive innovations, (1) air travel within the commercial air sector continues to be mass produced and mass delivered for the bulk of travelers, and (2) traveler frustration at various touchpoints has been increasing. With respect to the first point, even though progress has been made in the area of personalization (for example, cabin and seat selection, boarding priority, lounge access, and baggage pick-up and delivery), some customers want more personalization. Their behavior and expectations are changing faster (based on their experiences in other business sectors) than the airlines' delivery of personalized products and services. With respect to the second point, traveler frustration has been increasing for most passengers traveling in the economy cabins, especially the infrequent travelers, as airlines have implemented strategies to reduce costs and generate higher levels of revenue – through more and tighter connecting banks at mega-hubs, rigorous capacity control, higher load factors, franchising of feeder services to low-cost bidders, and unappealing loyalty programs for infrequent travelers. Think about the recent confusion regarding the size of carry-on baggage.

Although outside of airlines' direct control, complexities of airport security and infrastructure constraints have also increased traveler frustration, not to mention the insufficient expansion in airport capacity relative to the increase in demand. Airport capacity is clearly not growing to keep up with the increase in demand that is expected to double between 2014 and 2035. Consider London Heathrow Airport that "operates at 99% capacity and has done so for more than 10 years."[4] While some airports have begun to change their operating model strategies and customer–tenant segmentation and relationships, there is more room to improve the airline–airport symbiotic relationship.

Then there is the frustration relating to online shopping through websites that are difficult to navigate, difficult to obtain relevant and contextual information, and difficult to undertake comparison shopping – areas that are within an airline's control. For a given trip (say, from Cape Town, South Africa, to Warsaw, Poland), how can an infrequent traveler find out the best price–service combination or the best airline–airport combination for the trip to meet the needs of this particular individual? For comparison shopping the hotel websites seem to be ahead in that not only do they provide information on the number of stars the hotel has achieved, but also the reduction in price compared to the full rates. The non-top-tier travelers also continue to be frustrated because, until recently, airlines have focused more on the needs of top-tier travelers and the deployment of technology more to improve operations than customer service.

While airline efforts to improve customer service, reduce customer frustration, and enhance customer experience are all movements in the right direction, on a scale of change where incremental changes are at one end and disruptive changes at the other end, the needle has not been getting closer to disruptive innovation from within the industry for the infrequent and non-premium fare travelers. On the other hand, given (1) the available technology (information, the depth and breadth of mobile apps, and the availability of customer and predictive analytics), and (2) insights on best global business practices, it is possible to bring about disruptive innovation relating to customer experience in the air travel industry to a much larger segment of passengers through changes in systems and processes as well as partnerships within the ecosystem if management can bring about changes in culture.

The reasons given for the slow progress in this area generally relate to the complexities of the airline business, their legacy systems, and the constraints under which the airline industry operates – government regulations and regulatory policies, fixed capacity of an airplane with variable demand, constraining labor contracts, and operations dependent on weather and capacity-constrained infrastructure. However, although difficult, it is possible to find ways to work around the constraints. Apple did it to deal with the constraints within the music industry when it introduced iTunes. Integrating design into products and services, while working around the constraints, appears to be the hallmark of Apple's success, showing an amazing reported market capitalization of around $750 billion at the end of May 2015. Uber is continuing to work around the regulatory constraints in introducing its version of taxi service in cities around the world and is now, as noted in Chapter 4, entering the air travel sector.

Management at traditional airlines does understand disruption and recognizes the value it could bring to both travelers and airlines – better customer service and experience as well as an increase in profitability that is sustainable. But, it appears, there are three groups of executives who see challenges relating to the introduction of disruptive innovation. One group views it to be "difficult, painful, and slow," given the constraints of legacy technology systems and international regulations (slowing down, for example, IATA's Fast Travel Program Project). Then there are the widespread ongoing challenges with workforce motivation and management, whether one attributes this to labor unions or regards it as a management responsibility. The pain and the slow speed can be explained by the fact that legacy systems, processes, and human resources need to be kept working while an airline transitions to new models. A second group sees disruptive innovation as a "threat to existing revenue streams." Think about the slow speed at which IATA's New Distribution Capability (NDC) transitioned at the beginning for the aforementioned two reasons. The third group views the industry to be "immune to disruption" because of the existence of regulatory policies for reasons of "safety and national security." Consequently, while the management of airlines does have good ideas, the implementation of the good ideas continues to be a struggle for most, partly because of the mindset and partly because of the reluctance to make major investments, given the continuous focus on cost reductions that, in turn, leads to the continuation of customers' frustration with service experience.

Airline Improvements

However, there is a small group of older-generation and newer-generation airlines working on transformational changes that could eventually lead to disruptive innovation. Here are just four examples of airlines based in four different regions.

Delta Airlines, having (1) merged with Northwest, (2) reduced its debt level, (3) changed the ratio of fixed costs to variable costs, (4) acquired equity in a number of non-US airlines (Aeromexico, GOL, and Virgin Atlantic), (5) rationalized capacity and hub structure within domestic and international markets (exemplified by the reduced focus on Cincinnati and Memphis and added focus on Seattle, London Heathrow, and Shanghai), (6) reconfigured its loyalty program, and (7) developed a Delta Jets division to improve the experience of its most valued customers, and is now reported to focus on its brand attributes – thoughtful, reliable, and innovative – and the change of culture to make these attributes a part of the decision-making process at all levels within the organization. More discussion on Delta is available in Chapter 7.

British Airways, having (1) become part of the IAG, leveraging a desirable holding company structure, (2) gained more slots at London Heathrow through the acquisition of British Midland, (3) developed a cooperative working, and a restructured, relationship with labor, (4) re-aligned its international network that includes a leading transatlantic position and a retuned hub at Heathrow, (5) facilitated an equity investment from Qatar Airways and facilitated its entry into oneworld, (6) initiated the strategies to leverage technology to improve its customer service and personalization of products and services for external customers and more efficient operations for its workforce (mobile enablement for crews and maintenance, for instance), (7) further strengthened its already well-recognized brand, and (8) acquired Aer Lingus to diversify its hub structure, and is further along the change spectrum toward disruptive innovation by looking at new ways to provide value and benefit from it.

Qantas, having (1) started a dual brand with a different type of low-cost subsidiary with foreign bases – Jetstar – (2) re-aligned its capacity worldwide using a partnership with Emirates, (3) undertook major cost-cutting initiatives, (4) improved its balance sheet, (5) constructed a mutually acceptable relationship with labor, (6) re-aligned its fleet and configurations, (7) developed strong marketing partnerships and joint-ventures with other airlines, (8) capitalized further on its loyalty program (for example, through the introduction of Qantas Cash – a prepaid multi-currency payment mechanism built into the Qantas loyalty card), and (9) expanded into new strategic businesses to smooth out the business cycles, and is now moving rapidly to focus on its product and customer experience initiatives by leveraging the breadth and depth of its customer insights.

Azul, having (1) begun operations from a non-conventional airport (Campinas Viracopos, in Brazil), (2) started with a new fleet of Embraer jets instead of the conventional Airbus 320s or Boeing 737s, (3) added complexity by introducing a second category of aircraft (ATRs), (4) acquired a competitive low-cost airline (TRIP), (5) started bus service to feed traffic, (6) acquired yet another type of aircraft (wide-body A330) to start intercontinental operations, and (7) started to develop partnerships with other airlines (jetBlue and

United), and has now acquired TAP Portugal to expand rapidly in long-haul international markets and very recently established strong ties with China's Hainan Airlines Group through a massive investment by Hainan Airlines. More discussion on Azul is available in Chapter 8.

Besides the older generation of traditional airlines, there is a younger group (within the low-cost, hybrid, and full-service sectors) that is trying to dramatically transform the airline business. These newer-generation airlines have no allegiance to conventional pricing systems, revenue management systems, scheduling processes for airplanes, crews, and loyalty schemes. Examples of these relatively young airlines include Ryanair and Etihad. Ryanair could start transatlantic service with narrow-body aircraft, develop websites that enable comparison shopping, increase the sale of travel-related products (hotel rooms, car rentals, and so forth), and increase its penetration in the business segment of the market (as discussed in Chapter 8). Initiatives to inter-line with long-haul network carriers are under discussion. Etihad could synchronize its physical and digital operations, for example, by introducing an app that facilitates an improvement in every part of the travel experience, promote a universal travel profile for each customer, and extend further its operations virtually through the networks of its partners, introduce personal pricing systems, and establish special areas in economy sections where passengers traveling in economy cabins could purchase higher-quality meals and have access to lie-flat beds for a certain number of hours. Moreover, if one believes in the viewpoint that value and profits are generated at points of integration then Etihad could become an example of an integrator that not only integrates networks of its equity partners, but also information within the ecosystem (airlines, airports, hotels, car rental companies, and tourist service providers).

There are many other nimble operators (Vueling, Spirit, Allegiant, Alaska, and WestJet) that have been strong innovators with smaller footprints. Vueling is setting records in profitable growth by balancing its strategy – offering valuable products for both business and leisure travelers in both O&D markets as well as markets that feed the IAG partners. Spirit is expanding within the ultra low-cost group in secondary and conventional markets. Allegiant is expanding in a special niche market by operating low-frequency service in mostly non-competitive leisure markets. Alaska was the first to provide a service guarantee along with its bag fee. Alaska has now announced its decision to acquire Virgin America to strengthen its network. WestJet aligned its workforce and management through an employee share ownership plan, created a lower-cost subsidiary that operates turboprop aircraft, and now a designated small fleet offers service in intercontinental markets. Although these types of airlines have not taken over the world, they have successfully defended their turfs and solved some of the issues with which the large carriers struggle. Azul, not even a teenager yet, appears to be managing well the complexity of different aircraft in the fleet – ATRs, Embraer jets, and A330 wide bodies. The experience in managing complexity and business agility should lead to a rapid and smooth integration between Azul and TAP. Hawaiian Airlines has been using an increasingly successful new model in which a non–state flag carrier is striving toward building a franchise as a premium airline to a premium destination.

As in other business sectors, the key force behind the movement to disrupt the business landscape is the changing customer behavior facilitated by the rapidly changing technology and the availability of real-time information. There has been a shift in the power from businesses to customers. Customers are increasingly looking for: (1) personalized products and services to fulfill their unmet and unstated needs; (2) further empowerment to control their travel, before and during their journeys; and (3) good value that encompasses price, experience, brand, and quality. The experience component could be one reason that people with the ability to pay higher fares are not willing to buy higher-fare tickets as the perceived difference in experience does not warrant the price differential. Keep in mind customers' willingness to pay higher prices for the Uber on-demand service in return for improved customer experience. Within the airline industry, customers' painpoints continue to exist for travelers and, in some areas, have increased – experience in shopping, dealing with irregular operations, boarding airplanes, traveling in short and medium haul, and low–density markets. Although airlines have been implementing strategies to improve customer service and experience, their continued focus on the bottom line, although necessary, has slowed the process to eliminate the painpoints for customers, especially when customers compare the services provided by airlines in comparison to the services by best-of-breed businesses. Consequently, the perception of customers that airlines have not been improving customer service may be related to two developments: (1) that customer expectations are being set by service providers in other business sectors; and (2) that the bar relating to customer service is being raised both inside and outside the airline industry.

There are three encouraging signs, however. First, at the industry level, in his Thought Leadership Piece in Chapter 10, Eric Leopold of IATA provides an excellent overview of IATA's Simplify the Business (StB) program's achievements during the past 12 years. Second, as stated earlier, some airlines, having achieved financial success, possibly even on a sustainable basis, are beginning to focus on personalization and customer experience. Third, technology-empowered organizations and platform-focused entrepreneurs might seize opportunities not to start new airlines themselves even with different business models, but to focus on air travel-related spaces around the airline business where painpoints exist for customers – online shopping experiences, processing at airports, and receiving relevant information at various touchpoints in the journey, for example. The outsiders will most likely focus on profit margins, and target and pick-off the profit concentrations in travelers' journeys. Keep in mind that innovation-focused groups recognize that the latent value in consumer discretionary industries lies in the customer information and the use of customer analytics and predictive analytics to uncover hidden patterns and relationships to make more informed marketing decisions (see the section on distribution management in Chapter 4 and the Thought Leadership Piece by Dan Wacksman in Chapter 10). Outsiders could develop the customer-serving and the revenue-generating networks that programmatically address the mobility needs of a broader spectrum of travelers better than the networks developed by airlines. It is also possible that the information-rich companies could monetize their assets and become fourth-party logistics providers (4PLs) or, simply, sell the information back to some aggressive airlines, enabling them to become the disrupters. (Consider the role of 4PL in the cargo sector as described in the Thought Leadership Piece by Guo Xianqin in Chapter 10.) The airlines, in turn, could create and market personalized services and prices or they could develop strategic alliances with the information and analysis-based organizations.

As indicated in Chapter 1, in the survey of airline CEOs conducted by PwC, 92 percent of airline CEOs believe that new market entrants will disrupt their industries during the next five years. This belief supports the research conducted by the author which concludes that uncertainty relates only to the timing, the intensity, and the pace of disruptive innovation. Assuming this to be the case, the message is relatively clear. The adaptive airlines are trying to pursue disruptive innovation or, at least, implement some forms of dynamic and transformational changes. They are exploring ways to create new value by re-defining what is possible (through new business models, new strategies, and new products) to meet the needs of a growing number of customers for simplicity, and personalized and experienced-based services. Customers prefer to be empowered through self-service capabilities, coupled with abundantly rich and relevant information. Empowering customers involves, however, much more than an improvement of current processes. It is about transforming the corporate culture and, in turn, processes, systems, and staff so as to add more value. They are also trying to maintain and grow the relationship with their customers to prevent technology-powered businesses entering businesses outside the core product of the airline industry – that is, flights.

At the other end of the spectrum are airlines working with a business-as-usual mindset and culture for incremental change only. They could be disrupted in the long run – obtaining, at best, a lower average fare, a lower share of the profit from travelers' journeys, or, at worst, by being acquired, by becoming irrelevant, or becoming a supplier of seats to disrupters that make products more affordable and/or more accessible, not to mention handle the high-margin aspects of the customer relationship. It is worth noting that while scale and consolidation can work in favor of network efficiency, inertia and integration issues can be huge challenges for the larger and more mature enterprises. Most, but not all, of the innovation globally has come from either smaller startup or niche players. Some of the biggest failures have come about when legacy carriers have tried to execute their own versions of disruptive models (Ted and Song, for example, in the USA). There do seem to be some encouraging signs of successful shifts by big enterprises, as pointed out in this book. United's embracing of Uber, Qantas teaming up with Emirates, and some good examples of multi-brand strategies, all point to better outcomes ahead. Some airlines face a substantial challenge in introducing significant change as they work with entrenched labor groups and have large system integration issues.

Takeaways

While airlines introduced a multitude of improvements across the spectrum in the products and services offered, only a couple of these improvements can be classified as disruptive innovations – the introduction of low-cost, low-fare airlines and their variations such as services offered by the ULCCs and services offered in longer-haul intercontinental markets. However, some improvements come close to being disruptive innovations, such as the introduction of fast and efficient jets in long-haul markets, the development of hub-and-spoke systems, and various aspects of e-commerce.

The more extensive innovations were facilitated by the outsiders, such as aircraft manufacturers with respect to airplane and engine technologies and governments with respect to liberalization policies.

Despite the ongoing improvements, evolutionary innovations, and disruptive innovations, (1) air travel within the commercial air sector continues to be mass produced and mass delivered for the bulk of travelers, and (2) traveler frustration at various touchpoints has been increasing.

A small group of older-generation (for example, British Airways and Qantas) and newer-generation airlines (for example, Azul and Ryanair) are working on transformational changes that could eventually lead to disruptive innovation.

Besides the older generation of traditional airlines, there is a younger group (within the ultra-low cost, low cost, hybrid, and full-service sectors) that is trying to dramatically transform the airline business.

New players, airlines, and related businesses are beginning to emerge that could change the landscape.

Notes

1 "Low-cost line-up," *Airline Business*, June 2015, p. 27.
2 Spirit Airlines Presentation, available on the airline's website, dated May 2015. The data are derived from the US Transportation System, Form 41 and adjusted for the length of haul.
3 CAPA – Centre for Aviation, "Redefining airport hubs," *Airline Leader*, 28, May–June 2015, p. 67.
4 Newton, Graham, "Bright thinking," *Airlines International*, 55, April–May 2015, pp. 24–7.

3 DISRUPTIVE FORCES AND THEIR CONVERGENCE

The timing and the breadth and depth of disruptive innovation depend on the impact of a number of forces, including the following four primary ongoing and reinforcing forces. Although these are not new forces, they have become more powerful and begun to move at a faster pace, and their convergence is leading to one fundamental change – a shift in power from businesses to customers. Businesses are well aware of this shift and are adopting strategies, although at different paces, to change their business models to respond to the challenges and to capitalize on the opportunities created in the marketplace by this shift in power. This chapter provides an extremely brief overview of the four primary forces. Since there is a strong correlation between the dynamics of economies and the dynamics of air travel, it makes sense to start with a brief synopsis of just a couple of aspects of how the economies are changing worldwide. This sketch follows a brief review of changing customer expectations, increased competition facing airlines, and the role and impact of changing technologies.

Changing Nature of Economies

Demographic-Related Trends

The *Global Market Forecast: 2015–2034* developed by Airbus shows that in 2014 there were 6.3 billion people in developing and emerging regions (primarily in Asia, the Commonwealth of Independent States, Eastern Europe, Africa, and Latin America) compared to one billion in developed regions of the world (primarily in Western Europe, North America, and Japan). First, the populations of the developing and emerging regions are forecast to grow at higher rates compared to the growth of populations in developed regions. Second, people in the developed regions are getting older, leading to declines in populations of developed regions, such as parts of Europe and Japan. Third, the economies of developing and emerging markets are growing at faster rates than economies of developed regions. Fourth, within the developing and emerging regions, populations have been moving to cities, leading to an increase in urbanization. These trends alone illustrate the shift in the center of gravity. Consider some eye-opening forecasts made by three directors of the McKinsey Global Institute and their potential impact on air travel. In 2010, Tianjin, a city located 120 kilometers southeast of Beijing, in China, had GDP approximately equal to that of Stockholm, Sweden. In 2025, Tianjin is expected to have GDP approximately equal to the whole country of Sweden.[1]

Next, not only are the populations of the developing and emerging regions expected to grow at higher rates than the developed regions, but even more important, the middle classes of the populations in emerging regions are expected to grow at much higher rates. Figure 3.1 shows that the middle class within the developing and emerging markets compared to that within the developed markets grew at a much higher rate between 2004 and 2014, and this differential in the growth rates is expected to continue for the next 20 years. In 2014, the middle class in Europe and North America totaled 703 million people, and in the emerging regions totaled 2,001 million. In 2034 it is forecast that the middle class will grow to 744 million in the developed regions (a growth of 5.8 percent) and to 3,977 million in the emerging regions (a growth of 98.8 percent). From this perspective, another conclusion of the McKinsey Global Institute report is not surprising. Whereas in 2000 about 95 percent of the Fortune Global 500 (the world's largest international companies) had their headquarters in developed economies, in 2025 China will be the home of more large companies than the USA or Europe.[2] On top of this, there is a force that represents a shift in the flow of "capital, people, and information" from major well-known trading hubs to emerging hubs.

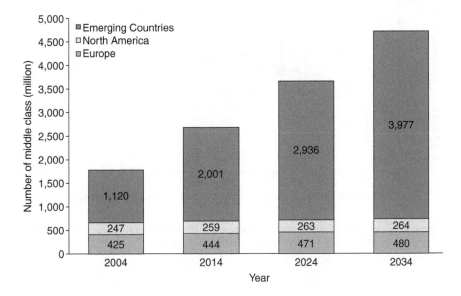

Figure 3.1 Growths of Middle Class Segments (source: Airbus, *Global Market Forecast: 2015–2034*, 2015).

The report by the McKinsey Global Institute provides one compelling example: The volume of trade between China and Africa increased from $9 billion in 2000 to $211 billion in 2012.[3]

To see some implications of this aspect of the change in economies on air travel, let us turn back to the *Global Market Forecast* by Airbus. Up to now, trips per capita has been highest for countries in Europe and North America, but the increase in this measure will be the highest for countries in the developing and emerging regions. From the perspective of propensity to travel, 25 percent of the population of the emerging countries took a trip in 2014. However, in 2034, 74 percent of the population of the emerging countries is expected to take one trip per year. Figure 3.2 shows, for example, that while people in Europe and North America are most willing to fly, by 2034 people in India will reach the same level of propensity as China in 2014, and people in China will reach the same level as people in Europe!

These demographic changes will have an enormous impact on the patterns of air travel and networks of airlines. For example, according to the analyses by Airbus in its *Global Market Forecast*, in 2014 there were 47 aviation mega-cities in the world, representing 22 percent of the world's GDP. There were 900,000 passengers per day flying in long-haul markets to, from, and via these 47 markets. In 2034, there will be 91 mega-cities in the world, located in many developing and emerging markets, representing 35 percent of the world's GDP. And there will be 2.3 million passengers per day flying long haul to, from, and via these mega-cities.[4]

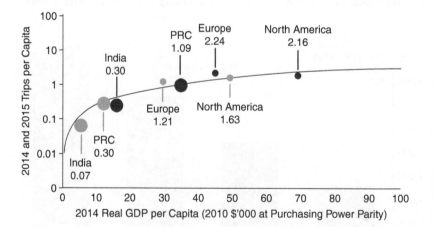

Figure 3.2 Trips per Capita (source: constructed from the information contained in Airbus, *Global Market Forecast: 2015–2034*, 2015).

Changing Characteristics of Economies

Besides the changing demographics of economies, there are a number of other characteristics that will have a significant impact on air travel.

1 New technology companies are becoming powerful components of economies. In the USA, Amazon.com has a higher market capitalization than Johnson & Johnson, and Facebook is almost equal to General Electric.[5]

2 Economies are increasingly becoming digital and are transforming the business landscape.[6] Some business analysts point to the starting point being the introduction of the web and the internet, leading to the proliferation of websites and dot-coms. These two developments were followed by the proliferation of social media and the emergence of web-based analytics. Don Tapscott lists 12 key themes of the new economy: knowledge, digitization, virtualization, molecularization, integration/networking, disintermediation, convergence, innovation, prosumption, immediacy, globalization, and discordance.[7] These 12 themes have different ramifications for different business sectors. Of significant interest for the airline industry are the themes relating to digitization, disintermediation, integration/networking, prosumption, immediacy, and globalization. Consider, for example, the theme of disintermediation and its impact on what was called distribution. Consider, next, prosumption, which relates to the shift from mass production to mass customization, an extremely important attribute for airline strategies. And we have already seen the tremendous impact of social networking technology (one of the arrows in Figure 3.10) on airline marketing.

3 Continuing the discussion on the second theme by Tapscott, digitization, Ray Wang points out that businesses need to pay much more attention to the trend that shows that customers want more than basic products and services. They want experiences and outcomes. And given the range of social and mobile technologies, the economies are taking on the characteristic of "peer-to-peer" or "people-to-people," providing connections between customers, between suppliers, between partners, and between employees. Businesses can therefore not only recognize where communications are taking place, but also how to become engaged in the relevant communications to get insights on what the customers' needs are and how to fulfill these needs. Wang describes these trends in the economies as "consumerization of technology," calling for the need to transform the businesses, for example, to deliver mass personalization at scale.[8] Again, there are insights for airlines.

4 The "peer-to-peer" characteristic of economies is also related to the term *sharing economies*, meaning sharing of the access to goods and services by leveraging information. Ride-sharing businesses, such as

Uber Technologies, have been impacting not only the travel sector but also the workforces. The number of active US Uber drivers increased from almost nothing in November 2012 to about 400,000 in November 2015.[9] Leaving aside the debate as to whether a sharing economy enhances money-earning opportunities for more people or whether it is a reduction in secure jobs and an increase in part-time jobs, the sharing economy feature has led to the emergence of new businesses such as Uber and its competitors, the San Francisco-based Lyft and Sidecar, the New York-based Gett (GetTaxi), the China-based Didi Kuaidi, and to some extent the France-based, BlaBlaCar. An example within the hospitality sector would be the growth of Airbnb. This characteristic of the sharing economy has a significant impact on air travel. The services of Uber could be combined with airline services to provide door-to-door services. The services of car-sharing companies such as BlaBlaCar could have a short-term impact on air travel. For example, if a person shared a car between a small city in France to Paris, the person could connect for the long-haul portion of the trip on a competitor of Air France, whereas if the person took a flight on Air France from the small city to connect in Paris, the probability is high that the person would stay on Air France all the way, or at least on an alliance partner.

5   Another business analyst points out that economies are becoming "intention economies" in which "customers take charge." In this context, whereas businesses are trying to use information and analytics to get close to their customers, customers are also deciding which personal information to provide to businesses, where to build their loyalties, and to let the businesses know their terms for making the purchases. Within this context, Doc Searls describes the shift from businesses using customer relationship management (CRM) to customers managing the relationship, resulting in vendor relationship management (VRM). In its simplest form, in intention economies it is customers saying this is what I am willing to buy and having sellers make offers to customers.[10] Think about the impact on distribution within the airline industry. Not only could companies such as Google enter the marketplace by better managing customer relationships, but companies such as Facebook could also enter the marketplace by representing groups of customers to increase leverage.

6   Peter Diamandis and Steven Kotler describe yet another aspect of the changing nature of economies: crowdsourcing and crowdfunding. Crowdsourcing relates to the acquisition of services, ideas, and activities from groups of people leveraging online communities, with contributors acting on their own initiatives. Similarly, crowdfunding relates to the acquisition of capital for projects from numerous people who support projects by leveraging "platforms" that connect the two groups. Two examples of companies in the US using crowdsourcing

to get innovative ideas are General Mills and Anheuser Busch to develop and deliver new products. An example of crowdfunding is Kiva.org, a website that began to make small loans (typically under $100) to entrepreneurs in developing countries.[11]

7 The changing economies also show the emergence of platform-focused integrators who can leverage the resources of others, a task that can be facilitated by technology. Therefore, disruptive innovation could enable existing information-rich organizations and some platform-focused entrepreneurs who could rapidly expand the market by organizing end-to-end services for customers who are not only connected and influence-driven, but are also looking, and willing to pay, for personalized, self-controlled, and value-driven services. The platform-focused entrepreneurs are also known as business re-definers. There is a trend toward individual entrepreneurs, more than corporations, leveraging the "platform" ecosystems to bring innovation to the marketplace to create new businesses in the uncontested market space. This means the conventional business rules will have less relevance. These entrepreneurs lean toward a smart "test-and-iterate" type of planning with customer feedback more than elaborate and intensive planning.

Customer Expectations

There is no reason to repeat the extensive information that already exists on what customers want, except to re-emphasize:

- that the power has and is still shifting from sellers to buyers;
- that customers now want more than just products and services, they also want experiences, outcomes, and choices;
- in the case of air travel, the rank-ordered areas where passengers want to see improvements are different from where airlines see their priorities;
- there is a significant disconnect between airline passengers and airline executives on customer satisfaction with the air travel experience; and
- on a global basis, customer expectations and appropriate solutions often look very different and may evolve even more rapidly.

Customer Priorities

So, what do airline passengers want? According to a recent study on *Airline Customer Experience*, conducted by the Economist Intelligence Unit in cooperation with Sabre, the most important factor was to spend less time in airports (Figure 3.3). The next four important factors were, in order of importance, more enjoyable experience in flight; improved on-time performance; improved baggage handling; and streamlined search and booking systems that operate industry-wide.

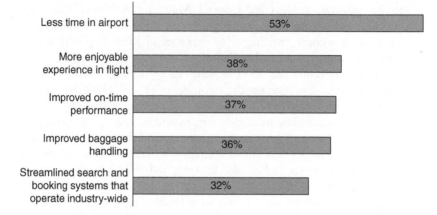

Figure 3.3 Preferred Improvements in Air Travel Experience Over the Next Ten Years (source: Sabre Airline Solutions, *Airline Customer Experience: Vital to Long-Term Success, A Special Report*, 2015, p. 7).

Management Priorities

On the other hand, according to this report, of the top six priorities of airline executives over the next ten years, priority number one is reducing operating costs. Improving customer experience is number three in the list of priorities. It is also interesting to note, according to the report, that whereas poor customer experience erodes loyalty, airline executives list building customer loyalty as the second priority but ahead of improving customer experience (Figure 3.4). The airline industry's focus on costs is understandable, given the extremely thin profit margins generated historically and, as such, the unwillingness of management to invest money in non-core areas. As the fourth section in this chapter will highlight, investments in emerging technology can help in improving customer experience, but airlines typically spend only around 2 percent of their revenues on technology. It may, in fact, be worse than this. As some analysts have pointed out in the past, if one breaks down what the technology spend is used for, it is probably heavily skewed toward overhaul and maintenance (certainly justified), integration (especially for consolidated players, also justified), administrative and other internal functions, and then customer-facing technologies. Unfortunately, the legacy systems probably require inherently heavier investment and maintenance simply because they are older and often bespoke or proprietary systems. In contrast, deeper analysis could probably show that costs of customer-facing technologies and infrastructure have been declining and can also be more readily procured on a software-as-a-service (SaaS) basis. Although newer entries, as a result, have some great advantages, it does not necessarily follow that large enterprises should continue to underfund consumer-facing capabilities that may show greater return on investment.

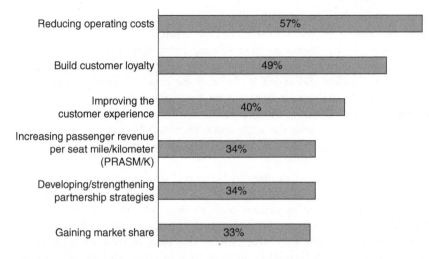

Figure 3.4 Top Strategic Priorities Over the Next Ten Years (source: Sabre Airline Solutions, *Airline Customer Experience: Vital to Long-Term Success. A Special Report*, 2015, p. 8).

While what customers want is not really new information, what is even more significant is the difference in opinion of what airlines think vs. what customers think of the response to customer needs. Not only does customers' desire for significant improvement in experience throughout the journey and expectation for personalized services continue to increase, but so does the gap between what customers think they are receiving and what airline executives believe they are providing (see the information on this gap shown in Figure 3.5). According to this survey, whereas a very high percentage of airline executives believe that customer satisfaction relating to the air travel experience has increased significantly, the percentage of customers that agree with this statement is small. It is possible that both groups are correct. One

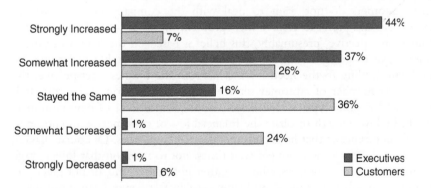

Figure 3.5 Customer Satisfaction with the Air Travel Experience (source: information provided by Sabre Airline Solutions).

explanation in the gap could be due to a different interpretation of the air travel experience between passengers and airline executives. An executive may look at the numerical number relating to on-time performance or lost baggage, while the passenger may be looking at her experience of a problem and what the airline did about it. Another explanation could be that while the data may be correct, it may not be the right data. Passengers may be including the experience at the airport as part of the total experience. Executives may be considering the experience provided by just the airlines and claiming that the experience provided by airports is not under their control – a subject discussed in Chapter 6.

It might be helpful to distinguish between "personalization" and "relevance." True personalization, in the one-on-one sense, is an ambitious goal and can still be defined in various ways in terms of how it is supported in both the digital and real world. "Relevance" is perhaps a lower hurdle, and it may be easier for airline executives, in the allocation process, to grasp and to execute. Structuring information flows so they provide relevant information, at the right time and in the right way, vastly improves the odds of positive outcomes for the consumer and the supplier.

Another point highlighted at the beginning of this section was that customers want more than just basic products and services. What are customers looking for in the area of customer service beyond the basic service itself? For example, there are some who want to be served and there are others who want to do the work themselves. There are still businesses who would like to talk with customers on the phone as they feel that this form of customer engagement increases customer loyalty and lifetime value. Two companies reported in the media are Zappos, which sells shoes, and Zipcar, which provides a car-sharing service. Tony Hsieh, the CEO of Zappos, is reported to have said that the lifetime value of a customer who makes a call, for any reason, is 5–6 times higher than a customer who does not call.[12]

Contrast this with businesses that have almost no customer service employees – including, by the way, Uber. These types of companies believe that customers do not want to deal with the company customer-service employees and prefer to resolve their problems in other ways. From the customer's perspective, presumably, this belief is based on the length of time it might take to get someone on the line and still not be able to resolve the problem, leading to the need for a call. From the business' perspective, the lower the number of customer service employees, the lower the cost. It is true that for some types of businesses the acquisition cost of new customers might be low enough to offset the financial loss of customers who choose to buy from businesses that have customer-service employees. Of course, having fewer employees leads to longer wait times, not to mention that lower-wage customer-service employees who are either not trained and/or not given the resources to solve customers' problems may, in fact, cause even more irritation for customers. How do airlines balance these considerations? Today it is fairly common for airlines to impose fees of $15–25, whether to penalize or as a disincentive for customers to make reservations by phone. In some other industries, though customers may not be encouraged to use voice vs. online channels, contact with engaged consumers is prized as a positive and as an opportunity to reinforce relationships and provide additional services. And some consumers prefer to utilize online chat services for convenience and because they automatically provide a permanent record.

Evolving Competitors

The big discussion in recent years has been on the role and impact of: (1) the three relatively new full-service airlines based in the Persian Gulf and the older Turkish Airlines – the four sometimes called "Super Connectors"; and (2) the expansion of the low-cost carriers (LCCs), including their expansion in long-haul markets. It is true that both groups are providing an increase in competition for existing airlines. However, based on some historical data for the past dozen years on passenger traffic and airline services (destination, frequency, and average fares), admittedly cursory, for both the Super Connectors and the LCCs, it seems that the increase in competition has benefited consumers by providing access to more and further diversified services (more destinations and higher frequencies, for example) and in some cases at lower fares, not to mention the often-reported contribution to "innovation, product quality, and service standards." The added value to consumers brought about by the LCCs is illustrated by analyses of services in domestic markets in three countries: India, Brazil, and the USA.

The Super Connectors

To put in some perspective the role of the Super Connectors, let us look at the extent of their operations on a worldwide basis. Although they have grown at a rapid rate during the past dozen years, on a worldwide basis their share of global passenger traffic was still only about 7 percent in 2014, based on the data compiled from the Global Demand Data of Sabre Airline Solutions Group. On the other hand, while their market share on a global basis is still pretty small, in some regions their market shares have become more significant. For example, during the dozen years examined, between Europe and the Indian subcontinent and between North America and the Indian subcontinent, the Super Connectors doubled their market share from about 20 percent to about 40 percent. However, not only did consumers have more destinations and more frequent services, the average directional fare charged by incumbent airlines decreased by about 25 percent between Europe and the Indian subcontinent and about 15 percent between North America and the Indian subcontinent between 2003 and 2014. It is true that the Super Connectors may have only reduced their fares for connecting services when competing in markets with non-stop service, and kept the fares the same or even increased the fares in markets where both types of carriers provided connecting service, but (a) there is now more service and passengers have options, and (b) the average fares are still lower than before their entry.

Was the traffic carried by the Super Connectors in these regional markets stimulated or diverted? In the Europe to the Indian subcontinent region, the Super Connectors transported almost twice as many passengers in 2014 compared to the incumbent carriers. However, both groups transported more traffic than they did in 2003, presumably, as a result of lower fares and more service. Similarly, in the North American to the Indian subcontinent market, the Super Connectors transported a few more passengers than the incumbent carriers, but both groups increased the amount of traffic they transported between 2003 and 2014. Therefore, it appears, based on this rudimentary analysis, that new competition stimulated the total market, producing more passengers for both groups in each region, showing stimulation rather than diversion. The data were compiled from the Global Demand Data of the Sabre Airline Solutions Group.

These new competitors have also changed the landscape in some regions. Consider the breadth of service provided by Emirates, for example, between Africa and the Asia-Pacific region. It is truly impressive (Figure 3.6). In the first week of October 2005, Emirates connected ten airports in Africa with 23 airports in the Asia-Pacific region. In the first week of October 2015, Emirates provided connecting services from 20 markets in Africa to 40 markets in the Asia-Pacific region. Again, people can now fly conveniently between, say, Brisbane, Australia and Luanda, Angola. Looking at the schedules on October 9 for travel on October 19, 2015, itineraries vary from service on three airlines involving three connections (in Singapore, Bangkok, and Addis Ababa) and taking 45 hours and 45 minutes to service

Figure 3.6 Emirates Airline's Network between Africa and the Asia-Pacific (source: OAG Schedule Analyser and Mapper).

involving one carrier (Emirates) with one connection (in Dubai) taking 26 hours and 50 minutes.

Similarly, Turkish Airlines is now connecting passengers on its network to more destinations in Africa than any other airline. As shown in Figure 2.2, Turkish flies, as of August 2015, to over 40 destinations in Africa compared to just five in August 2005. And compared to Emirates, which flies all of its services with wide-body aircraft, Turkish flies to most of the destinations with narrow-body aircraft, leveraging the geographic location of its hub in Istanbul. The services operated by Turkish benefit not only local passengers but also passengers connecting from smaller cities in Europe, the Middle East, and Asia to smaller cities in different countries in Africa. Destinations and frequency will undoubtedly increase with the opening of the new airport in Istanbul, bringing further advantages to travelers.

Although this section described Emirates Airline and Turkish Airlines in some detail as two of the Super Connectors, the other two Super Connectors equally play a significant role as new evolving competitors in the global marketplace. And each of the three full-service network Persian Gulf-based carriers is operating with different business models, other than that all three are operating through large connecting hubs. Etihad, the smallest of the three, has developed substantial cooperative and equity partnerships. In some ways, Etihad has been developing its own strategic alliance with reported equity to get around the constraining rules regarding foreign ownership and control. As of the fourth quarter of 2014, Etihad had the following ownership percentages in eight airlines: in Airberlin (29 percent), Aer Lingus (4 percent), Air Serbia (49 percent), Air Seychelles (40 percent), Alitalia (49 percent), Etihad Regional[13] (33 percent), Jet Airways (24 percent), and Virgin Australia (22 percent).[14] Unlike other alliances, the equity partnership alliance formed by Etihad will achieve much greater benefits for both the generation of revenue and the reduction in costs. In addition to the direct impact on the bottom line, this unique partnership will spread the risk during downturns and enhance the opportunities during upturns. Qatar Airways, the second biggest of the three Persian Gulf-based carriers, is developing a brand; known as the "World's 5-star airline," it is now a member of the oneworld Alliance, and has 9.99 percent equity in IAG, the parent of British Airways. There are other differences also, such as that Qatar operates all-business–class flights from Doha to the UK with Airbus 319LR aircraft. Although the data are not readily available, it is worth thinking about how this would compare on a revenue/profit vs. market share basis. If the new-model Gulf carriers are growing revenue and profit faster than their shares, the end result could look more and more like the smartphone business, where Apple has a low two-digit share, but the vast majority of industry profit.

Low-Cost Airlines

In India, although Air Deccan started flying in 2003 and Kingfisher and Paramount joined in 2005, it was 2006 when three more low-fare airlines entered the marketplace – IndiGo, SpiceJet, and Go Air. In less than ten years the traffic transported by the new LCCs had more than doubled the traffic transported by the existing incumbent carriers in domestic markets and raised the total traffic carried by both groups of carriers by more than 100 percent. Prior to 2006, the domestic market was served by Air India, Jet Airways, and Jet Lite. At one time there were five LCCs serving the domestic markets – IndiGo, GoAir, AirAsia India, Air-India Express, and SpiceJet. Subsequently, three carriers left the domestic marketplace – Kingfisher, Paramount Airways, and Indian Airlines (which merged with Air India in 2011). While the total traffic carried by the incumbent airlines did decrease from about 30 million passengers in 2006 to about 20 million in 2014, the traffic transported by the new LCCs increased from about two million in 2006 to about 44 million in 2014, indicating a significant amount of stimulation compared to diversion (Figure 3.7).

How did the new LCCs stimulate the market? First, they introduced new services; and second, they reduced fares. The average fare in 2009 was more than 50 percent less than in 2002. However, this fare competition, coupled with a very challenging operating environment in domestic markets – high operating costs, inefficient infrastructure, and out-of-date government policies, just to name three – did result in losses for all airlines. Then, starting in 2009 the average fare stabilized until 2013 and then increased sharply in 2014, producing a profit for some LCCs. During the FY2015, for example, while GoAir is reported to have achieved breakeven results, IndiGo posted substantial profits. And, unlike in other regions, the full-service airlines continue to lag behind the LCCs.

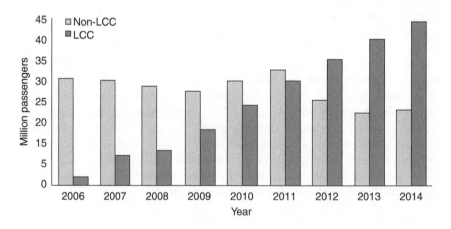

Figure 3.7 Domestic Airline Traffic within India (source: Global Demand Data provided by Sabre Airline Solutions).

In Brazil, domestic markets were served by TAM and GOL (each with about 50 percent of the market) until about 2007, when Ocean Air started service. Azul entered the domestic marketplace in December 2008. The name Ocean Air was re-branded as Avianca Brazil. Figure 3.8 shows the traffic carried by each of these four carriers within the Brazilian market. TAM and GOL have not only maintained the traffic, but each has managed to increase the traffic it carries. In addition, Azul and Ocean Air also have been increasing the traffic they carried between 2007 and 2014. Thus, the entry by Ocean Air and Azul produced a significant stimulation in the marketplace, with Azul growing at the fastest rate of all four airlines and ending up with almost 25 percent of the total traffic in just five years. As in the case of India, the stimulation resulted from the introduction of new services and the reduction in fares by all four airlines. Based again on the Global Demand Data provided by the Sabre Airline Solutions Group, the additional service, coupled with lower fares, increased the total traffic in domestic markets by almost 250 percent between 2005 and 2014.

In the USA, Spirit and Frontier continue to expand as the two ultra low-cost airlines. Chapter 2 provided some data that showed the lower fares offered by Spirit relative to its competitors. Figure 2.5 also showed how the ultra low-cost airline is stimulating the market more than diverting traffic from existing airlines. And Spirit is continuing to expand its capacity, given its significantly low costs per available seat mile. The established LCCs have been changing their business models in response to the new competitive marketplace. Southwest, whose costs are no longer low, has been increasing services in long-haul markets (for example, Newark–Las Vegas, with a stage length of about 2,200 miles), including some that are international that came from the acquisition of AirTran. JetBlue and Virgin America have been

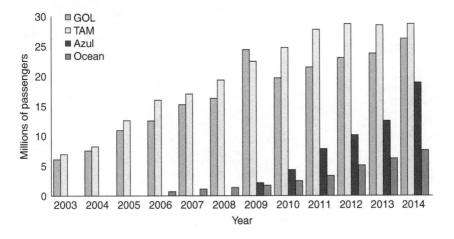

Figure 3.8 Domestic Airline Traffic within Brazil (source: Global Demand Data provided by Sabre Airline Solutions).

moving toward hybrid business models to remain competitive with the ultra low-cost airlines below and the full-service airlines above. As an example, jetBlue has been expanding its premium product in transcontinental markets in the USA and could start flying across the Atlantic with a two-class service.

Finally, low-fare airlines are no longer limiting their services to domestic and regional markets. It was mentioned in Chapter 2 that there are at least seven airlines offering scheduled services in intercontinental markets with long-haul aircraft. And that number is increasing. For example, WestJet, based in Canada, which started serving Ireland with a narrow-body aircraft with a stop in Halifax, has announced that it will serve London Gatwick non-stop with the Boeing 767-200LR. Also:

- AirAsia X flies to destinations within Asia and Australia with a fleet of 20 Airbus 330-300 aircraft.
- Airberlin serves destinations in the USA, the Caribbean, Africa, and Southeast Asia with a fleet of 14 Airbus 330-200s.
- Cebu Pacific flies to destinations within Asia and the Middle East with a fleet of six Airbus 330-300s.
- Icelandair operates a hub-and-spoke system at Reykjavik Airport, serving more than 40 cities on both sides of the North Atlantic with a fleet of 24 Boeing 757-200s (Figure 3.9).
- Flynas serves Europe and Asia with a fleet of 26 Airbus 330-200s.
- Jetstar serves destinations in Asia and Australia with a fleet of 11 Boeing 787-8s.
- Norwegian flies to destinations in Asia and the USA with a fleet of eight Boeing 787-8s (see Figure 2.6).

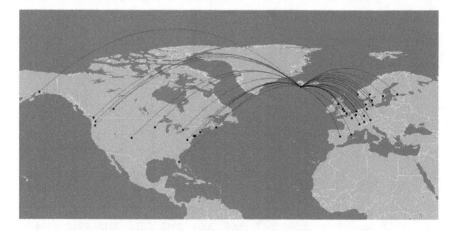

Figure 3.9 Icelandair Network, October 2015 (source: OAG Schedule Analyser and Mapper).

Enabling Technologies

Think about how technologies have been, and could be, changing economic and social life. Think about the following:

- India overtakes the USA in the number of internet users after China.[15]
- The enormous impact that social networking channels, such as Facebook and WeChat, have had in the marketing of products and services.
- Apple's Siri, a technology system embedded in the Apple smartphone, that has been working as a personal navigation assistant.
- IBM's Watson, containing a cognitive system, that can process a natural language, has a learning capability, and can develop deep insights from processing unstructured information.
- Apple's Watch, which contains technology that monitors a person's fitness attributes and works with a wirelessly connected smartphone to make calls and send text messages.
- Google-acquired Waze, a technology that generates maps and traffic information through electronics and crowdsourced reports generated by users.
- Driver-assist systems in cars that provided previously visual and audible signals and can now deploy physical ways to avoid dangerous situations.
- 3D printers that can create three-dimensional solid products from digital files.
- The Internet of Things (IoT), in which billions of things are already connected to the internet. Expansion of the IoT environment, leveraging further advancements in transmitters, networks, and sensors, is leading to a machine-to-machine (M2M) world.[16]
- Google's "self-driving" cars that have already been test-driven more than a million miles and could enter the marketplace in less than five years.
- Virtual reality, where people can not only now "sense" virtual places and environments, but also will be able to "feel" them.
- Peer-to-peer systems, facilitated by Bitcoin, that can enable direct transactions, eliminating the need for intermediaries.[17]

Moreover, the speed of adoption of new technology by consumers is increasing. In a report issued by the McKinsey Global Institute, one chart shows the following times taken to reach 50 million users: 50 years for the radio, 13 years for the television, four years for the iPod, three years for the internet, one year for Facebook, and nine months for Twitter.[18] This trend is expected to continue as digital technologies – relating to the innovative use of advancing computers, software, and communication networks – and digitized information produce machines that can beat humans, as IBM's Watson did in Jeopardy! and as Google's "self-driving" car could do relatively soon. As for airlines, the Thought Leadership Piece in Chapter 10 by Koops and Engelen of Accenture point out the potential emergence of a digital airline, from digital strategy to airline strategy.

Convergence

The enabling power of technologies is increasing not only because of the advancements in each type of technology, but also because of their convergence and synergies. Consider, for example, a dozen aspects of advancements in technologies shown in Figure 3.10. Think about the value of digitization alone – converting information into ones and zeros to make it easier to process, transmit, and store – to facilitate the conversion of some physical products and services into virtual products and services. Instead of buying a printed book a person can buy an e-book. Physical transactions can be done through online platforms such as eBay. The availability of incredible amounts of information, huge bandwidth, storage space, and sophisticated

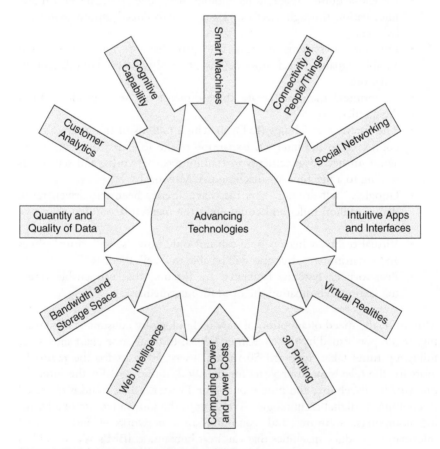

Figure 3.10 Advancing Technologies and their Convergence.

visual analytics is leading to the capability of visual images displaying multi-media content. Distribution of physical products is being impacted by the availability of 3D printers. Figure 3.11 shows some potential applications for the use of 3D printers. How much of an impact would 3D printers have on the air cargo sector, particularly for products where the transportation costs are high relative to the total production costs?

Advances in digital technology and digital intelligence are leading to the "era of cognizance" in which systems can understand (all kinds of data and in different forms such as a spoken language), they can learn, process information to reason, and influence thinking through reasoning. The comprehensive platform behind IBM's Watson represented almost two dozen engines and about four dozen technologies. Now this capability is being leveraged in many sectors, such as the healthcare sector. Think about some type of cancer and the hundreds of therapies that could be considered by a doctor. This capability will help doctors to customize treatment at unforeseen levels. Cognitive technology is much more than artificial intelligence. Artificial intelligence is an integral part of cognitive technology. And, as for working with data, most businesses work with only a fraction of the total data that exist but are not being utilized. Some data scientists claim that "more than three-quarters of the data are dark today."

In the case of the airline industry the deployment of emerging technologies represents huge opportunities to address all six priorities of airline

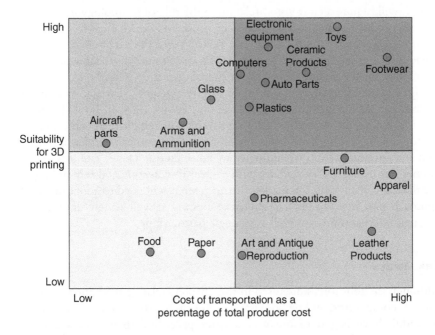

Figure 3.11 Potential Areas of Application for 3D Printers (source: Pricewaterhouse-Coopers).

executives listed in Figure 3.4, with a focus on improving the bottom line and customer experience. Think about the previous statement. If billions of things are already connected to the internet, then it should be possible to leverage connectivity – people, processes, products, and information – to create and market new value. By leveraging artificial intelligence to understand natural language instructions, Siri can answer relatively simple questions such as where is the nearest Starbucks or a gas station. The same technology can be used to answer, for now, simple questions from passengers – where is gate A34 in Terminal 2? How about the development of next-generation self-service machines at airports for passengers to process themselves, as well as through their mobile phones – not just for printing boarding passes and baggage tags but also for re-accommodations on an airline's flights as well as its alliance partners. Further out, think about the role of customer analytics, in particular predictive analytics that are embedded in cognitive technology that can inform an airline what different passengers want or will do before they know it for themselves.

Resources

However, the strategic deployment of advancing technologies (particularly digital technologies) will take much more than simply a higher investment that is currently, as stated earlier, averaging about 2 percent of the revenue base. It will require a clear vision relating to the role of technology in meeting the emerging customer and management needs and the changes in corporate culture, organizational structures, and skills to get the technologies implemented in a timely manner. Perhaps it will also require a fundamentally different way for the enterprise to look at capital allocation. Clearly, in a cyclical industry it may not always be possible to "overweight" strategic investment in customer-facing technology, but if the time is ever right, it should be now, when growing discretionary travel demand, more efficient aircraft, and, at least temporarily, lower fuel costs, are all cause for optimism. And as information and communication technologies are advancing at a faster rate than many airlines can manage, for example, with respect to detecting and responding to the dramatic changes in the markets, management will need to adopt different approaches to leverage the availability of existing as well as new information through internal sources as well as strategic partnerships.

Takeaways

Although the four forces discussed in this chapter (relating to economies, customers, competitors, and technologies) are not new, they have become more powerful, have begun to move at a faster pace, and their convergence is leading to one fundamental change – the shift in the power from businesses to customers.

The changing nature of economies (relating to demography and economics) will have a huge impact on air travel. According to research conducted by Airbus, whereas 25 percent of the population of the emerging markets took a trip in 2014, this number will increase to 74 percent in 2034. Consider the impact of this statistic in combination with the current population of emerging markets and their higher growth rates relative to mature markets.

There is more innovation, disruption, and transformation going on in the rest of the world than in the mature economies. Some businesses have learned *how to learn from* foreign markets and import or upstream business models, rather than just following the same strategies and exporting the head office version.

While airlines are well aware of customer expectations (for example, as they relate to customer experience), there seems to be a significant gap between the opinion of what airlines think and what customers think of the response to customer needs.

Competition in the airline industry will increase even more with the expansion of the four Super Connectors (the three Persian Gulf-based carriers and Turkish Airlines), the LCCs (particularly those with long-haul operations), and the ULCCs that have been stimulating the market more than diverting traffic from existing carriers.

It is the convergence of the technologies (smart machines and customer analytics, for example) and outcome (reduction in the price of computing power, for example) exemplified in Figure 3.10 that will allow technology to be an enabler of disruptive innovation. However, it is the C-Suite that needs to develop a vision based on what it "can sense, see, and extract" in the information about the needs of customers. And it is cognitive technology that will be a game-changer – the ability to acquire and process information and apply knowledge.

Brynjolfsson and McAfee point out that advances in technology would enable people to receive more of everything, physical products and digital products and services, and to lower prices, resulting in an increase in the variety and volume of people's consumption.[19]

While there is some value in understanding the important trends that are shaping the future, it is more important to know how to use the information on the key trends to shape the future.[20]

Notes

1 Dobbs, Richard, Manyika, James, and Jonathan Woetzel, *No Ordinary Disruption: The Four Global Forces Breaking All the Trends* (New York: Public Affairs, 2015), p. 5.
2 Ibid., p. 5.
3 Ibid., p. 7.
4 Airbus, *Global Market Forecast: 2015–2034*, Toulouse, France, 2015.
5 Clark, Don and Strumpf, Dan, "Technology stalwarts soar to new highs," *Wall Street Journal*, October 24–25, 2015, p. A2.

6 Brynjolfsson and McAfee argue that measuring GDP in the traditional way may not be reasonable in the information age. See Brynjolfsson, Erik and McAfee, Andrew, *The Second Machine Age: Work, Progress, and Prosperity in a Time of Brilliant Technologies* (New York: W.W. Norton, 2014).

7 Tapscott, Don, *The Digital Economy: Rethinking Promise and Peril in the Age of Networked Intelligence* (New York: McGraw-Hill, 2015), chapter 2.

8 Wang, R. "Ray," *Disrupting Digital Business: Create an Authentic Experience in the Peer-to-Peer Economy* (Boston, MA: Harvard Business Review Press, 2015).

9 "New rules for the gig economy," *Wall Street Journal*, December 10, 2015, p. A2.

10 Searls, Doc, *The Intention Economy: When Customers Take Charge* (Boston, MA: Harvard Business Review Press, 2012).

11 Diamandis, Peter H. and Kotler, Steven, *BOLD: How to Go Big, Create Wealth, and Impact the World* (New York: Simon & Schuster, 2015).

12 Mims, Christopher, "Customer service: from touchy feely to do it yourself," *Wall Street Journal*, November 2, 2015, pp. B2 and B5.

13 Previously known as Darwin Airlines.

14 The equity position in Aer Lingus will most likely change now that Aer Lingus has been acquired by the IAG group.

15 McLain, Sean, "India to overtake US in number of Internet users," *Wall Street Journal*, November 18, 2015, p. B6.

16 Diamandis and Kotler, *BOLD*, pp. 46–7.

17 Vigna, Paul and Casey, Michael J., *The Age of Cryptocurrency: How Bitcoin and Digital Money Are Challenging the Global Economic Order* (New York: St. Martin's Press, 2015).

18 Dobbs *et al.*, *No Ordinary Disruption*, p. 43.

19 Brynjolfsson and McAfee, *The Second Machine Age*.

20 Canton, James, *Future Smart: Managing the Game-Changing Trends That Will Transform Your World* (Boston, MA: Da Capo Press, 2015).

4   ADAPTATION STRATEGIES
    BY AIRLINES

Airlines worldwide have been adapting, although at different paces and different levels of intensity, to the forces and their convergence and intersection described in the previous chapter. This chapter outlines the adaptation strategies in four broad areas: (1) consolidation, in various forms, to improve the bottom line, to be able to compete more effectively in the coming years, and to smooth out the financial performance during cycles; (2) network alignment to remain competitive, be poised to access strategic global markets, and achieve operational excellence; (3) proactive customer management in the information-led and increasingly connected world to win and maintain loyalty; and (4) the distribution space where airlines face challenges, not just on the decision of simply direct vs. indirect, but also on whether or not to partner with existing and new distributors. Examples are provided that show a variety of adaptation strategies of a broad spectrum of airlines worldwide. Limiting the discussion to just these four areas does not mean that airlines are not adapting strategies in other critical areas, such as the re-alignment of their balance sheets (by restructuring debt, for example) and corporate diversification. Delta, for example, reduced its debt by $10 billion between 2008 and 2014, which led to a significant decrease in interest payments and much higher ratings from agencies.

Consolidation

Given some unique internal characteristics of the global airline industry (for example, the constraints of bilateral agreements and ownership rules) and the intensive leverage of external events (such as deep downturns in economies and swings in the price of fuel), airlines have always felt the need to develop various types of partnerships. Unless an airline is fairly small, operates with a limited network in a small region, and serves a small segment of the market, there is value in some form of partnership to remain viable and to grow. Decades ago airlines developed inter-line agreements followed by code-share agreements that benefited airlines – providing access to markets that were closed due to bilateral agreements – and benefited passengers through efficient itineraries in the globalizing world. Then strategic alliances were developed, enabling the partners to share assets and resources such as schedules, loyalty programs, and airport lounges. With the availability of anti-trust immunity, airlines developed joint-ventures through which they could not only share costs and revenues, but also "coordinate" schedules and fares.

In 1997, Northwest and KLM received approval to establish a joint-venture that was so successful that it started a trend. It helped both airlines to reduce some operating costs, such as those relating to sales in both regions, and it helped to improve the scheduling process by maximizing the connecting passengers from "behind" and to "beyond" cities, optimizing the number of aircraft needed, and the spreading out of departing flights during the day (avoiding the creation of bunches around peak times). For example, flights leaving Detroit for Amsterdam on December 1, 2015 show departure times at 4:02 p.m., 6:05 p.m., and 8:52 p.m. (an almost five-hour spread). Without the joint-venture the two carriers are likely to have only two flights instead of three, and departures at times very close to each other instead of a five-hour spread. The fleet optimization process also frees some aircraft that can be operated on other routes.

It is estimated that, whereas at the beginning of this century only about 5 percent of the seats were flown in long-haul markets around the world by airlines with joint-ventures, 15 years later the number is closer to one-third of the total flights. There are many reasons for the increase in the developments of joint-ventures. A prominent reason is the increase in competition from low-cost airlines and the expansion of the relatively new carriers based in the Persian Gulf. To remain viable, the large legacy full-service airlines lowered fares in short-haul markets, decreased service in these markets, and increased service in long-haul markets to the extent possible within their operating authorities. However, to be able to fly significantly more in international markets required some sort of partnerships, including joint-ventures.

The Open Skies agreement between the USA and Europe (2008) led to the desire for, and the possibility of, even more joint-ventures. The end result is clear. The joint-venture between Air France-KLM, Alitalia, and Delta now involves around 250 flights each day across the Atlantic and offers connections worldwide. This joint-venture alone accounts for about 25 percent of the total capacity between North America and Europe. Then there are other powerful joint-ventures between Lufthansa, United, and Air Canada, as a second large group, and between American, British Airways, and Iberia, as a third group. Delta, in fact, has yet another powerful joint-venture with Virgin Atlantic that, in some ways, competes with Delta's joint-venture agreement with Air France-KLM. The markets between North America and Europe now have numerous joint-ventures. Therefore, airlines in North America and Europe are beginning to develop joint-ventures with airlines in developing markets such as with airlines in Latin America and Africa.

The content of the joint-ventures varies significantly. Generally they all encompass the "metal neutrality" element – sharing of, at least, revenue, if not profit proportionately, regardless of who carries the traffic. While the concept itself is relatively straightforward, the implementation has been difficult given such considerations as the treatment of the "beyond and behind" traffic, sharing customer data, and ancillary revenues. And, although strategic alliances (in which airlines can sell the seats of each other and pool some operating costs) have been around for much longer, it is the "metal neutrality" attribute in the agreement that provides one differentiation between joint-ventures and strategic alliances. Other differences in joint-ventures relate to the degree of competition a joint-venture creates within a market. The powerful joint-venture between Air Canada, Lufthansa, and United is designated as the A++ transatlantic joint-venture (see Figure 7.2 and Table 7.1) whose government approval required some concessions to maintain competition. Its government approval called for, for example, Lufthansa giving up a slot to a competitor between New York and Frankfurt. However, alliances, with their relatively loose coordination rules, lack the power of integrated airline groups where there is a much stronger governance, given the asset-driven relationship of the consortium.

From a consumer point of view, short of a full merger and subsequent integration efforts, various forms of partnerships and alliances have resulted in a mixed and confusing set of attributes. Code-share flights often involve very different equipment and operating standards; loyalty program benefits vary widely across alliance partners and are typically curtailed or unavailable on "partner" flights; functions as mundane as advance seat assignments on alliance flights are far from seamless, even for elite travelers. Consumers have to search out these issues for themselves, a frustrating and annoying task. Overlaying revenue management issues and benefits that shift with fare classes further erodes trust.

The ultimate desire on the part of many airlines in partnerships has been to achieve full consolidation through mergers, a process that has been slow due to the government approvals needed and the length of the approval process. And although the consolidation process through mergers has been underway for some time, the pace has accelerated to achieve more control in managing capacity and prices and to deal more effectively with the changes in the marketplace brought about by the swings in fuel prices, regional conflicts, changes in the economies, and natural disasters. Since the beginning of this decade: in Europe British Airways and Iberia merged in 2011, having created the International Airlines Group (IAG). In 2012, British Airways acquired British Midland International. In 2013, IAG took control of Vueling, the Spanish low-cost airline based in Barcelona. In 2015, IAG acquired Aer Lingus. In the USA, United and Continental merged in 2012. The same year, LAN and TAM merged in South America to form LATAM. Back in the USA, during the period 2013–14, American Airlines and US Airways merged to create the world's largest airline in terms of fleet size and revenue base. If the government of China allows Air China and China Southern Airlines to merge, a reported possibility, it would create the largest airline in the world in terms of the size of its fleet.[1]

Some mergers created ripple effects, leading to further organizational changes. The merger between LAN (a partner in the oneworld Alliance) and TAM (a partner in the Star Alliance) created a need for the merged carrier LATAM to choose one or the other alliance. LATAM chose oneworld, leaving a void for members of the Star Alliance in Brazil. This development led both United and TAP Portugal to develop equity partnerships with Azul. Given the fact that Azul now is the third largest carrier in Brazil, there are discussions for Azul to join the alliance, a major development given that Azul is a low-cost carrier (LCC).

Another form of consolidation has been the development of equity partnerships to create "virtual global networks." As pointed out in Chapter 2, Etihad has various levels of equity in seven airlines around the world. The partnership in these airlines clearly provides synergies. For example, through such partnerships with Alitalia and Jet Airways, Etihad was able to negotiate some strategic slots at Heathrow Airport in London. It is also relatively easy to integrate networks and frequent flyer programs. Similarly, Delta has acquired equity in the Mexico-based Aeromexico, the Brazil-based GOL, and the UK-based Virgin Atlantic. The HNA Group has acquired equity stakes in Africa World Airlines (based in Ghana), Aigle Azur (based in France), Azul (based in Brazil), Comair (operating as a British Airways franchise), as well as an LCC, Kulula (based in South Africa), Hong Kong Airlines as well as Hong Kong Express (based in China), and MyCargo (an all-cargo airline based in Turkey). Airlines with these "virtual global networks" have been able to achieve significant benefits in scheduling their combined fleets, optimizing their revenue, and managing their loyalty programs once they found and installed an efficient governance structure.

The key benefit has been in the area of optimizing the networks based both on the strength of the airlines in the portfolio and membership in an alliance, especially where airlines have signed joint-ventures. Take, for example, the three major European operators, the IAG, the Lufthansa Group, and Air France-KLM. Each group has increased its transatlantic capacity in terms of both frequencies and seats during the past ten years. The increase in frequency of the flights operated by the Lufthansa Group was more than double the increase posted by Air France-KLM. The percentage increase in the seats was also the highest for the Lufthansa Group (about 40 percent) compared to Air France-KLM (about 20 percent) and much higher than the IAG (about 5 percent). And, whereas both the Lufthansa Group and Air France-KLM increased the average size of their fleet (from 272 seats to 303 seats and from 288 seats to 310 seats, respectively), the IAG decreased the average number of seats in its fleet (from 311 to 270).

Has the consolidation process achieved its goals? Figure 4.1 shows the airline enterprise value by region estimated by the Association of Asia-Pacific Airlines. If one combines all the initiatives taken by airlines worldwide (different forms of consolidation, network alignment, managements of customers, and so on), the biggest gains seem to be made by the four major airlines based

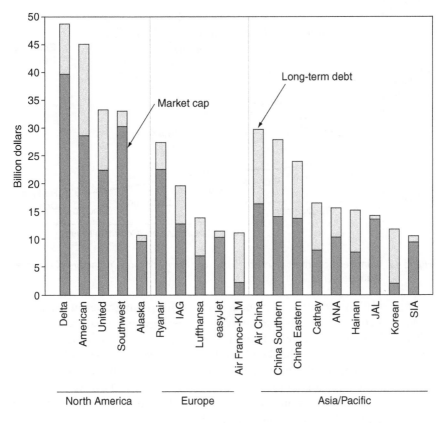

Figure 4.1 Airline Enterprise Values by Region (source: Association of Asia Pacific Airlines).

Note
Market capitalizations as of 5 November 2015.

in the USA in terms of enterprise value and Earnings Before Interest and Taxes (EBIT). The primary reason might be that consolidation, through actual mergers (as opposed to subsidiaries within a group), led to better control of capacity and, to some extent, pricing power. The four large airlines in the USA, having gone through mergers and having restructured their operations and balance sheets, now have the highest levels of market capitalization in the world, with Delta not just leading the group in the USA, but the whole world.

Network Alignment

An airline's network has a disproportionate leverage in the generation of total revenue – estimated to be about 80 percent (Figure 4.2). As a result, leading airlines are making major changes to their networks based on different types

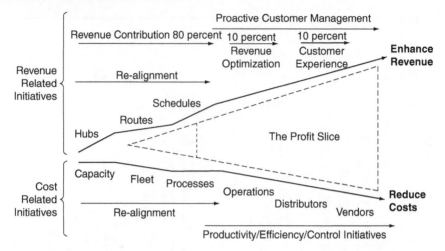

Figure 4.2 Relative Revenue Contributions of Network and Proactive Customer Management.

of consolidation processes, described above. Also, playing roles in the alignment of networks are advancements in technology and data, described in Chapter 7. As for the value of networks, we need to look no further than the successful expansion of the LCCs and newer-generation network airlines, particularly based in the Persian Gulf, and also the recent re-alignment of Japan Airlines' network and fleet. What is now different, however, is a new level of vision and intuition and new types of data and technologies that are being used to optimize an airline's network.

Traditionally, airlines have used five types of basic input in the analysis and planning of their network, fleet, schedules (frequency, capacity, and times of departure and arrival), and cabin configurations. The most important input came from the size and seasonality of the origin and destination (O&D) traffic. The second input related to market demographics; the third input referred to competitors (schedules and frequency); the fourth related to partners (inter-line initiatives); and the fifth input came from local sales teams in each market. While these five considerations are still important, the importance of each input has been evolving significantly, and technology has changed to enable optimization to be at the enterprise level for an independent airline and at the group level for partners such as those within the IAG and the Lufthansa Group. Even for a single airline the optimization now is achieved from a system perspective as opposed to a functional level, on a piecemeal basis, and a sequential basis. New perspectives on these five areas are given in Chapter 7.

Consider, for example, the third input relating to competitors. The competitive analytics are changing. First, airlines that were not considered serious competitors are now serious competitors. Not too long ago major US airlines did not consider Southwest to be a direct competitor, as the latter sold the product directly through one channel, in purely domestic short-haul markets, and to and from secondary airports. Now Southwest sells through multiple channels, offers long-haul flights, and operates to and from major airports, and in some near-international markets. Additionally, airlines that were partners may now be competitors, or vice versa – for instance, the changing relationship between Delta and Alaska Airlines in the USA. While they have been code-sharing for some time, which way is the relationship headed? India's powerful conglomerate, TATA, has an interest, along with Singapore Airlines, in Vistara. TATA also has an interest in AirAsia India along with AirAsia. Will the common owner, TATA, consider these two upstarts to be partners or competitors? In Australia, Qantas is still an anchor in the oneworld Alliance, but is also re-defining its network through collaboration with Emirates. And, perhaps most noteworthy, not only are there discussions about LCCs connecting with each other, but LCCs connecting with full-service airlines.

While network and schedule planning in the past relied more on the rigorous use of sophisticated analytical models and operations research techniques, and less on vision and intuition, the balance in focus between science and intuition is being revisited, with an increase in uncertainty in areas of regulatory policies, the state of economies, and the staying power of new-generation competitors, whether they be large, full-service global players, sophisticated hybrid airlines, or LCCs with increasingly viable business models for service in intercontinental markets. Think about the role of science vs. vision and intuition when

- Singapore Airlines decided to add one more subsidiary to its portfolio of airlines, Scoop, to maintain and increase market share;
- Etihad decided to create a virtual global network via strategically aligned partners as well as membership in a traditional alliance;
- Turkish Airlines decided to offer service to more than 40 destinations in Africa from its hub in Istanbul;
- Norwegian Air Shuttle decided to offer transatlantic service between the UK and the USA (and more recently between France and the USA) to compete with not just lower fares, but also with marketing initiatives through social network platforms;
- Delta acquired 49 percent of the equity in Virgin Atlantic Airways, despite its partnership with Air France-KLM;
- IAG decided to go aggressively after Aer Lingus, based not so much on the value of its slots at Heathrow Airport in London, but its hub in Dublin that would add strategic value to the three other hubs of the IAG – London, Madrid, and Barcelona; and
- United announced it will fly non-stop between San Francisco and Singapore.

The idea behind the new thinking in network and schedule planning is not just a conventional computation of the share of the market, but also the potential to develop the market. And it is this latter vision and intuition that is explaining, presumably, the growing network of the Super Connectors. Clearly, vision, intuition, and market development potential must have played a role in Emirates' decision to run five trips per day between Dubai and London Heathrow with the Airbus 380, four trips per day between Dubai and Johannesburg with the Boeing 777, and a double daily between Dubai and Mauritius with the Airbus 380. Think about Qatar Airways' decision to put a non-stop flight between Doha and Philadelphia, a relatively thin market.

Below are some specific examples of airlines changing their networks to adapt to the forces mentioned in the last chapter, including: Lufthansa, British Airways, All Nippon, Delta, and Azul. Let us start with Lufthansa.

Facing strong competition from LCCs (Airberlin and easyJet, for example), and ultra low-cost carriers (ULCCs; such as Ryanair and Wizz Air), Lufthansa created some time ago a low-cost subsidiary, Germanwings, to operate in short-haul markets that did not serve destinations from its major hubs in Frankfurt and Munich. In other words, Germanwings served markets within Europe that did not include Lufthansa's two main hubs in Germany. It flew in and out of Cologne/Bonn, for example. As a result, Lufthansa flew from its two hubs in Germany in small and medium size markets within Europe with twice as many seats as Germanwings did from other cities in Germany to destinations within Europe, even though Lufthansa has been reducing the number of seats it flies relative to those flown by Germanwings. However, the cost structure of Germanwings, while lower than Lufthansa, was still much higher than the other European LCCs. And even though the average fare charged by Germanwings was higher than that charged by competitors, it is reported that Germanwings experienced losses. One reason reported for the higher operating costs of Germanwings was that its pilots worked under the Lufthansa group-wide labor contract.[2] And it is the differential in this cost structure between Germanwings and other LCCs that has been encouraging Ryanair to expand its service, to, from, and within Germany.

Not having succeeded with the introduction of Germanwings, Lufthansa started to divert capacity from Germanwings to Eurowings (another low-cost partner) and also have Eurowings offer capacity on some long-haul routes, from Cologne, operated for the time being by SunExpress Germany. Presumably, Eurowings has lower operating costs than Germanwings partly because of different contracts with labor. Eurowings is forecast to have a fleet of 89 aircraft in 2017, 82 Airbus 320s and seven Airbus 330-200s.[3] With its lower operating costs and long-haul fleet, Eurowings is reportedly expected to fly in long-haul markets such as Boston, Las Vegas, Miami, and Cancun to the west, Mauritius to the south, and Bangkok and Phuket to the east.

In response to the Persian Gulf-based carriers, Lufthansa has developed a revenue-sharing joint-venture agreement with Singapore Airlines that includes flights of the subsidiaries of both airlines (Austrian and Swiss on the Lufthansa side and Silkair on the Singapore Airlines' side). According to

CAPA (the Centre for Aviation), the joint-venture will cover about one-third of the capacity flown by the Lufthansa Group and Singapore Airlines on a non-stop basis between Western Europe and Southeast Asia.[4] The joint-venture provides benefits for both sides to compete not only with the three powerful airlines based in the Persian Gulf, but also major players based in Europe, such as British Airways and KLM, and some based in Asia such as Thai Airways and Malaysia Airlines. It is interesting to note that both Lufthansa and Singapore, while in the same strategic alliance, have not only tried to remain independent but, in fact, have been competitors in some ways. Now they have a joint-venture as both need to compete more effectively with the Gulf-based three airlines.

As for British Airways, it has been strengthening itself in many different ways. The previous section already mentioned the formation of a holding company made up of British Airways, Iberia, Vueling, and Aer Lingus to be an effective competitor for the traffic going across the North and South Atlantic, as well as traffic destined for Asia. It has also been strengthening its powerful hub in London by carefully selecting the non-stop markets that served to maximize the value of half of the slots it holds at London's Heathrow airport. While British Airways has been focusing on its network across the North Atlantic (adding, for example, second-tier cities such as San Diego, California, and Austin, Texas), Iberia has been focusing on its network across the South Atlantic, growing its destinations between 2010 and 2015. New routes include Montevideo, Santo Domingo, Havana, Mexico City, and Panama City.

British Airways' hub at Heathrow is very different to Air France's hub at Charles de Gaulle and Lufthansa's hub at Frankfurt. The very large O&D market at Heathrow makes it less dependent on connecting traffic and the lack of capacity at Heathrow; also, the nature of the traffic coming to and from Heathrow enables British Airways to charge premium fares. Take a look at the top 20 long-haul markets in the world. Many are to and from London. In fact, the connecting traffic from regional airports in the UK that cannot make connections easily at Heathrow may be impacting the connecting traffic of Air France and Lufthansa more than British Airways. And British Airways is developing intriguing relationships with other airlines, again to maximize the value of its Heathrow slots. Consider the equity of Qatar Airways in IAG, enabling Qatar to transport traffic from the UK to the Indian subcontinent. Sometime in the future, LATAM could be integrated under the IAG umbrella.

Next, think about the value that Aer Lingus brings to IAG. It had the third largest number of slots at Heathrow after British Airways and Virgin Atlantic. And British Airways had already acquired British Midland International in 2012. So, for British Airways, Aer Lingus provided not only a lot of extremely valuable slots but, even more important, a hub in Dublin that can, in some ways, be considered to be the equivalent of a third runway at the constrained Heathrow Airport. And given that Dublin (as well as Shannon) has US immigration pre-clearance facilities, British Airways would

be able to connect some of its westbound traffic through Dublin. As for competing effectively with the Super Connectors mentioned in the previous
chapter, British Airways, by deploying innovative strategies and leveraging its
global hub strength, increased its non-stop service, for example, from London
Heathrow from four destinations in India in 2002 to five destinations in 2014,
while charging a premium fare relative to the Super Connectors and benefiting from the overall growth in the market. This analysis is based on the
Global Demand Data provided by the Sabre Airline Solutions Group. Consequently, it is intriguing to note that whether an incumbent loses or gains
market share in competing with the Super Connectors may depend on
whether it is reactive or proactive in its strategies to leverage its network, on
its own or with partners, in the face of new competition.

The IAG organizational structure is clearly working to compete in the
highly competitive marketplace. The group has been able to develop an
integrated framework in which each major entity (for example, British
Airways and Iberia) competes for resources while maintaining its own brand.
Iberia, which had been losing money since 2009, did not get the resources
until it fundamentally changed its operating and financial structure. The
changes not only resulted in a financial turnaround in 2014, but also enabled
it to obtain more resources that led to further profits in 2015. Similarly, IAG
is really benefiting from the exploitation of synergies, with respect to both
revenues and costs, through the strategic alignment of networks, fleet, and
back-office functions and processes. The group posted a real return on
invested capital of 12 percent for the year 2015 and is aiming to be at 15
percent for the coming period. And whereas the average share price of the
Lufthansa Group and Air France-KLM has been declining during the
2014–15 months, it has been increasing sharply for IAG.[5]

All Nippon Airways in Japan has taken a slightly different strategy to
compete with LCCs. To begin with, the penetration of LCCs in Japan has
been minimal compared to the Philippines, Indonesia, Malaysia, Thailand,
and even Korea. There could be five reasons: high operating costs, shortage
of pilots, a difficult environment relating to distribution, the availability of
good ground transportation (particularly from high-speed trains), and the
service-minded public in Japan. As such, until recently, Japan Airlines and All
Nippon did not really have any significant low-cost competition on domestic
routes. The business models of the three, supposedly, LCCs, Air Do,
Skymark, and Starflyer were not significantly different from the business
models of Japan Airlines and All Nippon.

As a result, the domestic market did not grow for almost the first 15 years
of this century. Around 2010, the government did start discussing the possibility of low-cost entry through the liberalization of government policy,
including the privatization of secondary (regional) airports. These signals led
to the formation of joint-ventures between Japan Airlines and Jetstar (a subsidiary of the alliance partner Qantas) and between ANA and AirAsia. The
government needed to be very careful in implementing policies to encourage

low-cost competition as it had just facilitated the bailout of Japan Airlines in 2011. This may explain the rationale for the development of joint-ventures with LCCs, especially for Japan Airlines. In any case, both full-service carriers were mindful of the fact that the low-cost subsidiaries of full-service carriers had failed in other parts of the world. In fact, the joint-venture between All Nippon and AirAsia was also terminated. The LCC Peach entered the marketplace in 2012, basing its service in Osaka at Keizai Airport, and All Nippon acquired a significant equity share in Peach Aviation. Peach operates domestic routes to major airports and secondary airports as well as to nearby international destinations such as Seoul and Busan in Korea, Hong Kong, and Taipei and Kaohsiung in Taiwan, and Okinawa. Another LCC, Vanilla Air, started in 2013, this time with a relationship with All Nippon. For its long-haul network, All Nippon has relied heavily on its partnerships.

In the USA, the situation relating to low-cost competition is different. To begin with, Southwest, jetBlue, and Virgin America are no longer low-cost competitors as their costs have increased over time. At the same time, Spirit and Allegiant are also not in the category of low costs as their costs are even lower and they are in the category of ULCCs. And, while Spirit has been growing at around 20 percent per year since 2010 and has a nationwide network including service to 84 percent of the top 25 metro regions, it still only represents 2 percent of the seats in the USA compared to Ryanair, which represents around 10 percent in Europe.

As for Allegiant, this niche ULCC operates a very different business model. It deploys very old aircraft with low-frequency service in leisure markets and focuses strongly on ancillary product lines. The airline trades off low aircraft utilization and high maintenance costs with low aircraft ownership costs, and trades off low aircraft utilization with the ability to match capacity to demand. In addition, labor productivity is high, airport costs are low, and the product is kept very simple. Schedules are established to bring crews home each time, saving crew costs and reducing maintenance costs at non-home airports. Allegiant appeals to price-sensitive customers in thin markets that are under-served. These markets are too thin for the larger carriers and even too thin for the other ULCCs on a non-stop basis. And the yield is so low that they are insignificant to the larger airlines or even other ULCCs. Allegiant selects markets very carefully to avoid competition. There is only competition on about 10 percent of Allegiant's routes. However, it has started to go for medium-size cities from Las Vegas and Orlando.

Given the situation in the USA, Delta has been rationalizing its capacity and hub structure within domestic and international markets (exemplified by the reduced focus on Cincinnati and Memphis and added focus on Seattle, London Heathrow, and Shanghai). It is expanding in international markets by leveraging equity positions in foreign airlines, leading eventually to joint-ventures. It is aiming to expand its equity in Aeromexico, for example, to 49 percent, the same level as in Virgin Atlantic. Delta already has small equities in GOL and China Eastern. Delta also tried to acquire an equity position in the lower-cost airline Skymark, based in Japan. Through significant equity stakes and joint-ventures, not only is Delta getting access to new markets but also the ability to exert some influence on the design of networks and the optimization of revenue for the partners. Greater access to strategic routes is important to balance its network in foreign markets and to stay competitive with other airlines. Within the USA–Mexico market, the second largest international market from the USA, Delta's share of seats in November 2015 was around 8 percent, compared to United at 21 percent and American at 23 percent.[6] Similarly, while the economy of Brazil has been down, it is still an enormously powerful region and its economy will turn around eventually. Consequently, the equity in GOL will strengthen Delta's position in Brazil. The partnership with Virgin will help with the capacity in the USA–Heathrow market where Delta's share of seats is 8.5 percent, United's is 13.4 percent, and American's is 18.4 percent.[7] Similarly, Delta has a lower seat share compared to American and much lower compared to United between the USA and China, a market that could increase significantly as a result of the discussion on Open Skies between the two countries, explaining the equity stake in China Eastern.

In South America, Azul has been responding to the changing marketplace with aggressive and rapidly changing strategies. First, it began operations with new Embraer 190s rather than the conventional old Boeing 737s or the old Airbus 320s. It developed a vast network connecting secondary markets in a large emerging country with large bases at Viracopos, Belo Horizonte, Santos Dumont, and Curitiba airports. Azul began to offer low fares to compete with bus transportation in the short- and medium-haul markets. Then it added complexity by acquiring the smaller ATRs to compete in even thinner markets and uses bus transportation to provide some feeder traffic. It also merged with a domestic LCC, TRIP, to manage competition and obtain scale quickly. Next, it added even more complexity by acquiring Airbus 330s to operate long-haul routes to the USA. Next, it developed a partnership with United in which United took an equity stake in Azul. For United the arrangement meant connecting traffic in Brazil, given that the Star Alliance partner, TAM, had merged with LAN and the combined airline, LATAM, decided to become a partner in the oneworld Alliance, as mentioned previously. For Azul, it meant potential feeder traffic in the USA for its new long-haul operations and the possibility for an even deeper relationship in an emerging environment, given the discussions between the USA and Brazil regarding Open Skies. This development could lead to code-share agreements with not only United but also jetBlue, given jetBlue's strong bases at Fort Lauderdale and at New York's Kennedy Airports.

Next, in conjunction with a group of investors, Azul acquired a 61 percent stake in TAP Portugal, the largest carrier in the Brazil–Europe market. TAP, a small European carrier, had been struggling for some time and had been up for sale for some time. However, although small, it had a strategic location and a relatively strong network within Europe, Africa, and North and South

America, particularly Brazil. Although short-haul routes within Europe faced competition from LCCs, they were needed to provide feeder traffic for long-haul routes out of its base in Lisbon. On the other hand, except for the long-haul routes to Brazil, TAP had strong competition from the larger hubs of Air France, Lufthansa, Iberia, and British Airways. However, Brazil played an important role given the heavy business traffic to and from Portugal and heavy leisure traffic from Brazil to Europe via Lisbon. TAP already flies from Portugal to 12 destinations in Brazil and, according to Azul; there could be eight additional destinations in Brazil for TAP. The equity stakes of United and TAP, both partners in the Star Alliance, could lead to the possibility of Azul, an LCC, joining an alliance.

To top it all, on November 24, 2015, there was an announcement that the HNA Group would buy a 24 percent stake in Azul to strengthen the air transportation market between Brazil and China. These initiatives hardly represent the typical strategies of LCCs – keep costs low by avoiding complexity. On the contrary, Azul has been adding complexity, but it also has been opening up opportunities for future growth worldwide, and at a rapid pace. And investments from the likes of the HNA Group, having postponed its own IPOs, will enable Azul to fund its rapid growth and fleet orders of not only the Airbus 320s but also the Airbus 350s, not to mention positioning Azul to capitalize on the eventual turnaround of Brazil's economy.

Airlines have always been well aware of the fact that the value delivered to passengers depends not just on the quality of an airline's network but also on the quality of its operations. But now operational excellence is becoming a competitive force. As such, in addition to aligning their networks, airlines have now also begun to put a much greater emphasis on operational excellence, and that depends heavily on the complexity of the airline business relating to operations. There are many reasons behind the complexity of the airline business. Just one is that many assets of an airline are mobile and remote – aircraft and flight crews, for example. Another is that an airline operates in an extremely fast-changing environment brought about by rapidly changing weather patterns, airport congestion, and unforeseen maintenance events during the "day of travel," resulting in irregular operations. The financial performance of an airline that operates with extremely thin margins is therefore highly dependent on the efficiency of its decisions during irregular operations that, in turn, are affected by the mobility of an airline's assets and the continuously changing environment during the "day of operations."

Forward-thinking airlines are now beginning to understand more clearly that suboptimal decisions made by operations management impact not only costs and revenues, but also value – in terms of the traveler experience, for example. Recently, airlines have been managing their operations proactively when they have fairly good notice that, for example, a major ice storm approaching within the next 24–36 hours will affect a major airport for a whole day. However, operations become much more challenging when operating conditions deteriorate without much notice and problems are compounded. Given the capability to integrate data and communications available within different silos of the operations department, leading airlines have begun to "connect the airline" and to deploy advanced optimization techniques to reduce costs and enhance experience as well as value – see the discussion in Chapter 7.

Customer Management

As shown in Figure 4.2, about 80 percent of the revenue of an airline is generated by its network and schedules and about 20 percent by various aspects of customer management. Of the 20 percent relating to customer management, about half is related to revenue management and half to customer experience. As indicated in the previous chapter, customer expectations are increasing in areas relating to product personalization and customer experience that, in turn, depend on customer engagement. And given the availability of mobile devices and connectivity, customers want instant fulfillment of their needs – relevant services delivered anywhere and at any time. Leading businesses have made significant progress in satisfying customers' expectations using three building blocks: (1) availability, in *real time*, of holistic information on customers; (2) smart communication technologies and connectivity; and (3) the culture and skills to leverage both.

From a higher-level perspective the ongoing challenge faced by airlines is how to reduce operating costs and increase revenue while improving the customer's experience and brand loyalty. In recent years, however, in the US airline sector, strategies to decrease costs have, in many cases, led to deterioration in the passenger experience. Examples include the installation of higher-density seating configurations to reduce unit costs, elimination of meals, pricing strategies to maximize revenue per flight, reduction in the mainline non-stop services in lower-density markets, reductions in call center staff and/or additional charges for reservations made through call centers, and so forth. Similarly, industry-wide strategies to increase revenue – baggage fees and complicated rules, reservation change fees, seat location fees, and reduction in the number of seats available for redemption on desired flights in the loyalty programs, not to mention charges for redeeming loyalty miles – have led to an increase in dissatisfaction and a loss of loyalty.

Airlines, while reactive and initially slow in transforming their businesses to improve customer experience, are now becoming much more proactive, given the turnaround in their financial performance in recent years. For decades, and as a group, airlines did not make profits on a consistent basis and, as such, were focused more on operation, product, and process centricity than on customer centricity. With razor-thin margins, airlines focused on market shares and the efficiency of their operations, adapting reactively to the changing dynamics in the marketplace – proliferation of mobile devices, social media, and the desire for superior customer experience in the purchase and use of products and services.

Now, some airlines (a) having made noteworthy progress in getting their financials in order, having recently made profits, and having some confidence that the profitability trend is sustainable, and (b) having some experience with the role of technology to facilitate business model changes, have started to make investments in technology, systems, and processes to balance focus on operational efficiency with customer experience. On the operational side, for example, leading airlines are looking into the possibility of the breakdown of silos, the integration of data, and the use of predictive analytics with the possibility of saving millions of dollars to deal with irregular operations.

The previous section described the progress made by British Airways to deploy the IAG structure to position itself for the longer term. The group has begun to develop strategies to leverage the common technology base to improve its customer service and the personalization of its products and services. Similarly, Delta is now committing financial resources to focus on the use of technology and retailing strategies to de-commoditize its products and services, while identifying which segments are valuable and how they should be served.

To improve customer experience, airlines have enabled passengers to shop, check-in, obtain the status of flights, and find their way around airports using smartphones and their apps. Airlines are now working on initiatives that will enable passengers to receive dynamic and relevant offers, re-accommodate themselves, and personalize their in-flight entertainment and Wi-Fi activities, leading to an increase in personal experience. For further improvements, the challenge relates to the availability and use of information, specifically: (a) passengers' willingness to provide it; (b) airlines' ability to process it analytically and cross-functionally; and (c) the travel chain members' willingness to share it and use it proactively.

Airlines have a lot of information on customers and are trying to get more – for example, by monitoring customers' behavior on the web and at different touchpoints. On the other hand, and rightfully, there are customers' concerns relating to privacy and the commercial use of the information. For example, a 2015 SITA report, *The Future is Personal*, cites that 72 percent of travelers are willing to share their location or personal data with travel providers. However, far fewer travelers are willing to share personal information if they either do not see the benefit or if they feel it will be used for invasive commercial purposes. For example, according to the same SITA report, only 29 percent are willing to share personal information for commercial purposes, while 40 percent are willing to do so if the information is to be used to improve travel.

Until recently, the information that airlines do have on their customers has been residing in various disparate functional areas. Airlines are now beginning to integrate this information across functions to provide holistic views of customers, within the limitations of the available data. Two interconnected key attributes being focused on are that the information is in real time and it is holistic. Real time means having information that is current and having it accessible when and where it is needed. Unfortunately, right now, much of the information that is in real time tends to be narrow and incomplete. This person has been on the website three times looking at the same flight. Let us make her an enticing marketing offer – a narrow view. But what do we know about her to make her a compelling offer based on her needs? This action would require holistic information on the customer and the context.

A few airlines have begun to consider using customer analytics to interpret customer information, to understand customer behavior, and to manage customer experience. Some are even exploring the use of predictive analytics to make valuable predictions about the impacts of, for example, website improvements and proposed marketing offers. Some are considering the possibility of using programmatic analytics to make real-time offers based on the context of the search. If a male or female traveler has made reservations for two, one adult and one child, and provided information that there is also to be a third traveler, a child under two years of age, and if they have a relatively tight connection at an intermediate airport, the airline makes an automatic offer for the meet-and-greet service as well as the fast transfer service feature at both, the point of origin and the point of connection. Based on the experience of the trendsetting airlines, these marketing initiatives require changes in culture and skills, knowing not just the breadth of merchandizing but its depth with respect to having analytic-based customer-merchandizing insights.

The third point about information is the sharing of information among the travel chain members, between airlines and airports and between airlines and agents, for example, to improve the experience on the ground. Some airlines have already made significant progress (with the limited personal information they have on their customers) with the development of smartphone apps to improve the customer experience and make relevant commercial offers to increase revenue. They are now able to inform passengers not only of the status of their flights, but also information on the best time and the route to take to the airport (using data from sources such as Google Maps), and information on food and beverage service onboard. They are now working on providing the capability for self-service re-accommodation in case of irregular operations, at airport kiosks and eventually via smartphones.

The availability of internet access and Wi-Fi onboard is also enabling airlines to improve the onboard customer experience through personalized products and engagement with customers. Although just becoming available on airplanes, these systems are showing the potential to provide in-flight content (content that can be viewed on a customer's choice of mobile device) based on a passenger's background with information derived from social media. As for engagement with customers, crews are now being equipped with systems and in-flight connectivity to solve travel-related personal problems, while on board, such as that a connection will not be made and a rebooking will be required. These airlines are balancing the need for ancillary revenue through the sale of internet and Wi-Fi services and the value of providing free Wi-Fi service vs. mining data on customer behavior.

To various degrees, airlines have already been developing tiered processes to improve the experience of their most valuable customers. For this very small percentage of their very high-valued customers, airlines do provide some combination of:

- 24/7 dedicated numbers at call centers that are staffed with skilled and empowered personnel;
- limo services to and from airports;
- meet-and-greet services at curbside (with boarding passes and baggage tags in hand);
- separate check-in terminal buildings;
- escort services throughout the airport (including private car service for those with tight connections) and at the doors of arriving aircraft for passengers making connections;
- guaranteed accommodations on the next flight in the case of irregular operations;
- reservations on competitors' flights if necessary, regardless of the cost;
- free access to airport lounges with coupons for meals;
- constant tracking of customers and their baggage;
- expedited delivery of the mis-connected baggage to the customer's hotel, with arrangements with the hotel's customer relations staff to provide the customer with the needed items; and, in very limited cases private jet services.

Different airlines provide different levels of the aforementioned services depending on the status and value of the traveler. However, airlines are realizing the existence of two serious challenges.

First, even though some airlines provide such levels of service to their top customers, the experience delivered has been inconsistent and/or based on a profile of a customer that is different from the one in the database. A customer's profile changes from trip to trip or even for the same trip, depending on the situation and direction. The cause of the variation in the customer experience can be related to the fact that an airline may not have real-time information that is comprehensive (providing a 360-degree view of each customer), may not have deployed the essential technology and processes to make the information actionable, or may not have the skilled staff or business rules to know what to do even when information is available regarding what has happened. It is recognized that even with the necessary information and even with the availability of the information in an actionable form, the operationalization aspect also requires a transformation in corporate culture coupled with the need for talented staff that are at ease with the use of digital information to meet the personalized needs of customers at different touchpoints throughout the journey. This has been a challenge with an increase in the number of touchpoints, for example, as a result of the increasing use of mobile devices and customer expectations for solutions on a 24/7 worldwide basis and within an omnichannel framework – at airports, through call centers, on the web through desktop or mobile devices, or with alliance partners. In fact, a passenger expects to receive fast and consistent information while talking with a call center agent on her mobile phone and looking at the website of the airline on her iPad at the same time.

Second, even though airlines have been implementing technologies coupled with the needed changes in the relevant processes and human skills, they are seeing a need for scalability. Customers of lower status also expect an improvement in their experience. Forgetting about a better experience for 100 percent of the customer base, some airlines are simply aiming for about 10 percent, as opposed to the current 1 percent representing the most valuable customers. So, what is wrong with continuing to provide the excellent experience to the most-valued customers – say, the top 1 percent? Some airlines make two points: First, this group is more likely to be the most loyal segment anyway and will continue to travel with the airline. As such, their margin is not likely to increase much more. Second, it is the next segment, between 1 and 10 percent of the total customer base, that could easily be the really high-margin segment. Improving the customer experience for this next segment will most likely increase the value of the most-valued customers. And it is technology, coupled with a transformational change in culture and talent, that will enable scalability and much higher margins.

As for personalization, some airlines are moving toward incorporating dynamic pricing and dynamic inventory into their online marketing strategies – for example, with the display of advertising campaigns and Google AdWords. An airline can include, for example, instant savings to incentivize booking on the spot. The challenges to overcome include hundreds of millions of stock-keeping units (SKUs) (for a large airline) and the use of legacy systems to deal with personalized alerts. As such, traditional display advertisements have been too general, such as saying there are low fares to Asia from Los Angeles. Now, airlines experimenting with dynamic pricing and dynamic inventory are getting much more specific, such as $1,239 in economy class and $2,396 in premium economy to HKG for the shopper who is online. Show the tag, here is the "Best Price." It is not in economy or business class, for example, but in premium economy. These airlines have concluded that they should not rely on a customer finding a low fare based on trial and error or even the deployment of AdWords, with its low conversion rate. For dynamic pricing and inventory there is a need for comprehensive information and it is difficult to extract proficiently this time-sensitive information using existing legacy systems. As such, these airlines are encouraging customers to sign up for sale-fare alerts on specific routes and between specific dates. Some airlines are even considering a communication that they will match any published fare.

A key point in the proactive management of customers is to optimize revenue based on dollars per customer, based on information derived from processing transactions as well as analyzing information on customer behavior, expectations, and experience, and customer acquisition costs. And it is this information (coming from websites, mobile apps, airport kiosks, loyalty programs, and so forth) that can be monetized to dynamic retailing and generating value, including through user-generated content. It is this information-generated value (derived from integrated and active data warehouses as well as the use of non-relational data management systems) that feeds back to build relationships that increase the dollar per customer. The communication of the information is in both directions. An airline needs to provide, for example, specific information that the customer is seeking – the specific fare and seat availability rather than general information on a service, such as the forthcoming new seat configurations. If the customer has been targeted (separating those who are just shopping vs. those who are looking for specific information to make a purchase) then the airline needs to provide the information sought and incentivize the purchase immediately.

Distribution Management

The second area of customer management relates to distribution, an area that has been changing very rapidly during the last five years. Here are some reasons.

Initially, there were large OTAs such as Ctrip and Expedia, and smaller ones like BookIt.com, CheapOair, and metasearch engines such as Kayak and Skyscanner, all backed by solutions and/or data from the Global Distribution Systems (GDSs) who have continued to play a significant role in low-fare search. These distributors displayed the basic product reasonably well, given that the content – schedules, prices, and availability – was basically a commodity. Consumers could rank order the offerings from airlines by duration of the trip, time of departure, and price. And the metasearch engines directed the traffic to the selling airlines. However, questions were still raised, for example, when a distributor provided information on a schedule that had an exceptionally long layover and combined the airline seat with other travel products. An airline may have wished that this information was pointed out to the purchaser and options suggested, even if they involved a higher price. There were also concerns about the compliance of fare rules – local fares vs. O&D fares, for example. Airlines tried different approaches to dealing with distributors. Some time ago, for example, American removed its content from a major OTA and Delta removed it from a group of smaller agencies and metasearch engines for brief periods. The idea was not so much to reduce distribution costs but the desire to gain control of the shopping and booking experience. At the time, Delta provided a realistic example. A person in the USA can buy an Apple product from a general store like Best Buy or from an Apple store. However, while the product is the same, the experience is very different.

Subsequently, airlines unbundled their products and began to sell ancillary products and services, adding complexity to the displays. Furthermore, some airlines began to make investments in their brands and offered branded products and needed information on the individual, making the search and the relevant conditions at the point of sale so as to optimize revenue per customer (not seat) and customer retention. Think about airlines that invested in their products, such as high-quality lie-flat beds and direct aisle-access seating configurations (Figure 4.3). The challenge became how to show this rich content and to display it effectively (not just with text but also with high-quality images and video) through different channels to impact a customer's choice decision. Partly with this in mind, IATA launched the New Distribution Capability (NDC) initiative to address some of the limitations of the existing distribution system and to enable airlines to transform the way their products and services could be marketed, thus enabling airlines to display full and rich content as well as a more transparent shopping experience. Although GDSs may have resisted at first, they are now onboard to assist airlines with ancillary distribution, using the NDC XML standard. Two large North American airlines are now enabled to sell ancillary seats via a GDS using NDC XML.

There were other developments that impacted the distribution of airline products. There is the shift that began to take place from the use of desktops and laptops to mobile smartphones (next, possibly to wearables), to an

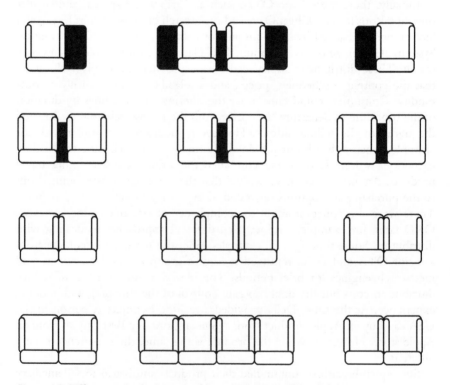

Figure 4.3 Differences in the Layout of Seats in Business Class Cabins.

increasing number of and more sophisticated apps, to mobile merchandizing, and to the delivery of personalized products and services. Accompanying this shift was the shift that started to take place in the way people conduct search for their travel products. Not only do they want to spend a lot less time conducting the search but, increasingly, search appears to be done in spurts and spread over a longer period of time. And consumers expect the "system" to have a memory relating to the search conducted over time and in brief moments. And while searching for travel, people want the results fast and with limited and customized offers, not with dozens and dozens of flights listed with detailed schedules and hotel options with all kinds of text and photos, but rather just a few that are relevant to the user. Around the same time, whereas the metasearch engines previously directed the traffic to airlines' websites (even though the fulfillment may have taken place on the metasearch engine's website), some metasearch engines began to think about making the booking themselves.

As a result of these developments new distributors began to show an interest in the travel space (for example, Amazon.com started with the hotel sector as an extension of the Amazon Local app), and Google, the powerhouse in the search space, has caught the attention of airlines and existing distributors. Even though Google had acquired ITA Software some time ago and developed products such as Google Flights and Google Hotel Finder, it now has come out with a specific system – *Book on Google* – a comprehensive destination-related search tool with a booking capability. And in December 2015, Uber was given the patent for *Uber Travel*, an interface similar to metasearch sites but with the ability to order a taxi for what Uber calls the "last mile" of a trip. And Uber has started to penetrate not only the business sector with its ground-based car service, but just announced its decision to broaden its services by offering on-demand helicopter services in partnership with Airbus – *UberChopper*.

The challenge for airlines will now be to capitalize on these trends while not losing control of (a) distribution costs, (b) the relationship with customers, and (c) customers' loyalty. Admittedly, anywhere between 25 and 40 percent of air travel is corporate travel, traditionally the most loyal, or at least the most locked-in sector due to corporate travel management programs. Due to travel policies, some of the trends discussed here are more difficult to apply to the corporate travel sector. However, consider the shift to mobile. It has significant implications. The screen on smartphones is small to begin with and it is clumsy to have multiple screens open at the same time. Users are reluctant to visit multiple sites, let alone make bookings on multiple sites that require users to remember multiple passwords and the use of a credit card multiple times. Next, since people want to spend less time on their search, they find the use of apps to be more valuable. This point explains the popularity of Uber's transportation product. A couple of clicks and the transaction is complete! On the flip side, some consumers do not trust airline prices – that is, they do not know if they are getting a good deal.

As mentioned, Google saw an opportunity to capitalize on these trends, especially if the NDC would allow it to get the rich content directly from the airline. Assuming that at least one half of the people begin their trip planning by searching for information on Google anyway, and given that Google had in its portfolio most components for destination trip planning and booking, it was just a matter of integration of its available resources. Besides the capabilities of the ITA Software, Google Flights, and Google Hotel Finder, there were Google Maps, Google+, and the Zagat Survey – adding to the functionality and comprehensive features for planning trips, especially on smartphones. Through its integrated platform Google began to offer comprehensive information on airlines, hotels, restaurants, and sites. Google can combine data it has from various sources such as searches made on its site on content, locations, the related products, and points of interest. Google has even acquired Frommer's branded travel guidebooks, but recently it has been reported that Google may sell that product back.

Although existing OTAs can also offer comprehensive packages, the feature promoted by Google is the ability to offer context-based travel searches to a customer using a sophisticated set of preferences that are relevant at the time of the search. Google can use, for example, the data on itineraries from Gmail and GPS destination-related information and make recommendations based on the knowledge of a customer's interests and preferences. Next, it is the quality of the information provided, relating, for example, to inventory such as the promotional price of the airline ticket and hotel room at the specific time and their availability. Then there is the ability to make the booking on the spot and pay for the entire package using the Google payment capability.

Airlines recognize that for search relating to travel there is clearly a difference between desktop and mobile sites and, furthermore, a difference between mobile websites and apps on mobile phones. Airlines also know that the experience varies among the three, even on the mobile phone – for example, between the use of the mobile web and a mobile app. It would also appear that the conversion rate would be higher for a person using an app on a mobile phone compared to someone using a website on a mobile phone. And Google can capitalize on the importance of this experience and conversion rate for its segmented customer base whose needs are, presumably, not met by airlines' mobile sites and apps for shopping and booking easily and seamlessly. As such, the *Book on Google* channel will appeal to the segment looking for an on-the-go experience and within this segment the sub-segment that is focused on micro-moments – short bursts of travel planning. These searches reflect questions raised with respect to destinations or events for very short periods of time – a minute or two as well as over a short period itself, such as the past few weeks or couple of months.

Some hotels within the USA have already begun to partner with Google. There are some European airlines that have also decided to partner with Google, at least for now. Lufthansa, for example, has become a partner given that the user is being directed to the airline's website when it is time to book the flight and, presumably, the airline pays for these leads. So the identities of the actual seller and the service provider are made clear. Presumably, Google suggests an airline based on the interest and intent of the user. As such, Google is not acting as an agent for the seller, but is a provider of information and enabler of transactions. Some analysts are claiming that this is consistent with Google's desire to be a "platform" that sets the standards for transactions, and not be just another agent, warehouse, or service provider. In his Thought Leadership Piece in Chapter 10, Dan Wacksman of Outrigger Resorts provides another perspective on the new entrants in the distribution space.

Some airlines are raising questions in two areas. Is the decision to direct traffic to a particular airline's website based on the results of organic search or paid search? Who owns the CRM? Will the seller feel that its product has been displayed in the right context? Although the partnership could lead to a win–win situation, the outcome depends on the answers as to who owns the customer relationship and how the search engine and the transaction facilitator is compensated and whose brand is being promoted – the airline, the hotel, or the distributor – and the strength and awareness of an airline's brand vs. the distributor, particularly Google. Some OTAs are also evaluating the competitiveness of the new powerful entrant. But, then, why would Google compete with an OTA, if the OTA provides advertising revenue and, say, a hotel is willing to discuss different methods of commission payments – percentage commissions or pay-per-click charges. Assuming that the advertising revenue from the OTAs comes from the commissions paid by the airlines to the OTAs, then it is possible that Google would get that money directly from the airlines if their ability to present offers in a contextual way is better than that of the OTAs.

So, airlines are looking at options since their decisions go much further than simply direct vs. indirect and whether or not to partner with distributors and, if yes, which distributors. Such decisions lead to some basic questions.

First, is the airline ready to make investments so that it can market its rich, branded content effectively, protect the content it owns, control it, and market to an emerging segment that wants to make an instant booking – the moment-to-moment segment? This aspect includes the need for not just new "shopping centers" (given that airlines represent the front door to travel) but also to establishing proactive mobile platforms leveraging the NDC with the ability to interact and achieve higher conversion rates and not be overly concerned about thinking of ways to bypass some channels. Keep in mind that the need is to invest enormous amounts in smarter technology, such as the capability to provide a single mobile app to address concerns and experience relating to the entire journey, not just from one jet way to another jet way for airlines and for check-in to check-out for a hotel.

Second, can the airline achieve greater flexibility to vary the product offering, such as with respect to price, not just within the 26 booking classes but also within various aspects of the ancillary products and services? In other words, the ability to introduce modular fare options. This question leads to two other requirements – digital thinking and upgraded revenue management systems. Digital thinking calls for investments in customer-centric dynamic retailing, pushing the relevant content to the relevant customer at the right time and at the right price. A distributor might push for the lowest available fare without identifying all the features related to this fare, whereas an airline may wish to push branded fares. The second requirement calls for the availability of a new revenue management system that leverages real-time pricing capabilities.

Third, can the airline recognize the person or organization making the inquiry and tailor the offers accordingly? This capability also calls for the availability of a recommendation engine dealing with what product to offer to a specific customer at a specific time. The quality of the recommendation engine would depend on the ability to perform sophisticated semantic search that is based on much more information than matching keywords.

Fourth, while there is value in forming partnerships, the question is how an airline can create and control its product content and its distribution and manage not just engagement with the customer but also the pricing aspects in the era of mobile pay and wearable technology.

Fifth, can the airline balance its decision relating to short-term vs. long-term relationships? In the short term, getting the reservations directed to the airline and even making some payments is reasonable, but what about the longer-term potential concern when a distributor begins to mine its enormous database and exercise some control on the referrals? This leads to the need for an airline to establish key performance indicators (KPIs) to measure the success relating to the fulfillment of its strategic intent and the financial aspects, both in the short and long term, of distributing through different channels. The KPIs are well established for travel agencies using the GDSs; however, these and new entrant channels will all require some tuning in order for airlines to make the most efficient use of the expanding travel marketplace.

So, what about the potential ramifications of new entrants into the distribution space? Are there some insights from the experience of low-cost carriers entering the marketplace? Initially, they were considered to be threats by the legacy carriers. Now the two sectors seem to have found a way to co-exist. One could even conclude that the LCC generated more new passengers than they diverted passengers from legacy carriers. Could airlines look at Google, Uber, and Airbnb – which is also expanding into the business sector – the same way as the experience with LCCs? And could customers be more satisfied with the services provided by these organizations since the power has shifted from sellers to buyers of travel products?

Takeaways

Consolidation, particularly in the case of full mergers, has provided the greatest benefit for the four major carriers based in the USA. Some analysts are claiming that consumers are getting "streamlined" offers but at higher fares.

Realizing the continued importance of the network in the contribution of revenue, around 80 percent, airlines have been finding new ways to optimize the network, fleet, and schedule (with more focus on vision and intuition) and through equity stakes in foreign airlines.

Of the remaining 20 percent, 10 percent can now be generated by optimizing the revenue by adding ancillaries and loyalty in the optimization process and the remaining 10 percent by improving customer experience through data-driven customer intelligence and not just business intelligence. In both cases, the object now is to manage customers proactively and to optimize revenue per customer, not revenue per seat.

Low-cost carriers are having discussions to connect with each other as well as with full-service carriers.

Distribution strategies impact not only costs but also the management of customer relations. New and powerful players are finally entering the distribution space, offering the capability for search that is seamless, semantic, and connected, not to mention comprehensive booking functions – now all through mobile devices.

On a global basis, with a large number of new and innovative entrants and rapidly growing access to air travel by new or first-time travelers in developing and emerging markets, there are new forms of go-to-market initiatives, communication and payment systems, merchandizing, and distribution. And the initiatives in all of these areas are evolving rapidly. For established airlines that make the effort, a closer watch on these areas may yield valuable insights into the future.

Notes

1 Chinese merger plans pose risk," *Wall Street Journal*, December 10, 2015, p. B1.
2 CAPA (Centre for Aviation), "Germanwings has preserved Lufthansa's market share, but still has too many legacy issues for a LCC," October 14, 2014.
3 CAPA, "Lufthansa to Germanwings to Eurowings: long haul and lower cost as Lufthansa seeks solutions," November 26, 2015.
4 CAPA, "Lufthansa, Singapore Airlines respond to Gulf competition with a limited JV: there is scope for more," November 13, 2015.
5 "IAG: delivering on its promises," *Aviation Strategy*, 211, November 2015.
6 CAPA, "Delta Air Lines increases its Aeromexico stake and broadens its influence in the US–Mexico market," November 23, 2015.
7 Ibid.

5 ADAPTATION STRATEGIES

Developing and Emerging Markets

Whereas the previous chapter exemplified adaptation strategies mostly within developed regions, this chapter attempts to provide an overview of the adaptation strategies being discussed and implemented in the developing and emerging markets. That raises a first challenge. What is a developing market or region and what is an emerging market or region? There do not appear to be any universally accepted definitions of what constitutes a market or a country to be developing or emerging. There are also other characteristics used to describe countries, such as frontier and newly industrialized. In the broadest sense, developing markets could be considered to include countries with underdeveloped industrial bases, even though some may have high rates of economic growth. Many countries in Africa, some in Latin America, and some in Asia would fall within this category. Similar challenges exist for defining emerging markets. Again, from a broad perspective, an emerging market could be one with some characteristics of a developed market and some of a developing market. Examples include a very broad spectrum of countries – Argentina, Brazil, Chile, China, India, Indonesia, Malaysia, Mexico, South Africa, South Korea, Taiwan, and Turkey. It is possible to include Persian Gulf States (United Arab Emirates and Qatar) in this list, given their rapid development status. In general, emerging markets tend to have higher growth rates for their economies than developed regions, but emerging markets can also have higher risks and greater volatilities. The variation with respect to the state of the economy, economic growth, risk, and volatility is enormous, even for the 12 countries listed above. Take the case of political unrest and its impact on the aviation sector. It has an impact not only on tourism but also on attracting and maintaining qualified executives and operating staff of an airline. The impact of the recent political unrest on Egypt and Egyptair is a case in point. Think also about the impact on travel of pandemic threats such as the case of Ebola in Western Africa in 2014, which had an effect on the rest of Africa with the association of this regional threat applying to the whole of Africa.

Within the boundaries of this challenge, this chapter provides some examples of adaptation strategies in Africa (representing a developing region) and Asia (representing an emerging region). In Chapter 2, a point was made that the best example of disruptive innovation within the airline industry was the introduction of low-cost services. These services were proposed by entrepreneurs, but their implementation was held back until governments changed their policies, in the USA enabling Southwest Airlines to enter the marketplace and in the UK enabling Laker Airways to do the same. In developing markets, such as Africa, disruptive innovation has been held back by the constraints of government policies to a much greater extent. But in emerging markets, such as those in Asia, the variation in government policies has been much greater, more conducive to low-cost carrier (LCC) entry in places such as the Philippines and Malaysia and less conducive in places such as China and Japan. As such, the benefits of disruptive innovations could easily be brought about in Africa through changes in government policies on liberalization of market entry (implementation of the Yamoussoukro Decision), ownership control rules, consolidation, taxation, and the rapid development of infrastructure. These changes, accompanied by a reduction in the constraining aspects of government intervention, would facilitate the availability of capital and the entry of new-generation aircraft. The benefits can easily be observed from the experience of the expansion of airlines in Asia – Indigo, Lion Air, and AirAsia.

Africa

While the 54 states in Africa represent 15 percent of the world's population (just over one billion people), they produce only 3 percent of the world's airline seats even though characteristics of the terrain and distances make transportation, other than by air, quite difficult. And given the economic characteristics, there is a need for affordable, and therefore efficient, air transportation to connect people and resources. However, the provision of air transportation services that are safe, secure, reliable, and affordable provides enormous challenges for airlines, despite the growing recognition that the marketplace represents enormous opportunities arising from the convergence of rising entrepreneurs, expanding businesses, and investments in technology. Some background might be helpful to put into perspective the differences in the adaptation strategies of airlines based in Africa. In his Thought Leadership Piece in Chapter 10, Barry Parsons, a seasoned airline executive, provides significant insights into disruption within the airline industry on both the supply side and the demand side.

There is great fragmentation in that there are almost 400 airlines in Africa, of which 32 are IATA airlines. There are probably 200 airlines that have Aircraft Operating Certificates from their states. However, only about six have the scale to compete in international markets. Although there are some relatively large airlines, such as Ethiopian, the top ten airlines based in Africa operate only a total of 454 aircraft (see Table 5.1), compared to 953 mainline aircraft in the fleet of American Airlines (as of June 2015), now the world's largest airline. For this comparison the size of an airline is based on the number of aircraft in the fleet in 2015, with the data extracted from various sources such as websites of airlines and the internet. In terms of the number

Table 5.1 Fleet Size of the Top Ten Airlines Based in Africa

Rank	Airline	Fleet
1	Ethiopian	76
2	South African	65
3	Egyptair	63
4	Royal Air Maroc	53
5	Air Algerie	50
6	Kenya Airways	45
7	Tunisair	32
8	Comair	26
9	Arik Air	24
10	Libyan Airlines	20
	Total	454

Source: Airline websites and the internet.

of seats offered, even the largest airports (Johannesburg and Addis Ababa) are not in the list of the top 75 airports around the world.

The airlines are typically government owned (except for Comair and Arik Air in Table 5.1) and government intervention is typically very high. Almost all airlines are not commercially sustainable. There are exceptions such as Ethiopian Airlines, discussed below, and private airlines such as Comair. But government objectives for many of the unsustainable airlines may not be making a profit. One objective could be to provide strategic links for the connectivity of people and trade. Not only are the capital bases themselves weak, but the costs of additional capital tend to be extremely high. The government policy tends to be not only unconstructive but is often dysfunctional. Airlines have higher operating costs that have led to barely breakeven results during the past five years. Fuel costs are estimated to be 20 percent higher than the world average due to higher government taxes and levies. There are all kinds of government taxes such as taxes on passengers, tourism, and transportation. Airport charges are the highest in the world. Infrastructure, relating to facilities at airports, air navigation, and security is very poor, although some states are making progress in addressing these deficiencies. There was significant airport infrastructure development in South Africa in preparation for the World Cup 2010. New developments are being constructed in Gaborone, Maputo, Livingstone, Cairo, and Victoria Falls. Some other airports currently have infrastructure under construction or in planning phases, such as Nairobi, Harare, Lusaka, and Dakar. According to the published data relating to safety, the accident rate in Africa in 2014 was 11.18 per one million flights, compared to 1.92 for the world average.[1] It is also reported that the jet hull loss in Africa in 2014 was zero for all IATA and non-IATA airlines. The turboprop rate was higher, leading to a high average for all aircraft.

One particular area where costs are high is related to distribution. There are many reasons. First is that in developing regions more passengers access travel via indirect channels (as opposed to booking directly through an airline's website). This aspect also adversely impacts cash flow and the ability for LCCs to exploit one of the key benefits of their model to fund additional fleet. A second reason is that internet penetration tends to be low in developing countries compared to both developed regions as well as emerging regions such as China. Third, the quality and the high cost of the broadband have an impact. Fourth, the percentage of travel coming from the corporate sector vs. the leisure and personal sectors has an impact on distribution costs. However, to provide an example of progress made in Africa, Kenya has become known as the country with the most advanced digital payment system using simple texting technology on simple mobile phones – the M-Pesa system.

The value propositions tend to be uncompetitive relating to network, schedules, and products, and this uncompetitiveness has a disproportionate negative impact on yield. One can look at the expansion of foreign airlines – Emirates and Turkish Airlines, and to some extent the Lufthansa Group and Air France-KLM – into Africa after markets were opened up. These expansions made the value propositions of the African airlines even less competitive when comparing schedules, cabin products, and loyalty programs. Consider the service between Johannesburg and London offered by South African Airways and British Airways. Even when both airlines offered the same frequency, South African Airways offered a two-class product, whereas British Airways offered a four-class product in its Airbus 380s. The schedule may not be important if there is no effective competitor in the marketplace. Between Windhoek, Namibia and Frankfurt, Germany, Air Namibia has a non-stop flight, whereas British Airways, Etihad, Ethiopian, Lufthansa, and South African Airways offer service with connecting flights. So the schedule may be less important if the quality of the schedule and frequency aspects appeal to business travelers. Otherwise, the airline based in the developing region ends up transporting mostly leisure travelers and possibly even group leisure travelers that may produce even lower yields. There are, of course, exceptions such as Ethiopian Airlines, Air Mauritius, and South African Airways.

An airline based in a developing market can compete effectively with more recognized airline brands if it offers non-stop service compared to a connecting service, has a good loyalty program, and some benefit in the area of government travel contracts. Looking at the schedules on December 7, 2015, in the market for Johannesburg and Cairo, South African Airways showed (on Expedia's website) a non-stop flight that took eight hours, while Etihad showed multiple flights, with one taking 13 hours and 40 minutes. Interestingly enough, for a round trip (returning on December 14) South African Airways showed an economy class fare of $796.55, whereas Etihad shows a fare of $974.55. Clearly, either Etihad believed its brand to be of higher value to command a higher fare despite the service being connecting, or South African believed its brand to be of lower value to warrant a lower fare despite the fact that the service offered was non-stop. On the other hand, if South African Airways code-shares on Egyptair's flights and if Egyptair's product is not comparable to Etihad, then it would be a comparison between Etihad and Egyptair and not South African Airways. But would a passenger go this far to make the comparison?

The relatively small size of the aviation sector can be seen from another perspective. Figure 5.1 shows the names of the top ten largest urban areas (each with a population of at least five million) with lines that show the availability of non-stop airline service. According to the OAG study cited below, of the total 45 city pairs (connecting these ten cities) only 22 city pairs have non-stop service. And even though these 22 city pairs had non-stop service, the frequencies offered in 2014 were minimal in long-haul markets such as Nairobi–Abidjan, Nairobi–Lagos, Johannesburg–Cairo, and Johannesburg–Lagos. It is interesting to note that to travel between some city pairs of reasonable size within Africa, passengers have had to travel to Europe or the Middle East to make connections – fly north for 1,000 or more miles and then fly south again. One reporter recently pointed out that the fastest way to travel between Algiers, Algeria to Cape Town, South Africa would take 18 hours, with the passenger flying to Lisbon, Portugal and then to Luanda, Angola, and finally to Cape Town.[2]

Consider also the fact that Nigeria, the largest state in Africa by population, has neither a strong airline nor a large airport with a connecting

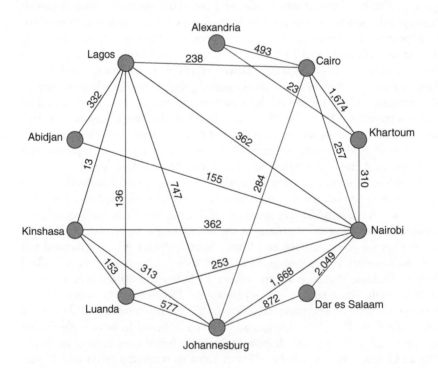

Figure 5.1 Non-Stop Service Connecting the Top Population Centers in Africa (source: OAG, "The big five," 2015).

hub-and-spoke system. Nigeria-based Arik Air is a relatively small airline in comparison to the size of Nigeria. Consider the size of Ethiopia, with about half the population of Nigeria, and its flag carrier, Ethiopian Airlines, which has been expanding globally – see Figure 5.3 for Ethiopian's strategy of expanding its network with equity, strategic partnership, and technical support involvement in airlines, discussed below. And, Ethiopian is profitable. Consider also the size of the airport in Addis Ababa. Even South Africa, with a population that is less than one-third that of Nigeria, has a reasonably sized airline, even though it has been struggling for some years. And considering that air transportation of people and goods plays an important role in developing economies, the government should establish policies to facilitate the development of a powerful airline based in Nigeria with a high level of services to North America, Europe, the Middle East, and Asia, particularly to China, given the high level of interest by China in making investments in Nigeria.

The penetration of low-cost airlines in Africa has been minimal relative to other regions of the world. To the extent that this sector does exist, it is concentrated in South Africa. Table 5.2 shows the top ten airlines in the LCC category, again based on the size of the fleet. It should be pointed out that this table does not show Comair Limited (based in South Africa) as a low-cost airline as it is a franchise of British Airways and a oneworld Alliance affiliate airline of British Airways. However, Comair has a low-cost airline (Kulula) that is a division of Comair and Kulula is listed in this table. Comair has a fleet of 15 Boeing 737s and Kulula has a fleet of 11 Boeing 737s; it serves six destinations.

In Africa the capacity operated by the LCCs is only about 13 percent of the total capacity, compared to about 26 percent on a worldwide basis.[3] Most of this capacity of LCCs is either in international markets or in South African domestic markets. Low-cost capacity from Europe is to destinations in North

Table 5.2 Fleet Size of the Top Ten Low-Cost Airlines Based in Africa

Rank	Airline	Country	Fleet
1	Kulula	South Africa	11
2	Fly540	Kenya	11
3	Mango	South Africa	10
4	Fly Safair	South Africa	7
5	fastjet	Tanzania	5
6	flyafrica.com	Zimbabwe	5
7	Air Arabia Maroc	Morocco	4
8	Jambojet	Kenya	4
9	Air Arabia Egypt	Egypt	3
10	Skywise	South Africa	2
	Total		62

Source: Airline websites and the internet.

Africa; the fast-growing LCCs from the Middle East are also serving destinations in Northern Africa. These developments could be explained by the 2006 EU–Morocco Open Skies Agreement as the catalyst; the proximity of the Maghreb states to the EU makes them different to sub-Saharan states for LCC penetration. Flydubai later came into the northeastern states of Africa on a similar proximity basis.

As with full-service carriers, LCC penetration has been held back by government policies. Low-cost competition varies significantly by country. Royal Air Maroc and South African Airways both face strong competition from LCCs. For example, in Morocco the capacity offered by the LCCs is about 40 percent of the total seat capacity. It is currently very high in South Africa also, with about a 40 percent market share. The growth and development of the private LCCs Kulula and 1time Airlines forced South African Airways to establish a low-cost subsidiary, Mango Airlines. In the case of Kenya, Kenya Airways also faced strong competition from the private LCC Fly540, and later fastjet in Tanzania developed a low-cost subsidiary, Jambojet, more to fortress the market than to start an efficient LCC. Despite these few regional competitive areas, there is virtually no low-cost competition on the continent as a whole. There are only 62 aircraft in the fleet of the top ten airlines[4] (at various times during 2015) compared to 634 aircraft in service with the top ten airlines based in Asia (Tables 5.2 and 5.3). Given that international fares within Africa are the highest and markets are underserved, there is clearly a need for many more services from LCCs.

The LCC sector in Africa is small, but it is making some progress, although at a very slow pace. The need for this sector is evident when one considers the statistic that less than 10 percent of people on the continent have taken a trip on an airplane.[5] Clearly mass transportation would benefit the people and the economic development of the continent. However, the vision of the leadership of existing and new LCCs should be to develop new markets rather than divert traffic from existing carriers, low cost or full service. There are dozens of states with large cities and significant potential for developing domestic markets. South Africa is well known. But there are other states such as Algeria, Egypt, Kenya, Nigeria, and Tanzania. This is a region where innovation can play a major role in bringing about low fare services that are reliable and offer a reasonable frequency.

One key requirement for the development of air transportation is the movement toward deregulation. The Yamoussoukro Decision (YD) calls for the States signing the agreement to deregulate air services across the region. The implementation of this agreement has been very slow. According to a study commissioned by IATA, implementation of liberalization policies across 12 markets would have generated five million additional passengers per year, created an additional 155,000 jobs, and contributed $1.3 billion to the annual GDP.[6] Airlines are ready to provide the services if regulatory policies enable the skies to be open for these airlines to initiate the services. Examples include fastjet, the multinational brand. Initially 44 states agreed to implement YD

when it was signed in 1999. Now, after limited success, a new initia
launched in 2015, whereby the transport ministers of 11 states of the
Union (AU) have agreed to the implementation of a Single African
Market through the YD by 2017. Further AU initiatives are underway to
encourage more African states to join in this new initiative. Contrast this
action with the ASEAN equivalent (developing vs. emerging markets) and
consider how that changed the marketplace. It would also be helpful if states
agreed to the implementation of the World Trade Organization's Trade
Facilitation Agreement (TFA) that would reduce costs and make it easier for
the transportation of air cargo across borders, making goods more competitive
in the globalizing economy.

As for infrastructure, there are two views on investments. One view is that
governments need to make sufficient investments to facilitate the development of the aviation industry. The other point is to ensure that the investments are not too high, leading to higher operating costs and producing a
negative impact on the industry. This aspect is important for LCCs to keep
their costs low. Having separate low-cost terminals is also not an answer as
the LCCs would like to be in the same terminals as the full-service airlines to
be able to make connections. The answer, of course, is to spend sufficient
and quality time with the current and potential users of the infrastructure
before the projects get funded, let alone built and operated, to discuss the
type and size of facilities needed and the expected level and timing of
demand. There is some airport infrastructure development via the Chinese
groups (for example, in Mozambique and Togo) that is part of China's push
into Africa.

Historically, African governments have protected their home markets from
other African airlines, and to a lesser extent from non-African airlines.
Another reason is the sheer number of countries in Africa, compared to, say,
South America. The expansion of non-African airlines is evident from the
fact that the Super Connectors (the three Persian Gulf-based airlines plus
Turkish Airlines) have expanded their capacity significantly in recent years.
Turkish now flies to over 45 destinations in Africa, while Emirates flies to
about 25. However, while Turkish flies to more destinations and with a
higher number of flights, Emirates operates with much larger aircraft, almost
twice the size of the average aircraft operated by Turkish Airlines. Consequently, Emirates offers about twice the amount of seat capacity compared
to Turkish Airlines. Even though non-Africa based airlines have been
expanding their operations to and from Africa, the numbers need to be put
into some perspective. While it is true that the capacity offered by non-
African airlines to and from Africa has increased over the past 15 years, the
overall increase has not been at exponential levels. Consider the results of a
recent analysis conducted by OAG, illustrated in Figure 5.2. While within
the Africa–Europe market the non-Africa-based airlines increased capacity
significantly between 2005 and 2010, the level did not change very much
between 2010 and 2015. However, within the Africa to Middle East market,

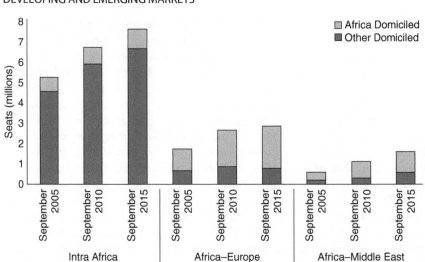

Figure 5.2 Capacities by Domicile of Carrier to, from, and within Africa (source: OAG, "The big five," 2015).

the capacity offered by the non-African carriers continued to increase significantly between 2005 and 2010 and between 2010 and 2015. But, then again, the percentage of the total seats represented by the Africa to the Middle East sector is only around 13 percent. Taken as a whole, according to the OAG analysis, the share of seats to, from, and within Africa operated by non-African carriers has been reasonably stable, varying between *29 and 32 percent.*[7] From this analysis it appears that the governments have continued to protect their national carriers from other carriers based in Africa more than from non-African carriers. Examples include the difficulties faced by fastjet in expanding its operations in different parts of Africa.

Despite the challenges facing the airline industry in Africa, there are also enormous opportunities being brought about by the exceptional growth in and transformation of the economies of some states and regions. While businesses continue to see the existence of poverty, conflict, corruption, and dysfunctional governments, as well as some states' dependence on foreign aid and foreign investments, there is also evidence of the growing emergence of business entrepreneurs, growth in technology-based initiatives, the expansion of business sub-sectors such as entertainment and fashion, and the increasing size of the middle classes. Although the continent is extremely complex, given its diversity, it is on a path to becoming connected within the globe and becoming mainstream.[8] Besides the development of economies, a Nigerian-American journalist sees Africa as a bright continent based on her belief in the *kanju* trait – creativity of pioneers to deal with the challenges in Africa.[9] In light of the previous brief background, how are airlines based in Africa responding to the changing marketplace? Following are two examples.

South African Airways

South African Airways has been struggling for years, costing "the taxpayer more than Rand 20-billion in subsidies over the past 20 years."[10] The media provides two views on what needs to happen. One view discussed is that the airline should be liquated and sold to the private sector. This way the assets (the best aircraft, routes, and staff, for example) are not likely to disappear, but will be better managed by private investors. The second view is that the airline should be owned and supported by the state on the grounds that it plays an important role in the economic development of South Africa. The proponents of this view argue that the amount of subsidy is relatively small compared to the contributions the airline makes to the economy. Moreover, if the airline was to receive help just for having its interest on its debt taken care of in the last couple of years the airline would have posted profits.[11]

South African Airways has had a relatively high-cost structure. It faced a disproportionately high level of competition from LCCs, as well as from the traditional full-service carriers based in Europe (British Airways, for example) but also the relatively new carriers based in the Persian Gulf, particularly Emirates. It has had an inefficient fleet to compete effectively with powerful competitors from Europe (British Airways), from Asia (Cathay Pacific), and the Persian Gulf (Emirates). It has had to deal with an overly complex situation relating to a fragmented and dysfunctional aviation policy framework and the intervention of the government that has not only brought in numerous new senior management teams, but also different Boards. The result of these changing leadership teams and government control of decisions relating to fleet renewal has been negative for the development and implementation of survival strategies. What has been clearly needed is an understanding on an agreement of objectives between the operating management, the Board, the Shareholding Ministry, and senior government policymakers. Whereas in typical private airlines there may be lack of coordination among senior management and possibly the Board, in the case of South African the lack of coordination is not only among the three major stakeholders, but within one group itself, namely among various levels of the government, transport vs. tourism vs. finance, for example.

Take the case of the impact on fleet renewal. Not only has the capital base of the airline been weak, but the cost of additional capital has tended to be high. There are many reasons, leaving aside the fact that the financial performance of the airline and its positioning relative to competitors in the markets it serves are unfavorable. The lenders also look at such factors as the capability of management, not in the absolute sense, but management's ability to perform given the interference from government policymakers (as well as from their elected Board members) not to mention the political risk relating to a country. All these factors combined may have meant that the funds may not have been available, or if they were available the influence of these attributes was factored into the cost of capital and the conditions of the loan, and the requirement for government guarantees that, in turn, created even more government intervention.

The airlines based in developing markets tend to have a high level of debt on their balance sheets anyway. South African Airways is a case in point. There is one development that is changing the landscape in Africa – the entry of investors from China. In Chapter 4 it was mentioned that the HNA Group has invested capital into African World Airways, based in Ghana, and Comair Limited, based in South Africa. However, this source of funding cannot be counted on as it depends on the interests of China, either for enhancing the opportunities for the airlines based in China or the trade between China and particular countries in Africa. Think about the case of Ethiopia, where in 2014 the ICBC Financial Leasing Company signed a Memorandum of Understanding with Ethiopian Airlines in which the Chinese leasing company agreed to provide financial support for the fleet replacement and expansion of Ethiopian Airlines.

Leaving aside the challenges relating to fleet renewal, South African has been aligning its network by reducing long-haul flights in a number of international markets out of Africa and increasing flights in regional markets. It has also been exploring strategic links with partner airlines to make its schedules and products more competitive. The key area, representing both a challenge and an opportunity, has been the working relationship with partners in the developed region, not just relating to networks and schedules but also the potential for equity stakes and conditions. The challenge for an airline in a developing region is always to demonstrate the value of the strategic link with partners so as to get fair treatment, for example, within an alliance. It can be done, based on the experience of Kenya Airways and its partnership with KLM and Air France and its membership in the SkyTeam Alliance. In the case of South African Airways, while there have been mutual benefits within the Star Alliance, South African may not be getting the optimum value, especially in markets where some alliance members have joint-ventures and of which South African is not a member. As equity stakes by foreign airlines would add much value for the airline in the developed region, it is interesting to note that two large airlines have not negotiated a deal yet – South African Airways and Aerolineas Argentina; both are entirely owned by their states. Is the actual and the potential intervention by the governments playing a role or is it simply the strength and the location of the airlines, or both?

Aviation professionals sometimes ask why the South African government could not follow the example of the New Zealand government and transform South African Airways. South African Airways' own, much publicized, long-term turnaround strategy appeared to be seeking a similar path. However, its implementation seems to continue to be stalled due to government intervention. In 2001 the New Zealand government effectively re-nationalized the then privately held Air New Zealand in exchange for a bailout. It is now one of the great state-owned success stories and the government has diluted its share down to close to 50 percent. Air New Zealand is expanding (with new routes to Houston in the USA and Buenos Aires in South America) and making money. South African Airways, in contrast, has a strategy that appears to be difficult to implement in light of the government intervention and a very high level of debt.

Ethiopian Airlines

Ethiopian, the largest airline in Africa, continues to grow while South African, Egyptair, and Royal Air Maroc restructure dramatically, and Kenya Airways looks for ways to survive. Ethiopian has not only passed South African in size, it also makes money. The reasons are the supportive and functional government policy, stable and focused board and senior management, and, maybe, that the LCCs have not made much progress in becoming competitors of Ethiopian for a number of reasons. The major barrier has been the slow implementation of the Yamoussoukro Decision even 15 years after it was agreed. Ethiopian has been extremely aggressive and proactive in its expansion. It has been increasing its capacity at rapid rates, particularly since 2005. It has an excellent geographical location, even relative to the three Persian Gulf-based airlines, for traffic moving between Africa and Asia, particularly China, which is making significant investments in Africa. Ethiopian is capitalizing on the growth of the trade in products and services between Africa and China exemplified by its services between Addis Ababa and Beijing, Guangzhou, Hong Kong, and Shanghai. While Kenya Airways also tried to capture traffic between Africa and Asia, it has been suffering from a deteriorating security situation. To capitalize on the growth in trade, Ethiopian also operates a fleet of ten freighters: two Boeing 757-PCFs, six Boeing 777Fs, and two MD-11Fs.

Ethiopian's proactive transformation is also evident from its pursuit of partnerships within Africa. It has had an equity partnership for many years in ASKY, a small airline based in Togo in the western part of Africa. More recently, it has developed a partnership with and an equity stake in Malawian Airlines and a technical support agreement and a strategic partnership with Rwandair, enabling the airline to start flying to India and China. These partnerships provide operating bases in the Western, Central, Southern, and Eastern parts of Africa (Figure 5.3). Moreover, these partnerships could lead to the possibility of Ethiopian becoming a pan-African airline in the future if (a) it can develop an acceptable brand throughout Africa; and (b) it begins to enhance connectivity among the large cities in Africa. Think about the visions of Ethiopian Airlines. In addition to its service to three destinations in North America (Washington Dulles, Los Angeles, and Toronto, Canada), it has announced its plans to offer service between New York and Lomé (Togo), where passengers would be able to make connections with its partner, ASKY. Moreover, Ethiopian plans to increase its services in the USA to Chicago and Houston. Could it offer more service to the USA from Dublin, Ireland, a city from where it is already serving Los Angeles?

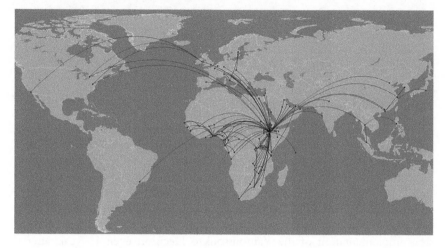

Figure 5.3 Networks of Ethiopian Airlines, ASKY, Malawian Airlines, and Rwandair (source: OAG Schedule Analyser and Mapper).

Asia

The movement of the aviation center of gravity to the east is not a new development. It has been discussed for the past two decades. One contributor has been the growth of the aviation industry in the Persian Gulf. This was discussed in previous chapters. Second is the growth of the LCCs in the Asia-Pacific region. For example, there has been enormous growth in capacity offered by the LCCs in India. Chapter 3 shows some data on the increase of the traffic transported by the LCCs in India. In 2006 the LCCs had a share of 8 percent of the domestic market. In 2014, their share had increased to 68 percent. Figure 5.4 shows the network of IndiGo as an example of an airline that did not even exist ten years ago and now is the largest low-cost airline in India. In 2015 it had 98 aircraft in service (Airbus 320-200s) and 430 on order (Airbus 320neos). In October 2015 it succeeded in completing an initial public offering at $459 million, valuing the company at $5.7 billion.[12] Moving further to the east, there are ten low-cost airlines with a fleet of 634 aircraft in service (Table 5.3). This scale of operations of these ten airlines alone explains not only how the center of gravity for the aviation industry is moving to the east, but also how the scale is so much different than in developing regions such as Africa. The third contributor to the shift in the center of gravity is the relative stagnation of the aviation industry in North America and Europe. Consider, for example, that the number of flights in North America has declined by about 10 percent between 2010 and 2015, due in a large part to consolidation. To a lesser extent, while the scheduled flights in Europe have not decreased, they have also not grown, except for the flights flown by the LCCs.[13]

Asia is a very diverse market, with some regions much more developed than others. The demand for air travel is high in some short markets and low

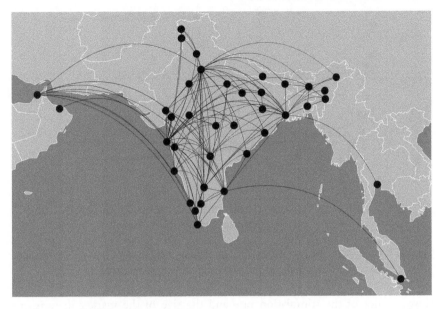

Figure 5.4 Network of IndiGo Airlines (source: OAG Schedule Analyser and Mapper).

Table 5.3 Fleet Size of Low-Cost Carrier Groups Based in Asia

Rank	LCC Group	Fleet
1	Lion Group	230
2	Air Asia	170
3	Cebu Pacific	55
4	Jetstar	49
5	Citilink (Garuda)	35
6	VietJet	29
7	Nok	28
8	Tigerair (SIA)	24
9	Scoot (SIA)	10
10	Golden Myanmar	4
	Total	634

Source: Airline websites and the internet.

in some thin and long-haul markets. Consider the short-haul markets on the high side such as Sapporo–Tokyo, Beijing–Shanghai, and Hong Kong–Taipei. At the other end might be markets such as Delhi–Guangzhou and Mumbai–Beijing. On top of these differences there is the huge variation in infrastructure. A recent analysis conducted by OAG of numerous markets in emerging regions shows that in thin markets where new or additional service was introduced the markets experienced relatively high stimulation rates within short periods of time after the initiation of new services. Figure 5.5

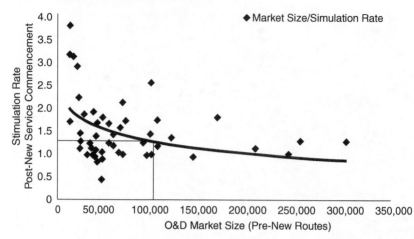

Figure 5.5 Stimulation Effect in the Asia-Pacific – Selected Markets (source: OAG, "Moving east, Asia: the dynamo of the airline industry for years to come," 2015).

shows a plot of the stimulation rate and the size of the market in terms of O&D traffic prior to the start of new routes. The stimulation rate varied between just under one to just over two for markets with fewer than 100,000 passengers per year. Figure 5.6 shows the new routes launched vs. their O&D size. According to this analysis, there is enormous potential for stimulation of thinner markets, estimated to number just under 2,000 in the Asia-Pacific

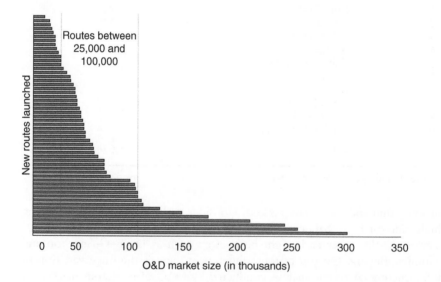

Figure 5.6 Selected Markets in the Asia-Pacific – O&D Sizes per New Route Launch (source: OAG, "Moving east, Asia: the dynamo of the airline industry for years to come," 2015).

region, with between 25,000 and 100,000 passengers per year.[14] There are two insightful Thought Leadership Pieces in Chapter 10 that illustrate the potentially game-changing role of new aircraft technology. First, Nico Buchholz, with Bombardier Aerospace, provides insightful information on how new-technology airplanes can enable airlines to re-align their networks with smaller aircraft that have similar unit costs to larger aircraft. Second, John Grant, with OAG, provides a case study of what an ultra long-range narrow-body aircraft could achieve in markets around the world.

Unlike within Africa, airlines in Southeast Asia have been struggling, but due to different reasons – overcapacity – and more recently weaker economies and political instability even though fuel prices have declined. Overcapacity is a concern even in the long term, given the number of aircraft on order. In Southeast Asia there were about 1,800 aircraft in service at the end of 2015. And there were over 1,500 on order. That is a concern for the continuation in overcapacity despite the forecast of growing economies and rising middle classes numbers. The LCCs have begun to slow their growth and the full-service carriers are restructuring. The LCCs increased their capacity by a factor of ten between 2005 and 2015, whereas the full-service airlines increased it only by 50 percent. LCCs now account for almost two-thirds of the capacity in Southeast Asia.

Before going on to a discussion on the restructuring movements relating to full-service carriers, it might be helpful to consider why some LCCs did not succeed in both Africa and India. For example, in South Africa it is known that 11 airlines failed since deregulation of the domestic airline industry in the 1990s. Mainly in the 1990s and early 2000s, this list includes not only LCCs (such as 1time and Velvet Sky), but also full-service carriers (such as Flitestar, Nationwide, Phoenix Air, and Sunair). Reasons could probably be related to overcapacity and high levels of competition in the market, high operating costs (including operations with older aircraft and high fuel prices). There were failures in India too. On the LCC side there were Kingfisher Airlines and Paramount Airways. On the full-service side it was Indian Airlines, which merged with Air India. It is interesting to note not only that Kingfisher Airlines started with high growth, but that these airlines did not survive in the high-growth market in India. One could speculate whether the reasons related to overcapacity or poor management, or both.

The primary reasons for restructuring by the full-service carriers – for example, Garuda, Malaysian, Philippines, and Thai – is the increase in capacity by the LCCs and the Super Connectors. The second reason has been the weakness in the economy and political unrest in some regions. Thailand, the second largest market in Southeast Asia in terms of demand for travel, is a case in point. Passenger demand is being impacted by political unrest and economic weakness. And there is the shift in tourism. For example, the Chinese are traveling more to the northeast (Korea, for example) than to the southeastern destinations (Malaysia and Thailand, for example). The restructuring strategy of the full-service carriers has been to cut long-haul flights and work more closely with partners. Even Singapore Airlines has been restructuring, given that, in the long run, the LCCs will grow.

In 2015 the LCCs in Southeast Asia had about 500 aircraft. These carriers had another 1,200 aircraft on order. Almost 1,000 of these 1,200 on order were from just two carrier groups – the seven airlines in the AirAsia group and four in the Lion Air group. The market will undoubtedly grow in the lower end segments as the middle classes continue to grow. In the short term there have been some setbacks in travel due to political instability, slowdown in economies, and change in currencies.

The current size of the fleet in Asia is smaller than those of both North America and Europe. However, after the orders have been accepted the fleet size will be more than that of the fleet in North America and Europe combined. It is simply due to the size of the region and the expected growth. There are about 600 million people in Southeast Asia. Some will be flying for the first time, but many will fly multiple times. The orders are from the LCCs, not the full-service carriers. Although only moderately, the LCCs are growing; the full-service carriers are not. This will change the balance significantly. Liberalization is expected to increase. Unlike Africa, Asia has been more proactive in the restructuring process, resulting in not only more service from LCCs, but also the growth of low-cost subsidiaries of full-service carriers – Scoot and Jetstar, for example. The LCCs operating long-haul routes are ordering wide-body aircraft – the Boeing 787s by Jetstar and the Airbus 350s and the Airbus 330neos by AirAsia X.

This model – LCCs ordering wide-body aircraft – is new to Asia. Norwegian has been doing it for a while. The reason for the expansion of low-cost, long-haul carriers is based partly on the fact that the full-service carriers have been suffering because premium travel has not been growing at the old rates and cargo has not been contributing as much in the past five years, an area in which LCCs do not participate. Full-service carriers also have much higher operating costs to compete for the lower yield traffic. Think about the unit operating cost per seat mile for All Nippon and Japan Airlines compared to AirAsia on an adjusted stage length basis. The other reason for the expansion of LCCs in long-haul markets is the greater level of connectivity, discussed below. As such, the full-service carriers have been adapting more rapidly. They are doing it by establishing low-cost subsidiaries – Silkair and Scoot by Singapore Airlines – with the exception being Cathay Pacific, which already has a somewhat lower-cost subsidiary, Dragonair.

In addition to the greater penetration of the low end of the market, the LCCs have been making progress in two other areas. First, given their network, reliability, and frequency they are beginning to make inroads in the corporate market. And the introduction of some sort of premium seating is also appealing to the corporate sector. And if they start distributing the product through channels such as GDSs, the penetration of the corporate market would increase even further. However, it is the second development – connectivity between LCCs – that will bring about major transformational changes in the airline industry. Connectivity within the network was the key differentiator of full-service airlines – enabling passengers to make connections, whereas LCCs transported passengers from one point to another point. Within the low-cost sector some passengers have been making their own connections by purchasing two separate tickets.

The self-connection process has been in operation for many years for airlines such as Southwest, Ryanair, and AirAsia. However, it has been inconvenient, taking extra time for two check-ins and sometimes more risky in the case of missed connections. And LCCs did not want to add to the complexity involved in transporting passengers on connecting services. Now, LCCs are becoming more aggressive in this area. The key breakthrough came with the operations of AirAsia X when it began to make connections at the new, dedicated terminal at Kuala Lumpur Airport, known as the KLIA2, which started making connections with AirAsia's short-haul operations. The reason it worked is because AirAsia had so many flights that there were plenty of opportunities for connections, just as Southwest has so many flights at some airports that about 20 percent of the passengers have been able to make their own connections for years ("incidental" hubbing). This connectivity is critical to the success of any long-haul, low-cost carrier, including AirAsia X. The critical need for connectivity can be explained by another factor. In narrow-body, low-cost operations about 60 percent of the difference in the unit costs of LCCs and full-service carriers is due to the higher asset utilization and greater seat density of the aircraft. According to CAPA, in 2014 more than half of the passengers on AirAsia X were transfer passengers.[15] And AirAsia X, with an average length of haul of about 3,000 miles, has just about the lowest seat mile costs. It is the convergence of the aforementioned trends that can explain the evolution of the air transport industry in the dynamic Asia-Pacific region – see Figure 8.8, developed by CAPA, that shows the evolution of this industry from the legacy full-service network carriers to the network, low-cost/hybrid carriers.[16]

The key aspect relating to the emergence and viability of the network low-cost/hybrid carrier is the availability of high levels of connectivity at airports. OAG recently published a report in which it developed a connectivity index to rank hub airports around the world. The index reflects the ratio of possible scheduled connections (online plus inter-line) to the number of destinations served by an airport. Hub airports based on this connectivity index show a different aspect of an airport than just the number of flights. This index shows the effectiveness of an airport from the viewpoint of making connections. The analysis conducted by OAG shows Atlanta Airport in the USA to have the largest connectivity index in the world (2503), followed by Chicago O'Hare, and Dallas Fort Worth. Brazil's São Paulo Congonhas is the first airport outside the USA that shows up in the list, ranked seventh with a connectivity index of 880. The first airport in the Asia-Pacific region is Indonesia's Jakarta Soekarno-Hatta, ranked seventeenth with a connectivity index of 652. There are no airports in Africa that show up in the list of the top 50 mega-hubs from the viewpoint of this connectivity index. Surprisingly, the first airport in India in this list, Mumbai, with an index of 599, ranks above the first airport in China, Shanghai Pudong, with an index of 482. From the viewpoint of the distribution of the top 50 mega-hubs share by region, Asia has 32 percent, Latin America 8 percent, and Africa has 0 percent.

India, China, and the Connectivity between the Two

What a difference between India and China, two countries with large land masses, similar sizes of population, high growth rates in the economies of both countries relative to the rest of the world, and large numbers of middle class, including their rate of increase. Yet within China the aviation sector has developed at an incredible level compared to India, even though China built in parallel a vast network of ultra high-speed trains, operating at 200 miles per hour over distances of 1,500 miles. In terms of the number of airline seats, whereas China is the second largest aviation market after the USA, India is number five.[17] Although there are many factors that explain the difference in the development of the aviation industry in the two countries, the two primary factors are the policies of the government and the propensity to travel. With respect to government policy, in China, the government has seen aviation as a catalyst for the development of economies, and the government adopted policies to promote its development by developing the infrastructure. The government also protected its carriers both within domestic markets and in international markets by controlling the operating environment. In India, while the government also recognized the value of air transportation, it chose different aviation policies for enabling the development of the air transportation sector. Consider just the rules relating to the start of international services by domestic carriers and the services to and from remote places. There has been the requirement of the five-year/20-aircraft rule – five years and 20 aircraft before a domestic operator can fly in international markets. There are the obligation requirements related to Route Dispersal Guidelines (RDGs) that refer flights to new routes to improve connectivity.[18] Then there is the Domestic Credit Formula that shows the relationship of domestic flying to international flying. The second reason for the differences in the size of the air travel markets relates to the differences in the propensity to travel. According to a report by OAG, in 2014 there were 63 air passengers in India traveling to, from, and within India for every 1,000 of population. The number in China was 242.[19] There is the difference in the growth rates of GDP in the two countries; GDP is a primary driver of the propensity to travel. China has an excellent GDP growth record.

In addition to the difference in the size of the air travel market in India and China, the number of airline services between these two major countries is insignificant relative to the size of their populations. The map shown in Figure 5.7 shows the only three cities in India and four cities in China that

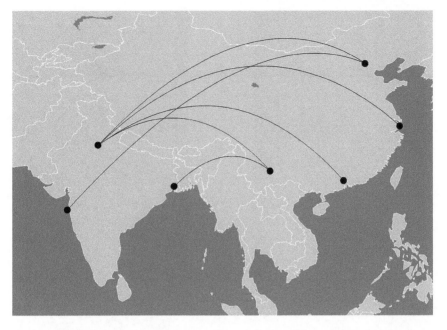

Figure 5.7 City Pairs with Non-Stop Service between India and China (source: OAG Schedule Analyser and Mapper).

had non-stop service during December 2015. From India, non-stop flights are operated only by Air India, and from China by Air China, China Southern, and Shandong Airlines. There are only six non-stop flights each day between the two countries (India with a population of around 1.3 billion and China with a population of around 1.4 billion) flown by the four carriers, one from India and three from China. To the extent that there is demand for air travel between the two countries, it is satisfied by carriers offering connecting services through airports such as Singapore, Bangkok, and Hong Kong. Direct services are apparently controlled by regulatory policies.

It is also possible that the priorities of the two countries are very different. For example, these two countries may be more interested in trading with strategically connected countries in developed regions or other developing countries rather than between themselves. An example could be China's interest in trading with countries in Africa, and India's interest in developing trade with the UAE and Southeast Asia. On the other hand, even though China does have a little more service to and from Africa than does India, the additional amount is marginal. As shown in Figure 5.8, there is non-stop service between just eight cities in Africa (including Mauritius) and just three cities in China. Moreover, there are still only eight non-stop flights per day between Africa and China, despite the fact that China has an enormous interest in Africa's raw materials and is interested in making potential investments. The additional services reflect not only China's interests with respect

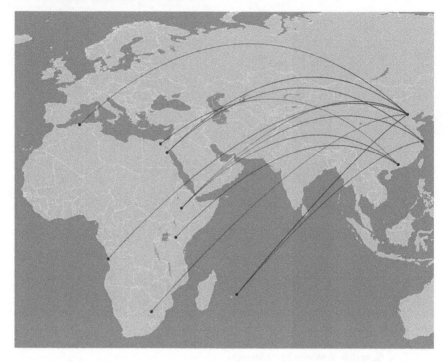

Figure 5.8 City Pairs with Non-Stop Service between China and Africa (source: OAG Schedule Analyser and Mapper).

to trade, but also the interests of the public and personal travel. While there are only six non-stop flights each day between China and India, there are between 16 and 17 non-stop flights each day between China and Australia, from nine cities in China and five in Australia (Figure 5.9). Once the "low-hanging fruit" in the developed regions has been picked by both India and China they will, presumably, increase air travel between each other as well as other developing markets such as Africa, facilitated by the introduction of more commercially viable aircraft such the Boeing 787s and the Airbus 350s.

In the long run, there is an incredibly huge potential for development of leisure traffic between China and India. This may take another decade or two, but it could be enormously beneficial, especially for India, if India strategically develops its inbound tourism market and provides safe, secure, and appealing options for the Chinese travelers. With master-planned resorts, shopping, and dining, and accessible sites of historical interest, India might expect Chinese tourists by the millions – or tens of millions – each year.

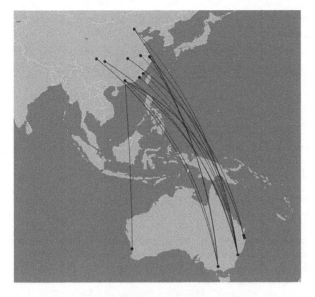

Figure 5.9 City Pairs with Non-Stop Service between China and Australia (source: OAG
Schedule Analyser and Mapper).

Takeaways

The center of gravity of the aviation industry is shifting to the east, facilitated
by the growth in the Gulf states, the growth of LCCs in the Asia-Pacific
region, and the stagnation of growth in North America and Europe relative
to the growth of low-cost airlines in Asia.

The highest growth will be in Asia, within the low-cost sector due to the
expected growth in the middle classes. The orders of airplanes reflect this
forecast. By historical accident, the current growth of LCCs in the developing and emerging markets is occurring during a period of lower fuel costs,
greater efficiency of new-generation aircraft, and the rapid adoption of
mobile digital technology. Although all airlines are benefiting, the LCCs are
in a sweeter spot on the growth curve, with a lower installed base.

In developing regions disruptive innovation could be facilitated by changes
in government policies on liberalization, ownership, consolidation, taxation,
and infrastructure.

The existence of greater liberalization in emerging markets in Asia relative
to developing markets in Africa shows the relative difference in the development of aviation services in the two regions.

Connectivity is a key development among LCCs, not just between short-
haul markets served by LCCs, but also between short-haul and long-haul
markets served by LCCs.

Full-service carriers based in developing regions (for example, Africa) are
developing partnerships, and in emerging markets (for example, Asia) are

adapting to the dramatically changing environment by developing low-cost subsidiaries and partnerships.

The size of the air travel market within India is very small relative to that in China, and the non-stop frequency between the two largest countries in the world is insignificant.

Notes

1 Remarks of Tony Tyler, DG and CEO of IATA, at the AFRAA Annual General Assembly, Brazzaville, September 11, 2015.
2 Cover story, "How Africa can capitalise on its skies and seas," *African Business*, July 2015, p. 33.
3 CAPA (Centre for Aviation), "Liberalisation seeps into African aviation policy: when what is needed is a flood of new services," *Airline Leader*, 26, February 2015.
4 The fleet size of different airlines must be considered carefully. For example, Fly540 has a mixed fleet. At the time of writing there was some talk of Flyafrica.com being shut down by the government. There was a good chance that Skywise would cease operations due to a lack of cash.
5 Mwanalushi, Keith, "Flying on a budget" *FlightCom: African and Middle East Aviation*, 80, May 2015, p. 16.
6 InterVISTAS, "Transforming intra-African air connectivity: the economic benefits of implementing the Yamoussoukro Decision," July 2014.
7 OAG, "The big five: disruptive strategies for African aviation," 2015.
8 See, for example, Bright, Jake and Hruby, Aubrey, *The Next Africa: An Emerging Continent Becomes a Global Powerhouse* (New York: Thomas Dunne Books/St. Martin's Press, 2015).
9 See Olopade, Dayo, *The Bright Continent: Breaking Rules & Making Change in Modern Africa* (New York: Mariner Books/Houghton Mifflin Harcourt, 2014).
10 "Should SAA be liquidated?" *FlightCom: African and Middle East Aviation Magazine*, 79, April 2015, p. 20.
11 Leitch, Guy, "Should SAA be liquidated?" *FlightCom: African and Middle East Aviation*, 79, April 2015, pp. 20–4.
12 "Ascending above the turbulence," *The Economist*, December 19, p. 97.
13 OAG, "Moving east, Asia: the dynamo of the airline industry for years to come," 2015.
14 Ibid.
15 CAPA, "Asia's Full service airlines could become endangered unless they adopt new strategies for sustainability," *Airline Leader*, 25, October–November 2014.
16 Ibid.
17 OAG, "An end to boom and bust for Indian Aviation?" 2015.
18 CAPA, "India starts to sparkle again: and it could just be for real this time!" *Airline Leader*, 26, January–February 2015.
19 OAG, "An end to boom and bust."

6 ADAPTATION STRATEGIES BY AIRPORTS

Airports have also been adapting to the forces of change described in Chapter 3, although not at the same pace as airlines. There are some good reasons for the differences in the pace of change for airlines and airports. For airlines the impact of the forces of change and their convergence was discussed in Chapter 3, and the transformational strategies being implemented by airlines were discussed in Chapter 4. Airports have been affected by similar forces, but to different degrees. For example:

- The governance structure of airports has been changing. Whereas in the old days airports were generally operated by different divisions of governments, beginning with the 1980s they started to be operated by private organizations, or public–private partnership organizations, or not-for-profit organizations.
- To some extent, competition has also increased for airports. Take three very different cases. In the first case, there is increasing competition for Paris Charles de Gaulle, Frankfurt, and London Heathrow Airports from Abu Dhabi, Doha, and Dubai Airports for passengers traveling from the smaller cities in France, the UK, and Germany to Asia. In the second case, for passengers living in the greater London area and traveling short distances within Europe (say to Amsterdam or Geneva), there are five competing airports: City, Gatwick, Heathrow, Luton, and Stansted. In the third case, there is significant competition from high-speed trains, at least in Europe, China, and Japan.
- Consumer behavior and expectations are forcing airlines to re-align their value propositions – more personalized services and enhanced customer experience, for example. Airports face similar demands from their tenants' customers – passengers – for more customer-centric processes and services relating to required activities (check-in, boarding, and so forth) and discretionary activities (shopping, dining, and so forth), not to mention operational excellence (Figure 6.1). While there is an ongoing discussion over whose customer the passenger is, the view that makes sense is that members in the travel chain should view passengers as shared customers as everyone provides some product or service to the traveler.

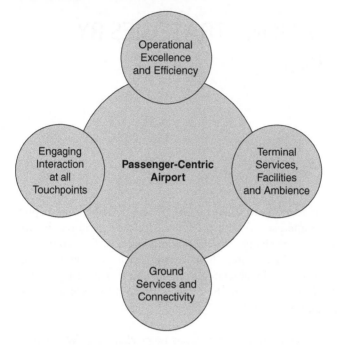

Figure 6.1 Passenger-Centric Airport.

- Technology is enabling airlines to transform their services and now it is available to airports as well – airport beacons and proximity sensing; systems for tagging, tracking, and moving baggage; human-sized airport virtual assistants; customer-centric robotics; and biometric identity management. One clear game-changing technology is the development and implementation of Automated Border Control and Automated Passport Control systems developed by Vancouver Airport in Canada.

However, unlike airlines, airports have been changing their business models at a slower pace for a number of reasons. First, airports cannot consolidate to the same degree that airlines have been doing to take advantages of the economies of scale and scope and to face the challenge of increasing competition. However, global airport companies, such as Fraport, have been acquiring airports in other parts of the world, an initiative that does provide some economic benefits. Second, whereas airports also have high fixed costs, they cannot shift their assets to balance supply and demand. They also have longer planning cycles and face "lumpy" investment decisions, measured in billions of US dollars for a new runway. In the USA, mergers between Delta and Northwest and between Continental and United had significant impacts on the operations of airports in Cincinnati and Memphis, and Cleveland, respectively. Similarly, in Europe, the failure of Malev and Spanair did have some impact on the operations at Budapest and Barcelona Airports, respectively. Third, it is somewhat easier for a full-service carrier to introduce new fares to compete with low-cost carriers (LCCs) than for a large airport to charge lower prices for the facilities and services to LCCs occupying space right next to the full-service carriers. However, Cologne Airport did this to become a large low-cost carrier hub even though it was built for full-service carriers. Fourth, airports work with very different regulatory constraints than airlines – not just those coming from the national government regulatory divisions, but a large number of other regional and national bodies such as local authorities and security services. Multiple airports located in the same region (San Francisco and London, for example) can be operated by different organizations and governed by different authorities. The impact of these regulatory constraints and governance is evident from the time it takes airports to implement changes in their business models, such as adding retail facilities and expanding airport infrastructure, such as building a new runway or a new terminal or getting service provided by a subway line or a highway.

This chapter provides an overview of four areas in which airports have been changing their business models (general framework, low-cost terminals, customer experience, and airports as destinations) and concludes with a brief perspective on some areas where disruptive innovation could take place.

General Business Model Changes

Based on a research report produced by Michael Gerra at Sabre, Table 6.1 shows changes in the business models of airports during the following three periods: between 1950 and the 1970s; between 1980 and the 2010s; and since the beginning of this decade. This research shows that the focus relating to customer service and ambience has changed in the past 60-plus years from efficient but limited functionality through standard retail (such as the sale of duty free products) to an increasing spectrum of targeted retail, and the offer of experience-based events and services. From the perspective of change to business models, the focus has shifted to meet the changing needs of airlines. Initially airlines set up their operations to serve O&D markets. Then they began to develop hub-and-spoke systems. Airports adapted to this change by the airlines. From the viewpoint of goals, airports' focus has changed from operational efficiency relating to airline and airport operations to serving the needs of a much broader spectrum of tenants than just airlines.

Initially the objective of a typical airport was simply to provide safe and efficient operations – customers were basically the airlines. Now there are many more tenants – ground service providers, retailers, parking operators, and, of course, government agencies to monitor border control, and an external player, the local community. And the coordination among these major players has not been easy. Prior to travel, the customer works with an airline or a distributor. During the day of travel, the customer works with ground service providers and airports. While at each airport there is a relationship

Table 6.1 Evolution of Airport Business Models

	1950–70s	1980–2010s	2010+
Primary Model	Take-offs/landings	Network hub, regional origin and destination	Air city, destination anchor, regional/national multi-modal hub, low-cost terminal
Business Goals	Operational efficiency	Operational efficiency, optimized passenger throughput	Customer experience, operational efficiency, increasing non-aviation revenues
Primary customer	Airline	Airline and passenger	Traveler (and increasingly non-traveling partners, retailers, other value chain participants)
Aviation Revenues (e.g., landing fees)	95 percent	70–90 percent	30–50 percent (or less)
Ownership	Usually local government owned or nationalized	Local or regional public–private partnership	Global public and/or private businesses. Usually multinational
Customer Ambience	Functional, basic customer services	Functional, crowded, growing but limited retail, mostly duty free goods.	Experience-oriented, broad and luxury retail; brand-name dining, comprehensive customer services

Source: Sabre: Michael Gerra revised this chart based on the one he included in his unpublished report "Airports reimagined," 2015.

with retailers, the airport is the connection with the airline and ground service providers on one side and the retailers on the other side. The airport serves the needs of many groups – airlines are looking for operational efficiency, local communities are looking for contribution to the local economies and passengers are looking for ease of travel, good experience, and comprehensive facilities.

As for sources of revenues, the focus has changed from reliance on revenues generated from the services provided to the aviation sector to revenue generated from non-aviation tenants and the services they provide. Currently, and going into the future, just as with airlines, the interest of airports is also to become powerful and sophisticated retailers and to diversify their revenue bases. Figure 6.2 shows that in 2014 the split in the revenue base of airports based in North America was 55 percent from aeronautical sources and 45 percent from non-aeronautical sources. And within the non-aeronautical sources of revenue the two biggest contributors were parking/ground transportation and rental cars, generating 60 percent of the non-aeronautical revenue. These large sources of revenue from non-aeronautical activities could easily be under attack from some of the forces discussed in the last section of this chapter, relating, for example, to the sharing feature in the economies and the development of self-driving cars. Even without such radical changes, this dependence on relatively inefficient and relatively poorly integrated ground transportation is seen by some airports as a planning failure (especially in North America) and something some leading airports are looking into ways to avoid in the future. Moreover, it appears that in Figure 6.2, passenger facility charges in the USA and airport improvement fees (the equivalent charge in Canada) are included in the aeronautical revenue component. There is a debate as to whether these charges and fees, which are charged to passengers by airports and collected by airlines on their behalf, should be in the aeronautical revenue category.

Facing the forces discussed in Chapter 3, managements of airports have been adapting to the changing environment in three primary areas: (1) keeping up with the increase in demand; (2) fulfilling the needs of not only an increasingly divergent group of tenants but sub-groups within the airline sector (full-service vs. low-cost carriers), not to mention the needs of tenants' customers – namely, passengers; and (3) the diversification of their revenue base.

Let us start with the challenge of keeping up with demand. Think about just four airports around the world and the challenges they have been facing.

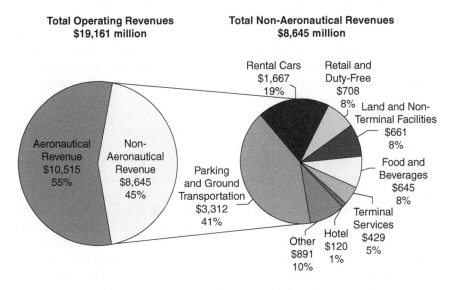

Figure 6.2 Summary of Aviation and Non-Aviation Related Airport Revenues in the USA, 2014 (Million Dollars) (source: Airports Council International-North America, based on data from US Federal Aviation Administration, *CATS Report 127*).

Istanbul's Atatürk Airport recorded the largest increase in passenger movements between 2013 and 2014. Shanghai's Pudong recorded the second largest increase in passengers. Dubai International Airport, where the total number of seats flown by airlines now exceeds the number at London's Heathrow Airport (see Figure 8.3), is looking to the new airport Dubai World Central (Al Maktoum) to handle not just cargo but also passengers. As mentioned in Chapter 2, London's Heathrow Airport is operating at 99 percent of its capacity and has been doing so for the past ten years. Looking into the future, on a global basis, the number of passengers traveling through airports (3.3 billion in 2014) is forecast to double in the next 15 years (7.3 billion in 2034), causing airports to re-think their business models, not just from the viewpoint of how to process this number of passengers efficiently but also to understand airports' roles in meeting the needs of the communities they serve.

To accommodate the growth in travel, facilities at existing airports are being expanded as fast as possible – an additional runway at either London's Gatwick or Heathrow Airport, for example. New airports are under development – in Beijing and in Istanbul. Beijing is planning to have a second major airport in Daxing. Istanbul, which already has two large and fast-growing airports (Atatürk and Sabiha Gocken), is scheduled to have a mammoth third airport in 2017. As for meeting the needs of local communities, regions are looking at how their economies would be impacted with the shift in the center of gravity discussed earlier in this book. Since there is a direct correlation between connectivity provided by airlines and airports, communities in Europe are looking at changes in connectivity resulting from the development of the three mega-hubs in the Persian Gulf region and how they would impact their regional economies.[1] The Yangtze River Delta region in China is the largest single metropolitan region in the world, with a population of about 120 million, about 85 million of which live in the urban environment. Which airport is going to meet the needs of this region for travel and how will connectivity impact the growth in its economy?

For terminals the focus is on smart design to accommodate more traffic (efficiency) while improving customer experience (reduce stress), conserve energy, and enhance ancillary revenues. Seoul's Incheon Airport is a case in point. The design of its facilities focuses on efficiency and the protection of the environment from the operational point of view, and it targets, for example, tourists from other emerging markets such as China by developing commercial facilities that include a shopping mall, a hotel, and a casino. While some processes within terminals may not seem to have changed much at airports – baggage arrival and pick-up, for example – they are being upgraded. Although passenger boarding still requires the display of boarding passes, airports are installing machine-readable systems for both boarding passes printed on paper as well as displayed on mobile phones. There are also facilities for self-boarding through automated gates.

On the ground side, a big development has been the emergence of transportation network companies (TNCs) at airports – representing "ride-sourcing" and "ride-sharing" companies. They leverage the technology behind mobile apps.[2] Uber is the global brand in the TNC sector, operating its services in about 300 cities in around about 60 countries. Other examples of TNCs are goCatch in Australia, 99Taxis in Brazil, Didi Kuaidi in China, GrabTaxi in Singapore, and HailO in the UK. Some questions facing airports are whether they should issue licenses to TNCs, assess safety standards, provide security clearances, and charge money to TNCs. Can geo-fencing – the capability to locate a vehicle as it crosses a particular point – be used to collect money? Would local governments impose drop-off fees to encourage passengers to use public transportation? Would TNCs become part of the airline booking and payment systems now that it is possible to make micro-payments through ordinary phones, not even smartphones? These are some challenges and opportunities facing airports with respect to emerging ground transportation systems, starting with the need to address air-to-rail connections. Passengers clearly see the value of the ease of making connections with rail transportation while they are in the terminals of airlines at airports such as Frankfurt and Munich in Germany. They also see even greater value in being able to check bags through to rail connections in Switzerland. These facilities clearly represent best practices at the present time – practices which airports need to work closely with government agencies to facilitate. Vancouver Airport in Canada is an example of an airport that worked with the government in Canada to develop and fund the new technology-based Automated Passport Control system.

Low-Cost Airports and Terminals

Initially the LCC sector favored the development of its services from low-cost airports. Examples include Ryanair in Europe inaugurating services from London's Stansted Airport and Frankfurt's Hahn Airport, Southwest from Dallas' Love Field Airport, Azul from the Campinas (near São Paulo) Airport, and AirAsia from the Senai International Airport in Johar Bahru, located near Singapore. These airports had lower charges, no congestion, and facilities to grow. And since LCCs transported point-to-point traffic, there was no reason for them to operate out of higher operating cost and congested airports served by the full-service network carriers. Moreover, some LCCs, specifically Ryanair, were even able to negotiate favorable marketing agreements with the low-cost airports in terms of incentives to provide service at those airports.

By being disruptive innovators, the LCCs began to grow at fast rates. As they began to grow and get accepted into the mainstream travel system they began to show interest in conventional airports, but in separate terminals located at these airports. On their side, the airports recognized this trend and started to develop separate low-cost terminals for the LCCs, exemplified by the initiatives taken by Marseille Airport (MP2), Singapore Airport (budget terminal), and Kuala Lumpur Airport (KLIA2). Now that LCCs provide a little over one-quarter of the total airline capacity, on a global basis, they are showing significant interest in connectivity, discussed in Chapters 5 and 8. As such, more and more LCCs would like to operate out of the same airports as full-service carriers. This interest is partly based on the desire to attract business travelers and partly on the desire to make connections, not only among the LCCs themselves, but also between low-cost and full-service carriers, to capture more traffic. AirAsia and AirAsia X are already connecting with each other in Kuala Lumpur's KLIA2. Mango, a low-cost subsidiary of South African Airways, was just accepted as a member of the Star Alliance and will therefore be making connections with full-service carriers.

The trend to serve conventional airports now exists around the world. Southwest has been moving in this direction for some years, having started services at airports such as Denver, Los Angeles, and San Francisco. Recently, Southwest has added services at Atlanta, Boston, New York's La Guardia and Newark, and Washington's National and Dulles Airports. Ryanair, which served Charleroi (Brussels South) Airport is now serving Belgium's main airport in Brussels. It is reported that in the next five years about one-half of Ryanair's growth will be at conventional airports.[3] Ryanair is not only beginning to serve conventional airports, but is beginning to also increase its frequency at both secondary and conventional airports.

The impact on airports of LCCs moving to either dedicated low-cost terminals at conventional airports or to the standard terminals at conventional airports has been mixed. In some cases the low-cost airports have begun to struggle financially. Frankfurt's Hahn Airport is an example. At the other end of the spectrum is Singapore Airport, which built its budget terminal in March 2006 and then decided to close it in September 2012. But then, a year later, in November 2013, the airport decided to build a new budget terminal (Terminal 4), which is expected to be completed in 2017. Given the acceptance of the service provided by low-cost carriers, including by the increasing percentage of business travelers, Singapore's Terminal 4 plans to have state-of-the-art facilities and services – kiosks for self-check-in, self-bag tagging and self-bag drop-off locations, biometric technology for fast movement through security, not to mention lots of retail space. With respect to the last point, would passengers traveling on low-cost airlines spend more money at airports since they are spending less on fares? One line of thought is that since there are no airport lounges and no food on airplanes, passengers would spend more money at airports. Another viewpoint is provided by London's Gatwick Airport, which claims that point-to-point traffic will grow at higher rates at airports such as Gatwick than traffic at major hubs such as London's Heathrow Airport, and that an increasing number of passengers are willing to make their own connections. Based on this belief, Gatwick has been developing an initiative that enables passengers to make their own connections with the facilities and services provided by the airport. And, as support, Gatwick Airport, in what is a first for airport operators, is offering GatwickConnects, an online service for travelers to shop and book connecting flights between low-cost and full-service carriers.

Airports are also recognizing that some attributes that LCCs started with are no longer valid. For example, many LCCs do not want to stay with the point-to-point model or the single aircraft model or the short-haul services only model or the low-frequency model. These low-cost airlines are not full-service network carriers, they are hybrids – Azul being a good example. Then there is easyJet, which is clearly moving toward carrying a lot more business traffic, which calls for service out of conventional airports and with high frequency, possibly even with bundled fares and distribution through GDSs. Then there is jetBlue, which is seeking code-shares. So, if the objective is to divert traffic from traditional full-service carriers then LCCs must operate to and from conventional airports.

Based on this potential growth of LCCs and the potential for them to become powerful hybrid carriers (as discussed in Chapters 5 and 8), the interest by airports in Asia is strong for building low-cost terminals and low-cost airports. Manila's airport (Ninoy Aquina International Airport) has been discussing the construction of a fifth terminal dedicated as a low-cost terminal rather than building a third runway. There are also plans to construct low-cost terminals at the Clark International Airport, about 50 km north of Manila and at Kansai Airport in Osaka. Even Narita Airport in Tokyo has indicated the possibility of building a low-cost terminal. However, airports are also keeping in mind two other developments in Asia. First, while there are numerous large independent LCC groups – AirAsia and Lion Air being the prime examples – the low-cost subsidiaries of full-service carriers are growing – Singapore Airlines' Scoot and Qantas' Jetstar being the prime examples. Second, there are also cross-border joint-ventures such as between Japan Airlines and Jetstar. These developments will impact the decisions on separately located low-cost terminals from the viewpoint of connecting traffic.

As for the development of low-cost airports, in Thailand the old Bangkok airport – Don Mueang – decided to convert itself into a low-cost airport now that Bangkok has a new airport – Suvarnabhumi Airport. Ibaraki Airport, located about 50 miles from Tokyo, was converted from a military base to a commercial airport, facilitating the entry of LCCs such as Spring Airlines from China. In India the interest in new low-cost airports is really strong given that two-thirds of the capacity in domestic markets is flown by LCCs and it is a region where low-cost airports can be built with relatively less money than conventional airports. Relating to the last point, for example, the low-cost facilities could exclude air bridges and enable greater space for parking airplanes on the apron, work with thermal cooling instead of air conditioning, and have minimal non-aviation facilities in the terminals. The airport could exclude push-back tractors and could design terminals for rapid turnarounds. The government of India appears to be thinking of developing greenfield low-cost airports in tier-II and tier-III cities (airports costing under $10 million, for example) to provide facilities for LCCs whose services would provide greater regional connectivity for the public. Even though about 50 were initially planned, only about a half-dozen seem to be under development. There are two other considerations that should not be overlooked. First, an airline, such as AirAsia India, could develop a disruptive network by connecting up the tier-II cities. It would mean that airports would need to reduce their operating costs significantly (along the lines mentioned above) to incentivize airlines such as AirAsia India. Second, airlines such as IndiGo, the largest LCC in India, could decide to join an alliance, in which case it would need to serve conventional airports.

Focus on Customer Experience

Airports have clearly been changing their business models (as shown in Table 6.1) based not only on the changing needs of their tenants, but also the changing needs of the customers of tenants, particularly in the case of the airlines. In the beginning, airports were basically operationally oriented, served the needs of just one group – the airlines – and provided them with efficient and sufficient air-side and terminal-side facilities as well as adequate parking for passenger vehicles. Now passengers, customers of both airlines and airports, want not just services that are efficient and hassle-free, but also services that are personalized, engaging, and experience-based. According to passengers there is a lot of stress at airports resulting from flight delays, gate changes, difficulty in finding gates (especially at large hubs), exceptionally long walking distances between gates, long waits for luggage (not to mention lost luggage), rental cars available off-site from airports, and so on. However, while airports are working on improving the customer experience, there are many challenges for adding the experience component to the services provided at an airport.

- First, passengers going through an airport are not in a homogeneous group. There are the younger digital natives from developed regions at one end of the spectrum to the elderly people from developing and emerging markets at the other. Even within a single demographic segment from a given region there are road warriors at one end and people who travel for personal reasons once every couple of years at the other end. Customer experience and satisfaction mean different things to different people.
- Second, the term *experience* is a very broad term – different touch-points involving different organizations. In some cases the standard key performance indicators still relate to operations (aircraft, passengers, and cargo) as opposed to customer experience and customer satisfaction, not to mention the value of sharing information among the different groups and businesses located at airports.
- Third, despite the desire of both the airline and the airport to enhance the customer experience, the question of which entity "owns" the customer at the airport remains open. Airlines and airports are still at odds, especially when it comes to sharing data and processes. There is some improvement but there is a long way to go.

- Fourth, different organizations (airlines, airports, government agencies, and so on) have different objectives and use different measurement concepts and criteria at different touchpoints. Consider the difference in the goals of airlines and retailers. An LCC may want to process passengers at a very fast rate and move passengers in and out of an airport in record time. Retailers, on the other hand, may want passengers and non-flying visitors to linger, spending time and money shopping and dining at airport facilities.
- Fifth, different airlines and other service providers may lease space from airports and operate differently, thereby creating fragmented approaches to, for example, customer service. Where airports provide common operating processes – for example, for check-in and baggage processing, and more recently, security – the problem is less severe.

Working around these challenges, airports have been changing their processes to enhance the experience of passengers going through airports. Examples include:

- Airlines and airports are mapping the passenger touchpoints and looking into where the painpoints are and how to eliminate them by eliminating and/or changing processes and systems and by introducing new technologies. Difficulties arise due to the involvement of government agencies that have not only very different objectives but very different processes and systems at different airports. There are no global standards for border control and tags embedded in bags, for instance.
- Airports are deploying a broad spectrum of technologies to improve customer experiences, starting with digital signage and wayfinding services – enabling the display of dynamic information – in different formats (text, images, and videos) and in different interactive and personalized ways – touch, type, and voice. Next, there are beacons, smart gates for boarding and passing through immigration and emigration (passport control) and customs with checkpoints with electronic stations that can read passports and facial features, sophisticated systems for tagging, tracking, and moving baggage, as well as permanent radio-frequency (RF) enabled tags installed in the bags (embedded technology).
- The check-in process has already become decentralized – online, via kiosks, and via mobile apps. Technology is being implemented to monitor traffic and open up lines and staff to accommodate based on predictive analytics and fluctuating demand, and some airports are looking into the development of interchange points where bags could be dropped off and from where passengers could walk to the terminals.
- At some airports border control is becoming almost fully automated, with roaming agents available to pull people out of lines if necessary.

Airports are looking into security systems that could be made more recognizable so that passengers are aware of how they work. Multiphase screening is being investigated. People could walk through without unpacking and undressing. Laser-powered security scanners and facial recognition technology located at multiple points could capture expressions and body movements. Laser molecular scanners could scan the contents of clothes in great detail. Multiple people could be scanned at the same time and from a distance in a non-invasive way.

- Some airports have also installed human-sized airport virtual assistants (including holographic imaging) that are now delivering relevant information and branding information at airports. Examples include New York and London's Luton.
- Airports, while generally behind airlines, have started to develop smartphone apps (even though there is a limit as to how many apps a person will have on a smartphone) to improve customer experience (real-time information on how to get to the airport, wait times at security, immigration and customs checkpoints, status in parking lots, and location of eating and shopping facilities, based on some degree of personalization).
- Airports have also started to develop their own loyalty programs – for example, *Thanks Again* – to build relationships with customers. This program allows a customer to automatically earn frequent flyer miles or hotel stay points when the customer parks the car at the airport or shops and dines at the airport.

Relating to the above points, the forward-thinking airports are looking into three specific areas for improving customer experience and satisfaction. First, airports gather vast quantities of data for operational control and to increase the effective utilization of their assets. Now they are beginning to supplement those data with data collected from partners at airports and couple them with analytics (particularly, predictive analytics) to engage with customers proactively to improve passenger experience. They recognize that engaging with customers not only can improve customer service and experience, but also lead to new sources of revenue.

Second, the leading airports are attempting to establish greater coordination between airports and airlines, and other third parties, such as security agencies and ground transportation service providers. At the higher level there are opportunities for joint operations. Terminal 2 at the Munich Airport is owned by Lufthansa and the airport company on a 50:50 basis. It is financed and operated jointly. Following are some examples of coordination at the lower levels. Some airports are exploring the implementation of Bluetooth beacons (wireless detection devices) that can send contextual information (notifications or promotional coupons) by triggering an alert on a smartphone. By increasing the coordination between airlines and airports, decisions on the location of these devices can enhance the customer experience. Airlines have begun to know the location of passengers to provide relevant information – mobile boarding passes, time remaining before the aircraft door closes, navigation to the gate, and so on. Similarly, more coordination is being considered between agents working for airlines and airports, such as via mobile passenger concierge tablets. For an airport to be able to engage with a passenger is not an easy task if the airline does not even have the contact information for the passenger if the reservation was made by an agent.

Third, the forward-thinking airports are slowly beginning to re-design facilities and services based on traveler-centricity. For experience, the attributes may relate to the availability of real-time information. For ambiance and mood, the attributes may relate to having higher ceilings and skylights and natural lights, not to mention sweeping views, a sense of place, for example. For efficiency the attributes could be the existence of high-speed processing through self-service systems and processes (self-tagging capabilities, self-drop-off locations, gates that enable self-boarding, and self-clearance through immigration and customs). Airports are looking into technology to engage with customers – for example, where a passenger can tap their phone to get information about flights, gates, and restaurant locations, and order food from one side of the security line and pick it up at the other side. Airports are contrasting passengers' experience of being at an airport to the passengers' experience of being in a hotel lobby or a restaurant. Should there be iPad stations for people to order food or get information on the wait times in security lines and check-in lines? Some of these features are not only being examined for existing airports such as Singapore's Changi, but will appear in the new airports being built, for example, in Mexico City and Istanbul, with facilities that are not just energy efficient (solar energy), but feature gates within reasonable walking distance and facilities for high-speed connections between terminals. Passengers do point out that there are two parts to the customer experience at airports – performing activities that are necessary, and often stressful, such as check-in, security, and boarding, and those that are discretionary, but usually enjoyable, such as shopping and dining. The idea is not just to make existing processes more efficient, but to re-define and re-design processes that reduce stress and enhance customer experience through personalization and engagement. Keep in mind the shift from desktop to web-enabled mobile devices, not to mention engagement through social networking that has brought in enormous changes, including changes in design thinking. The connectivity feature will change even further as technology provides more speed and greater bandwidth.

Airlines and airports are looking at best practices inside and outside of the industry. Inside the industry insights could be drawn from the experience of Qatar Airways, which operates out of two separate terminals, one for premium class and one for economy class travel, buses all passengers to and from the airplanes, and has separate ground processes for inbound and outbound passengers. Lufthansa operates a separate terminal for first class and top tier passengers. There is valet parking, check-in while seated in a lounge chair, a short walk to service areas, security and immigration with no lines, and transit to aircraft in limousines. Could such a first class terminal be scaled down to a business class terminal if an airline was to give up boarding all passengers from one gate through jetways?

While airports (and airlines) are looking into insights from other business sectors such as hospitality and, in some cases, both airlines and airports are referring to passengers as customers and even guests, the strategies to improve experience needs to be real and measured from the viewpoint of customers. For example, even though airlines say the customer satisfaction has improved, passengers do not agree. Figure 3.5 shows the answer to the question: Do you strongly agree that customer satisfaction has increased with respect to air travel? Forty-four percent of executives said yes, while only 7 percent of passengers said yes. Add this information to that shown in Figure 3.4, asking what the top priorities of airline management are. Airlines listed the top priority as reducing operating costs and the third priority as improving the customer experience. While passengers may have accepted the fact that processing at airports will take longer and that free amenities offered by airlines have disappeared, it does not mean that customers are more satisfied.

Airports as Destinations

Some airports are re-focusing on their missions. Should they be places to get on airplanes or should they also be destinations, something in between, or something else entirely? Singapore's Changi Airport has always tried to develop and maintain its status as a destination. Now other airports, such as the new airports in Abu Dhabi, Doha, and Dubai, have been developing their facilities and services to become destination airports. Becoming a destination airport does not mean simply more and a greater variety of retail outlets, conference centers, and hotels, but also areas for other activities such as relaxation and prayer, and to provide a greater sense of outdoor places and appealing spaces as opposed to just functional spaces and places. It also means aligning the interests of airports with the interests of local communities, and again not just in terms of contribution to the local economies, but also in terms of showcasing local culture and attractions and even aspects of national pride and identity. And, importantly, these destination airports aim to serve not only passengers, but other visitors as well.

Changi is re-designing its terminal, which will include an eye-catching palace of glass encompassing retail stores, entertainment activities, and places to relax such as gardens and walking trails. There is a plan to have a "Rain Vortex," a 40-meter waterfall flowing from the roof of the glass dome, accompanied by a light and sound show. Singapore Airport's initiative, known as Project Jewel (to be completed in 2018), will connect seamlessly the existing terminals and encompass airport facilities (ticketing, boarding passes, baggage transfer) and retail outlets and leisure activities, hotel space, multiple gardens, retail, and casino. The new complex is also planning a theme park and a medical center. Early check-in facilities at the complex will allow passengers to check-in and drop-off luggage ahead of regular check-in times. Subways will be available to connect to all terminals as well as to the city's mass rapid transit (MRT) network. By re-designing their facilities and services, airports can not only improve customer experience but also their ancillary revenues by appealing to travelers, non-travelers, and those planning events for the general community.

Areas of Disruption

The role of the airport and its relationship with the surrounding community, not to mention its look and feel, is likely to change in significant ways over the coming decades. The shift in airport revenue diversification, away from aeronautical-related services and toward a broad range of ancillary services, is an indicator of a significant upcoming change. It indicates how airports across the globe are envisioning their roles within a broader services context that touches travelers, airlines, and the greater community. The airport of the future is likely to be characterized by a much more dynamic role within the travel ecosystem, driven by travelers looking for a more engaging and relevant customer experience and by airlines operating much more like retailers. Airports are innovating and changing their roles to manage disruption from different sides based on the evolving needs of airlines, the continuously-changing needs of travelers, and the possible future role of changes in the air traffic control system with respect to the impact on runways and other infrastructure needs. A few airports are even taking the view of "disrupt or be disrupted."

Airport as Regional Economic Engine

Since the beginning of this decade there has been a discussion on the development of "Aerotropolis," an area where aviation-related businesses and activities (for example, time-sensitive manufacturing and distribution facilities, including the deployment of 3D printers) as well as multi-modal transportation systems, are centered on an airport. In other words, the airport is the center and it is surrounded by the community.[4] This concept is not just an academic discussion. It has been discussed in great detail with respect to its application in the Ekurhuleni area (near Johannesburg) in South Africa and in the San Diego region in California.

Airport as Intermodal Community Hub

Some airports, rather than becoming cities, are likely to remain or evolve into inter-modal or simply transportation hubs. The management of inter-modality is critical. Even today, consider the value of Shanghai's "domestic" airport. It is close to the intersection of two interstates, has three high-speed rail lines in an adjacent terminal plus two subway lines. Within a concept of transportation hub, what is now called "an airport" would simply become a large off-airport parking lot/rental car hub/short- and long-distance train terminal, where passengers could be seated until they are boarded into buses (or limousines) and driven right to the aircraft. This would eliminate the need for endless concourses (eliminating long-distance walking for the passengers), push-back trucks, and complex taxi procedures for arriving and departing travelers.

Disappearing Airport Services

Since airlines have now begun to charge up to $100 for each bag, could it be possible for third parties such as UPS and FedEx to succeed in making compelling value propositions to passengers to have their bags picked up from the points of origins and delivered to their points of destination for similar fees? If a significant number of passengers selected to use the services of these third parties, could not the baggage collection and delivery system at airports be disrupted? Stretch the imagination a little further. Could 3D printers be used to "print" most of the articles transported in passengers' bags, eliminating the need to ship bags through airlines or third parties?

When, not if, the self-driving car becomes a reality, what could happen to the huge parking garages at airports? A passenger could ask the car to drive her to the airport and then ask the car to park itself somewhere until it is required to return to the airport to pick up the passenger again. This scenario would reduce the revenue generated by parking at airports and free up the space currently used by the garage building. Keep in mind the data shown in Figure 6.2, that 45 percent of the revenue of an airport in North America comes from non-aeronautical sources and 41 percent of that revenue is generated by parking and ground transportation. Continuing the thought in the same area, could the peer-to-peer economy and the growing car-sharing business lead to a reduction in the number of cars rented at an airport? This activity generates 19 percent of the non-aeronautical revenue at an airport according to the data in Figure 6.2. FlightCar is an example of the ongoing disruption to airports. The company offers peer-to-peer car rental services at an airport where a departing traveler can leave her car at the airport for rental to an arriving traveler. The departing traveler receives a rental fee and the company earns a middleman transaction charge. What does the airport get – another area for some disruptive thinking on ways to integrate airport traffic with parking data into in-car information systems?

Consumer-Centric Disruptions

Some processes surrounding baggage are already moving off the airport as travelers prefer to check-in remotely and print their own bag tags from the convenience of their homes or offices. One of IATA's Fast Travel initiatives to improve airport experience relates to promoting standards and best practices for self bag tagging and fast baggage drop-off. Airlines can obviously provide real-time information to passengers through their smartphones. This process will clearly have an impact on airport check-in facilities, including kiosks. It is also possible that biometric identification technologies may change the process at airports, including the possibility of the process being performed at off-airport locations. What would happen to the infrastructure related to security? And how will the airports and some tenants (for example, dining) be impacted if airlines improve significantly their service recovery processes and systems along the lines suggested in Chapter 7, including, for example, through the use of predictive analytics?

Long-Term Disruption: Hyperloop, Drones, and Self-Driving Cars

These are just three examples of the areas where disruptive innovation could occur. Let us start with the development of the "Hyperloop," envisioned by the futurist entrepreneur Elon Musk. This is a high-speed transportation system in which pressurized capsules travel on an air cushion. It is reported that a full-scale prototype could be seen as early as 2016. This transportation system would reduce significantly the number of passengers traveling in short-haul air travel markets and reduce the need for additional capacity at many airports. Amazon could enter the business of transporting packages either through dedicated airports or using drones. One could scratch off these thoughts as dreams. Keep in mind, however, that Amazon did not even exist until 1994 and now it has been experimenting with the deployment of drones to deliver packages. Google did not even exist until 1996 and now it has developed a self-driving car.

Takeaways

Airports have been changing their business models in four areas – general framework, low-cost terminals, customer experience, and airports as destinations.

Airports are also adapting, although at a slower pace than airlines, to the three major forces of change (and their convergence) discussed in Chapter 3 – competition, consumer behavior, and technology.

In some areas the goals of airlines and airports are the same – improve the customer experience and enhance ancillary revenues, for example. However, in some areas, the goals are diametrically opposed. Airlines prefer to move passengers through the airport as quickly as possible. Airports prefer for passengers to spend as much time as possible to increase the retail-related revenue stream.

Despite the desire of both airline and airport to enhance the customer experience, the question of which entity "owns" the customer, at the airport, remains open. Airlines and airports are still at odds, especially when it comes to sharing data and processes. This lack of communication often results in missed opportunities between the airport and the airline, creating an opportunity for disruption.

By re-designing their facilities and services, airports can not only improve customer experience but also their ancillary revenues.

The desire by the LCCs to connect to their own flights as well as with full-service airlines is bringing about dramatic changes in airports and other organizations, such as within alliances. The emergence of major hybrid airlines, requiring cost-effective connectivity, will bring about major transformations within airports.

Airports, having used vast quantities of data for operational control and effective use of assets, are beginning to use the data, coupled with analytics (particularly predictive) to engage with customers proactively and improve passenger experience and generate more revenue.

Opportunities for disruptive innovation exist in the areas of airport facilities (parking and car rental, for example), and baggage collection and delivery (through the involvement of third parties such as fast-delivery service providers).

Notes

1 Airports Council International Europe (in partnership with SEO Aviation Economics), "Airport industry: connectivity report 2004–2014," 2014.
2 CAPA (Centre for Aviation), "Uber at airports: TNCs, airport policies and the issues surrounding them: CAPA Survey," November 26, 2015.
3 CAPA, "Low-cost airports and terminals are changing shape," *Airline Leader*, 26, January–February 2015.
4 A concept promoted by Dr. John D. Kasarda, a professor at the Kenan-Flagler Business School at the University of North Carolina, USA.

7 AIRLINE TRANSFORMATIONAL OPPORTUNITIES

For decades the largest percentage of an airline's revenue has been generated by the sale of its basic product (revenue generated by the combination of its network, fleet, and schedules). This number can be in the 80 percent range. The next 10 percent is estimated to have been the result of managing revenues, based initially on the combination of inventory and price and, more recently, on the sale of ancillary products and services. Now airline strategists are looking at the final 10 percent coming from various aspects of customer service and customer experience – not only the high profit margin component but, in some ways, also the differentiator among competitors. This chapter provides an overview of the transformational opportunities that are being followed by leading airlines in these three areas. The first section of this chapter begins with a brief overview of the strategies leading airlines are following at the corporate level to grow. The three sections that follow discuss transformational strategies at the functional level: network, fleet, and schedules; day of operations; revenue management; and dynamic merchandizing that calls for a high level of cross-functional integration within airlines. These functions are not new except for dynamic merchandizing.

Given the size and complexity of the problem within each function, airlines have relied heavily on the use of analytical techniques to optimize the use of their resources. Many of the planning systems airlines used worked well in the past partly because the operating environment was *relatively* stable, at least in the near and medium term, and partly because the technologies incorporated in the planning systems were becoming increasingly sophisticated for the systems used within each function – aircraft and crew scheduling, activities within operating systems centers, and revenue management, for example. In recent years, the amount of uncertainty facing all businesses, and even more the uncertainty facing the airline sector (given its high visibility and government involvement), has been increasing as a result of the forces and their convergence described in Chapter 3. This exponential increase in uncertainty is necessitating a need for (a) more input relating to vision, flexibility, and agility, and (b) more advanced planning systems, not so much with respect to an increase in sophistication for optimization within each functional area, but, instead, to achieve optimization on either a system-wide basis or in real time, or, hopefully, both, and to start new initiatives such as dynamic merchandizing.

Corporate Level

Airline leaders are clearly looking for ways to grow in the increasingly changing marketplace while working within the constraints of the airline industry (government regulations relating to bilateral agreements and government policies regarding ownership and control), remain agile and flexible, and take on complexity that is manageable. While these management attributes are not new within the airline industry, what is new is the consideration given to the need for long-term vision and the concept of "design" that now applies not only to products but also to the planning framework itself, including "designing" innovation and even strategies.

Consider some examples. After emerging from bankruptcy in 2007, Delta carefully navigated through the process of merging and integrating with Northwest, implemented an employee stock ownership plan, and purchased equity stakes in GOL, Virgin Atlantic, Aeromexico, and China Eastern Airlines. In terms of transforming its own business, Delta acquired an oil refinery to have some control over the fluctuations in the price of oil, started to reduce debt to reduce the enormous level of interest payments, and changed its loyalty program (switching the credit given from miles flown to dollars spent) to reward the high-value customers. At the end of December 2015, Delta was reported to be establishing an overseas subsidiary to reduce its tax obligations. With respect to its reach, Delta re-aligned its domestic and international networks and deepened its partnership and/or joint-venture relationship with Air France-KLM and Alitalia to maintain a higher level of control on capacity and the relationship between capacity and demand to reduce costs and generate more revenue. With respect to operations, Delta reclaimed control of the reservations system and data to get more insights into customer behavior and invested resources (money and capabilities) to move higher up on the operational excellence curve. And Delta invested heavily to enhance its products and services in its business class and economy plus cabins to attract and maintain higher-paying customers.

These initiatives reflect the leadership attributes discussed above. Given that the growth in air travel is forecast to be much higher to, from, and within other parts of the world than in the USA and given the strong possibility that governments worldwide are not likely to change their policies with respect to ownership and control rules in the foreseeable future, acquiring significant equity stakes in carefully selected airlines around the world represents sound judgment. The selection process involved a careful analysis of the current amount of travel to and from the USA, expected growth in travel, and mutual value for both parties. For example, since the largest air travel market by dollar value is between the US and the UK (Figure 7.1) it is hardly a surprise that Delta took a 49 percent stake in Virgin Atlantic. It added value

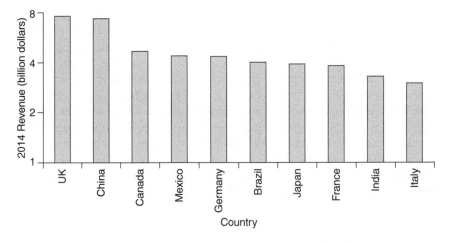

Figure 7.1 Top Ten US48 to International Markets (source: Delta Investor Day 2015 presentation).

for both airlines by providing a greater market share for Delta across the Atlantic and making Virgin a more effective competitor of British Airways. The arrangement – representing the design attribute mentioned above – was more than just an acquisition of the equity stake. Clearly there was a meeting of the minds as Virgin re-aligned its international capacity by reducing services to Asia and increasing services across the Atlantic.

Similarly, Delta is planning to increase its equity in Aeromexico to 49 percent, given the dollar value of the travel between the USA and Mexico, the fourth largest market in the top ten (Figure 7.1). A similar rationale explains the investments in GOL and China Eastern. Delta is either an equity partner and/or in a joint-venture for travel relating to the UK, China, Mexico, Brazil, France, and Italy. In Japan, Delta has a major hub at Tokyo's Narita Airport. It is reported that through these equity partnerships and/or joint-venture relationships Delta is most likely to be asked to give advice on managing the airline business.[1] And, given the size of the revenue base of travel between the USA and India, at the end of December 2015 Delta was reported to be working with Jet Airways, based in India, to develop a partnership.

There are a number of other examples of airlines planning for the uncertain future. Chapter 4 mentioned British Airways not only establishing and becoming a key member of the IAG but also acquiring Aer Lingus, not just for its slots at London's Heathrow Airport (at least in the long term) but mostly to acquire an ideally located fourth hub for IAG. Aer Lingus' Dublin hub provides diversification for IAG and enables British Airways to expand outside the UK, where capacity will continue to be limited at London's Heathrow Airport even when expansion does finally begin. Consider the initiatives taken by Etihad, having acquired equity stakes in and developed strategic partnerships with numerous airlines around the world (Aer Lingus, Airberlin, Air Serbia, Air Seychelles, Alitalia, Jet Airways, Etihad Regional, and Virgin Australia).[2] Through these arrangements, Etihad has established its own unique strategic alliance with one major difference. Having provided a significant amount of money, negotiated membership in the Boards, and having placed senior executives in key positions, Etihad should be able to exercise significant control in the decisions relating to fleet, network, schedules, airport facilities, and planning systems, such as reservations and revenue management. The concept is valid if Etihad can place the strong leaders at conventionally managed airlines such as Airberlin and Alitalia. As a third example, take the case of Air Canada, Lufthansa and United with respect to their powerful joint-venture across the Atlantic. The coverage in terms of frequency and capacity provides significant control in terms of managing capacity and demand relative to competition – see the information provided in Figure 7.2 and Table 7.1.

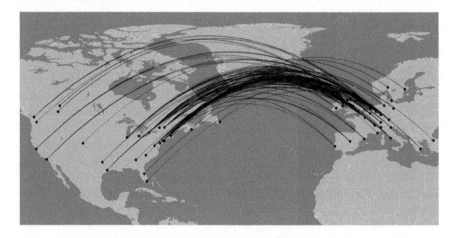

Figure 7.2 Transatlantic Networks of Air Canada, Lufthansa, and United (source: OAG Schedule Analyser and Mapper).

Table 7.1 Frequency and Capacity Offered by Three Airlines with a Joint-Venture in the Star Alliance

Carrier	Average Daily	
	Seats	Flights
Air Canada	5,471	20
Lufthansa	9,674	29
United Airlines	11,434	52

Source: OAG Schedule Analyzer.

Network, Fleet, and Schedules

To appreciate the value of an airline's network there is no need to look further than the successful expansion of low-cost carriers (LCCs) shown in Figure 2.3 and the newer-generation network airlines, particularly from the Persian Gulf. In more recent times, one could look at the re-alignment of Japan Airlines' network and fleet (immediately following its emergence from bankruptcy) and Hawaiian Airlines. While recognizing the importance of an airline's network is not a new insight, what is different now is a growing appreciation of (a) the importance of vision and intuition, (b) the relationship of the network to other areas such as partners (alliance or equity) and distribution, and (c) the value of new types of data and technologies that can now be used to optimize an airline's network. The key to "designing" innovation is to integrate the physical hub-and-spoke system with the digital hub-and-spoke system.

Let us start with the growing importance of vision and intuition. While network and schedule planning in the past relied more on the rigorous use of sophisticated analytical models and operations research techniques, and less on vision and intuition, the balance in focus between science and intuition is being revisited with an increase in uncertainty in areas of regulatory policies, the state of economies, and the staying power of new-generation competitors, whether they are large full-service global players, sophisticated hybrid airlines, or LCCs with increasingly viable business models for service in intercontinental markets. Think about the role of science vs. vision and intuition when:

- Singapore Airlines decided to add another subsidiary to its portfolio of airlines, Scoot, to maintain and increase market share;
- Etihad decided to create a virtual global network via strategically aligned partners as well as membership in a traditional alliance;
- Turkish Airlines decided to offer service to more than 45 destinations in Africa from its hub in Istanbul;
- Emirates and Qantas decided to develop a virtual network through their partnership;
- Norwegian Air Shuttle decided to offer transatlantic service between the UK and the USA to compete with not just lower fares, but also with marketing initiatives through social network platforms;
- Delta acquired 49 percent of the equity in Virgin Atlantic Airways, despite its partnership with Air France-KLM;
- WestJet started thinking about offering one-stop service between Canada and Ireland and the UK; and
- Copa faced a decision on where to put the capacity withdrawn from Venezuela after the currency crisis.

The idea behind the new thinking in network and schedule planning is not just a conventional computation of the share of the market, but also the potential to develop the market. And it is this latter vision and intuition that can explain the growing network of the four Super Connectors discussed earlier. Clearly, vision, intuition, and market development potential must have played a role in Emirates' decision to put five trips per day between Dubai and London Heathrow with the Airbus 380, four trips per day between Dubai and Johannesburg with the Boeing 777, and a double daily between Dubai and Mauritius with the Airbus 380. Think about Qatar Airways' decision to put a non-stop flight between Doha and Philadelphia, a relatively thin market.

Such visions of market development cannot be evaluated with the use of standard market share techniques. The conventional models (for example, the Quality of Service Index – QSI) had to be changed dramatically to take into account the quality of the product as well as the desirability of the brand. The Persian Gulf-based carriers are offering higher-quality service, at least in premium cabins, at competitive if not lower fares. Making connections at their hubs is considered more desirable in light of the facilities and services available at the more modern airports that are open around the clock. And they have better presence in social media platforms. It was recently reported in the press that Qatar Airways was awarded the title of the most "liked" global airline on Facebook, an incredibly popular social media networking site. Think also of the experiential aspect in market share models of the proposed facilities and services in the first class of Etihad Airways.

Some readers might feel that "vision and intuition" is a bit fuzzy, but it is not necessarily the case. Suppose that we think of an airline's future business choices as a portfolio of investment choices. The vision and intuition supporting the bold and innovative options represent the investment decision supporting the commitment. As in any portfolio, the investment decision can either prove itself objectively or, if not, become a basis for an exit. In this sense, the "vision and intuition" is more than a hunch, and it is also more than a mechanistic by-the-numbers decision. It is also more than "trial and error," as the vision entails an internally consistent scenario and is subject to disciplined metrics when it comes to sustaining the position.

Next, as mentioned above, defining an airline's network and strategy lays the foundation for other key strategic decisions relating to fleet, products, partners (alliance or equity), and distribution. Consider, for example, the distribution sphere that has also been changing rapidly. To begin with, low-cost carriers and airlines from emerging markets have been growing at fast rates and now they both want a larger part of the corporate market. Second, new third parties have begun to synthesize vital information on customers, insightful information that could be sold to airlines. Third, digital advertising has begun to increase. And, fourth, the metasearch landscape is moving from a marketing platform toward a distribution channel.

Past network and schedule planning exercises relied more heavily on the rigorous use of sophisticated analytical models, operations research techniques, and forecasting processes, such as the QSI, and less on intuition. This worked as the environment was reasonably stable at least in the short to medium term. However, this is no longer the case given the significant increase in uncertainty in the long term, but also in the short and medium term. The situation has been changing as uncertainty has been increasing in the areas of regulatory policies and the state of economies.

So, what about the role of new data and new technologies for optimizing the network? Let us start with the central piece of information shown in Figure 7.3, the size of the origin and destination (O&D) market. While this will continue to be an important factor, the experience of LCCs and the new players based in the Persian Gulf suggest that the market has the potential to be developed to incredible levels, while being ready to respond to new marketing initiatives. Many LCCs started service in markets, often at secondary airports, where the reported O&D traffic was insignificant. Yet by offering services in unserved or underserved areas they developed those markets – for example, Southwest in the USA, Ryanair in Europe, Azul in Brazil, and Spring Airlines in China. Similarly, Emirates Airline's entire network, fleet, and schedules could hardly be considered to be built around the traffic to and from Dubai.

As for demographics, they clearly have been and will be changing in emerging markets. A few carriers are aligning their networks radically to

Figure 7.3 Factors Influencing Network Planning.

capitalize on the opportunities. For example, the capacity offered by IndiGo in 2015 within the Indian domestic market was almost double the capacity offered by Air India and more than the total capacity offered by all other LCCs combined – SpiceJet, GoAir, AirAsia, Air Costa, and Vistara. Also, the planned capacity of Emirates to and from India is likely to approach that of Jet Airways. On the other hand, it is interesting to note the low level of penetration of LCCs within domestic markets in China relative to the situation in India. Moreover, it is also puzzling, as mentioned in Chapter 5, to see the insignificant non-stop frequency and capacity between the two largest countries in the world based on the size of their populations.

Continuing with the changing importance of demographics, it is now becoming important to consider the value, and not just the number, of customers in a market. This customer value goes beyond passenger yield or average fare or even wallet share. Customer value also includes aspects of loyalty and advocacy in social media platforms. A passenger buys tickets on an airline that has more than 80 percent of the flights out of a given airport. Is that considered loyalty or patronage? Similarly, a passenger who is likely to be a supporter of an airline's products and services in social media platforms has much higher value than one who is neither active in social media nor a promoter. Customer value can now be scored and analyzed in ways that can play an important role in the analysis and planning of networks and schedules.

It is now also important to consider new O&D marketing approaches and technologies. Within a market, demographics and consumers' outlook toward emerging consumer technology can play an important role in dynamic customer acquisition, growth and retention, supported by agile business and customer intelligence. In other words, some markets may not just have a greater proportion of business travelers but a new generation of travelers who have greater expectations of the use of consumer technology. They may require and respond to different marketing value propositions. It is worth considering how people, including those residing in emerging markets, use their mobile phones to access information relating to travel and even pay for travel products and services. The availability of the internet on mobile devices is calling for new strategies given that, according to some estimates, more than two-thirds of the "webtime" is spent on mobile devices.

Then there is the expanding role, and changing nature of, partnerships. In the formative days there were inter-line partners, followed by code-share partners, and most recently, alliance partners. Now, there are joint-venture partners and equity partners. Figure 7.2 showed the power of the joint-ventures for three airlines operating a joint-venture across the Atlantic during the first week of December 2015. Table 7.1 showed that among the three they operated 101 flights per day on average, with a capacity of 26,579 seats per day. These new partnership arrangements make a big difference as to how the basic network-related product is aligned in a given market, which then significantly affects the outcomes of revenue-generating efforts. For example, Delta must execute its transatlantic network with great care now that it has acquired equity in Virgin Atlantic, essentially competing with fellow SkyTeam Alliance founder Air France for the same global traffic flow in key markets.

What about input from local sales? In the early days, this played a key role. Frequency and schedules were impacted significantly based on the input and commitment from sales at one or both ends of a market. With the use of centrally based planning systems, input from local sales decreased, leading in some cases to scenarios of "Here is the schedule, now go and sell." With O&D-based revenue management systems, the dynamic between field sales and revenue management is as loaded as ever. Yet, the changing demographics and the availability of locally targeted marketing technologies that develop new traffic and defend against emerging savvy competitors have made input from local sales vital again.

Besides new sources and types of information, network optimization can now also benefit from the availability of more advanced analytical techniques. In the past, market selection, capacity, frequency, schedules, and so forth had to be performed on a piecemeal and sequential basis due to technological limitations. Then adjustments were made, almost always manually, for constraints such as airport slots and noise restrictions. Then there were also maintenance and crew assignment considerations, not to mention day-of-week schedule changes to allow for peaks and troughs. And the potential for cannibalization from having airlines-within-airlines cannot be overlooked – Eurowings within Lufthansa, Jetstar within Qantas, Scoot within Singapore, and Rouge within Air Canada, for example. Now, with improvements in optimization techniques, including computation power and speed, it is possible to perform simultaneous optimization processes. With the availability of more precise data on customers and customer-centric forecasting techniques, it is now also possible to undertake targeted network, fleet and schedule planning. Knowing that passengers travelling in premium cabins generate a disproportionate percentage of the revenue and costs, it is possible to introduce cabin profitability in the network–fleet–schedule–cabin configuration optimization process.

Drilling down further, within scheduling, for example, and deciding on the correct balance between capacity and expected demand has become even more challenging given various levels and types of uncertainty. For airlines with a mixed fleet, it has been possible, to some degree, to adjust capacity between 30–45 days prior to departure to obtain the extra demand (or reduce spoilage) through processes known as "demand-driven dispatch" and "close-in-re-fleeting," a concept that the express freight carriers (such as FedEx) have been using for a long time. Now, with dynamic merchandizing, discussed below, it is possible to increase revenue as well as achieve higher load factors. By including ancillary revenue and loyalty into the revenue optimization process (also discussed below), the fleet-schedule combination can be adjusted much closer to departure to better match capacity to demand. Again, this aspect of planning requires the use of "close-in-re-fleeting" techniques as well as a totally integrated revenue optimization model in which optimization is based not just on inventory and price, but also ancillary revenue and loyalty.

Clearly, within network and scheduling, on every flight an airline now competes on price and service delivered by the brand as well as ancillary revenue generated by context-based offers that enhance experience. Therefore, the network must be optimized to fulfill the stated and unstated needs of the targeted current, and future, customers. The object now is to optimize revenue per customer, not revenue per seat, while building the brand and loyalty. The new commercial planning framework can now enable an airline to adjust price and service levels to not only meet market competitive dynamics, but also brand promises and expectations. Moreover, the network and schedule planning systems can now also enable an airline to take into account the revenue from cargo.

There is one all-encompassing piece missing in Figure 7.3 that integrates all other pieces and that may be more important to some carriers than others. The workforce is an integral part of network planning. If it is not part of the vision or if its role ends up being played out of character (or off-brand), then risk and/or cost increase, jeopardizing execution. All of the factors define the brand, in the holistic sense, for the traveler. If the elements are soundly integrated and work to a common purpose, then the brand fulfills the vision.

Day of Operations

As with network, fleet, and schedules, the planning capability is also improving with respect to operations based on the availability of more comprehensive data and technologies for optimization on a broader basis. Consider, for example, that for the day of departure, it is now possible to incorporate proactive service recovery systems and processes into an airline's network operations center. Emerging technologies can now enable an airline to undertake scenario planning well in advance of an irregular operation and produce optimal solutions for the crew and aircraft movements as well as for strategic groups of passengers.

Typically, there are four major inter-related considerations within operations when operations fall apart due to, say, a major thunderstorm passing through a large connecting hub airport – aircraft, crew, gates, and landing slots. There are also two other groups involved – the systems operations control center and flight management (Figure 7.4). The challenge has been to operate the schedule with minimal disruptions when there is uncertainty about the length of time it would take for the thunderstorm to pass and the intensity and duration of lightning. Compounding the problem, there can also be mechanical failures with mechanics unable to even go on the ramp to inspect the aircraft and diagnose problems, given the on-and-off lightning situation. Such a situation requires not only the integration of data and communications in *real time*, but also the resolution of contradictory departmental objectives, both within operations and outside of operations, such as

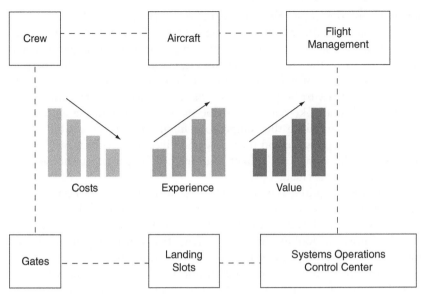

Figure 7.4 Connecting the Airline to Deliver Value.

reservations, sales, loyalty, and even further out, for example, with the relevant groups at the airport. The optimization process must take into consideration five inter-related elements: costs, revenues, consistency of customer experience, long-term customer loyalty, and customer value.

From a broader perspective, staff in the departments, shown in Figure 7.4, work with two challenges. First is the analytics challenge – determining which items can be juggled and which one comes first. Second is the challenge of coordinating the resources in real time – aircraft, crews, gates, tow trucks, and so forth. After connecting the airline within the operations department, shown by the dotted line in Figure 7.4, with respect to these two challenges, operations communicates with departments outside of operations. For example, it is important to know not only that there are 20 passengers who will miss connections if this flight is delayed, but *who* the 20 passengers are, how their plans would be impacted, and what options can be provided to each passenger to meet his or her unique needs and willingness to pay. Where are these 20 passengers at the airport? What is the priority of re-accommodation – with respect to time and the transporting airline, the affected airline, its alliance partners, or its competitors? Re-accommodating passengers on the airline's other flights, or even the flights of its alliance partners, is not sufficient if the process does not meet the needs of customers. The challenge is either to find out each passenger's needs or to present each passenger with personalized and viable options.

Imagine the reaction of a passenger who is informed that she will be accommodated on the airline's next flight that is four hours later, would therefore miss the connection at the international gateway, but would be accommodated on the international segment the following day, when the passenger, in fact, sees on her smartphone a flight on a competitor that would allow her to make the connection at the international gateway. But the passenger cannot walk over to the counter of the competitor, given that the electronic ticket has to be processed by the airline with the irregular operation. Would it not make sense to provide the passenger with the option that a seat can be acquired on the competitor's flight about to depart but it will mean an additional charge and there is a possibility that the bags may not be transferred to the competitor's flight in time? Let the passenger choose from the list of options provided.

Optimization requires, as mentioned, the availability of, in real time, integrated and actionable information and its dissemination, and the use of advanced systems. However, there is also a need to change processes. For example, instead of looking first at the items that can be juggled and then looking at the coordination of resources in real time, why not first ask for information on the impacted passengers, not just the number, but who they are and the priorities for re-accommodation. Clearly, the unaccommodated minors would come first. But then what? Those with earned status and in what order? If the operations department was to start with input from the commercial sector, the optimization process might be based on long-term value as opposed to short-term costs. And this information must come directly from the commercial group that is working, in turn, with reservations. It is very difficult for operations to figure out *quickly* the O&D of each passenger based on the information contained in the Passenger Name Record (PNR). And getting relevant information from the commercial group is not easy either. At some level of the airline, tough decisions have to be made. Should the airline focus only on the top 10 percent of its passengers that generate 50 percent of the revenue, or the top 20 percent that generate 80 percent of the revenue? What about the other 80 percent? Should they all be treated equally, or differently?

All resources are now available to operate a "connected airline," given the availability of mobile devices for communications, the convergence of technologies to collect, integrate, and disseminate information, and the availability of a broad spectrum of algorithms suitable for different categories of airlines – low-cost and full-service carriers, for example, based on corporate strategy. But, it is the change in processes, systems, and culture to "connect the airline" that will lead to an acceleration in the decision-making process to optimize not only costs and revenues, but also customer value and customer satisfaction of all passengers, not just the premium-fare and high-loyalty program status passengers.

Think about the relatively minor but ongoing challenge that can easily be addressed in a more customer-friendly way. When booking a normal connecting flight within a globally branded alliance, even the top-tier customer cannot access seat selection on the partner flight. The website (if the traveler knows where to look and reads the fine print carefully) will provide a note, and the airline may even provide a telephone number and/or the alliance partner's alternate confirmation number so the traveler can complete the awkward process. Since airlines have come this close to integration within an alliance, it should be relatively easy to make it work end to end.

Revenue Management Planning

The function of revenue management has been a game-changer within the global airline industry for more than four decades, allowing carriers to offset some of the negative factors associated with a perishable product, fixed capacity, high fixed costs, and low variable costs. The fixed costs are high given that airlines offering scheduled services operate with a published schedule as a commitment to operate even during times when the demand is insufficient. In the early 1970s, one of the earliest adopters of revenue management, British Airways (then BOAC), began to experiment with capacity-controlled discounted fares based on early bookings, otherwise known as segmental demand. This was soon followed by American Airlines' 1977 experiment with Super Saver fares, implemented again on a capacity-controlled basis. Since then, airlines have been using advanced knowledge of analytics and consumer behavior to optimize their revenues, a practice that was adopted by many businesses in other sectors, notably hotels, car rental companies and entertainment companies such as Disney World. However, some of these retailers have capitalized further on this practice and benefited even more than airlines. By spending more time understanding the lifestyles and behavior of their targeted customers, these retailers have not only mastered how to price inventory more effectively, but also how to promote the product in ways that catch the attention of carefully segmented and targeted customers, motivating them to make purchases and to pay attention to the omnichannel experience.

In recent years, the airline industry has posted higher levels of profit, resulting from networks, fleet, and schedules (including significant consolidation with the resulting control in capacity and pricing), and the generation of high levels of revenue through the sale of ancillary products and services through the process of unbundling the product and charging for some services that were included in the basic fare. With respect to the latter, on a global basis, ancillary revenue has already reached a level above $50 billion in 2015 and is estimated to be well over $100 billion within five years. The debate now is not on the size of this number, but how:

- airlines can capture a large percentage of the forecast ancillary revenue for themselves rather than new distributors emerging in the market – businesses with a much greater focus on customer centricity leveraged by relevant information and predictive analytics; and

- an individual airline can increase the size of its profit slice, the difference between the cost trend line (incorporating productivity, efficiency, and control initiatives) and the revenue trend line (incorporating proactive customer management initiatives) during its planning horizon (see Figure 4.2).

The idea now is to optimize revenue based on dollars per customer, based on information derived from processing transactions as well as analyzing information on customer behavior, expectations, and experience. And it is this information (coming from websites, mobile apps, airport kiosks, loyalty programs, and so forth) that can be monetized for dynamic retailing and generating value, including through user-generated content. It is this information-generated value (derived from integrated and active data warehouses as well as the use of unrelational data management systems) that feeds back to build relationships that increase the dollar per customer.

Until recently, airline revenue managers focused on two basic parameters: inventory and price in a given market, shown in Figure 7.5 by the two circles

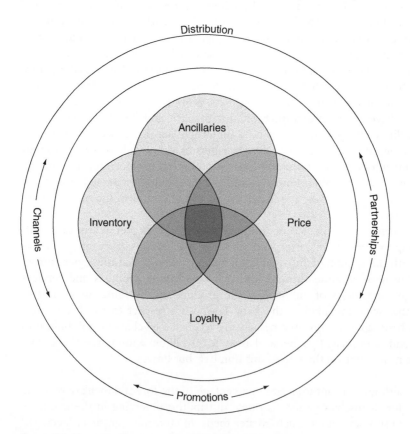

Figure 7.5 Changing Components of Revenue Management.

and their intersection. Within this context, they used sophisticated techniques to optimize trip revenue, taking into consideration factors such as booking patterns, load factors, and the nature of the itinerary (local segment, or a connection, including details such as whether the connection is inter-line, intra-line, or with an alliance partner). Sophisticated carriers went further and analyzed not just the inventory within different buckets, but also the makeup within each bucket. For example, company A in the corporate bucket might get a 10 percent discount while company B in the same bucket might get a 15 percent discount. Similarly, the more advanced airlines looked at whether it was an alliance partner, equity partner, or a joint-venture partner requesting a seat before authorization was provided.

Now technology is available to integrate at least two more functions in the optimization process, ancillaries and loyalty. Optimization can now encompass the intersection of all four circles in a given market – a more complex task, but one that promises to provide a significant improvement in not just revenue, but also customer experience, assuming that the airline has the technical capability, the right systems, and an organizational structure to achieve this level of optimization at the enterprise level.

Clearly, within network and scheduling, on every flight an airline now competes on price and service delivered by the brand as well as ancillary revenue generated by context-based offers that enhance experience. Therefore, the network must be optimized to fulfill the stated and unstated needs of targeted current and future customers. According to some airline executives, around 75 percent of customers are totally price sensitive and will go for the lowest price. An airline still cannot ignore this group and must gain its market share of this component. Therefore, an airline must find out more information about the passengers in this large group as to: (1) who they are; (2) how valuable; and (3) how they behave and respond to various offers. The object now is to optimize revenue per customer, not revenue per seat, while building the brand and loyalty.

The analysis can start with questions such as who are the targeted customers, what they buy, what are their propensities to buy, what channels do they prefer, and how does the analyst maximize wallet share. The next process, optimization, is much more complicated. Revenue managers do not know how much people will spend on ancillaries when they are making reservations months ahead of the travel date. The analyst cannot optimize something they cannot forecast. This leads to the execution process and the use of predictive analytics. Again, the forward-thinking airlines have already begun to experiment and build a database. Who purchased what ancillary product or service at what price and at what time in the travel cycle – day of reservation, day of flight, prior to check-in, or during the flight? In a particular bucket, who purchased X and also purchased Y? They are experimenting with prices, up-selling, cross-selling, and using market intelligence. A person making a day trip is not likely to be interested in a lower price for checked bags. A person on a long-haul flight that is almost full might be interested in a seat with extra legroom. A person with an exceptionally long layover might be interested in a lounge pass for part of the day, but not the whole day. The evaluation process, a difficult task within a service sector to begin with, involves not just an analysis of how each functional silo is doing but how commercial planning – the combination of all four functions – is performing. Even within a functional silo, evaluation is required in real time – for instance, on how a certain promotion is doing. Is it cannibalizing a premium product? Feedback is needed in real time, not two months after the promotion. This is where metrics and key performance indicators enter the evaluation process.

Despite a desire to take the revenue optimization process to the next level, even the ambitious airlines face monumental challenges. Just within commercial planning, are the four functions, represented by the four circles in Figure 7.5, integrated? Is there a conflict between branded fares developed by marketing and ancillary products and services being sold by revenue managers? The integration relates not just to the sub-functions within each of seat inventory, price, ancillaries, and loyalty, but across all four functions. Would inventory control open up a bucket if the passenger asking for a seat had negative experiences during the past three trips? Would inventory control even have this information without human intervention? Would sales be able to get a bucket opened up for a special customer that falls in the category of being an "influencer"?

In addition to the four basic functions shown in Figure 7.5, the revenue management optimization process must also take into account input on the value of customers and distribution – channels, partnerships, and promotions as shown in Figure 7.5, not to mention an alignment with business strategies and brand strategies dealing with, for example, onboard digital experience. It is the total integration within commercial planning, within operations planning, and between the two that will transform an airline's business strategy into brand strategy and, in turn, lead to a customer strategy.

The onboard digital experience relates to what used to be referred to as in-flight entertainment (IFE), including hardware and software, and now includes access to in-flight Wi-Fi or broadband, access or ability to use a device for voice communications, access to power and/or connectivity with onboard systems or devices, and customized communications systems to a screen at a passenger's seat.

The onboard experience has been improving, and it is poised to leap forward in the next 3–5 years and could transform as much or more as the early mobile phones morphed into the near-ubiquitous smartphones. Airlines can learn from the experience of hospitality and the automobile sectors. In the hospitality sector, initially, third parties were responsible and the hotel guests were not served well. Then capabilities improved, but could not keep up with the bandwidth needs. Legacy assets and operators were at a big disadvantage because of costs and execution challenges. Even shortages of electrical plugs were amusingly but frustratingly troublesome. New, lower-end hotels offered free service, while old-line business properties set up paywalls and extracted money from their best customers. Then free connectivity became a perk for the guests with elite status, and then again, bandwidth demands became a challenge, necessitating a tiered guest-status approach. The auto industry experience is also relevant in terms of the relationship of onboard connectivity to the model cycle and the longer-term platform generation cycle.

The insight for airlines is to move faster. As in hospitality, the internal (workforce) dimension will be of near-equal or greater importance. And as in the case of the auto industry, the airline industry is also challenged by the mismatch between rapid cycling of consumer (and business) technologies that cycle much faster than their respective model and platform generations. The immediate result is onboard systems that either fail to sync and/or fall short of consumer expectations. The risk is that more of the capability, content, and profit potential in the manufactured product and services are captured by the faster-moving technology providers. In the smartphone business, for example, the business offering the best customer-facing ecosystem captures a larger share of the profit.

Should every airline undertake this extremely sophisticated revenue optimization process? A global, full-service airline, of course, is clearly a candidate. An ultra low-cost airline, on the other hand, could use a far less sophisticated optimization framework, depending on the vision of the leadership with respect to the current and future customer base and the complexity of the operations required to meet the expectations of the customer base. Even low-cost airlines need to do some level of segmentation to move from mass marketing to segment marketing to target marketing. Those low-cost airlines that provide service in intercontinental markets (AirAsia X, Jetstar and Norwegian Air Shuttle, for example) need to go much further to identify and interact with customers to optimize revenue by up-selling and cross-selling. And for the large global, full-service airlines, especially those who aspire to become successful retailers, optimization of revenue at the *enterprise level* will increase margins that are incredible for airlines, but normal for high-end retailers. However, the process requires much more information on customer behavior, with a focus on customer insights, not just customer friendliness, and the long-term value of building and maintaining a brand, and not a desire to build for scale.

Dynamic Merchandizing

Once the traditional and the new aspects of network, fleet, and schedules, as well as the major components of revenue management discussed above, had been analyzed, attention in recent years has been turning to the management of customers not just from the viewpoint of experience but also merchandizing to enhance revenue. Based on the early returns from the merchandizing of airlines' own initiatives as well as the experience of state-of-the-art techniques used by retailers, interest now has moved from static to dynamic merchandizing. However, if an airline wants to become a high-margin retailer, as appears to be the case with numerous large global carriers, then it needs to circle back to the practices of successful retailers: ease of use regardless of channel, consistent brand experience at every touchpoint, customer and data-centric personalization – at least based on enriched customer profiles of the targeted segments – and optimization at an enterprise level (not within a silo). Retailers learned from airlines the capability of sophisticated revenue management. But they took the practice to new heights by understanding customer behavior and building genuine relationships with different customers at different levels by offering the right product to the right customer at the right time through the right channel and at the right price. Airlines can now learn from successful global retailers.

Let us start with technology that can enable an airline to take the passenger experience (and personalization) as well as dynamic merchandizing to a much higher level. There are five fundamental building blocks:

1   The establishment of a centralized and comprehensive database on customers that is updated in real time.
2   The deployment of a broad spectrum of commercial analytics to (1) clean data; (2) identify customers and their value scores; (3) develop profiles; and (4) analyze and predict behavior.
3   The development of personalized and situation-based trigger rules.
4   The capability to create and make dynamic and personalized retailing offers throughout the journey.
5   The implementation of an integrative technology system that sets into motion a sequence of events and offers by extracting information from one or more of the above four databases and enables the relevant staff to take specific action.

The first block calls for the existence of a centralized and comprehensive database with real-time customer profiles. It can be developed by extracting data from internal marketing/sales and operational data banks (reservations, departure control, ticketing, loyalty management systems, and customer relationship management programs). Critical information is also needed from external sources (social media, travel partners – hotels, car rental companies, credit card companies). It sounds fairly simple, but many airlines have not even synthesized information from their internal sources, let alone gathered information from external sources. And this is only the first building block.

For the second block, a few airlines are now beginning to use a broad spectrum of commercial analytics that are facilitating the development of customer profiles containing customer identification and value scores, relevant customer touchpoints for different segments and past experience at each point. They are also using analytics to correlate profiles with customer behavior, actual and predicted. The primary component in this block is the calculation of customer value, a computation that includes many more variables than just the price of a ticket. Information is also needed on frequency of travel and the potential influence of a customer in social media.

For the third building block, airlines can now develop comprehensive menu-driven sets of business trigger rules. If this happens to a customer of this tier status at this touchpoint and in this situation, make the following offer: an upgrade, access to a lounge, meal voucher, no baggage fee, no reservation change fee, priority boarding, and so forth. If the premium cabin is full or if the passenger is already traveling in the premium cabin, then find out, instantly, if the passenger has an upcoming flight and then offer a free upgrade in the next reservation, assuming that the reservation is in a similar sector.

The fourth building block relates to the creation and marketing of dynamic and personalized offers. At the present time, marketing offers are made in a static environment. For example, there is a fixed menu that shows prices for the transportation of baggage (by the bag number, weight, and so forth), seat location, access to a lounge, and so forth. However, this list can be made dynamic so that the price for the transportation of a bag and reservation for a particular seat would vary by flight and access to the lounge would vary by day of the week and time of day, as well as the duration of the stay. The price of a service feature would be dynamic, with variation based on the customer's profile and customer's situation, as well as the demand for the services in real time.

The fifth building block, just beginning to be deployed by a few airlines around the world, is the deployment of integrative technology systems that extract the relevant information from each of the four building blocks and enables different staff members to take different actions in different situations (Figure 7.6). An event could be triggered by observing that a known customer is on an airline's website or an incident such as a report from a ramp agent that one of the two bags belonging to a particular passenger did not get loaded onto the flight that just pushed back. It is the integrative technology system that starts the process by accessing the relevant data, making it available to all key staff, accompanied by action items. The action items are provided to the relevant staff members at relevant times and in relevant manners for the actions to be taken in a timely manner. Gate agents are not likely to have the time or the knowledge to know which passenger should not be charged for overweight bags or which customer can get to take a second bag free and why. An integrative technology system can provide agents with the needed information in a timely manner and format to meet the needs of customers on a contextual and situational basis. However, there is a need for a designed feedback loop in Figure 7.6. The journey never ends and the cycle needs to incorporate outcomes and customer input and feedback.

All five building blocks for moving up the experience curve and dynamic merchandizing are now available in the marketplace. What is needed is not just the enabling technology, but the transformational change in culture to prepare for the digital future in which customers want more than products and services. They also want consistent experience and personalization at all

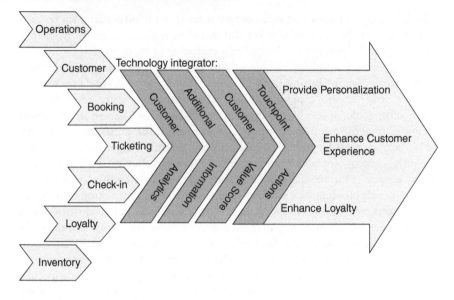

Figure 7.6 Technology Integrator to Develop Personalized and Experience-Based Services for Dynamic Merchandizing.

touchpoints based on their value expectations, and are willing to pay for such services. Airlines do have incredible amounts of data that can be leveraged to understand and respond to the constantly changing dynamics of the market-place, as well as access to advanced technology and analytics to offer value-adding propositions and to monitor, interpret, and evaluate performance. But, do they have the right systems to provide a single, transparent, 360-degree view of the product to a customer? Do they have the systems, skills, and pro-cesses to create a unique solution for each customer along the lines of what Amazon and Netflix have done? To their credit, the ambitious airlines have begun to focus on areas where there are opportunities for personalization and dynamic merchandizing. Areas under consideration include:

- the sale of ancillary products and services within the various inventory buckets, including opportunities to up-sell and cross-sell on a dynamic basis;
- granular customer demand segmentation based, at least, on customer personas rather than traditional segmentations based on purpose of trip;
- demand for these personas based on specific purchasing behavior that, in turn, is based on numerous parameters, and in as close to real time as possible, rather than just price, network and schedules;
- use of consumer decision choice models rather than forecasts of market share based only on price and schedule (number of stops, total elapsed time), but including factors such as affinity to the brand and fare rules;

- deployment of rule-based analytics to transactional data (that is, if this, then do this);
- event-driven market and competitor conditions and dynamics;
- customer loyalty based on customer centricity and customer experience, as well as customer relationships;
- current and predicted lifetime value of customers; and
- implementation of key revenue performance metrics, based, for example, on (a) wallet share within a given bucket and not just seats sold, (b) customer acquisition and retention costs for various buckets, and (c) the costs to and benefits for other divisions within an airline.

The technical capability is now available to optimize revenue on a dynamic basis and at an enterprise level rather than on a static basis and within individual functions. What is needed is a change in corporate culture to acquire and retain the skilled staff and develop strategic partnerships with technology businesses to help implement the relevant systems and the enabling processes to analyze, optimize, execute, evaluate, and provide feedback.

Takeaways

Airline leaders are clearly looking for ways to grow in the increasingly changed marketplace while working within the constraints of the airline industry, remain agile and flexible, and take on complexity that is manageable. While these management attributes are not new, what is new is the consideration given to the need for long-term vision and the concept of "design" that now applies not only to products but also to the planning framework itself, including "designing" innovation and even strategies.

The key to "designing" innovation is to integrate the physical hub-and-spoke system with the digital hub-and-spoke system.

All resources are now available to operate a "connected airline," but it is the change in processes, systems, and culture to "connect the airline" that will lead to an acceleration in the decision-making process to optimize not only costs and revenues, but also customer value and customer satisfaction of all passengers, not just the premium-fare and high-loyalty program status passengers.

It is the total integration within commercial planning, within operations planning, and between the two that will transform an airline's business strategy into brand strategy and, in turn, lead to a customer strategy.

There are five fundamental building blocks for designing and implementing dynamic merchandizing strategies: establishment of a centralized and comprehensive database on customers; deployment of a broad spectrum of commercial analytics; development of personalized and situation-based trigger rules; capability to create and make dynamic and personalized retailing offers throughout the journey; and the implementation of an integrative technology system that sets into motion a sequence of events and offers by extracting information from one or more of the four databases and enables the relevant staff to take specific action.

Notes

1 Bachman, Justin, "How many airlines does Delta really run?" *BloombergBusiness*, December 22, 2015.
2 The equity stake in Aer Lingus could be renegotiated now that Aer Lingus has been acquired by IAG.

8 POTENTIAL DISRUPTIVE INNOVATORS AND SCENARIOS

The viewpoint presented in this book is that disruptive innovation in the airline industry will continue to happen, maybe more slowly in some parts of the world than in other industries due to institutional constraints – regulatory policies, constrained infrastructure, and control by traditional airlines of hard assets, not to mention culture. Disruptive innovation is likely to come both from within the airline industry and from outside of it. From within the industry, in some ways, it has already been started by the aggressive, less constrained, and well-financed Persian Gulf-based Super Connectors (in particular, Emirates). From the low-cost carrier (LCC) sector it has originated with carriers such as Ryanair, AirAsia, Azul (and lower-cost carriers such as easyJet) who are innovative, aggressive, and fast-moving. From outside the airline industry, information-rich technology organizations as well as unencumbered entrepreneurs see personalization, customer experience, and retailing as ripe areas for disruptive innovation through initiatives that provide travelers with exactly what they want, when they want it, and how they want it throughout the entire trip. Some of these potential disrupters may challenge the conventional wisdom of the airline industry and believe that the environment has changed sufficiently to transform dramatically the way the industry operates, despite the limited success of some initiatives that had been tried in the past.

Experience with Disruptive Initiatives

Some commentators (within the airline industry, related businesses, and outside the airline industry) have always questioned the airline industry's conventional beliefs about how and where value is created and the associated notions that support such beliefs. Following are some examples of beliefs and the associated notions:

- The airline business is a commodity business, incredibly complex, and a low-margin business and, as such, will not be of interest to outsiders.
- Integrators will not be able to offer airline tickets as their "ancillaries" as they will find the management of seat inventory purchased from airlines to be difficult and complex.

- Business travelers focus mostly on the network, frequency, and schedules.
- For the most part, schedules must be created a year in advance with relatively minor changes throughout the year.
- Leisure travelers focus mostly on price and will switch airlines for a difference of a few dollars. Therefore, cheaper fares are everything.
- All frequent travelers are profitable and provide the most useful feedback.
- The most important components of revenue management are the mix of fare buckets and the inventory in each bucket.
- Low-cost airlines will find it extremely difficult to succeed in producing and marketing low-cost and -fare services in long-haul intercontinental markets.
- Serving single segments (all business class seats across the Atlantic, for example) is not a viable proposition.
- Airlines should stick to their areas of expertise, namely flying airplanes between airports, and not get involved with operating other businesses such as hotels and car rentals.

Based on such conventional beliefs, a number of initiatives have been taken to create and market new value propositions. Some initiatives failed, some are struggling, and some have achieved significant success.

- In the mid-1980s, the leadership at United Airlines set up the Allegis organization (airline–hotel–car rental conglomerate) with two brand-named divisions of United – Hertz and Westin Hotels. The failure of the integrated travel company was blamed on the insufficient time given by the internal stakeholders and the financial marketplace to exploit the synergies.
- Four lower-cost carriers did start to offer all business class services across the Atlantic and all four failed – Eos Airlines, L'Avion, Maxjet, and Silverjet. Reasons given included the change in the price of fuel, the state of the economies, the lack of scale and scope, and the deployment of uneconomic aircraft for the missions.
- Skybus Airlines tried to be a disrupter by setting up a base in the US Midwest and offering a limited number of promotional $10 fares and branded aircraft (selling advertising space inside and outside of the aircraft) with service to mostly secondary markets, and was the first airline to charge for the transportation of baggage. The slogan was "Only birds fly cheaper." Again, the reasons for failure, after less than a year of operation, included the soaring price of fuel and the state of the economy.
- POGO Jet Air Taxi was an attempt to sell the entire aircraft (about six seats) for the day instead of selling individual seats to business people traveling between small community airports in the USA. The strategy

was to promote the idea that the price would be similar to full-fare tickets purchased on the same day. The plan was to use the Eclipse 500 or the Embraer Phenom, or the Adam 700 small aircraft. The plan did not materialize as both of the organizations behind the Eclipse 500 and behind the Adam 700 filed for bankruptcy.

- Skymark, a lower-cost airline based in Japan, ordered the Airbus 380 and announced its plans to fly between Tokyo Narita Airport and Frankfurt, London, New York, and Paris with 394 seats (114 in business and 280 in premium class). These plans did not materialize and the airline experienced significant financial stress.
- Surf Air is a California-based airline in the USA that offers to members only a flat-fee all-you-can-fly service. For about $1,700 each month a passenger can fly as much as he or she wants between select cities north and south in the California coastline. The company set up the service in 2013 using eight-seat turboprop aircraft.
- AirAsia X, the low-cost, long-haul carrier based in Malaysia, offered a two-class service to London and Paris using the Airbus 340, but canceled these services in 2012 due to the high fuel costs of the aircraft and, presumably, the lack of sufficient connecting traffic.
- Jetstar, a subsidiary of Qantas based in Australia, was started as a dual-brand strategy of Qantas and has proven to be extremely successful in Asia using Boeing 787s.
- The TUI Group, the largest leisure travel and tourism business (encompassing travel agencies, airlines, hotels/resorts, cruise ships, and tour operators), is committed to delivering an end-to-end experience across a traveler's entire journey. Thompson Airways alone, one of the six airlines in the TUI Group, has about 60 aircraft. TUI has articulated a clear vision for how it plans to serve its customers – from trip ideation to engagement after the trip to follow-ups. This vision is supported by investments in digital and physical capabilities, as well as the development of the brand, to deliver personalized services on a consistent basis.
- Since the early 1980s American Airlines has tried to offer the flat-fee unlimited flying concept, starting with its AAirpass for a one-time $250,000 price for unlimited travel in first class. American has experimented with a number of price–service options, including an option for a lower amount for travelers who spend at least $10,000 per year on its flights. The passenger gets a fixed rate that is high but still better than buying seats closer to the flight. On the other hand, the airline gets a reasonable amount of money and the more the customer flies the more revenue the airline generates.

Despite a disproportionately large number of failures of new ideas, an increasing number of "rule breakers" from both inside and outside the airline industry has been working diligently to challenge their conventionally minded competitors and introduce new ways to create, measure, and market value.

One could divide these "rule breakers" into four categories: (1) Re-Inventors; (2) Super-Regionals; (3) Disruptive Leaders; and (4) Global Enterprises.

Airlines in the first two groups, Re-Inventors and Super-Regionals, have become large in scale and have made bold, disruptive moves that threaten and/or preempt the business of their potential competitors. Qantas, British Airways, Air New Zealand, and Delta would be examples of Re-Inventors for some reasons discussed in Chapters 4 and 7. Emirates, discussed in this chapter, would be an example of a Super-Regional. To paraphrase Lou Gerstner, the former Chairman of the Board of IBM, most elephants cannot dance, but some can. There have been more failures than successes when large legacy businesses tried to re-invent themselves. However, there have been exceptions – Qantas and Air New Zealand. Another insight from outside the industry is that transformation and innovation initiatives may be just as important from the viewpoint of success as they are from the viewpoint of failure. The new insight of "fail fast" is more about fast cycling, constant experimentation, organizational learning, and cultural change than it is about achieving operational perfection in every initiative.

The third group, Disruptive Leaders, represents upstarts with leaders from the outside – Herb Kelleher, Sir Richard Branson, Michael O'Leary, Sir Stelios Haji-Ioannou, and Tony Fernandes, for example. Would there be Virgin Atlantic, or AirAsia, or easyJet without Sir Richard Branson, Tony Fernandes, and Sir Stelios Haji-Ioannou, respectively? Leaving aside visionary leadership and laser-focused leadership, these upstarts demonstrate that, contrary to conventional wisdom, it is not impossible to enter into the airline industry with different ideas. Although the industry is capital intensive, capital is available worldwide if a business case can be made as assets are "commodities" and can be traded and moved around the world.

The fourth group, Global Enterprises, represents businesses that dominate large sectors of the new economy, leveraging leading-edge transformational technologies. These businesses have invested enormous resources in R&D and experimentation in the marketplace. And since travel is a large sector, with airlines alone generating over $700 billion in revenue, and since airlines do depend heavily on technology, there is an incentive for these large enterprises to explore opportunities in this industry. Examples of these Global Enterprises include Google, Amazon, and Facebook, as well as some large online travel agents (OTAs). As discussed earlier, they have already had significant impact on the airline industry by shaping consumer behavior and expectations by providing best practices in search, online retailing and merchandizing, as well as sharing information. If Google can develop the self-driving car that has the potential to shake up the auto industry, then can it do something similar in the area of distribution within the airline industry, as discussed in Chapter 4?

The key enabling tools that all four groups of innovators now see are: (1) the technologies to explore the digitalization aspects of the airline business; (2) their unconventional thought process to strike a balance between efficiency and costs, as well as an increasing interest of travelers in customer satisfaction and customer experience with the brands; and (3) the pursuit of market-expanding models into new profit zones within an expanding global universe of travel. This chapter begins with a discussion on the key area of concern to customers (varying levels of stress relating to air travel) followed by some examples of potential disrupters from within the airline industry, and the potential role of outside businesses with expertise in the use of new technologies and customer relationship management.

Stress Relating to Air Travel

Recently, entrepreneurs (from inside and outside of the industry) have been focusing on the high level of stress that air travel has caused passengers, partly by the airlines' increasing focus on costs and the increasing complexity of services offered. Airlines started to become laser-focused on costs after the industry became deregulated and even more after the emergence of lower-cost airlines that were not saddled with legacy cost structures resulting from legacy systems, processes, and labor contracts. The focus on costs continued when the newer generation of full-service airlines, such as those based in the Persian Gulf, began to expand their operations. These airlines had no burdens of legacy systems, processes, and labor contracts and they had the benefits of excellent geographic location, abundant airport and terminal space, as well as the financial strength to acquire cost-efficient aircraft with ideal payload performance. The pressure on traditional airlines to reduce their costs had significant impact on customer service and experience and the reluctance on the part of traditional airlines to make sufficient investments simply added to the customer experience challenge. As mentioned earlier, airlines have improved various aspects of customer experience. However, the bar has been raised high both within and outside of the airline industry.

Major areas of customers' concern start with shopping (searching and making bookings) and then continue to the airport experience, in-flight experience, and the reliability of operations, especially the experience during irregular operations. As for shopping, many shoppers for air travel find that airlines' websites, while improving, do not provide good information, are not user friendly, and may not provide security for the information given. With respect to information, concerns relate to the quality of the information, its usefulness and detail (seat features, ease of airport connections, taxi services, currency exchange rates, weather, and so forth), and the presentation of information (text vs. pictures vs. videos, for example). With respect to ease of use, problems can start with the lack of recognition that different users have different comfort levels with the use of technology. Second, the layout does not make it easy to navigate – functionalities relating to searching and finding content (on the airline product and related products), and making reservations and payments. Third, most shoppers now would like to have transportability so that a user can switch from one device to another device within a session.

The second stress-contributing factor relates to the airport experience, both in terms of normal operations as well as during irregular operations. In the case of normal operations, consider the hassles involving check-in, passing through security clearance lines, boarding, navigating, making connections at major hubs, and the process for requesting upgrades by both the frequent and the infrequent travelers. The problem with security clearance is not only the time it takes, but the uncertainty about the time it could take. The problem with making connections is related to airlines making their connecting banks tighter and adding more flights to the connecting banks to improve financial perform-ance. During irregular operations the stress arises from the lack of timely information and the re-accommodation processes. Then during the flight itself, there is stress concerning space and insufficient personalization. Customers, both frequent and infrequent travelers, are also stressed about the loyalty pro-grams. The only travelers that seem to accept the programs are the point-game players who are trying to "beat the system" and maximize the points gathered. Stress relates both to the unattractiveness of the redemption systems as well as the supplemental charges required for redemption. Take, for example, a married couple where one passenger is short on the points needed to qualify for a trip and wants to transfer some miles from the account of the partner. There is a significant charge for the transfer of the points. Finally, there is stress relating to traveling on the flights of alliance partners. An airline joins an alli-ance primarily to widen the scope of sales by offering a much wider network to its customers and providing a greater choice of destinations with, presum-ably, a seamless itinerary. However, according to some passengers, seamlessness is in theory only. Airline products are different (for example, seats) as well as practices (for example, upgrades). And, switching travel plans to an alliance partner, whether in the case of irregularities or because plans have changed, is a cumbersome process.

There are about three dozen touchpoints encompassing the air travel process that starts with inspiration for a trip and ends with sharing memories in the case of personal travel and recalling the outcomes in the case of busi-ness travel. At these touchpoints, airlines have an opportunity not only to eliminate relevant painpoints, but also to make customer-friendly offers. At the moment, the strategies appear to be to generate ancillary revenues through cross-selling, up-selling, and seat add-ons. Airlines justify this focus on ancillaries on the grounds that in the past 20 years the average fare itself has declined about 15 percent in real terms.

It is ironic that one area where airlines did not invest sufficiently is techno-logy, and yet investments in this area would have improved customer experi-ence and lowered operating costs. And poor customer experience, in turn, led to lower brand loyalty as cost pressures further commoditized the products and services offered. It is also interesting to note the results of a survey of customers and airline executives reported in a major study conducted by the Economist Business Intelligence Unit and Sabre. Whereas customers ranked their experi-ence as the top factor of importance, airline executives listed it as number three, with number one being the need to reduce costs, number two being the need to build loyalty.[1] However, now that airlines (at least in the USA) are beginning to make money, they have begun to pay more attention to the experience by making investments in two areas. First, technology is being used to collect, analyze, and share much more information within the organization to provide much more personalized services. Second, airlines are looking at other business sectors to gain insights on best global business practices – online retailers such as Amazon for shopping and hotels for customized products.

Part of the reluctance in investments in technology came from the concern that some technologies were new and untested – for example, access to Wi-Fi onboard that can be used on a broad spectrum of mobile devices. It is interesting that this technology would not only enable customers to personalize their services but also enable airlines to collect valuable information on how passengers communicate. In terms of personalization, some passengers might use the Wi-Fi for entertainment purposes, while others might use it to improve their work productivity relating to office work. Availability of onboard Wi-Fi can also reduce costs (let passengers use their own devices for entertainment purposes) and enhance revenue-generation opportunities through merchandizing – directly by airlines as well as in partnership with third parties. Cost savings come from not only the lack of need to wire the aircraft, especially the older versions, for entertainment but also through fuel savings due to the lower weight of the aircraft. Providing tablets to passengers is one benefit (cheaper than rewiring the aircraft) but making them available to crews is another benefit. Crews can provide much more customized services, starting with recognition of who is onboard and what their likes and dislikes are. And then there are the advantages for operations when crews, mechanics, and other ground service providers can communicate using voice, data, and video in real time using the plane's built-in communication platform. In his Thought Leadership Piece in Chapter 10, Leo Mondale, President of Aviation at Inmarsat, provides good insights on the emerging role of onboard technology.

The third area where insufficient investments were made relates to the understanding and deployment of social media. Social media can be critical in two-way communications – answering customers' questions and resolving customers' problems as well as making relevant offers, for example. The fourth area of stress relates to distribution. Airlines appear to be focusing on knowing what people buy at what touchpoint and what bundles to create to maximize ancillary revenue rather than eliminating painpoints. Some have tried to create bundles that reduce the level of painpoints – early boarding, lounge access. However, one painpoint now is that people want to shop around and compare products and prices through all channels. Should they shop through third parties who might be able to help in the decisions relating to product differentiation? Hopefully, the implementation of IATA's New Distribution Capability (NDC) will help reduce the stress relating to transparency. It will enable greater transparency as well as the capability to differentiate products, especially when airlines decide to offer comparison shopping.

While the above discussion relates to stress areas and painpoints, as reported in the media in North America and Europe, in some developing and emerging markets the concerns may relate simply to the lack of access to convenient, affordable, and accessible air travel. On a global basis there is more potential for incremental revenue and profit in targeting underserved, or not-yet-served markets across most of Africa, parts of Asia, and parts of Latin America than there is in the developed regions of the world. The Super Connectors are serving the long-haul markets and connecting with and stimulating the underserved markets. There is, however, more value in addressing the underserved markets with new, best-practice models than fixing embedded pain in the developed regions of the world. Certainly there will be setbacks and failures, over-expansion, skill shortages, and so forth, but there will also be stabilization, profit, consolidation, and new best practices well attuned to these expanding markets for first-time air travelers and growing discretionary middle classes and business travel.

Potential Disrupters

Global Customer-Centric Airlines with New Value Propositions

In 30 years Emirates Airline has already become a true powerhouse – having developed a global network around the hub in Dubai and a globally recognized brand. Figure 8.1 shows the current network that extends from Australia in the Asia-Pacific region to the Middle East, Africa, Latin America, and the West Coast of the USA. In addition to the breadth of Emirates' operations it is also important to note the depth of the airline's operations. Figure 8.2 shows the distribution of the percentage of routes served by the level of frequency. Only a couple of percentage points of the routes are served by less

Figure 8.1 Emirates Airline's Global Network (source: OAG Schedule Analyser and Mapper).

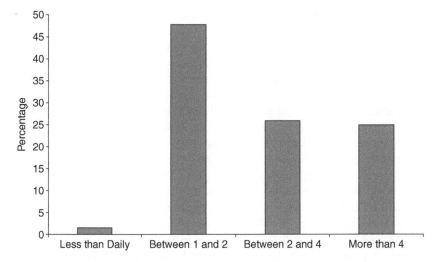

Figure 8.2 Emirates Airline's Percentage of Routes Served by Frequency (source: OAG Schedule Analyser).

than a daily flight. Both the number of destinations and the frequency will increase as the airline takes delivery of the airplanes on order, as the airline is able to get clearance on the capacity restrictions implemented by governments relating to bilateral agreements, and as more capacity becomes available at its operating hub in Dubai. The airport in Dubai is already handling more seats than London's Heathrow Airport (Figure 8.3).

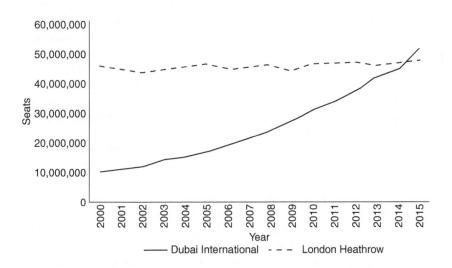

Figure 8.3 Growth of Total Seats Offered: London's Heathrow vs. Dubai's International Airport (source: OAG Schedule Analyser).

Emirates already offers non-stop service on a number of ultra long-haul routes and plans to add more routes such as the non-stop service between Dubai and Panama City, with flights taking between 17 and 18 hours to cover a distance of about 8,600 miles. The modern airplane is capable of flying even further to provide non-stop service by Emirates between Dubai and Mexico City and between Dubai and Auckland, New Zealand, a distance of more than 8,800 miles. Ultra long-haul flights began in 2004 by Singapore Airlines (Singapore–New York) followed in 2005 by Thai Airways (Bangkok–Los Angeles) and later by American Airlines (Chicago–Delhi). They were popular among business travelers, given the enablement of an increase in productivity. However, they began to be eliminated when fuel costs increased and demand decreased, relating to the downturns in the economies. Now, with even higher efficiency of new-generation aircraft, better management of passenger traffic (alliance partnerships and joint-ventures), and the lower price of fuel, airlines have started to re-introduce ultra long-haul flights with non-stop service – by Qantas between Dallas and Sydney and by Air India between Delhi and San Francisco, for example. Singapore Airlines has announced its plans for non-stop service again between Singapore and New York, taking about 19 hours and covering a distance of just over 9,500 miles.

From the technical side, a non-stop flight is possible even between Sydney and London and between Dubai and Mexico City. New generations of aircraft, besides being more fuel efficient, are also capable of providing cabin pressure that is the equivalent of 5000–6000 feet above the sea-level environment, compared to the conventional figure of 8,000 feet. The question relates, however, to the economic feasibility of such flights. While there are passengers willing to spend up to 20 hours and pay premium fares to gain productivity, this segment of passengers is relatively small. The leisure segment is not likely to pay premium fares, especially to travel in premium cabins, given the basic comfort needed for such long-haul flights, not to mention the potential medical concerns, such as deep vein thrombosis. The cost side could become a challenge again if the price of fuel increases or if the requirements change with respect to the number of crew members, crew rest periods, and crew rotations. If there is an airline that is likely to succeed with the use of ultra long-haul flights it is Emirates, simply due to the size of its fleet and its ability to mix and match to accommodate the needs of different marketplaces.

Relating to the size and the rate of expansion of Emirates' network is the airline's potential to disrupt the industry by achieving an incredible level of operational excellence. Obviously all airlines are at the mercy of the unpredictability of weather and capacity constraints of airports at which they operate. However, there are many decisions over which Emirates can exercise greater control given its resources – the number and location of spare aircraft and crews, for example, as well as scheduling practices. Management can allocate a disproportionately higher level of resources to spare aircraft and crews and it can use sophisticated mathematical algorithms to optimize the location of these standby resources based simply on its size and frequency of operations. Similarly, with scheduling practices the optimization criteria could be changed from maximization of resources such as aircraft and crew utilization to maximization of on-time performance and customer satisfaction with respect to on-time performance and the making of connections. The decision criteria take on a very different meaning once the focus turns to the development of a brand based on operational excellence and its impact on customer experience and satisfaction. Figure 7.4 showed the value of a connected airline, not just in terms of reducing costs, but much more in terms of enhancing customer experience and providing value-added services. And Emirates is in a position to go to such lengths.

Going back to the data presented in Figure 4.2, which showed that about 80 percent of the revenue can be accounted by the network of an airline, let us turn to the remaining 20 percent coming from revenue management with optimization viewed from a much broader perspective (see Figure 7.5) and the proactive management of customers (see Figure 7.6). Both areas require: (1) the effective management of vast quantities of data (structured and unstructured, transactional and behavioral); (2) changes in marketing philosophies, for example, the implementation of digital marketing; and (3) the availability of extremely sophisticated Passenger Services Systems (PSSs). While the implementation of digital marketing practices is within the control of the airline (item number 2), for the other two items an airline needs to develop deep partnerships with other organizations. Let us start with item number 1, making sense of data. Emirates has taken some unusual steps in this area.

In October 2015, Emirates announced an arrangement with Oxford University in the UK to establish a data science laboratory to develop ways to understand customer preferences on one side and the airline's processes on the other side with the purpose of designing and creating more customer-centric products, services, and operations. Emirates can provide the data and the university can provide the multi-disciplinary staff from such departments as Mathematics, Engineering Science, Computer Science, and Statistics, and use the internet to conduct behavioral analytics to analyze the customer behavioral aspects of the data. The airline hopes to transform its business initiatives from the customer's perspective, leveraging technology-based innovations. A month later, in November 2015, Emirates announced a similar arrangement with Carnegie Mellon University in the USA, to set up an Innovation Laboratory to help Emirates re-invent its business practices enabled by smart technology, big data, and real-time analytics. As with the groups at Oxford University, the groups at Carnegie Mellon University will also represent multi-disciplinary teams. The Emirates team will work with Carnegie Mellon's Integrated Innovation Institute that, in turn, is a joint enterprise between the university's College of Engineering, College of Fine Arts, and the School of Business.

It is true that airlines collect a lot of data on their customers and on their operations. The challenges and opportunities relate, however, to the analyses and use of that data compared to other business sectors that make much better use of information and analytics to gain insights into customer behavior from a contextual viewpoint and to provide customers and management with control of the use of information. For example, while progress in artificial intelligence had been slow for decades, it is now gaining speed and beginning to be embedded in commercial products such as Apple's iPhone (Siri) and in driver-assisted cars, as well as in car-to-car communications. Using software and sensors, artificial intelligence is not simply replacing drivers (at least not right away), but instead making drivers safer and making driving more fun. Think about what artificial intelligence can do when deployed to assist passengers during regular and irregular operations. There is no doubt that, from management's perspective, data science, analytics, and visualization techniques (dashboards, for example) will help Emirates understand and anticipate what targeted customers want and then enable Emirates to develop, market, and monitor personalized and dynamic offers.

Turning to the digitalization process, it is fairly clear that economies are becoming digital and that customers want improvements in experience through personal engagements at one end and the provision of basic transportation and transactions at the other end. To achieve this objective it would be helpful if a business was to digitalize itself at the enterprise level by leveraging digitalization to facilitate coordination and integration within its different functions. For an airline, it is through the cross-functional integration of its processes that passenger experience can be enhanced by getting closer to the availability of seamless travel, for example. And it is through cross-functional integration that an airline can create compelling value in products and services that customers want to buy. But creating compelling value means that management not only design products differently, but they also test, create, and manage products differently.

Within the enterprise, in the hyper-competitive environment, the forward-thinking airlines are looking into the deployment of digital marketing that is quite different from conventional marketing. The key questions in marketing relate to connecting with an airline's customers to know who they are, what their needs are, and how to fulfill those needs. Moreover, externally, while it is important to recognize that what a good product feature is to one customer is different from what it is to another customer, internally, it is also important to recognize that what a good product feature is to a scheduler is different from the one to a revenue manager, from the one to a loyalty manager, from the one to an airport check-in staff member. The problem internally is that in general functionally focused managers think differently in this area. The object is not only to identify the different needs of different customers, but also the different viewpoints of different managers within the airline organization. Besides connecting the internal and external perspectives on good product features, digital marketing can allow an airline to measure the results of different investments in different elements of the marketing mix, such as tracking and measuring the benefits of a campaign and the coordination among different functional managers internally.

Using digital marketing, Emirates can know much more about its customers than ever before – for example, through two-way communications. Is Emirates' new marketing campaign sending the right message to the right customer or is the message being wasted? Think about the infrequent travelers. It has been difficult for an airline to engage with passengers who travel very infrequently. A major airline may have 70 percent of its customers who are not in its frequent flyer program. The number could be higher for Emirates, especially for passengers based in emerging markets as such in India. And even within the 30 percent that are in the airline's loyalty program, there could be 50 percent who travel so infrequently that it is difficult to engage with them in any meaningful way, let alone have sufficient information to develop ample portrayals of them. They may be infrequent travelers on an airline, but they do engage quite frequently with other businesses such as Google and Amazon and they are very likely to be serious participants in social media networks. And it is the digitalization process that will help data-driven airlines such as Emirates to engage with these infrequent travelers and learn more about their travel needs and the product features they desire. The key to this very large segment, as Emirates undoubtedly knows, will be to work with other organizations to make its brand known more to potential passengers from emerging markets who, for now, travel very little.

Digital marketing will enable Emirates to have two-way communications with both frequent and infrequent travelers to "market test and iterate" marketing campaigns through feedback. Each functionally focused manager needs to step outside of his or her function and "walk in the shoes of ordinary people." How does it feel to:

- sit in the middle of a nine-abreast row in the middle of the 40 rows, with a 31 inch seat pitch, on a 14-hour non-stop flight?
- have to pay $150 reservation change fee on the return portion of a $300 return fare ticket?
- be told that there are no seats available for exchanging frequent flyer miles for three months unless the passenger is willing to exchange double, or even triple, the number of miles?
- be told the flight has been delayed for two hours due to the delay in the inbound flight and the needed crew rest time when a salesperson will miss a make-or-break meeting with a client at the destination airport?
- be told that the bag was placed on a wrong flight and would be arriving in 24 hours when the passenger knows that it contains the custom-tailored clothes for participation in a wedding?

Although the functionally focused managers do keep the needs of passengers at the back of their mind, to the degree possible, their main focus is on their own needs. The scheduler is focused on aircraft utilization, airport slots, crew constraints, maintenance-routing requirements, and gate availability.

The revenue manager is focused on the dilution of passenger yield, onboard load factor, passenger no-shows, overbooking, and the change in the mix of local vs. connecting passengers. It is two-way communications with a broad spectrum of travelers and a cross-functional integration of perspectives that will enable a global airline, such as Emirates, to be able to meet the divergent needs of its customers, from those looking for the cheapest fares with minimal service features to those looking for customized services with appropriate prices.

Consider briefly the advertising component of marketing. Digital (online) advertising can help analyze demographic characteristics of potential buyers in an area. Marketing does not need to keep the content fixed and can vary it. In fact, the content being browsed by different individuals can be tracked and analyzed, with responses customized. From this perspective, digital advertising can be a game-changer. Instead of general advertisements in the media, digital marketing can be targeted at a decreasing size of segments with effective two-way communications between an airline and its potential customers by analyzing the behavior of the person browsing the content. The technology and analytics are now available to reach an individual with the capability to align specific content to a specific individual and at a specific time. Moreover, in programmatic marketing, a promotion can, in fact, be automatically prompted based on a type of occurrence and an offer made available based on a set of defined rules. If a potential passenger has looked at the same flight three times in a row, then make an offer – "book in the next four hours and receive 25 percent additional miles in your loyalty program" or "book now and receive a 5 percent discount."

Consider a different aspect of marketing – fares. A carrier such as Emirates would not need to discount its fares in many markets to compete with the incumbents. It can know which individual would be attracted by its value proposition more than a discounted fare. These individual customers can be diverted from other sites as they are now "trackable and addressable," including information on their socio-economic traits and based on their social media patterns. A person in Hyderabad, India needing to leave Hyderabad at a particular time and be in Mountain View, California, USA, at a particular time may be divertible by Emirates from websites of competitors that are promoting their services in general.

Think about customers' desire for transparency in the marketing of airline products and services. In some ways fare comparison shopping has become more difficult, while in some ways it is becoming a little easier. The difficulty has arisen from the unbundling process of the airline product that provided a new source of revenue streams. In some ways transparency has been facilitated by the proliferation of intermediaries, initially, such as Priceline and Expedia, and later such as Kayak, Skiplagged, Mobissimo, Hipmunk, and Baidu. The increasing use of social media provides even more resources to get more transparency. As a result, airlines will need to develop greater product differentiation; for example, through the development of seamless service leading to the development of brand preference. Here is where the digitalization process can help improve the passenger experience from the start of the shopping process at the beginning to shopping on the day of departure, to shopping onboard the aircraft, and even after the trip. In addition, digitalization can also facilitate the coordination between airlines (alliance partners and feeder service providers) as well as between airlines, airports, and surface transportation providers, and, ultimately, through the coordination with government service providers in the areas of security.

So, what is the status of Emirates' shift toward the adaptation of digital strategies? In an article in *Airline Leader*, published by CAPA (Centre for Aviation), Michael Hanke is quoted to have developed a "Digital Airline Score" that measures an airline's adaption and use of e-commerce across seven attributes. In Hanke's analyses four fundamental attributes relate to an airline's brand: digital performance, digital presence, digital brand appearance and protection, and digital data privacy. The remaining three attributes are differentiators airlines are likely to apply in their e-commerce value chain and include: online advertising and promotion, e-sales and distribution, and web customer.[2] Figure 8.4 shows the results of Digital Airline Scores for a sample of 35 airlines of different sizes, operating with different business models, and based in different parts of the world plotted with the four fundamental attributes on the *x*-axis and the three differentiator attributes on the *y*-axis. It should be noted that in this sample Emirates already scored really high on the *y*-axis (combination of the three differentiator attributes) and relatively high on the combination of the four fundamental attributes. Based on the

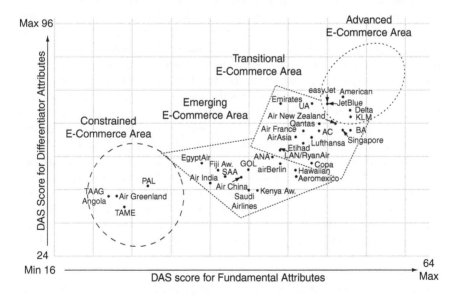

Figure 8.4 Digital Airline Scores (source: Michael Hanke, "Airline e-Commerce," *Airline Leader*, 30, October 2015).

extensive data that Emirates are collecting and the potential analyses to be conducted by the multi-disciplinary teams at the two universities through the arrangements previously discussed, Emirates should be at the leading edge with respect to the digitalization of the airline at the enterprise level.

While digital marketing is focused on being data-driven, Emirates' marketers are not likely to overlook the traditional fundamentals of marketing – message and creativity. Think about the story-telling aspect of marketing. Marketing communication needs to address the concerns of the passenger. The passenger residing in the southeast part of London does not say "I need to book a flight on airline XYZ for next Friday morning." She probably says, "Next Friday I need to be in Dubai for a meeting at 10 AM but I have a dinner meeting in Central London that evening and I am not going to have the car in the morning to drive to the airport as it is scheduled to be in the garage for service." The winner is the airline that can address the marketing communication in the lifestyle of the passenger in the form of "storytelling." This is not to imply that data- and analytics-driven marketing does not have a role to play, but rather that it has to supplement the traditionally successful aspects of marketing.

Think about how the large traditional consumer electronic brick-and-mortar retail chains in the USA (such as Best Buy) began to feel pressure from online retailers (such as Amazon) as traffic began to move from the physical stores to online retailers and some high-margin electronic goods started to become a commodity business. Just as brick-and-mortar stores recognized that they could not survive without heavy traffic through their stores (leveraging the space) airlines cannot survive without the high volume of passengers traveling in economy class to fill the planes. Just as the large brick-and-mortar stores began to transform their business models to become viable, so can legacy airlines. The key is in the revitalization of the organization's design for not just scale and scope, but also the agility to identify and respond to customers' changing needs. Best Buy, for example, implemented strategies to ship products directly to the locations preferred by the online buyers while matching competitive prices. Management also began to leverage the huge space in the stores by enabling companies such as Microsoft and Samsung to offer their own product line inside Best Buy stores.[3] It is reported that Walmart began to develop new strategies to meet consumer needs in a different way by enabling shoppers to store the contents of their DVDs in the cloud, with access to the DVDs on mobile devices.[4] The relationships that Emirates is developing with universities such as Oxford in the UK and Carnegie Mellon in the USA will help Emirates to balance its digital and conventional marketing initiatives to match the needs of the breadth of its customer base.

Finally, Emirates could be a leading airline, working with advanced technology partners to design, develop, and implement a truly state-of-the-art PSS. Traditionally, the centerpiece of a PSS is the departure control system for handling most of the processes prior to boarding. However, the advanced

PSS could contain features that enable a passenger to be able to control many functions herself and also to access numerous services provided by third parties – Uber car service, reservations and ticketing on surface modes, intermodal baggage transfers, and so forth. With the deployment of an advanced PSS, Emirates could make significant inroads into the door-to-door service for all travelers and not just for those traveling in premium cabins. This service could be provided without an increase in the complexity of making and processing door-to-door services on a broad spectrum of surface modes for transportation, not to mention the needs of passengers for accommodations, entertainment, and food and beverage activities. Moreover, an advanced PSS would also enable Emirates to evolve from a seller of seats to a sophisticated retailer. And, given Emirates' focus on the use of data, analytics, and digital marketing, the next step for Emirates could be to evolve from a seller of static products and services to dynamic products and services based on the needs (and willingness to pay) of individual customers worldwide and their real-time situations on a 24/7 and worldwide basis.

Ryanair Becoming the Amazon for Air Travel

Ryanair has the potential to become a disrupter by transforming its strategies in four areas. First, it appears to be determined "to become the Amazon for air travel." Second, it seems to be shifting its focus to catering to the needs of business travelers. Third, it could easily be the first airline to offer transparency in the comparison of fares. Fourth, it has been discussing openly the possibility of not if, but when, to start transatlantic operations. Ryanair has incredible strengths. It is the largest carrier in Europe (in terms of the number of seats flown) and has the lowest unit operating costs. It is a profitable airline and its management is totally focused and used to thinking unconventionally. For example, it was the first airline to negotiate openly with airports to receive incentives to start service at their bases. Let us start with the first point about becoming a smart retailer.

The airline industry as a whole has finally started to report large amounts of profits in the last few years. For the most part, it is the ancillary revenue that has been the main contributor to profits through the use of unbundled fares. The ancillary revenue can vary from less than $10 per passenger to over $60 per passenger within the industry, with the budget airlines being at the top end of the spectrum. As mentioned above, the experience with ancillary revenue is shifting airlines from sellers of seats to sophisticated retailers. It is in this area that Ryanair could easily become a disrupter by "becoming the Amazon for air travel." Ryanair appears to be committed to becoming a genuine retailer based on its announced decision to establish "Ryanair Labs," which can help Ryanair to leverage digital technology for online retailing. Ryanair will do whatever it takes to put the customer in control of what she wants to do. For example, it could easily develop really sophisticated apps for the mobile device, enabling a passenger to book not just air travel but any aspect of travel. Besides the ease of making the reservation, when coupled with the use of much more comprehensive data on customer behavior and preferences, it builds a stronger relationship between the customer and the airline.

For insights on best practices on online retailing, one can look at the experience provided by Amazon. Amazon is laser-focused on removing all obstacles to make shopping easier – emphasizing speed and convenience. One executive is quoted as saying that it should only be between 10–30 seconds between the thought of buying a product and buying it. Why is it necessary to type in the name of the product in the bar when looking at the website on a device, say a mobile phone? How about an app that shows the product when the device is pointed to an object? Amazon's "Flow" app for the smartphone makes shopping really easy. Just the convenience of the one-click payment capability demonstrates the power of the Amazon brand. The one-click payment can be made by any number of systems, such as with the use of traditional credit cards (Visa, MasterCard, and so forth) or, presumably, with the use of newer methods such as Paypal, Apple Pay, and Google Wallet. Some retailers are even gearing up for the usage of Bitcoin, a digital currency.

Next is the convenience of the fast home or office delivery (including same-day service) feature. Some shoppers went to brick-and-mortar stores to be able get the product the same day. Now online retailers such as Amazon and Google Express can provide the same delivery service for products that include groceries. Shoppers are clearly willing to pay for convenience, exemplified by the use of Amazon Prime and personal shoppers, who will make the purchase of the selected item and deliver it to the shopper's home or office. It is ironic that while online shoppers may be looking for lower prices they are willing to pay for convenience. Amazon Dash is a device that connects to a person's home Wi-Fi network on one side and her Amazon account on the other side. A shopper can speak a product's name into the device or use the device to scan a product sitting at home. Either way, it will be added to the shopper's cart. This device is targeted at people shopping for groceries. The object is to provide speed and convenience. AmazonFresh is an account with Amazon to buy groceries that can be ordered and delivered the same day or early morning the next day.

Second, Ryanair has begun to strategize to penetrate the corporate travel sector. For example, whereas LCCs, including Ryanair, went direct initially to reduce their operating costs (by saving on the distribution costs), they are now beginning to use the services of intermediaries such as GDSs to broaden the reach, including to the corporate sector. Ryanair is no exception. The intermediaries were at a disadvantage as they could not display the full content of the airlines' product. But with the initiation of IATA's NDC (enabling the display of the full content) intermediaries can help the LCCs penetrate the business sector. Ryanair recognizes that the business sector wants services in and out of conventional airports and with higher frequency, and as such has started to shift its strategies in this direction. For example, instead of flying just to and from Charleroi Airport in Belgium with low frequency, it has started flying also from Brussels International Airport and has started to increase its frequency. And, while Ryanair has been known to be less friendly in terms of its customer service, the strategy has shifted to become more customer-service oriented.

Third, Ryanair could easily be the first airline to provide transparency with respect to fares and succeed for two primary reasons. First, customers want this feature while they are browsing online. Second, since Ryanair has the lowest costs it will most likely have the lowest fares and, as such, have the benefit of showing its lower fares compared with the higher fares of competitors.

Fourth, Ryanair is probably in the best position to start and succeed in providing low-cost, low-fare service across the Atlantic. Ryanair has discussed this concept openly in the press, saying it would start such service as soon as the price of the smaller wide-body aircraft becomes viable. However, it is possible that Ryanair could revisit the aircraft decision given cost-effective capacity-performance characteristics of the new generation of narrow-body aircraft such as the Boeing 737 MAX8 and the Airbus 320neo. For example, the Boeing 737 MAX, with a maximum range of around 3,800 nautical miles and a capacity of around 150 seats, and the Airbus 320neo, with a maximum range of about 4,000 nautical miles and a capacity of around 160 seats, could make Ryanair a disrupter by bypassing conventional hubs on both sides of the Atlantic. Ryanair could start the service from Dublin, Ireland, an airport with US immigration and customs pre-clearance facilities, and land directly at smaller uncongested and lower operating cost airports in the USA. It is true that the lower level of O&D traffic between Dublin, Ireland and the small cities to be served in the USA would require Ryanair to change its scheduling practices to generate connecting traffic. Alternatively, it could start from bigger airports in Europe, such as London's Stansted or Cologne, Germany and land at conventional airports in the USA such as Baltimore Washington International Airport, where Southwest has a major hub. Could Ryanair disrupt the transatlantic market? Think about it. It has the size and scope with the breadth and depth of its operations in Europe. And although it does not have global services, its brand is recognized worldwide. Moreover, since social media is at the center of new events and their promotion, Ryanair has the potential to not only be present in social media but to leverage it to create a clear positioning of its brand and value propositions.

The almost ideal seat-cost vs. trip-cost characteristics of the new generation of narrow-body aircraft are making airlines rethink their decisions regarding the choice of aircraft for long-haul flights (Figures 8.5 and 8.6). According to the information shown in Figure 8.5, while the unit operating costs of a new-technology narrow-body aircraft may be slightly higher than a comparable technology wide-body aircraft, the smaller size of the aircraft reduces the financial risk, resulting in an acceptable risk–reward trade-off. Similarly, the information shown in Figure 8.6 provides a clear message that

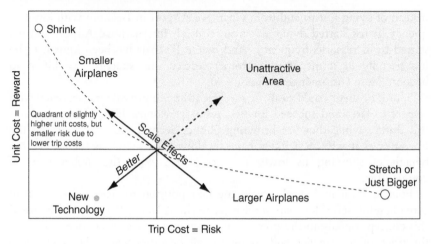

Figure 8.5 Aircraft Unit Cost vs. Trip Cost Relationship (source: Nico Buchholz, Lufthansa AG).

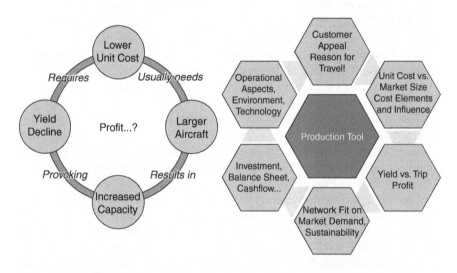

Figure 8.6 Aircraft Evaluation Decision Criteria (source: Nico Buchholz, Bombardier Inc.).

it may be possible to reduce unit operating costs by acquiring larger aircraft, but that could mean a dilution in yields that would put pressure on management to reduce costs. Smaller aircraft may also have greater passenger appeal if their operations result in non-stop flights in secondary markets resulting from a hub bypass strategy. And it may also be possible for an airline operating a smaller aircraft to offer greater frequency.

Evolving Network, Low-Cost/Hybrid Carriers

The third example of a potential disrupter is the AirAsia Group, founded by Tony Fernandes, to offer air travel to the masses in Asia and the ASEAN region – an airline offering a product with reasonable value and at affordable prices. Established in 2001, the AirAsia Group now serves almost 100 destinations with a fleet approaching 200, with operations in India, Indonesia, Malaysia, the Philippines, and Thailand. Table 8.1 lists the five brands that operate short- and medium-haul routes and a sixth brand, AirAsia X Group, that operates long-haul routes. The Philippines AirAsia brand also has one affiliate, AirAsia Zest. Figure 8.7 shows the network of the airlines within the AirAsia Group. Besides the six airline brands, the AirAsia Group also owns the Tune Group, QPR, and Caterham.

AirAsia has been leading the charge on innovative operations and innovative marketing. Given the restrictive rules on bilateral agreements and ownership and control, AirAsia found ways to work with local partnerships in different countries in the region and offer relatively consistent services under

Table 8.1 Airlines within the AirAsia Group

Thai AirAsia
Indonesia AirAsia
Philippines AirAsia (plus an affiliate AirAsia Zest)
AirAsia India
Malaysia AirAsia
Air Asia X (plus affiliates Malaysia AirAsia X, Indonesia AirAsia X, and Thai AirAsia X)

Figure 8.7 Networks of Carriers within the AirAsia Group (source: OAG Schedule Analyser and Mapper).

a common brand. As for marketing, it was one of the first airlines to promote the idea of setting up low-cost hotels in the region where passengers could spend time during journeys that involved extra-long times between connections. The idea was to maximize aircraft and crew utilization. AirAsia was the first airline to recognize that the traditional ways of reaching customers and building the brand may not be effective in the emerging environment, and that the new ways were through the use of social networks and social media. AirAsia was also one of the first airlines to establish new ways of accepting money from customers based in developing and emerging markets – for example, through local retail establishments.

AirAsia, having developed a recognizable brand within Asia to serve short- and medium-haul markets, then went on to develop a low-cost brand to serve long-haul markets through its subsidiary, AirAsia X. AirAsia X has been taking on a number of key features of full-service carriers, such as a premium cabin and, much more critical, the passenger transfer capability at its Kuala Lumpur Airport hub for its connecting passengers. It is the existence of these two features (some full-service attributes of the product and connectivity) that support the concept portrayed in Figure 8.8 of the evolving nature of the air transport industry in the Asia-Pacific region – the emergence of network, low-cost/hybrid carriers. AirAsia X already has much lower costs than the full-service carriers for comparable stage lengths, and the costs would go down even further with the introduction of more advanced airplanes such as the Airbus 350s and the Airbus 330–900neos. Table 8.2 shows the current long-haul fleet and the aircraft on order of the LCCs around the world.

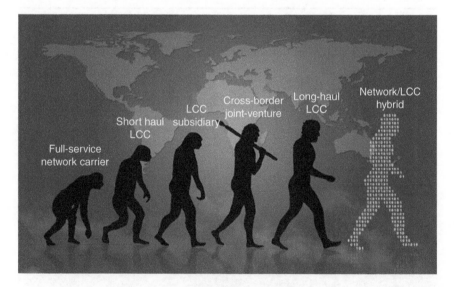

Figure 8.8 Evolution of the Air Transport Industry in the Asia-Pacific Region (source: CAPA, "Asia's Full service airlines could become endangered unless they adopt new strategies for sustainability," *Airline Leader*, 25, November 2014).

Table 8.2 Low-Cost Carriers: Wide-Body Aircraft in Service and on Order

	Region	Aircraft	In Service	On Order	Seats			
					Premium	Economy	Total
AirAsia X	Asia	A330-300	20	11	12	365	377
		A330-900neo		55			TBA
		A350-900		10			425
Azul	Latin America	A330-200	7	1	24	249	279
		A350-900		5			TBA
Cebu Pacific	Asia-Pacific	A330-300	8		0	440	440
Jetstar	Asia-Pacific	B787-8	11		21	314	335
Jin Air	Asia-Pacific	B777-200ER	3		40	353	393
Norwegian	Europe	B787-8	8		32	259	291
		B787-9		30	53	291	344
Scoot	Asia-Pacific	B777-200ER	2		32	370	402
		B787-8	3	7	21	314	335
		B787-9	6	4	35	340	375
Eurowings	Europe	A330-200	4			310	310
		B767-300ER	1			267	267
WestJet	North America	B767-300ERW		4		262	262

Source: Computed from information available from airlines' websites and the internet.

The desire to become a hybrid airline is also based on the movement to capture more of the corporate business. Businesses are looking into the use of the services provided by LCCs for, at least, the following five reasons. First, businesses want to reduce their travel costs, not to mention use the availability of the low-cost options to negotiate better deals from the full-service network carriers. There are many sub-segments within the corporate segment. The hybrid carriers are looking into who is the customer, the corporate travel department (with an interest in reduced travel costs) or the ultimate traveler (interested in convenient travel). The ultimate traveler is interested in having some control over the travel plan – for example, being able to make changes. And the "open booking" system can enable a corporate traveler to make her booking outside of the travel management company and still comply with the travel policies of the business. Second, low-cost airlines are beginning to provide features that corporate travelers want, such as broader networks, use of conventional airports, premium seats, flexible fares, bundled fares, bookings through distributors such as GDSs, and fast-track security. Third, at the same time, legacy full-service airlines have begun to adopt features of low-cost carriers. Fourth, a number of legacy full-service airlines have set up low-cost subsidiaries (in Europe and in Asia). Some of these carriers are listed in Table 8.2. Fifth, while LCCs face the challenge of not having attractive loyalty programs, the forward-thinking network low-cost/hybrid carriers shown in Figure 8.8 can develop really effective customer relationship management systems to personalize the trip for the more frequent customers. On the last point, some analysts have argued that loyalty programs in the airline industry have been "purchased" as opposed to "earned" from the delivery of better customer experience.

During the current transition period, the AirAsia Group is slowing down its expansion. At the end of 2015 the combined fleet of the AirAsia Group included 196 aircraft (172 Airbus 320s and 24 Airbus 330s). In 2018 it is reported it will have 208 aircraft (177 Airbus 320s and 31 Airbus 330s).[5] However, given the expected growth in the Asia-Pacific region, the potential opportunities for the emerging hybrid carriers, and the non-conventional thought process of the AirAsia management, it is clearly set on a path to be a disruptive innovator.

From a slightly different perspective, Azul could also become a disrupter as a network low-cost/hybrid carrier. In just seven years, from its start in December 2008, Azul has developed an enormous network in Brazil using three types of aircraft, started operations in intercontinental markets with wide-body aircraft, developed code-share arrangements with carriers in the USA, and acquired an interest in the Lisbon-based TAP Portugal, with an extensive network to and from Brazil, within Europe, and to and from Africa. Figure 8.9 shows the breadth of the combined networks of Azul and TAP Portugal. The image would become even more impressive if one were to add the selective portions of the network of jetBlue where Azul could make connections, such as in Fort Lauderdale now and New York-JFK later. Azul has

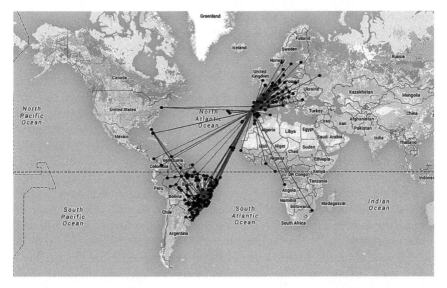

Figure 8.9 Combined Networks of Azul and TAP Portugal (source: OAG Schedule
Analyser and Mapper).

already proven that it can manage complexity by operating three kinds of aircraft (Embraer regional jets, ATR turboprops, and Airbus 330s) and having
acquired and integrated another LCC (TRIP). Given the equity stake that the
Hainan Airlines Group has taken in Azul, China's long-term interest in
linking up with Brazil, and the unconventional thought leadership of Azul's
management, it is fairly clear that Azul has the potential to be a disruptive
innovator. Keep in mind that it was Azul that introduced airline services in
Brazil that competed with fares offered by buses.

Partnerships with Outside Businesses

The outside disrupters are unlikely to start airline operations given, historically, the lack of profitability and the complexity of airline operations. Why?
Let us look at an insight from outside of the airline industry. In the hotel
industry, perhaps the single largest transformational change was the shift
to the "asset-light" model. This was started when Marriott, at the strong
suggestion of some Wall Street analysts, spun-off most of its real-estate
assets from its corporate balance sheet and put the assets into separately
traded entities that are essentially real estate investment trusts (REITs).
Now, all of the large global brands have taken this approach, and they only
have strategic assets on their balance sheets (hotels that are owned and operated). The benefit of this strategy has been to enable management to focus
totally on its brand and its customers (both guests and franchisees). In light
of this powerful insight one could assume, in today's world, that the

information-rich companies are not likely to start airline operations. In fact, one could ask if it would make sense for an airline to own any airplanes. It's another way of asking if a future disruptive innovation could arise from the financial structure side.

In light of the above point, the information-rich companies are much more likely to do business around airline operations, leaving the airlines to actually fly the airplanes at thin margins. The question that can then be asked is not if non-airline businesses will enter the travel business, but which aspect of the travel business they will attempt to enter, and why. Besides the monetary rewards of their entry, they would undoubtedly explore their risk of entry – the risk that airlines themselves would leverage technology and information, for example. However, airlines also know that they would require huge resources to match the pace of change and the very fast cycle of innovation to keep up with: (1) the fast-changing customer expectations and motivations, especially those relating to online customer experiences; and (2) the investments made by the information-rich companies that are not burdened, like airlines, with the challenges of maintaining and replacing their legacy systems. Consequently, the risk–reward evaluations on the part of both the airlines and the information-rich companies could lead to new forms of competition and/or cooperation in areas such as distribution, retailing, and end-to-end travel.

From outside of the airline industry, organizations with huge amounts of rich information, scale, and powerful predictive analytics could emerge to disrupt the non-core business of the airline industry. Examples could include the "marketing machines" of Google, Amazon, Facebook, Apple, Concur (now part of SAP), and travel-related businesses such as Expedia and Priceline. They recognize that the global travel sector is very large and growing. If these or other organizations can leverage their business models, new points of integration, and the exponential change in technology that is converging, they could scale and monetize their comprehensive information on the needs of actual and potential customers (not just from frequent flyer programs, but also numerous external sources). They could provide high-impact "travel solutions" and "total travel care" to all travelers, not just those in the very top tier of the loyalty programs. Besides the likes of companies such as Google, Amazon, and Facebook, there are travel-related companies that are already making significant investments in technology and their brands to improve processes and systems that serve customers much more than improve operations.

- It is reported that Expedia invested almost three-quarters of a billion dollars in 2014 to develop many new technology products cutting across its extensive brand portfolio, with over a dozen travel-related brands – Expedia.com, Hotels.com, Hotwire, and Travelocity, to name only a few. The objective could be to focus on distribution (regardless of the travel mode) and conversion (percentage of those who buy to those who shop). Just one example of the development and marketing of a technology product is the Scratchpad system that allows users to save the information they have searched for and continue their search and shopping across multiple devices.

- The Priceline Group, an organization created to help users obtain discount rates for travel-related purchases, has also been investing hundreds of millions of dollars in technology to position itself as a potential disrupter. The idea, presumably as with Expedia, is to improve customer service across its product line – Booking.com, Priceline.com, Kayak.com, and so forth. Priceline appears to be starting with a focus on the integration of their independent hotel partners who do not have the technology or the ability to develop and manage competitive websites. What could be the potential role of a company such as Priceline if prices of airline tickets become personalized?

Then there are dynamic tour packagers (such as the TUI group) that could distribute a much broader spectrum of products and services. As mentioned above, the TUI Group is the largest leisure travel and tourism business (encompassing travel agencies, airlines, hotels/resorts, cruise ships, and tour operators), and is committed to delivering an end-to-end experience across a traveler's entire journey. And as mentioned, TUI has already articulated a clear vision for how it plans to serve its customers – from trip ideation to engagement after the trip to follow-ups. This vision is supported by investments in digital and physical capabilities, as well as the development of the brand, to deliver personalized services on a consistent basis. The TUI brand is clearly visible on the ground, onboard the aircraft, and in the properties.

Would some "marketing machine" companies with rich information and sophisticated analytical skills compete or partner with airlines? Based on the low margins of the flying part of the airline business and the associated complexity, and the benefits of an asset-light business, companies from outside of the airline industry are likely to get into some aspects of distribution where they could add value by integrating their services with those provided by airlines, to provide much more personalized products and services accompanied by much higher levels of customer experience. The disruptive innovation is likely to result from strategic partnerships.

Takeaways

Some potential disrupters from inside the airline industry could include Emirates, Ryanair, AirAsia, and Azul. Emirates could expand and market further its global network, take the digitalization process to new heights through the use of its extensive data and the arrangements with multi-disciplinary teams at two leading universities, and simplify the air travel business (door-to-door travel) through the development of a state-of-the-art PSS. Ryanair could become the Amazon of the airline industry, develop an innovative website that shows transparency, and provide cost-effective long-haul operations across the Atlantic with narrow-body aircraft. AirAsia could succeed in converting itself into a network, low-cost/hybrid carrier in the fast-growing market in Asia. Azul could develop into a hybrid carrier of a different sort – one that provides extensive services within Brazil and within its neighborhood and in intercontinental markets with its own fleet, as well as through partnerships with carriers in the USA (United and jetBlue) and Europe (TAP).

Outside of the airline industry, entrepreneurs have always questioned the airline industry's conventional beliefs and the associated notions that support such beliefs about how and where value is created, and new ways to design and create compelling value propositions. Recently, insiders and outsiders have been looking at stress caused at various touchpoints in the air travel journey – from shopping to operations and disruptions – and how to reduce, if not eliminate, stress. Consequently, the risk–reward evaluations on the parts of both the airlines and the information-rich companies could lead to new forms of competition and/or cooperation in areas such as distribution, retailing, and end-to-end travel. As such, airlines could develop strategic partnerships with outside businesses, with expertise in technologies and customer relationship management, to offer personalized services all the way from very basic travel such as on high-speed trains at one end to customized door-to-door travel in comfort and style at the other end.

Notes

1 Economist Intelligence Unit and Sabre, "Airline customer experience: special report," 2015, pp. 7–8.
2 Hanke, Michael, "Airline e-commerce," *Airline Leader*, 30, September–October 2015.
3 Tancer, Bill, *Everyone's a Critic: Winning Customers in a Review-Driven World* (New York: Portfolio/Penguin, 2014).
4 Lee, Thomas, *Rebuilding Empires: How Best Buy and Other Retailers Are Transforming and Competing in the Digital Age of Retailing* (New York: Palgrave Macmillan, 2014), p. 3.
5 CAPA (Centre for Aviation), "AirAsia 1H2015 results: the region's leading LCC regroups for the long run, reining in expansion," August 26, 2015.

9 CLOSING THOUGHTS

Innovating in the Air Travel Space

Although disruption is not a new concept, it has become the business word of the past couple of years within the media. A typical question being raised is: What can happen to us that we cannot see coming until it is too late to respond or compete? However, think about the length of time that businesses have been asking similar questions relating to threats from inside or outside of their sectors. Businesses that adapted survived; those that did not, failed. As for new entrants, it was through the disruptive innovation processes that some information-rich organizations or unconventionally thinking entrepreneurs rapidly expanded some market segments, including the airline sector. From outside the airline industry consider seriously Jeff Bezos and Amazon.com, Reed Hastings and Netflix, Guy Laliberté and Cirque du Soleil, Dietrich Mateschitz and Red Bull, Mark Zuckerberg and Facebook, Amancio Ortega and Zara, and Salman Khan and the Khan Academy. From within the airline industry, think about Herb Kelleher and Southwest Airlines, Michael O'Leary and Ryanair, Sir Stelios Haji-Ioannou and easyJet, Tony Fernandes and AirAsia, Bjørn Kjos and the Norwegian Air Shuttle, and David Neeleman and Azul.

Now, some business analysts are predicting that businesses in general are ripe for disruption at a faster and deeper rate due to a number of forces, some of which were discussed in Chapter 3. Some analysts believe that air travel may be more vulnerable to disruptive innovation, given the widespread lack of customer satisfaction expressed by airline travelers, the large revenue base of the sector (airline revenues exceeded $700 billion 2015), and the role of emerging technologies to impact both the supply side as well as the demand side. This book also claims that disruption will take place in the air travel space; the only thing that is uncertain is its timing, extent, and areas. However, the airline industry, as a whole, has become more adaptive (as discussed in Chapters 4, 7, and 8) to changing forces, despite the existence of a complex web of regulations and other externalities within which airlines operate. One can easily see the strategies that have already been implemented to manage the controllable parts – costs, capacity, and competence. Moreover, the industry, as a whole, is continuing to become increasingly adaptive due to the same factors that cause creative destruction and also enable opportunity – for example, various kinds of technologies and the growing global demand. The Thought Leadership Piece by Rob Broere in Chapter 10 provides numerous examples of the technology-related changes that have been implemented during the past six decades. The previous chapter provided some examples of potential disrupters that could emerge from within the airline industry and some from related businesses and/or from outside of the industry, especially companies rich with information and analytics to profit from the management of the relationship between airlines, other providers of travel-related services, and travelers themselves.

Here are five trends (and their implications) that some C-Suite executives are monitoring to see how they can be more proactive in the disruption space.

1 Customer-centric technologies have been accelerating the pace of change with respect to the acceptance and adoption of new products and services, particularly by the newer generations. They are growing up with and using technologies such as a broad spectrum of apps when shopping, booking, and managing their entire trips, and they are participating in social media to read and provide reviews, not to mention their desire to share information about their travel experience. Think about the following statistic. It has been reported that in August 2015, one billion people logged on to Facebook in a single day and about 84 percent were on their mobile devices.[1] Besides being heavy users of technology, these generations are, as reported by business analysts, seeing the current providers of travel services (airlines, car rental companies, and hotels) as commodity businesses.[2] The forward-thinking airlines are looking at the implications of this trend and the need to scale-up at a faster rate and also to re-define value on a continuously changing basis.

2 In developing and emerging markets technologies are creating "leap frog effects." There is no need to wait for landline telephone systems when inexpensive mobile phones are available in the market. There is no need for desktop or laptop computers when smartphones are available. And, there is no need for small financial transactions to be conducted through established institutions when mobile phones with simple embedded systems are available to conduct ordinary, everyday transactions. So, if the world is shifting to mobile at an incredible speed, the aggressive airlines based in developing and emerging markets, for example, see the implication of this trend to develop incredibly user-centric apps for a very wide range of travelers with different skills to leverage technology.

3 Customers compare the quality of services among different business sectors. If it is possible to shop on the Amazon.com website with a few clicks, why is it necessary to spend orders of magnitude more time on airline websites? How can ALDI reduce complexity much more

easily than an airline? The innovation-focused airlines see the implication of this trend to be that they must compare themselves with businesses in other sectors and not just among their peers within the airline industry.

4   The center of gravity in the airline industry is shifting to the east and to the south due to the much higher level of growth – actual and predicted – within the emerging markets relative to mature markets. Moreover, some airlines based in emerging markets are developing innovative strategies to work around the challenges of constraining regulatory regimes to grow and expand the market using upstream business models. The proactive airlines based in developed regions see the implication of this trend to be that they must think of globalization within the airline industry as more than simply an extension of their networks using their own ongoing business models or simply adding services within an alliance framework. They should be willing to review and gain insights from emerging markets. They are looking into how the low-cost carriers in Asia are evolving into network, low-cost/hybrid carriers and how Azul is managing complexity while working with multiple types of aircraft and a broad spectrum of hybrid carriers.

5   Leading airlines recognize that human skills within this industry are not keeping up with the enabling capabilities of technologies. Some business commentators describe this situation with the following scenario. Imagine technology as the engine in the car that is being designed to run faster and faster. But is the driver able to keep up with the capability of the engine in the car?[3] The potential disrupters are now accepting that one prerequisite to become an innovator, if not a disrupter, is to attract and maintain staff with expertise in emerging technologies (for example, cognitive) and create a culture and environment and establish, for example, innovation labs such as a "No Hassles Lab" to eliminate painpoints. They also understand that the need for talent is not restricted to the technical skills. The leadership at these airlines might appreciate the insight from the research performed by some business analysts, that people to be recognized and promoted should have "producer mindsets" as opposed to "performer mindsets." A person with a producer mindset aims to create immense value by re-defining what is possible through new products and services, new strategies, and new business models. A person with a performer mindset, on the other hand, simply strives to shine in well-defined areas.[4] It will be the people with the producer mindset, inside and outside of the airline industry, that will either create disruptive innovation or respond to it proactively.

Within the context of above points, potential innovators, if not disrupters, can emerge from inside the airline industry if the C-Suite:

- develops a clear vision by thinking not only "outside of the box" but from a "different box." The business does not need to be a commodity business. Think about the competitive advantages Singapore Airlines enjoyed for decades. The airline was obviously looking at customer service as an area for investment, not as an expense. As for complexity, it can be reduced dramatically and managed cost-effectively. Think about the achievements of Pacific Southwest Airlines in the US West Coast and Eastern Airlines' Shuttle operations in the US East Coast decades ago, operating when the available technology was extremely basic.
- develops a culture promoting change, innovation, and open discussion instead of a defensive, silo-oriented, deeply hierarchical working environment. Instead of operating on a fixed schedule developed months in advance, can an airline schedule its aircraft and crews much closer to the time of departure using a non-conventional mindset, a non-conventional cost model, groundbreaking technology, and some insights from businesses such as FedEx?
- thinks of evolving competitive differentiators – organizational agility, for example, the speed to change business operations and practices to adapt to the changing market dynamics. Organizational agility requires a very different organizational culture – one where cross-functional teams look at, in sequence, "What happened? Why did it happen? What will happen? How can we make it happen?"[5] Such a framework requires (a) the availability of large amounts of, as close to as possible, real-time data, and the ability and willingness to analyze the data on a fast track; (b) digitalization of the airline business at the enterprise level (including the possibility of appointing a Chief Digital Officer); and (c) the culture to continuously experiment and learn.
- develops a truly customer-obsessed mindset that analytically attacks today's painpoints of travelers at multiple touchpoints along the whole travel journey, instead of from airport to airport. Such a mindset calls for "design thinking" that applies to more than the product. "Design thinking" has also "become central to strategy, innovation, and organizational culture."[6] Think about Amazon's culture to stay laser-focused on the customer – the ease of browsing, shopping, making the payment, and receiving the products. Focus on customer experience must consider all segments of travelers – those who might prefer the convenience of a simple shuttle service to those who may wish to be pampered by recognition of their names and the specifics of their beverages.
- does not reject some ideas that are being discussed right now relating to "Bold Technology, Bold Mindset, and the Bold Crowd."[7] Take, for example, 3D printers, Google's self-driving car, and Elon Musk's Hyperloop. Their entry in the marketplace would have an enormous impact on the air cargo sector, the parking facilities at airports, and the demand for air travel in short-haul markets, respectively.

- works within the ecosystem, not only within the direct travel chain (airports, surface transportation modes, hotels, car rental companies, and so forth), but also with businesses that are operating on the periphery of the air travel sector (the information- and analysis-rich technology businesses, for example). The latter will enter with their own business models in the space between airlines and travelers. Leveraging information, they could simply be in the business of customer relationship management and have a significant impact on the distribution area. Or, they could become travel integrators and facilitators and treat airline seats as "their ancillary products." Does it make sense to try to compete with them or to partner with them through carefully "designed" strategies?

The airline industry is not only large but also global and diverse. As such, there is no single answer for how to prepare for disruption or become a disrupter. As discussed throughout this book, from the perspective of functional areas, some airlines are better than others at marketing, others excel in cost structure, and some are more advanced in managing revenue. This book has also provided some examples of innovative and best practices in various disciplines from a number of other industries. The Thought Leadership Piece in Chapter 10 by Rob Solomon provides an insightful summary of the "lessons learned and issues that linger." Based on a discussion with him, here are four important questions.

As to the business model, can the airline fulfill its mission on a sustainable basis? If the mission is to be the flag carrier for the country and the business model is state ownership and government intervention, it can be sustainable for a while, but not forever if the mandate is not to remain dependent on the government's finance department. Within this context, think about the business models and challenges faced by such airlines as Air India and South African Airways. In other cases, if the mission is to be the lowest-cost operator in the "region" and the definition of the "region" changes, the position may not be sustainable without significant changes to the business model. For a large legacy group, if the mission evolves from being the largest and most profitable international airline brand to maximize the enterprise profit from a global asset base, then the business model needs to shift accordingly to manage multiple brands.

As to the aspect of asset allocation, is the airline putting its resources into the most productive areas to balance geographic (new markets) and organic growth, new and traditional market segments, and with respect to short-, medium-, and long-term profitability? What is the mandate, quarterly performance in the stock market or market positioning for the long term? If the mission is to penetrate the business sector, does the airline have the right assets and are they allocated correctly in the strategic areas? At the time this book was being written (December 2015) for US carriers the outlook for the US domestic market was favorable relative to the outlook for foreign travel in light of the weak currencies, the slowdown of the economy in China, the overcapacity in Asia, the relatively weaker economies in Europe, and security concerns relating to the problems in the Middle East. Should Delta, discussed in Chapter 7, continue its expansion overseas and try to find a partner in Japan?

With respect to execution, within the context of the business model selected by an airline to support the mission, is there sustainable competitive advantage in the dimensions that really matter for the future health of the business? Single aircraft in the fleet might have been ideal for prior missions, but is it still appropriate when the mission has changed to fly outside of the historical region? Again, there is no one answer. Southwest and Ryanair think one way and Norwegian and Azul think differently.

Even more important is the question about the sustainable alignment among the key stakeholders, including ownership, customers and employees. How does the airline stay on course when the strategy on paper can change in 90 hours, customer acceptance can take 90 days, and organizational engagement 90 weeks?

This approach, encompassing four basic elements, may sound simplistic, but if one puts aside externalities or uncontrollable events, arguably enormous value has been either created or destroyed by mis-matches within and among these four factors. Let us re-visit some examples from earlier chapters. If the single largest enabler of disruption is technology, is the business model sufficiently supported by resources allocated to the areas of technology that most impact future outcomes? If a powerful global trend is the shifting center of gravity in growth and demand, how is that reflected in strategy and execution? If the most intractable challenges for management are in stakeholder alignment, how will this be reconciled going forward? If the strongest influence on consumer expectations is from online behavior and purchases in other categories, not airline tickets, then what is the strategy for understanding and responding to these trends?

It's not a coincidence that these are all items on the leadership agenda, unless one assumes that evolution will occur through business as usual. In the earlier discussion of leadership in this book, vision and intuition were described to be playing a greater role in driving purposeful transformation within the airline industry. Their role will increase as, according to some researchers at the McKinsey Global Institute, "The world,..., not only feels different; the data tell us it *is* different."[8] And as the authors of *Bold* point out, entrepreneurs now "go from 'I've got an idea' to 'I run a billion-dollar company' far faster than ever before."[9]

Notes

1 Alex Dichter and Nathan Seitzman of the McKinsey Company interview Lee McCabe of Facebook, "Facebook and the future of travel," December 2015.
2 IBM Institute for Business Value, "The millennials monsoon: improving returns from a young generation of travelers," March 2015.

3 Alexander, Jan, "Technology alone won't change the world," *Strategy + Business*, Winter 2015, pp. 12–14.
4 Sviokla, John and Cohen, Mitch, *The Self-Made Billionaire Effect: How Extreme Producers Create Massive Value* (New York: Penguin Group, 2014).
5 Lovelady, Lauren, "Organizational velocity," *Ascend*, Published by Sabre, 4, 2015, pp. 34–5.
6 "The evolution of design thinking," *Harvard Business Review*, September 2015, pp. 55–85.
7 Diamandis, Peter H. and Kotler, Steven, *BOLD: How to Go Big, Create Wealth, and Impact the World* (New York: Simon & Schuster, 2015).
8 Dobbs, Richard, Manyika, James, and Woetzel, Jonathan, *No Ordinary Disruption: The Four Global Forces Breaking All The Trends* (New York: PublicAffairs, 2015).
9 Diamandis and Kotler, *BOLD*.

10   THOUGHT LEADERSHIP PIECES

THE MISSING LINK FOR THE AIRLINE INDUSTRY TRANSFORMATION

Rob Broere
Co-Chairman
IATA Simplified the Business Steering Group and Think Tank

Introduction

A lot has been written for many years about transformation of the airline industry. This has been mainly focused on customer self-empowerment driven through the internet and the latest consumer available (mobile) technologies, while underpinned by large amounts of data that the airlines can and should use to make better decisions in all aspects of their operation from customer analytics to revenue management, etc. This is all extremely valid, and shows areas that each airline has to focus on to ensure they stay competitive and respond to consumer demand. One area, however, that has not received the same attention is the fundamental question: Are the core of the airline passenger processes ranging from reservations to airport processing and from fare filing to revenue accounts, just to mention a few, in use by all traditional airlines across the globe, still valid? With my 35 years of relevant experience in the airline industry, with KLM and Emirates, this Thought Leadership Piece focuses on this relatively unexplored but, as I see it, crucial "missing" piece of the transformation puzzle.

Background (Simplified Version) in Three Leaps: 1960s, 1980s and 2000s

In the early 1960s automation crept into the industry when American Airlines together with IBM created Sabre. This automated the basic reservations process, creating PNRs (Passenger Name Records); however, fare calculation, ticketing and the airport check-in processes still all remained manual.

Fares were filed to governments to ensure they were all the same between airlines on a route and published by ATPCO in large books for reservation agents to enable them to calculate the relative fares. These were based on RBDs (Reservation Booking Designators) that depicted available buckets which the reservation systems were holding and allowed the airlines to do revenue management. Tickets were handwritten and you needed revenue accounts to be able to reconcile the flights and show how much revenue a flight had brought in, a process that often took many weeks after the flight had flown. At the airport flights were handled on dedicated counters where one or two agents, using a sticker-sheet holding each seat on the plane, could check-in a full Boeing 707 or Douglas DC-8 in 15–20 minutes, baggage tags were preprinted and just affixed, labeled to the destination. Life was so simple and actually very effective.

Initially all reservations started with huge central reservation call centers, close to the airline computer centers; but with communication links becoming available, terminals started to be installed across the airline's operation and customer offices, thus giving birth to airline telecommunication providers SITA and ARINC, who leased the very expensive data lines and combined traffic from various airlines to keep the cost under control.

Slowly more complexity entered the process stream. Travel agents, who until then had to call the airlines, were given airline terminals so they could make bookings themselves. This ended up with most travel agents being connected to the system of their home national airlines, so that all travel agents in France used the Air France system while travel agents in Switzerland used the Swissair system, etc. Travel agents, and airlines as well, needed to sell not just the home airline but any other airline, and as such airline systems created sales capabilities to sell other airlines as well. An agent could in the late 1970s book any airline and behind the scenes a Teletype or TTY, yes a Telex flowing through the SITA and ARINC networks, was sent from one computer to another and within seconds a confirmation arrived, "all fully automated." This was real e-commerce B2B, that airlines pioneered, decades before the internet was invented. Tickets started to get printed instead of being handwritten to simplify the workload of the agents. Fare calculations were automated as it was near-impossible to train a sufficient number of ticketing agents who fully could calculate a complex fare with all taxes, especially taking in the complexity that airlines used to define fare rules and optimize their revenue; I am sure many of us remember the weekend stay rules, etc.

In the airport automation also started to be used as airline systems were enhanced with the departure control functions, which now allowed many different desks to handle the same flights, while adding in automated baggage tags that could be labeled for multiple flights to go from A to C via B, for which passengers would also receive system-printed boarding passes. Levels of sophistication varied and improved year on year.

Fast-Forward to the Late 1980s

Reservation system providers, driven especially by Sabre, started to expand into overseas European markets, offering travel agents "neutral" availability instead of biased availability depending on the airline system they were connected to. This was more effective for travel agents and "neutral" availability rules slowly became law as well. The European airlines, recognizing the threat, wanted their own Travel Agent Distribution system; the fact that they could not agree completely meant that Europe ended up with two as they created Galileo and Amadeus. The global distribution system (GDS) was born. GDS took in the availability status from the airlines through AVS (AValability Status) messages – yes more telexes – which passed across status changes for RBDs on each flight when they happened. They combined that with the filed fares from the airlines through ATPCO and passed that to the agents before an automated ticket was issued. On the operation side, airlines were now capable of connecting the check-in systems as well through what is called IATCI (Inter Airlines Through Check-In), which meant you could print all boarding passes for a trip even if they were handled in two different systems. Three-way through check-in rules were also published but this became so complex that they were never really implemented. These IATCI messages were passed between systems in real time using a structured data format known as EdiFact. The same EdiFact standard also allowed the GDS to get real-time availability from reservation systems, instead of purely relying on pushed AVS telex messages. Airport counters that were shared by airlines started to become unmanageable as each airline put its own terminals, or PCs as technology progressed, and printers on the counters or used mobile trolleys. The solution was to create Common Use and the principle of CUTE (Common Use Terminal Equipment) was born, thus allowing airlines to share equipment owned mainly by SITA and ARINC and connect it through their communication networks back to the airlines.

Fast-Forward into the Twenty-First Century

Tickets moved from paper-based to electronic tickets (ETs). Airlines, who ironically created their own GDSs to keep control, started to sell their shareholdings into these GDSs and furthermore outsource their PSSs (passenger services systems) to the GDSs, mainly Amadeus and Sabre, as well to SITA who had always been the preferred system provider for the smaller end of the airline spectrum.

The business model of the industry also started to change. The low-cost carriers (LCCs), led by Southwest in the USA, Ryanair and easyJet in Europe, and AirAsia in the Far East, started to unbundle their products. Traditional airlines, starting in the USA, seeing revenue opportunities, started to do the same. This was the end of the standard package on which the industry had been built.

Why Does the Industry Need to Change?

The basics of how passengers buy travel and consume it has drastically changed over the last 50 years, but the industry processes that support this have not adapted to this change. This has created a number of issues. Some key issues are.

- *Unbundling of the airline products*
  The current core processes are historical, based on the fact that each airline is providing a similar product – a seat, a bag and a meal – which are being sold for a semi-fixed price. However, over the last many years this assumption is no longer valid. Airlines, on one side, have started to add many new product features, while, at the other side of the spectrum, the unbundling has come in.
- *Difficulty servicing customers*
  The current structure of PNR, TKT and EMD, who are not fully connected and are not bridged into departure control, make it very difficult to understand which products the customer has bought and if they have been delivered. This becomes even more apparent if the product delivery is taking place through another airline, even if the airline selling is part of the same alliance or partnership.
- *Rigid product offering*
  Product offering and corresponding pricing is very rigid and inflexible and that stifles innovation. It takes many months to years for an airline to add in new features that can be sold through all channels, and that is without having to worry that the execution is to be done through an airline.
- *Objective product comparison*
  Objective product comparison across the end-to-end offering of the airlines is near impossible with the level of product features and bundling/unbundling that each airline has. How do you compare the cost of a door-to-door trip, with a meal and a bag, between airlines? What do I get on this flight, and the specific aircraft deployed on the route, a lie-flat seat or just a reclining seat? The basic available comparison is, as it states, basic. The price is for a flight booking in a cabin without any consideration to the product and add-on you might get.
- *Ancient airport processes*
  Airport processes have not structurally changed over the last 50 years, other than that more and more complexity has been added. We still stand in queues and get our documents checked over and over again, each time being looked at as if you have never been seen before. Yes there are registered traveler programs that relieve the pain slightly in certain markets, but if you are a regular global traveler that does not add the value you are looking for. Why can all stakeholders not work together to provide a more pleasant but at the same time more secure

traveling experience in which passengers do everything only once and can more or less keep on walking through the process without having to stop? Most customers will have no problems sharing more of their data if this can facilitate a faster but more secure processing on a global basis. Technically this is not hugely complex to achieve, if all stakeholders, from airlines to governments, work together to deliver this.

- *Complicated back-office processes*
  There are a huge number of back-office processes that add cost and complexity and could be simplified or eliminated. This includes, but is not limited to, revenue integrity, revenue accounts, fare-filing, back-office reservations management and airport flight management. With PNR, TKT and EMD being loosely connected, in conjunction with fares that are externally being calculated by a third party, those processes are crucial to avoid revenue loss and fraud. However, in the modern retail world there is a single offer centrally calculated and there is an integrated order management system, and with that the need of many of these processes will diminish or cease to exist completely.

Where Do IATA and the StB Program Fit?

One of the key responsibilities of IATA is to drive messaging standards that enable airlines to operate with each other and with other stakeholders like government agencies, travel agents, ground handlers, airports, etc. What an airline can do itself, such as on its website, is out of scope of IATA.

The IATA StB (Simplify the Business) Steering Group is the voice of the IATA Board tasked to look at airline industry process innovation. It consists of around 15 airlines from across the globe. Each of the StB representatives is appointed by their CEO to ensure senior management buy-in. IATA facilitates the process and executes the projects which are high on the agenda from the IATA management as well as the IATA Board. StB is unique in that it spans across the commercial and operational areas as it looks at travel from a customer's point of view. This in general spans across various airline departments and does the same within IATA.

In 2011 the IATA StB program was coming to an impasse as most projects like electronic ticketing, fast travel or the Baggage Improvement Program were either finished or well defined. The group asked itself: are we finished – read, is the world (near) perfect? That was an interesting question as on the surface it looked like all was done. About everything was automated and running well.

To explore this further the StB created a think tank which consisted of five members from the StB Steering Group and a number of technology providers to the industry. It fast became apparent that real transformation had not even started. What had been done was airline industry automation, not transformation. The StB think tank set out to drastically revamp how the industry should/could work. Out of this a number of industry transformation initiatives have sprouted since 2011. Some of the major ones are:

- *NDC (New Distribution Capability)*
  NDC offers management for third parties, travel agents, in the new internet age. A lot has been written and stated about NDC and will not be repeated here as books can be written about it. For the purpose of this contribution it is crucial to know that NDC was the first significant transformational project that the StB think tank put on the agenda of the world. NDC has set the stage that airline industry transformation is possible and provides the blueprint of what went well and an understanding of what needs to be done differently.
- *One Order*
  Having done the offer management side through NDC, the next obvious area to completely redraw is the order management side. The objective of One Order, previously known as COT (Customer Order Transformation), is to redraw the order management process and bring it into the modern e-commerce retail world. This will mean the end of PNR, TKT and EMD as we know it, but is not just limited by just that. It needs to address many areas of weaknesses that are currently not addressed.
- *Travel Communications*
  The modern world of mobile customer empowerment has opened up a huge spectrum of information, that is available, which various entities from airlines and airports to travel applications providers need to use to give a complete picture to their customers. The one missing question, however, is where does the reliable information come from? Data like departure times to gates assignment, roadside traffic issues and queue length at various touchpoints is available, but often conflicting and different. This inconsistency makes it unusable and risky as drawing conclusion from wrong data is much worse than not drawing any conclusions at all. The Travel Communications project intends to address this missing element of "trusted" information across the value chain.
- *One Identity*
  One identity will address the linking of all stakeholders to enable the seamless and secure process of customer movement across the airport, from security lines, to emigration/immigration gate processes and gate processing. This is based around the fact that customers can be securely identified and processed based on their credentials, including biometrics. A level of opt-in might be required to ensure that customer privacy is maintained, but ultimately it means a massive simplification and reduction of duplication, while increasing the ability of security and immigration stakeholders to perform their vital tasks.

- *Future end-to-end experience*
  Over the years a lot of effort has been put into optimizing each step of the airport process. That has reached saturation with not much more improvement being possible. However, what has been missing is to see how these steps, if looked at a combined level, can be merged and simplified, and duplication taken out. The "future end-to-end experience" is all focused to look at the entire airport processes in a holistic way.
- *Airport optimization*
  Airlines are completely reshaping how they interact in real time with their customers. More and more, each airline will use a very different approach. To enable this, the future of check-in, check-in desks, common use and kiosks is highly overdue for transformation. I cannot envisage that for the vast majority of customers the airport process in 5–10 years will be anywhere close to what it is today.

All of the above topics can stand on their own, but the real power is to see them together, as that will really reshape the world we know.

Each of the above transformational projects were conceived by the StB think tank and then approved by the IATA Board to be taken forward as projects.

How to Start?

The best way to make real transformation possible is to ask the question: "What would the airline industry look like if we start it today?" and work backwards from there instead of trying to apply incremental improvements to reach an undefined end state. There are a few important aspects to this approach.

- *Think Airline Industry not just an airline*
  The airline industry is extremely integrated and allows interoperability, which is not something we should forget. As such the core should be how can we make the processes simple and seamless across the value chain of all stakeholders?
- *Create a high level business case*
  Airline industry transformation is expensive to execute and slow to implement. Unless there is a solid business case, showing the even greater financial rewards and improvements to customer service, even though it seems common sense, it is likely to fail. The challenge here is that most of the business cases here are not having an instant pay-back and some of them might not even have a pay-back within five years.
- *Start with minimal given constrains*
  Read: do not worry about what is there today as that would create a sub-optimal outcome. Naturally you need to make some assumptions to be realistic.

- *Ignore the migration (initially)*
  Initially do not worry about the migration aspect of how to get there. The migration of today to tomorrow is crucial and often more complex than the future end target state. However, if the aspects on how to achieve migration are embedded too early in the end state definition, the results will likely be a compromise and not be as far reaching as they could be.
- *What are other industries doing?*
  The idea is not to conceive everything from scratch. It is important to take advantage of learning from other industries like internet retailing and modern accounting practices and to take the best elements of those while making adjustments for the unique aspects of the airline industry.

What Will the Transformational Changes Do?

Ultimately the changes that are executed through the transformation projects and the future ones that are being conceived right now will have a huge impact.

- *Customer service can drastically improve*
  Whatever we do should be benchmarked to what it does for the customers. The current airline product in terms of how it is sold and serviced is complex and has many non-value-added components to it. The customer suddenly will be able to compare what he gets for his money. Airlines will be able to introduce new products much faster and have those reliably delivered through their value chain, which can include other partner airlines as well. The information flow will also be much more accurate and transparent and that again will improve customer satisfaction.
- *Airlines can sell their products like retailers*
  The airline business is moving more and more away from being a provider of a standard air-only product to a modern retail model. This gives significant new opportunities for revenue that airlines can exploit to provide a quality differentiated offering.
- *Revenue increases*
  The new opportunities for revenue generation can add billions of dollars to the airlines' bottom line and that will enable the airlines to have a good return on invested capital.
- *Complexity is broken down*
  The internal complexity of the industry is staggering. Trying to explain this to non-airline people is an uphill struggle. This complexity has grown over the years and until now there has never been a serious challenge to try to simplify this. Core processes that are simple and easy to understand and execute will drive efficiency.

- *Significant cost reductions*
  By tackling the complexity, significant costs are also taken out permanently from the cost base, making airlines more competitive and contributing to the bottom line. Many airline business processes and, with that, departments will no longer exist in the current form, taking significant costs out of the organization.

What Do the Experts Say?

Speaking to many airline management and also IT providers on all levels from middle management to CEOs, I received a lot of feedback that can be put into three categories.

1 *Skeptics*
  A significant number of internal airline stakeholders fit into this group. They have perfected the operation given a set of boundaries on how the industry works. Now these boundaries are being challenged and torn down it suddenly takes many out of their comfort zone. This often causes an initial reaction of unbelief and a response showing that it is too complex and cannot be done.
2 *Optimists*
  Outsiders who do not understand the full complexity and integration of the airline industry are the majority in this group. They think this is easy and cannot understand why the airline industry is so slow to adapt. Although the optimists are a force for change, their limited understanding of how the industry works is likely to hit road blocks sooner or later as the bigger picture has not been thought through.
3 *Realists*
  This group of people can see why the industry must change. On the other hand, they also see the task at hand as extremely complex and challenging. The airline industry has a few top-level executives that fit in this crucially important category, who want to drive forward. Ultimately airlines that embrace the transformation early on are likely to come out on top.

To make it work you need all three categories.

The drive should be by the realists as they have the vision and the big-picture view. They, with the support of the optimists for their free thinking, are the ones to keep the pressure and momentum going. The key role the skeptics can play is a reality check to ensure that the final goal, but even more, the migration path to get there, has been thought through. Over time it is likely that the optimists, after understanding more of the complexity, as well as the skeptics, after seeing the change is imminent and works, slowly converge into the realists.

What Could Hold the Industry Back?

Although doing this transformation seems obvious and long overdue, especially seen from a customer and an outsider point of view, there are a few areas that could hold the industry back:

- *Cost of the transformation*
  Due to the complexity of the industry and the number of airlines and other parties like travel agents, ground handlers and governments involved, the transition to the new world will take time and significant investment. In essence it means that all core IT systems that have billions of dollars invested in them will need to be rewritten and/or replaced to achieve the future target end state of the core processes. This is likely to cost a few billion dollars. The pay-back over a ten-year period or more is clear but will the airlines have an appetite to take this level of risk and investment? The initial answer could be no, this is going too far. However, the risk of doing nothing is not to be underestimated and is in my opinion directly linked to the long-term survival of the traditional airline business model, and with that any airlines that follow this model. Ultimately the change will need to happen if the airlines want to survive into the future and compete with new players like the LCC airlines, and that might be the straw that will justify this type of long-term investment needed to make it work.
- *Vested interest to keep the current situation*
  The future state will put new IT players at the same level of ability to service airlines versus existing suppliers that see their market domination likely to be challenged. Current IT providers to the airlines are making a healthy profit, being the highest out of the entire value chain. Now with the investments needed and with the future having more IT suppliers to compete with there is naturally a tendency to avoid or at least delay a transition to the future for as long as possible. With NDC this initially was already apparent and that is likely to repeat itself in other areas as well.

What Is Next?

The list of projects that have been stated will surely set the airline industry transformation on the right footing for the future, but there are other areas that can be taken on as well. The most obvious is baggage, where all stakeholders from manufacturers, to airlines, to airports should take a serious look and re-invent baggage from the ground up. Apart from baggage, some other potential areas could need a serious look as well, like code-shares to see if they are fit for future purpose.

Conclusion

The airline industry transformation is long overdue and will reshape how the industry works. It is not an *if* but a *when* and *how* this will be achieved, as ultimately it is the only way forward for the airline industry to survive. It is not simple, but a great challenge that some of the leaders will take on. Those that dare to lead will be remembered for showing that 100 years after the first commercial flight the industry is capable of recreating itself and having a new lease of life. Let the future begin.

JUST CHANGE OR DISRUPTIVE INNOVATION: A LOOK AT THE MOBILITY PROVIDERS AND THE ABILITY FOR A PASSION TO CHANGE

Nico Buchholz
Senior Vice President and Chief Procurement Officer
Bombardier Aerospace

The aviation industry has been and still is at the forefront of several technologies. However, there has to be a differentiation between the airline world and the original equipment manufacturer (OEM) world. While automotive, trains, ships, and air transport have all benefited from technology improvements, some even of disruptions like autonomous vehicles, we also have a disruption via protectionism in some segments of our industry. The focus here shall be on the aviation sector with a view on the aircraft.

At the same time globalization has had an impact on the change of both business models. While air travel in the early years was only for the lucky few, over one billion passengers per year and millions of cargo shipments have changed the landscape today. Fierce competition, ancillary revenues, and low-cost carriers (LCCs) have had a significant impact on growth and how we think about aviation today. Security measures have become a fact of life for travelers, implying longer ground times than before. The travel chain has changed. The path to today is littered with airline failures, struggling major carriers but also a lot of new carriers embracing new business models. Airlines provide a network, like the internet, but while some also have the internet onboard there have been disruptive changes only in very few airline business models. Airlines are part of a mobility-providing chain – for passengers and cargo alike. Again most of it has been evolution. Before trying to look forward, we ask how is the environment with the OEMs? We tend to walk in our comfort zones and mostly traditional patterns. Hence we are facing challenges when we square the circle and go beyond the usual. Customer behavior is changing to becoming more "value driven," unlike the value OEMs put on certain aircraft features. At the same time, aircraft are just production tools. So when trying to understand how to square the circle we face a couple of expected but also unexpected topics:

- emotion vs. logic
- what is a game-changing definition?
- small vs. big (just a feeling?)
- customer needs ... the seat plus?
- yield management systems
- "up-selling" ideas

- "baggage from the past"
- direct flying vs. large airports and the benefits of hubbing to reach a larger catchment and to provide services
- "groundtime" vs. "airtime"

The OEMs have changed the industry landscape significantly. About a century ago the magnificent flying machines started appearing. Today the aircraft manufacturers have become the mobility tool providers for the airlines. Yes, with all the emotion on the flying itself, the aircraft themselves have become production tools. They produce seat miles and ton-kilometers for the airlines, which will enhance the product of flying with emotions, cabin features and ground services – with a travel experience. While the focus has traditionally been on the aircraft manufacturers like Airbus, Boeing, Douglas (a fatality on the way, like Lockheed), Bombardier, Embraer, Fokker (another failed pioneer), and countless other smaller producers, we tend to exclude the marvels of technology which propel these aircraft. It would fill the book to argue who of these two – engine or airframe – have actually provided a disruptive change in our aviation world, but let us focus on some significant milestones that changed the landscape of the past before looking forward.

Small propeller aircraft slowly became bigger and faster, peaking with the high-complexity turboprops like the Lockheed Superstar, which in its time could fly for over 20 hours but at half the speed of today. The industry has become all about efficiency. So when the jet engine started its life, doubling the speed, a new era began. The 20-hour turboprop flight could suddenly be done in 12 hours, and the airframe manufacturers pushed the engine manufacturers for more thrust to allow them to grow bigger. This cumulated in the original B747, and more recently in the A380, placing them on a "normal trend curve" (see Figure 10.1). With these new technologies also becoming more reliable it heralded the ability to build twin engine aircraft the size of the original B747. Tomorrow these twins, like the A350, B777X, and B787, will dominate long-haul traffic. Pioneering technologies like fly-by-wire first saw a full civil application on the original 150-seat aisle aircraft, the A320. So what is revolutionary?

Bigger is better. Bigger is more effective. The OEM and airlines thrived very much along the Olympic line: faster, higher, bigger, and further. Nowadays we can reach about 90 percent of the world's population non-stop in more or less comfort depending on the willingness and ability to pay. Efficiency, however, has a new name: small is beautiful! And effective is only what embraces a standardized flexibility in combination with being reliably innovative. Before we focus on conflicting paradigms, one should look at facts long denied in many airline and OEM management teams – if small is really better, how flexible do these tools have to be to survive more than a heartbeat. We do look at technical product life cycles that are measured in decades, including the upgrades, rather than in months like mobile phones. Looking at supply and demand, there is the balancing act between restricting

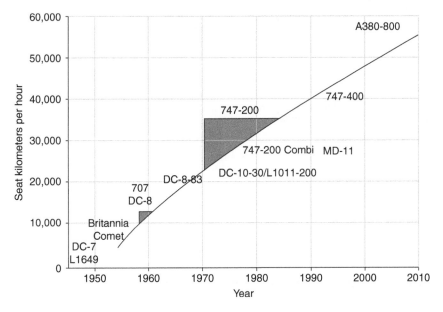

Figure 10.1 A Neutral View on Efficiency Improvements.

supply to keep prices up and discounting to create volume needed to be profitable with bigger units; some markets obviously have a basic large demand requiring less discounting to fill larger aircraft. This has long been the basis of all planning. Technology progressed. Not really noticed for various reasons and because of the small market size, the "old" Boeing 747 was revamped, with the key elements influencing operating cost in the long-haul business – new wings, the newest engine generation, plus other features. Suddenly the "old one" was operating at costs similar per seat on a comparable basis with the perceived newest, finest, and largest aircraft. But airlines had to fill about 100 seats less for this unit cost. It went further when Airbus and Boeing came onto the market with their respective new large twins. Suddenly the smaller aircraft offered more performance at an absolute lower unit cost base. This is a first in a century of flying, hence technology provided for a disruption. When looking at the key influencers of long-haul operational cost – fuel burn and weight – it becomes obvious why the smaller aircraft can beat the traditional four-engine and larger aircraft on cost.

Moving to the smaller aircraft, so-called single-aisle aircraft, we see a similar trend – the re-engine of existing families reduces noise and fuel burn significantly, but as the "rest" of these production tools stays as before, full advantage cannot be taken. Allow me an "unfair" comparison as it compares a newly designed 120–40-seat aircraft with an old 200–30-seat aircraft. The newest siblings from Bombardier and Embraer have similar or lower cost per seat as the old aircraft; however, only the Bombardier aircraft offers close to the same performance as Airbus and Boeing to be a real option. Comparing

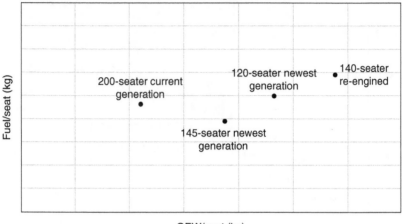

Figure 10.2 Efficiency Comparison of Selected Single-Aisle Aircraft.

more recent aircraft like A320NEO/B737–8MAX (both around 180 seats) with a brand new 145-seater shows the benefit of a full suite of new technology – no more advantage to growing bigger, similar seat mile cost at up to 20 percent lower trip cost. In Figure 10.2 the efficiency comparisons of selected single-aisle aircraft are based on the key drivers for cash operating costs. Note that the crew ratios, as the other large element of cost, are neutral in this comparison, as all of the aircraft compared need two pilots and a cabin crew per 50 passengers. "Growing" out of a cost problem is therefore no longer necessary, but more fundamental and sometimes more challenging business decisions have to be taken.

Having said all this, and knowing the countless times people have focused on hub bypassing, it is true that these new models have a more-or-less flat curve on unit cost over size if one is willing – large fleets can easily justify this – to "shop" for the most efficient model in each segment. Hub and spoke was created to generate enough connections and to have enough passengers to cover the operating costs of the aircraft. With now both ends of the scale – B787/A350 and NEO/MAX/CSeries – offering more attractive economics in the smaller segment, the challenge for airlines becomes how to competitively resize the hub network and which segments they can now bypass, satisfying passenger demand for non-stop rather than direct flight. CSeries, A321LR NEO, and B787/350/777X can be truly disruptive game changers. It will be interesting how and who in the airline community will first embrace these new abilities to attain a competitive advantage. This is not a guide to fleet planning including all the processes – you find these on the internet in some of my presentations – but rather to provoke new ways of looking at the whole process of thinking about aircraft and the travel value chain.

All manufacturers work on upgrades or new aircraft. Will the A321NEOLR replace the B757 or will Boeing enter this segment with a new model? In any case, these will offer the potential in some markets – e.g. China to Europe or for Turkish Airlines through their hub – to displace traditional traffic flows. Building a hub-and-spoke system with a smaller aircraft may make the chosen hub even more powerful – an option with the CSeries which could do this or longer flights. The smaller B787 and A350 models will allow airlines to rethink how to compete. Some carriers like Norwegian, Air Canada, and British Airways have already embraced the concept of downsizing (B777-300 into B787) or to open new routes previously not possible due to lack of passengers to achieve a profit. The smaller units provide the seat mile cost of before, but with a significantly reduced risk of failing to fill these seats. While there will always be some routes which require larger aircraft to maximize profit on high-density restricted airport links, the smaller aircraft seem to become the "flavor of the day" – their market is simply bigger and they offer more flexibility (see Figure 10.3).

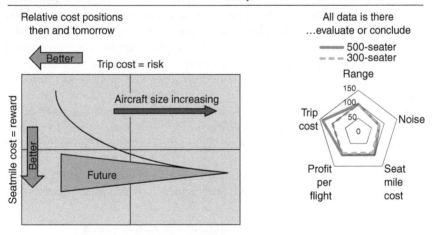

Figure 10.3 The New Cost Curves Paired with Innovative Reliability Provide Tools for Potential New Business Models.

FROM EVOLUTION TO DISRUPTION: THE NEXT TWENTY YEARS

John Grant
Industry Adviser
OAG

Cast your mind back a decade and spend a few moments thinking about how much aviation has changed in that time.

There was no A380 aircraft operating commercial services, the B787 was still only a paper plane and the A340 was being used by many carriers for ultra long-haul operations. There were six or seven major US international airlines. Low-cost carriers (LCCs) were in still in an evolutionary phase and travel agents were still prolific on the high street. The industry produced some 27.7 million scheduled flights each year and over 3.1 billion seats. With fuel at $57 per barrel IATA projected a $4.7 billion loss for the airline industry.

Returning to the present there is speculation that the A380 is already an aircraft past its "sell-by" date. The A350 is being talked about as an ultra long-haul 19-hour aircraft. The A340 is almost obsolete. Airline consolidation in the USA has seen the emergence of three major US international carriers, and LCCs have blossomed in nearly every part of the world. In 2015 the industry will operate some 33.3 million scheduled flights with some 4.6 billion seats, and operate some 5.12 trillion ASMs – an increase of over 58 percent in the last decade. And, ironically, IATA estimates an industry profit of $33 billion with fuel at an average price of $55[1] per barrel, some 14 percent higher than a decade ago. And how many travel agents can be seen on the high street?

The pace of change in the last decade has been phenomenal, and faster than most people would have expected (see Figure 10.4). Wireless connectivity,

LEAD TIME BEFORE REACHING 50M ACTIVE USERS

Figure 10.4 Innovation Cycles Have Massively Reduced in the Digital Environment and Create a Truly Unpredictable Future (source: OAG Connecting the World of Travel).

internet access to nearly every part of the planet, new mega airports in the Middle East, enhanced aircraft technology and increased consumer knowledge and purchasing power are just a few of the areas which have evolved almost beyond recognition. For the moment the industry may have found a way to be profitable, but individual businesses remain fragile. Innovation lead times are becoming shorter and shorter, and increasing effort and investment has to be directed at staying up-to-date in business processes, technology and customer relationships, as IATA's Simplifying the Business program has found.

It would be easy to look to the anticipated growth in air travel over the next decade and anticipate further evolution of the industry. After all, by 2034 the demand for air travel will have more than doubled to some seven billion trips per annum.[2] China will at some point around 2032 become the largest market in the world, having overtaken the USA, while India, Indonesia and Brazil complete the top five markets. The Chinese domestic market alone is estimated to be around 1.3 billion passengers by 2034,[3] accounting for nearly one-fifth of the world's travel by that point.

But what if the next decade is one of disruption rather than evolution? In this chapter we consider two challenges for the industry and their potential to disrupt current behavior and fundamentally affect the way consumers and airlines make choices about flying. These ideas are ours and there is no certainty about outcomes. All we know for sure is that the industry of 2025 and beyond will be very different to the one we know today.

Disruptive Technology, Disruptive Brands

As we look forward we see two potentially disruptive changes occurring in the industry. With both come challenges for existing players, but also opportunities.

The first is the aircraft technology. The history of aircraft development over the long term tends to lead to the notion that bigger is better. It's the large aircraft of the day which catch the headlines, not the smaller aircraft which are often the unglamorous workhorses of the industry. The growth trajectory of many airports has enhanced this with the need to create aircraft which can maximize slot utilization at the major congested hubs around the world.

Although the A320NEO and B737 Max have the potential to bypass hubs and extend the operating range of LCCs, they represent evolution. What if there were a new aircraft which offered a step change in fuel efficiency and long-haul narrow-body capacity? Could this have the potential to seriously challenge the legacy carriers, create global networks for low-cost airlines and provide point-to-point air travel for most of the world's population?

The second potentially disruptive change we see on the horizon is linked to the changing habits of consumers. The reach of the internet and the power of global brands could see a world in which consumers look to the likes of Google or Amazon to book their travel, and these brands invest in providing all the information consumers need at the point of sale – confidence, information, recommendations and ease of booking. In a world in which a global brand can "own" the customer relationship, what choices might airlines have? Will they simply be commodity suppliers of seats to the brand, or can they continue as brand owners?

The Future of Aircraft Technology

Bigger Aircraft for Bigger Airports

In no sector of the industry has there been as much technological advancement as in aircraft design and performance. Nineteen-hour sectors on two-engine aircraft using composite materials are possible today. By 2025 advancements in aircraft speeds, cruising altitudes and near 100 percent usage of bio-fuels could radicalize the way aircraft are deployed.

Much of the focus in recent years has been around the development of next-generation wide-bodied capacity, either in the mass market A380 or the longer, "thinner" B787 and A350 aircraft types. Demand has been driven by customers seeking to operate aircraft that meet the characteristics and constraints of their hubs. It is no surprise that Finnair have a preference for the A350 with their niche Helsinki hub, while the use of the A380 by Emirates equally meets their wider more expansive hub network.

Advancements in single-aisle aircraft look like offering the next phase of evolution which may just be perfectly aligned with a potential change in market behavior.

But a key question is, will the market in ten years' time behave in the same manner with new-generation single-aisle aircraft about to enter production?

Big airports create critical mass, driven in many cases by geographic position, enlightened air service development policies and an understanding of their competitive advantages. In a few cases local market demand has supported those hubs' growth, but some of the leading hubs such as Dubai, Singapore, Madrid and Chicago all have populations of fewer than 5.5 million and yet have established major market positions.

All of these hubs have built traffic on the basis of connectivity, joining smaller cities to global destinations. In many cases those connecting cities are well established; occasionally a niche city pair may occur. Might it be that the factors that made hubs attractive in the past could actually be a weakness in the next decade? With congestion and sheer size comes an increase in minimum connecting times, and infrastructure investment becomes cost prohibitive relative to either economic return or airline cost bases. Some of the discussion around the need for additional runway capacity in London confirms this, with airlines closely watching the required cost of such projects.

Take Dubai as an example. Is Al Maktoum International Dubai World Central actually the solution to a problem – or the creation of a new problem? On completion it would seem that an airport with five runways that is capable of accommodating 240 million passengers per year is ideal for the growing demand, but will that be the case a decade from now or will alternative solutions have been found for connecting inhabitants of one city or town with another?

Airline failure, consolidation, and strategic adjustments have previously left many airports with facilities that are either too large or over-engineered for their subsequent airline customer base. For some airports and markets, airport expansion may represent too large a risk for no guaranteed return. While many airports have flourished, others such as Brussels, Pittsburgh, Budapest, St. Louis and San Juan have all experienced dramatic changes in their customer bases that have forced significant changes in their business operations.

The Next Evolution of Narrow-Body Aircraft

Both Airbus and Boeing have new narrow-body aircraft waiting in the wings. The A320/1NEO and the B737-Max will be available for commercial operation in the next two years. Both aircraft will offer lower operating costs, estimated at around 20 percent per seat below current levels, as well as an enhanced aircraft range with a full commercial payload.

Initially the B737 Max-7 variant will offer a maximum range of around 3,800 nautical miles with a high-density 149-seat configuration, while the A320/1NEO will offer a range of up to 4,200 nautical miles in a 160-seat layout. With these ranges, established markets such as London to New York, Singapore to Sydney, and Miami to Buenos Aires will all be possible single-aisle aircraft opportunities where once conventional wisdom was for wide-bodied, long-haul classic services and product offerings.

With close to 2,900[4] firm orders already in place for the extended-range B737-Max and a staggering 4,400[5] orders for the A320/1NEO there is no doubt about market confidence in the expected performance of both aircraft types and there is no doubt about their intended use. It is no surprise that the majority of orders placed for delivery are for the emergent Asian and Indian markets and the bulk of orders placed by low-cost airlines, continuing the evolution of both market and airline trends.

Ten years ago both the Airbus and Boeing aircraft were "paper planes," just concepts for consideration; today they are close to reality. So where might the next evolution in aircraft technology take us? Could it be a single-aisle aircraft with a range of 4,500 nautical miles and a commercial payload of around 150 seats, faster flying speeds or indeed a combination of both? And indeed could such development rather than simply being an evolution disrupt the industry as we know it?

An Aircraft for Long Haul, Low Cost

The development of new aircraft technology has to be matched by a market need and perhaps more so by a current unserved market need. There appears to be a number of potential factors within the market, all occurring at the same time; that could bring about potential disruption.

In part the attraction of new-generation single-aisle long-range aircraft is to allow low-cost airlines to compete against their legacy competition with an aircraft offering lower seat cost, simplified product offerings and with a capacity that better matches the local market demand.

A classic LCC market entry strategy has been to fly head-to-head on major city pair markets, perhaps to secondary airports within or close to that city. That strategy has been built around a combination of: new market stimulation through competitive pricing; the securing of a share of the established market; and through an obsession with cost and efficiency that has been reflected in areas such as distribution, capacity per aircraft, working contracts and aircraft utilization. In many ways the emergence of LCCs in all markets around the world has been a wake-up call to the legacy and state-owned carriers about how to operate their businesses to the maximum effect.

In these situations the "contested" market has traditionally been the local point-to-point market segment which, on a RPK basis, has been higher yielding for legacy airlines. However, in recent years low-cost airlines have started building their own connecting traffic, initially in "self-connecting" formats but more recently through planned and coordinated scheduling. Airlines such as AirAsia X and Norwegian now support their long-haul operations on the basis of connecting traffic.

The introduction of new long-range aircraft opens up the opportunity to serve "long and thin" city pairs where existing market demand has not yet been able to support regular scheduled operations. Table 10.1 shows a sample of typical markets that are currently unserved with scheduled services and are in a range of 3,800–4,200 nautical miles, effectively in range for service from new-generation single-aisle aircraft.

These 20 city pairs highlight both the scale and the type of opportunity that may exist. In all cases, one of the two points is what would normally be described as a "mature market" e.g. London, Paris, Tokyo. At the other end is what might today be considered a secondary "emergent market," such as Dhaka, Colombo and Dar Es Salaam.

The attraction and opportunity of connecting a mature market to a secondary, or emergent, city cannot be overstated in the context of both the aircraft range and the disruptive potential created. The mature city destination provides a market size that allows substantial growth as well as stimulation typically attributable to new destination promotion and development. Alongside that, the emergent city offers access to a new growth market which can be rapidly stimulated by availability of low fares over a short period of time.

There are many examples of new long-haul market stimulation from the arrival of new entrants. Thirty-five years ago it was airlines such as People's Express and Laker Airways which pioneered air service and stimulated markets, more recently AirAsia X, Jetstar, Norwegian and Tiger Airways have

Table 10.1 Selected Current Unserved Local Market Demand within a 3,800–4,400 Nautical Mile Range

From	To	Indirect Market (Two-Way) July 2014 to June 2015	Nautical Miles
Dhaka	London (GB)	148,730	4,323
Kathmandu	London (GB)	109,998	3,969
Goa	London (GB)	93,016	4,089
Mahe Island	Milan	70,764	3,917
Male	Tokyo	69,977	4,134
Sylhet	London (GB)	67,990	4,326
Colombo	Milan	64,608	4,307
Mumbai	Manchester (GB)	61,838	3,962
Dzaoudzi	Paris	57,131	4,346
Kolkata	London (GB)	56,602	4,306
Dar Es Salaam	London (GB)	55,702	4,033
Colombo	Zurich	53,518	4,331
Male	Munich	51,751	4,106
Colombo	Munich	43,171	4,213
Male	Zurich	40,211	4,214
Mombasa	London (GB)	39,553	3,889
Delhi	Madrid	37,227	3,917
Dhaka	Seoul	35,742	4,255
Male	Vienna	35,231	3,922
Lusaka	London (GB)	35,137	4,265

Source: OAG Traffic Analyser, November 2015.

replicated those levels of market stimulation. Using airline booking data, OAG analyzed the levels of stimulation that had recently been seen in emergent Asian markets when new direct air services were introduced. Unserved indirect markets with fewer than 100,000 passengers per annum broadly grew by more than 50 percent when direct services were introduced, suggesting that significant opportunities for traffic growth exist from the opening of new services.

It is no coincidence that a mix of increased disposable income, relaxing regulatory environments and changing sales/distribution strategies allowed all of these airlines to stimulate the market. Sadly the long-term success of the early pioneers and disruptors was not realized, but the more recent experiences of the latest long-haul disruptors looks secure for the future.

Current expectations for market growth in the emergent Asian markets suggest that demand will double in the next decade and some 12,500[6] new aircraft will be required by 2034. Over two-thirds of those aircraft are also single-aisle next-generation equipment and with less than 10 percent of domestic capacity provided by low-cost airlines in China against a global average closer to 30 percent, there is reason to be optimistic that the expected growth levels will be achieved, if not exceeded, despite recent adjustments to industry forecasts.

By means of demonstration we have highlighted key potential emergent markets with their current propensity to fly and then assumed three different levels of propensity to fly in that market by 2025 placed on the expected levels of population growth over that time period.

Who Owns the Customer Relationship?

The Emergent Traveler

By 2025 today's schoolchildren will be taking to the skies for work and play. Globalization will give them reasons to travel and rising prosperity in developing countries will enable leisure travel by air to be affordable for many who might not fly if they had been born 20 years sooner. Propensity to fly in emerging markets is currently less than one-tenth of that reported in mature markets, so even modest increases in the desire and ability to fly will re-shape the patterns of global air travel. With no entrenched perceptions on airline, airport, comfort levels or ancillary products, these "new age travelers" are potential disruptors to the aviation industry.

Virtual reality will be in most people's homes or available on street corners in cafés around the planet. Internet access will be freely available to over 90 percent of the world's population and social media and meta-search engines will be the definitive source of all information. Many of these travelers will have "digitally traveled" in advance to their destination.

Bombarded by increasing media noise, consumers will have selected a cluster of trusted sources from which they purchase products; today we call them Weibo, Google, Amazon and in the travel sphere perhaps Expedia, Orbitz, Skyscanner and others. Tomorrow they may have different names but the consumer will rely on a few trusted brands for everything from food to finance management to travel. With that trust comes a desire for instant gratification, delivery of goods tomorrow or even perhaps in the next two hours, regardless of distance carried or complexity of logistics. Travel will be booked at very short notice; the ability to work from home will extend to working while on vacation and conventional holiday periods linked to school holidays will have changed as online learning becomes the prime source of education and knowledge.

Can Airlines Still Be Brand Owners?

All of these developments will create huge challenges for the travel industry. The mechanisms by which airlines revenue manage in such a highly dynamic market and how hotels will supply accommodation are but two of the many challenges to be faced. And perhaps more importantly how will airlines market to those consumers, or will they even bother? Building lifetime value relationships with customers is difficult today, the cost increasingly expensive, the ROI ever reducing as consumers shop around, use third-party search engines and social channels to find best-value offerings from a plethora of choice. Faced with several billion passengers who trust a selected group of lifestyle suppliers for their every need, is it realistic for an airline or tour operator to invest in trying to build that personal relationship?

Airlines face a real threat of being distanced from their consumer as much as today's farmer has been distanced from his consumer by supermarkets and retail brands. Loss of control is an inevitable consequence of wider choice and access to larger markets and increased sales opportunities. The car salesroom has become a location for affirmation of an already-made purchase decision and a trading floor for negotiation of the financial terms. Few products have managed to retain their exclusivity and personal service element, even fewer with a total market of over seven billion, so why should the airline industry expect to be different?

Air Travel as a Commodity

Is it therefore inevitable that by 2025 air travel will have become a commodity product? It may be that there will be some marginal brand differentiators that command premiums, perhaps based around punctuality and service, but the promotion, awareness and consumer's acceptance of those differentiators will be in the hands of Google and others. For many consumers the first point of reference for purchasing almost any product in ten years' time is likely to be via these intermediaries with their global distribution and power. Many airlines will be trapped, once again facing the constant dilemma of trying to "own" the customer when in reality the customer is owned by the meta-search providers and global brand owners. It is indeed possible that the level of knowledge between the meta-search provider and the customer will be such that the customer will be "reminded" of when to book their next travel itinerary based upon historic travel patterns and inserted profiles/demographics into that database.

When the potential material change in "customer ownership" is placed alongside the customer's future product expectations, then potential for disruption becomes very significant. Long-haul travel has historically been considered a luxury product with catering, in-flight entertainment and even for a while amenity kits in economy class! Today for many travelers long-haul flying offers a simple seat surrounded by discretionary product elements such as increased seat pitch, advanced seat assignment, selection of catering and baggage fees, all of which have been termed ancillary revenue streams for airlines as increased product transparency develops. All of which lends itself to the potential product offering from both those emergent markets and the new wave of travelers and the possibility of long-haul single-aisle aircraft services. IATA have attempted to address this particular disruptive threat through their New Distribution Capability (NDC) program, which gives airlines the ability to transparently offer individual product elements and services to the customer. Ironically, while the NDC program provides a welcome opportunity for transparency it also allows mega-distributors further access to airline prod-ucts and will, over time, allow them to further establish their position of trusted retailer to the consumer across all types of products and services aside from only airlines.

Since tomorrow's traveler has little or no product expectation other than a seat, they would not find it an unreasonable option to pay for ancillary ele-ments of the product such as those listed earlier. All of which plays directly into the hands of the Googles, Facebooks, TripAdvisors and Weibo's of 2025 and beyond, and leaves airlines struggling to build relationships with cus-tomers and corporate travelers. Indeed, now is a good time for airlines to be asking themselves if they should be continuing to invest in their brand and customer relationships, or whether the move toward dis-intermediation from their customer is inevitable and no longer avoidable?

Predicting the Unpredictable: Scenarios for 2025

The future is unknown but that doesn't stop us from having ideas, opinions and thoughts as to how the aviation industry will develop over the next decade. Many of those opinions are frequently discussed and common areas of agreement do exist.

The emergent markets which will be the future drivers of growth are widely recognized: China, India, Southeast Asia, Latin America and Africa. Aircraft technology and development is broadly shaped for the first half of the next decade. Increasing consumer power and choice is there to be seen and we see it in our own behavior. Airline distribution is changing every day. Regulatory environments are relaxing, albeit more slowly than some would like. New city pairs are served for the first time every week. Airport planners are already working on building the capacity needed to meet future demand forecasts.

So, we are aware of many of the potential "catalytic factors" that exist. What we all cannot be quite sure of is what the chemical reaction and sub-sequent results will be. In this section we explore some examples for how the aviation industry and market might look in 2025 and beyond and put them "out there" as our contribution to the discussion.

There is widespread agreement that the airline industry is ready for some degree of consolidation. Existing issues around ownership and traffic rights have been barriers to the type of supplier consolidation that has occurred in so many other market sectors. In the last few years business models based around franchises, joint-ventures, inter-airline equity ownership and ownership-based airline groupings, such as the International Airline Group (IAG) and the Lufthansa Group, have highlighted a desire among many for that consolidation to occur.

In many industries consolidation leads to a few, maybe three, major players which dominate a market. Over time and with more consolidation the size of the market which is dominated grows until there are just a few global players.

The Power of Three

One scenario for 2025 is the emergence of three global airline brands created from the recognition of, and grappling with, the need by legacy carriers to own the customer relationship. By investing in their own global brand and creating global networks where the details of ownership are invisible to the consumer and traveler, they defend their businesses and fend off the encroachment by low-cost airlines into long-haul markets. They compete globally with each other between every continent and country.

The Rise of the Low-Cost Carriers

Another scenario is one in which the low-cost airlines, with their healthy balance sheets and weighty aircraft order books are able to capitalize on the improved operating costs that new aircraft models afford, especially new-model long-haul aircraft. They do to the legacy carriers in long-haul markets over the next decade what they have done in short-haul markets over the past decade. Their networks may not be global but have distinct regional strengths, using new disruptive aircraft technology to provide air services between them. Legacy carriers have nowhere to go and the decade ends with the disappearance of some of the biggest names in airline history. Meanwhile, low-cost airlines make alliances with the technology firms, bringing all that modern data science has to offer to the customer relationship. The kids of today will benefit from low-cost travel anywhere integrated with their social media and technology habits.

Trying to Be All Things to All People

A third scenario is one in which airlines of all colors and hues focus so much on breaking down the product into distinct choices for the customer that they fail to see the non-airline competitors talking to those same customers. They lose control of the customer relationship to Google or Amazon or Weibo. In the future they will be suppliers of commodity seats, adding capacity where and when they are told to. They will increasingly be forced to compete on price alone. Legacy carriers might not survive.

The Law of Three

These scenarios are, inevitably, extreme versions of what will come to pass in 2025, but the challenges and opportunities are very real. Whether we see three global network carriers or the globe served by three sizeable and connected LCC franchises, or the disappearance altogether of airlines as brand owners, we know significant change is just around the corner. In early 2015, OAG published an *Insight Report* that outlined the concept of the law of three and how it related to the airline industry, or indeed highlighted how the industry currently avoids following this management law. Our analysis concluded that in time, with increased deregulation, changes in foreign ownership rules and increasing strategic partnerships the law of three will eventually apply to aviation as much as in the soft drinks or financial services sector. Since the publication of that report, small but significant developments have already taken place with senior management from competing airlines joining management boards of partner airlines and further European consolidation finalized, with IAG acquiring ownership of Aer Lingus. Speculation continues that further consolidation in Europe will take place in the next few years as smaller carriers seek protection from increasing competition, as evidenced by Croatia Airlines. While in a completely disruptive but potentially exciting opportunity for change, established low-cost airlines in Europe are openly discussing the potential for working with legacy airlines on building connecting traffic across their respective networks.

These factors outlined above, along with many already widely circulated pieces of research and various demand forecasts, lead us to conclude that by 2025 the aviation industry will be very different to what we see today. Many of the emergent pieces of thinking and commercial/distribution evolution will be impacting the market and have changed many existing ways of working and thinking. Distribution will be entirely different, third parties may well have built controlling relationships with their customers, airlines may struggle to build direct relationships with travelers, network structures may have changed, airline ownership structures may have changed, regulatory authority may have been eased in many markets and the price of oil may have risen back to 2012 prices. Today's next-generation aircraft will be the established workhorses for many carriers both within the low-cost and legacy airline sector which may indeed have blurred into a more generic term of "airlines" by that point, with product differentiation increasingly non-existent on short-haul sectors.

In summary, we may already be seeing the start of disruptive activity today and have some visibility as to the shape of the market in ten years' time, and the positive benefits of that spilling over across both consumers and suppliers. Are we already "peeking" behind the curtain? But what about in 2035, what could the industry look like then? We've made some bold predictions.

Based upon the development of new long-range aircraft, increasing use of composite materials and further advances in technology we predict that aircraft ranges will be stretched further by 2035, especially in the long-range single-aisle jet category. In the last 20 years the average flying time of sectors operated by this aircraft type have increased by 17 percent.[7] Among the same aircraft category the proportion of flights operated in excess of a 2,000 nautical mile range doubled from 1.0 percent in 2000 to 2 percent of all scheduled flights by 2015. With much of the short-haul market already served, the majority of that growth came in the serving of new longer-haul city pairs, many from emergent and secondary markets to major cities and hubs. By 2035, referencing Airbus' Global Market Forecast, there is an expectation that some 31,800 new passenger aircraft will be required, of which circa 20,000 will be additional, some 70 percent of which will be single-aisle types, equating to around 14,000 new single-aisle jet aircraft with more than 100-seat capacity by 2035. That is equivalent to two new aircraft per day leaving the production line for the next 20 years.

Extrapolating forward the advancements in average sector length that we have seen for single-aisle jet aircraft from 2000, then the possibility of increasing potential aircraft ranges from the current limits of 4,200 nautical miles could conceptually lead to a range closer to 4,900 nautical miles, which in turn would allow many of today's classic long-haul sectors such as London to San Francisco and Johannesburg to Sydney to be operated non-stop.

And with such advancement and possible disruption comes a very real opportunity that brings emergent markets and geographic position together to create a potential "round the world" network of low-cost airlines and operators to challenge the convention of the current mega-hubs and legacy carriers' network power.

In Table 10.2 and Figure 10.5 we have identified just ten potential city pairs that could be operated by a new aircraft type with an expanded range of up to 4,900 miles. Some of these cities are already established commercial centers, while others are reflective of emergent markets with large populations, growing disposable income and a very low current propensity to fly that will grow significantly in the next 20 years based upon current economic indicators. All enjoy either some geographic coastal advantage or are centrally located in a vast land-mass with high population density in the surrounding region.

For many of these markets there is already a level of low-cost service and clear potential for future growth in the coming years. By 2035, customers expectations will once again have moved further from those of today, and levels of service may have become completely transparent based around individual pricing for all discretionary elements of a journey. The possibility of one-stop "long-haul" low cost on single-aisle aircraft types is a realistic vision for 20 years from now. The creativity of the individual traveler combined with the infinite wisdom of their trusted travel adviser, perhaps Google-based for example, means that a one-stop global consumer could self-connect from city pairs such as São Paulo to Bombay via Casablanca within the operation of an LCC – in itself a connecting city pair that is possible today in a more traditional operating model, but in a low-cost type model with the cost advantages of a single-aisle jet and perhaps a better fit of capacity to demand that may just be pretty disruptive to what happens today.

Ultimately, we can all only second-guess the scope for further disruptive behavior in the industry over the next decade and further afield to 2035 and beyond. History is frequently a useful pointer, although equally fails to truly factor in the pace of change and innovation that we see in so many industries today.

The only certainty is perhaps that the success of the aviation sector and its ability to change, embrace innovation and bring communities together will inevitably bring levels of disruption and competition that will only benefit all. Waiting until 2035 and beyond to see the levels of all that change may in fact be the interesting part.

Table 10.2 City Pair Distances in Nautical Miles

From	To	Nautical Miles
London	Mexico	4,825
London	San Francisco	4,671
San Francisco	Tokyo	4,337
Bogota	Madrid	4,337
Casablanca	Bombay	4,325
Sydney	Tokyo	4,212
Sao Paulo	Casablanca	4,075
Perth	Bombay	3,931
Bombay	London	3,888
Tokyo	Bombay	3,640

Source: Great Circle Mapper, December 2015.

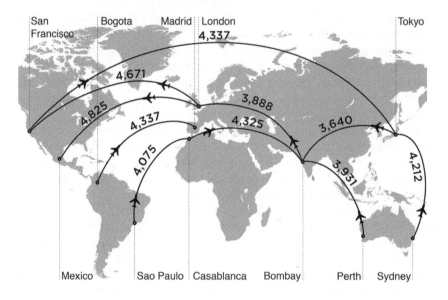

Figure 10.5 City Pair Distances in Nautical Miles (source: Great Circle Mapper, December 2015).

Notes

1 Based on November 2015 prices.
2 IATA 2015 Passenger Demand Forecast.
3 IATA Passenger Forecast, October 2014.
4 Boeing Aircraft Orders, November 2015.
5 Airbus Aircraft Orders, November 2015.
6 Airbus Global Market Forecast 2015.
7 OAG Schedules Analyser Analysis, December 2015.

THE UNDER-APPRECIATED IMPORTANCE OF HUBS AS DISRUPTORS

Peeter Kivestu
Transportation and Logistics Industry Consultant
Teradata

Hubs Matter

It's (Sometimes) Hard to Get There From Here

Transportation has always been about getting there. That hasn't always been easy. Two thousand years ago a Chinese emperor standardized the width of the axle, so that a consistent roadway network would make it easier to connect centers of commerce. Two hundred years ago industrialists raced to connect North America by a network of steel rail. One hundred years ago Juan Trippe was creating "airport infrastructure" so as to connect the globe by air.

All these events transformed transportation, and there have been a steady stream even since then. But if we ask, is it easy to get there now, the answer might not be straightforward.

Sometimes it's still hard to get there because the infrastructure is still not there. Or because of distance and aircraft capabilities; or the lack of population; or regulatory boundaries, the list goes on.

Sometimes it is not just about the physical connection, it is the time of day, the number of frequencies, the length of the trip, the price, and so forth.

How often do you get a trip that has most of those exactly the way you want it? How often do you find that your choice is affected by the presence of a hub?

Hubs in transportation are not new, as illustrated by the comment "all roads lead to Rome" or the "French railroad metric," a concept used by set theory mathematicians (to get from anywhere to anywhere requires a pathway through Paris).

Is there something special about hubs? How would we know? What will come next?

Hubs Are Natural in Network Enterprises

To see the power of hubs as a transformative force, let's start by understanding hub formation. Take a close look at what changed (and how quickly) in the airline industry after government controls were lifted in the late 1970s.

The top half in Figure 10.6 is a much simplified picture of how the airline industry looked prior to deregulation, and the bottom a similar image of hub-and-spoke structure that emerged even only two years into deregulation (and has grown more visible ever since). Why did that happen?

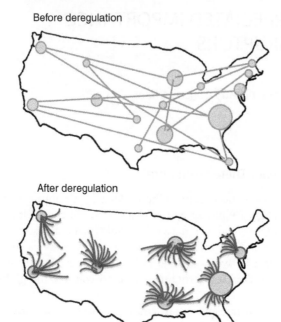

Figure 10.6 US Airline Domestic Route Structures.

Some years ago futurist Stan Davis said: "if you want to understand new business, you must understand new technology, and if you want to understand new technology you need to understand new science – new understanding of the very ways the world works." It turns out that the emergence of hubs has a lot to do with new science, specifically the new sciences of complexity.

Out of the sciences of complexity has emerged understanding that not all networks are created equal. While there are rich data here, one of the best ways to illustrate it is a famous experiment conducted in the 1960s by Harvard Professor Stanley Milgram.

Professor Milgram's experiment subsequently became known as six degrees of separation. It's the idea that any two people on earth are separated by just six intermediate links. In the experiment Prof. Milgram handed a large number of identical letters to random people in one part of the USA, asking them to forward the letters to anybody they knew, but with the objective of having the recipient re-forward the letter to someone they knew, in such a way that the letters would eventually end up with a certain individual in Boston, whose address was not provided. When all was said and done, it turned out that it only took an average of six intermediate steps for a letter to get there. It was an astounding discovery, and is often related as a "small world" story.

We now have enough science to understand that this is no accident, that human activity has a natural order about it that makes six degrees of separation possible. The insight is that networks are not random. A random network is what the airline industry looked like prior to deregulation. You saw nodes scattered across the page and links connecting the nodes and no particular order to the picture.

If networks were random, six degrees of separation would not work. It turns out that there is an inevitable hub structure in human activity, and it is best illustrated if you look at any map of the internet.

The map of the internet has a highly visible set of nodes scattered across the globe. Scientists studying the six degrees of separation experiment have used such maps to prove that six degrees is remarkably close to the actual number of links that separates any two of us in the internet world.

So there is an inevitable hub structure to human activity, and the best way of putting it is, *you are going to have hubs in transportation whether you want it or not – the only question will be, where are the hubs that matter, and are they working for you?*

Great Hubs Must Be Built (Through Data)

Looking back at airline deregulation, it took less than two years for a type of hub-and-spoke structure to emerge. How exactly did that happen? I suggest that while hubs are natural phenomena, and will occur regardless of planned activity, it is the truly great hubs that grow to be much larger than their naturally occurring structure – and that is done by using data.

I was in the airlines in that era and I can tell you that this progression was not obvious nor was it easy; let me provide a simple example.

On the very first day of deregulation in 1978, Braniff Airways announced service to some 16 new cities – major US destinations everyone wanted to go to – in the largest single-day expansion in the history of the airline industry. Meanwhile American Airlines (AA), somewhat around the same general era, announced new service to 11 tiny cities, such as Lubbock and Shreveport.

Just a couple of years later Braniff was bankrupt, while AA went on to build in Dallas–Fort Worth what was arguably the first new mega-hub of the deregulated airline era. They went on to dominate the airline industry for the next 20 years.

I was at AA when that happened and I can tell you there was a lot of skepticism about how one could possibly make money by flying large jets to small cities just 200 miles from Dallas. But I can also say that I was part of the team that did the analysis and I know that the data clearly showed that this balance of new cities, integrated with an existing route structure, was going to be a huge winner and indeed it was.

In any strategy, balance is the answer; however, it's not magic, it's in the data. The numbers clearly show the first law of hubs – which is the exponential benefit of creating more physical connectivity. Big hubs are exponentially more effective than small hubs, and being data-driven is one way to find that balance.

FedEx was actually way ahead of its time in using data and data science to build hubs to achieve specific objectives, in their case, a guarantee of absolutely, positively overnight.

In a data-driven O&D strategy, it is not just about understanding the number of shipments, but increasingly about richer understanding of underlying behaviors, such as types of shipments, types of customers, willingness to pay and a lot more. As a hub grows it almost always becomes possible to expand the range of services. In the case of FedEx, they added a whole layer, a second day air service hub right on top of their primary overnight hub.

One of the questions that always comes up is why everything has to go through Memphis, and the answer is it doesn't. The way to think of it is that each link in a hub network affects the entire network. If you choose to overfly Memphis you're probably doing that to build up another hub elsewhere in the country. One imperative of a hub strategy is the ability to conceive and grow a network of hubs.

I don't have a picture of the FedEx hub strategy, but I can illustrate the equivalent strategy for Northwest Airlines. In the decade of the 1990s, I experienced firsthand a ten-year O&D data-driven hub network expansion strategy, as shown in Figure 10.7.

We first spent over two years considering that our hubs were in cities that were too small and in the wrong places, and looked instead to build new ones in bigger and better places.

That's when data-driven analytics had its day: we discovered that our hubs in Minneapolis (MSP) and Detroit (DTW) were both undersized by about 25 percent in number of flights relative to the available O&D demand.

In the process of fixing the undersized DTW hub, the data led us to realize that it was not about growing domestic business, but growing worldwide business was the real opportunity now.

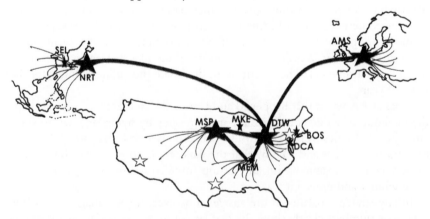

Figure 10.7 Northwest Airlines: Continuous Data-Driven Network Innovation.

That led to some remarkable next steps, because we had international hubs in Amsterdam (AMS) and Tokyo (NRT). It turns out that right-sizing DTW–AMS and DTW–NRT, and other markets that are called hub-to-hub markets, is essential to a successful multi-hub strategy.

In DTW–AMS, Northwest grew from a few services per week to five times per day over a ten-year period. While we don't have space to go into detail, such a ten times growth in capacity is no accident.

We also fixed the DTW–NRT connection. It is not that you could not fly DTW–NRT, because of course you could; you could also fly Boston–DTW–NRT, or you could fly DTW–NRT–Manila, but you could not do the double connection, Boston–DTW–NRT–Manila. Now you might wonder who would want to take such a double connection, but it turns out a lot of people did, and still do. It was one of the most successful company moves we made.

The purpose of describing these hub development scenarios is that while hubs are natural and are driven by concentrations of human activity, there are opportunities to strategically grow these hubs. By exploring the data, and complementary ways in which connections can be driven through the hub, it can help grow the vitality and strength of the hub. It's not magic, it's in having access to and using the available data. While it sounds relatively straightforward, it is much much harder to do than it seems.

Digital Hubs Matter More

Digital Hubs Are Not About Data

Physical hubs connect people, but the future will belong to transportation hubs that are increasingly a combination of the physical hub and the digital hub – insight that is emerging out of the fields of analytics and big data.

Hubs bring an enterprise closer together. While physical hubs bring people and freight shippers closer, connections between data bring the enterprise closer to the customer. Connections between data create new understanding – this is what we call analytics.

For example, the post-deregulation airline growth resulted in a phenomenal proliferation of physical hubs and flight connections. While these were all important, it was the airline reservations distribution networks that accelerated the growth by creating digital hubs of schedule/inventory data. These hubs greatly leveraged the physical airline hubs by dramatically improving accessibility to the available choices of flight connections.

However, it did not stop there. New *analytic* insights from the airline reservation systems emerged from the resulting data, and even though simple analytics, they nevertheless were of huge competitive impact. It turned out for example that how your flights were displayed relative to the competitors' flights mattered enormously. This one data-driven insight alone drove feverish follow-on analytics (and competitive posturing) in the early days of airline distribution systems.

The power of digital hubs is not only from what they do (connect data that are otherwise not connected) but also from what they enable (the creation of analytics), which are actionable competitive insights from the connected data.

Being data-driven is the use of ideas that emerge from this connected data. Data-driven is not just adding a little bit, or even a lot of data to some existing processes, but is actually letting the data reveal itself to you, suggesting new directions or uncovering new questions.

We would see a lot more impact of digital hubs across different industries if they just evolved naturally. But they don't. Just as we showed the challenges airlines faced in creating their great physical hubs, companies have many challenges in creating digital hubs.

It actually is a lot more challenging to build digital hubs, because the raw material of digital hubs is data. One of the challenges of using data is that it so easily changes form. For example, a passenger flies several flight legs on a roundtrip. During the trip, the customer data are captured many times: as a reservation, as a payment, as a boarding, as a flown coupon, as loyalty credit, as a revenue accounting transaction, and in passenger and flight performance statistics. And let's not forget changes that may have occurred along the way, or the effect of flight disruptions.

Each of these data is actually a copy, stored in various separate systems for the different business functions that need it. Each of the functions uses its own business rules to store only that part of the data that it needs. While this is easy to do, the result often looks like the left hand of Figure 10.8, with a crazy quilt of places where data comes together, but never in a way that is complete, and only to the extent needed to answer today's questions.

It is a mess. The way most data appears, you could call it a data swamp. A data swamp is land that is not firm enough to build on, and water that's not pure enough to drink. In short, it's unusable.

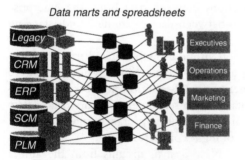

Data marts and spreadsheets

"Tell me how my department is doing
(but I do not need details from
other departments)"

[reporting]

Logical data warehouse

"Give me integrated, detail data
to help us all understand how
we affect each other"

[analytics]

Figure 10.8 Data Swamp or Data Lake?

Now imagine a CEO comes along who wants to focus on the customer experience. Possibly this is to provide refunds or points to all passengers who experienced a problem somewhere on their itinerary. Of all the passengers, which ones, through some fault of the airline, did not fly exactly according to the schedule they had booked (as of the morning of their departure)? To which system do you go to get the answer (remember to exclude those passengers who chose to make last-minute changes of their own accord, or for weather-related causes, etc.)?

There is not one system you can go to. The problem is one of connecting data. The data you need actually exist in more than one location and there are practical problems with how you might choose what to pick from what system. You probably will have a hard time answering the CEO's question. Certainly you could not do it accurately, or quickly.

The situation I describe is a real business situation (passengers who fly but for some reason are inconvenienced), for which a digital version does not exist (it could be captured this way, but usually isn't). The physical business is integrated (the passenger made it to their destination, although inconvenienced), but the digital version is in scattered pieces.

So a digital hub is about analytics – the result of integrated data. Without integration you have an incomplete digital picture of your business. Without integration you have the paradoxical situation where every department is doing its job, but the enterprise does not "comprehend" a situation that the customer understands almost intuitively. (This usually results in a poor experience.)

Digital Hubs Re-Define Profitability

Analytic insights into customers created by digital hubs can help the enterprise expand – sometimes well beyond its initial comfort zone. In one of the central lessons of the forces of disruption, Clayton Christensen[1] says that as products mature, competition moves upstream, moving toward new points of integration, and new sources of profits, as previous generations of products are commoditized.

This idea of integration as a source of profits leads us naturally away from more physical product innovation (where new integration gets harder and harder), toward data integration, where opportunities are getting richer and richer, partially because the available data are continually expanding.

So while digital hubs can help enterprises do existing business better, it is more likely that by combining, connecting, and deriving insights from customer data, these new integration points will lead to new sources of growth and profits. For one, digital hubs will connect elements of the enterprise that would not otherwise be easily connected. The enterprise will have data-driven insights into the direction that consumers are pulling them.

In the early days of deregulation American Airlines focused on making Dallas-Fort Worth a hub. Scarcely had they started this hub strategy, when the AAdvantage loyalty program was created, and almost immediately began to eclipse the physical hub in terms of importance and economic impact. But it didn't stop there. While AAdvantage was created to serve the airline, AAdvantage quickly evolved into a digital hub of affiliated travel partners.

Thirty years later the journey continues. At Qantas, their loyalty program is still undergoing transition, based on customer behavioral data. Like American, Qantas built a strong digital hub for its frequent flyer program. By cultivating analytics, the program has morphed into loyalty way beyond the airline, indeed way beyond the travel industry. Through analytics deeply explored through its digital hub, they discovered new directions for the program. Some of these directions were counterintuitive from an airline point of view, but data-driven from a solid digital representation of its customers' point of view.

In one case, they were examining the kinds of partners they should have. Could they go beyond the travel industry, more into day-to-day lifestyle partners, such as gourmet foods, wine, commodity purchases, and so forth? While the airline point of view suggested one choice of partners, the data point of view and the implicit preferences of customers were pointing to a broader set of partners.

Another area Qantas explored was the top loyalty tiers. Airlines often look to constrain the membership in the top-tier – a function of what the program is used for – e.g. rewarding highest tier members with upgrades, etc., which are all a limited quantity. But the data suggested they expand the top-tier eligibility, something that made sense as more and more of the redemptions came from outside of the core airline area.

Qantas says that while big data was key to these insights, it's still only the icing on the cake – without a strong foundation of an integrated understanding of the customer transactions, the impact of big data is harder to turn into big business value.

Digital Hubs Greatly Expand the Business

As big an opportunity (yet challenging) it is to create integrated digital hubs, they are about to grow more powerful, as new behavioral big data are emerging. Whereas in the past companies were limited to connecting various transactions data (bookings, tickets, upgrades, flight departures, delays, etc.), the growth is in behavioral data – what the customer sees, ponders, considers in the course of making a transaction.

Behavioral data are making visible – mostly due to internet, mobile web, internet of things, and related sources – what was previously invisible. Behavior data are fundamentally different from transactional data. It is much larger – from ten to one hundred times bigger – and reflects fast rates of accumulation and incredible variety of internet and mobile sources.

Not coincidentally, behavior data may have a very small signal to noise ratio. You may have to look at incredible volumes of customer behavior data to really understand customers' thought patterns, the context, and to connect behavior data with successful transactions.

These new data will greatly stretch the idea of a digital hub (Figure 10.9). While transaction data tend to be tightly linked across the enterprise, behavioral data may only be loosely connected. Knowing the customer's browse behavior before purchasing is potentially very useful, but is limited in what it is connected to – the booking dimension, and not much else. Of vast quantities of available clickstream data (e.g. pages viewed, offers scanned vs. clicked, entry and exit pages, length of sessions, devices used, etc.), these are only loosely coupled to the core bookings.

Behavior also includes a lot of data that may be almost unconnected to the enterprise, yet still important for providing context. For example, numerous social media sources outside the firm contain rich veins of customer feedback, user-generated content, and sentiment. While uncoupled from specific transactions, these data can be incredibly valuable to understanding customers.

Enterprises that want to put big data and low signal-to-noise sources to work cannot do so in a data swamp. They need to drain the swamp. They need to separate what they know for sure, which is "land" (their structured tightly coupled data warehouse) from their big data opportunities, which form the "lake" (the loosely coupled and uncoupled data).

The power of creating a data lake doesn't come just from a cost-effective way of managing volumes of big data. It comes rather from the creation of an

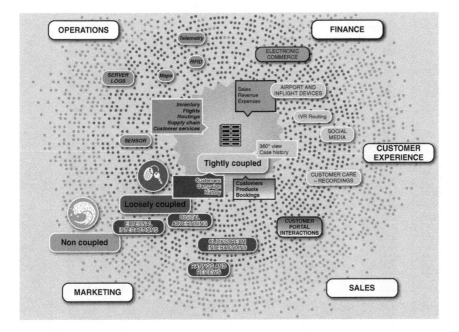

Figure 10.9 Challenge of Organizing for a Data-Enabled World.

architecture structured for extracting value from low signal to noise data. And for that you will need an expanded digital hub that has a unified data architecture as shown in Figure 10.10.

The broader purpose for having unified data architecture is enablement of deeper and more frequent business inquiry across widely varying data types. This is accomplished through a framework that provides for:

- *data acquisition*, "listening" for both real time and accumulating data history;
- *data engines*, landing places and connecting mechanisms for bringing together structured (relational) and unstructured (non-relational) data;
- *analytics*, a flexible connecting grid that can apply any of the wide array of available analytics tools from conventional to multi-genre analytics to the data; and
- *access to intelligence*, the means by which insights are shared and exploited across the enterprise.

While there is a natural tendency for data to be brought together across any enterprise in a variety of smaller digital hubs, the magnitude of the challenge has escalated with the emergence of big data. So for great digital hubs to coalesce, the connections within them need to be anticipated, supported, and grown. We showed that physical hubs, with the right focus, can be grown way beyond their natural size; and so also with great digital hubs.

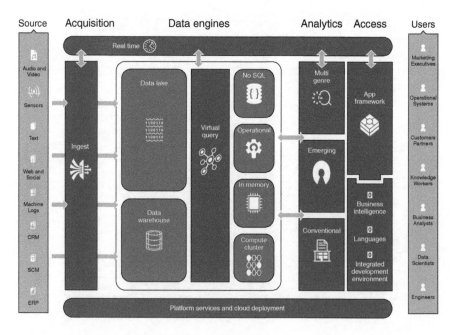

Figure 10.10 Architecture for Organizing a Digital Hub.

In a digital hub, the ultimate enablers of putting the data to work are people, users. With so much data accumulating so rapidly, we need new models of how to capture value from it. If we are to take data usage to a new level, we need to build tighter relationships between the people using this low signal to noise data, and more effective exchange of these ideas.

Great Digital Hubs Enable Connections between People

Recently a roadmap has been put forward called the Sentient Enterprise.[2] While the starting point for the Sentient Enterprise is an agile digital hub, covering the spectrum of tightly coupled, loosely coupled and uncoupled data, its future power comes from expected new frameworks for greater connectivity between people who are putting the data to work.

For example, today if someone discovers a new way to find value in big data, the method, the lines of software code, generally will not migrate much beyond the sphere of influence of the person coding it. In a Sentient Enterprise, however, there would be enablers of collaborative ideation, where the ideas represented in code could be passed on to others in the organization.

Already there are companies that can scan code (to find ways data are being parsed, used, and processed) and develop connectivity to help others in the organization who may just be beginning to think about how those kind of data may be used. It is a very fast way to pass on intelligence.

Another Sentient Enterprise concept leverages the concept of the app (as on mobile phones). In the future, a Sentient Enterprise may make it easy for a person who develops a short segment of useful code to create an app and put it out on a corporate framework, where it can be reused by others who have this need. Knowledge in this way is rapidly connected to others who need it.

You cannot build these kinds of thought-connecting hubs on a data swamp. The data have to be organized in a way that enables new kinds of idea-sharing methods to be established and to take root. The integrated architecture is what enables this.

As people are able to spend less time sifting through data, and more time creating content, knowledge spreads through framework enablers, like the app concept. There is not enough time or money to keep reinventing ways to get value out of big data – it has to be reused, and connected, and all readily accessible. That is what a hub does – build connectivity. And now collaboration on data-driven insights will become a new common language for creating value in the business.

Hubs are powerful, whether they are physical hubs or digital hubs. But with physical hubs, eventually there are limits to growth. Mathematicians call forces that limit growth "negative feedback loops." When each added resource adds less and less, when assets wear out or wear down, eventually growth tails off.

What is powerful about digital assets – such as digital hubs – is that they do not wear out, rather each insight actually grows more powerful on top of previous insights. It doesn't matter whether a data element is used once or all the time. When two pieces of data are integrated, the two do not change but in fact a new asset is created. When a useful piece of code created in one part of the organization is used to extract value for another purpose elsewhere, we have created an asset that grows more powerful each time it is used.

A Sentient Enterprise leverages these powerful "positive feedback loops," to become more closely attuned to its customers and business context. The Sentient Enterprise becomes one increasingly responsive to growing sets of opportunities in its digital environments.

User Experience (UX) Is the New Driver

UX Emerges from Digital Hubs Driven by Behavioral Understanding

Customer experience has emerged as a competitive force, largely because the behavioral data of customers from the internet, their mobile devices or their connected vehicles is readily available. While the customer experience is about a lot more than just what happens on the internet, the ready availability of behavioral information and the ability to tie it to transaction success or failure (e.g. purchases) has spawned entire new businesses.

The idea of the customer experience itself is not new. The concept was introduced some 20 years ago by Joe Pine,[3] arguably the father of the customer experience. At a time when only a handful of companies were creating revenues and profits from the customer experience, Pine foresaw that the experience would someday be a major trend, a natural evolution of the business cycle, which he described in something that looked very similar to Figure 10.11.

Pine foresaw the customer experience as a natural progression of business value generation. He saw that over time companies had progressed in the way they competed to create value. Having already moved out of the industrial era into a services era, the basis of competition for many companies was no longer the products they built but rather the additional services offered along with the products. In the case of airlines this has meant a range of ancillary services, loyalty programs, and various other added-value services. But even now we are nearing the end of the customer service cycle of the economy, and well into the fast-growth stage of the customer experience economy.

One interesting aspect of customer experience is that it cannot directly be measured. Products consumed/revenue created can be measured directly. Services consumed and revenue produced can be measured directly, but the customer experience cannot be measured directly. The customer experience is purely an integration of behavioral and transactional and other kinds of data that help us understand the customer frame of mind. And customer experience can only be measured via a digital hub, where you can connect the rich mix of data with its effect on customer valuation.[4]

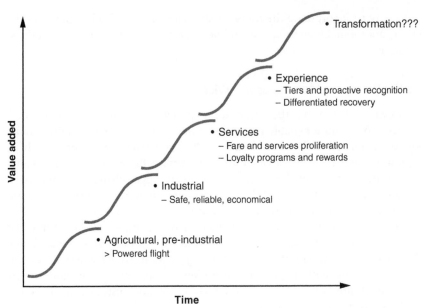

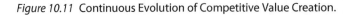

Figure 10.11 Continuous Evolution of Competitive Value Creation.

Although customer experience is still a new form of competition, we can already see the disruption it has created, because it is user experience that enables companies such as Airbnb and Uber to capture the hearts of consumers.

While the user experience is a lot more than digital, the effectiveness of the user experience at these companies is directly related to their digital hubs. Partially this is because the experience is a significant improvement over the status quo, and partially because these companies have introduced new experience elements and new dimensions with which they compete.

These new elements have been created by digital hubs. At Airbnb the user experience does not derive from the physical assets it controls (which are none) or the physical brand image at its locations (which does not exist) but rather from the ability to create digital connections between customers and providers. The user experience includes not just making a connection between customers and properties, but also connections with reviews from previous customers, and reviews from property owners on previous customers. The user experience is greatly affected by the level of trust created by an incredibly powerful digital hub.

And all this happened because digital hubs were carefully crafted not just around transactions (e.g. room-nights) but the associated behavior data (e.g. tell the property owner why you are traveling, etc.). The impact is similar at Uber. I once had the opportunity to ask someone familiar with Uber how it was they were able to take a very old-line business like the taxi business, and find a way to incorporate the mobile experience into it. Their reply: "it's the wrong question; Uber took the mobile experience and built a taxi business around it."

Are We Ready for Mobility as a Service?

Competition based on the customer experience in an increasingly app-enabled world will inevitably have a huge impact on how we consume transportation. Digital hubs that focus on the customer experience, such as Hipmunk, take the complexity out of displaying flight options and greatly expand the information they convey. And even bigger changes are underway as we come to think of "mobility as a service." It is a reflection of a world where the customer is increasingly in control.

Most transportation (increasingly even car ownership) is already purchased as a service today, so what do we really mean by "mobility as a service"? The idea rests on the premise that the customer just wants to get where they need to, on time, and with a great user experience – and choice of mode is just one derived dimension. Mobility as a service puts the customer at the center and looks for the best way to meet the need.

At the moment, we already purchase most mobility as a service, almost always after first picking a particular mode. But by providing a superior customer experience, "mobility as a service" may soon alter how we choose the mode of travel, by putting more focus on attributes that matter. Complexity can be taken out of modal choice by making "visible" elements such as convenience, time, cost, preferences, sustainability, or even non-traditional options. For example, when rail is a viable option, Hipmunk displays rail options side by side with air options, without the customer having to make a separate query.

More change is likely to impact multi-modal transportation. Multi-modal challenges include finding the right connections and in navigating last-mile situations (e.g. airport to city). In multi-modal situations, ease of making connections or reliability of last-mile transportation directly affects trip time variability, and is something with which traveler way-finding apps likely will help customers. Professor Mahmassani, Director of Northwestern University Transportation Center, suggests that reducing trip time variability is a dimension that customers value even more than trip time reduction.[5]

You can already see how software has transformed multi-modal transportation for transit connections, right there on your mobile phone. In the minds of transportation futurists, multi-modal trips such as bike-to-transit, Uber-to-transit, or shared car-to-transit, are not far behind. Multi-modal mobility as a service will continue to evolve as digital hubs increasingly capture a wider range of choices and better understand the underlying transactions and behaviors. This is not dissimilar to the way Airbnb and Uber have both introduced dramatic changes in the way we use lodging and taxi services.

As the multi-modal experience improves, single mode options, whether choosing your car or picking an air carrier for a trip, could be facing new competition. One could easily imagine a user experience that brings, for example, a European low-cost carrier that flies to the USA together with a search engine that creates connections to low-cost carriers onwards in the USA. A multi-modal app backed by a digital hub could dramatically alter the variability of the customer experience (of what we know today as an "interline connection"), create new sources of value, lead to emergence of new transportation providers, and expand effectiveness of the transportation ecosystem.

In his vision for the continued evolution of the drivers of competitive value growth, Pine asked the question, so what will come after the era of the customer experience? When competitive forces have leveled the playing field around the customer experience economy – what will enterprises be moving toward next?

Pine suggested that the "experience" is only a stepping stone toward a fuller realization of human potential. As we move from consuming products to services to experiences, a next level may appear in enabling human transformation. Pine argues that no one goes to the gym for the experience, nor students to school for the experience of exams. They all go for the promise and potential for transformation.

By stewarding naturally occurring hubs of human activity, by putting a focus on growing digital hubs to enable a world both physically and humanly connected – we can embrace a world that leads to open-ended expansion of human endeavor – something that Pine called the next era of human transformation.

Transportation is changing. "Getting there from here" has yielded to "mobility" and is accelerating toward "smart cities" and beyond. By driving growth of connectivity, hubs make a powerful impact on and accelerate the value growth in our transportation ecosystem.

Transformation of human activity has always occurred when people have been brought together. When we enable the development of both physical and digital hubs, we enable a level of connectivity where human transformation can really take place. That would be way beyond disruptive.

Notes

1 Christensen, Clayton, "Skate to where the money will be," *Harvard Business Review*, November 2001.
2 Ratzesberger, O. and Sawhney, M., "Sentient Enterprise: listen to data, sense micro-trends & make autonomous decisions." Video.
3 Unpublished presentation, Joe Pine at Teradata Partners.
4 Kivestu, Peeter "Leveling up on loyalty," Teradata white paper.
5 Mahmassani, Hani, "OpEd: express rail to/from O'Hare benefits region," *Chicago Business*, August 13, 2011.

THE DIGITAL AIRLINE: FROM DIGITAL STRATEGY TO AIRLINE STRATEGY

Dirk-Jan Koops
Managing Director Airline Industry
Accenture

Robert Engelen
Senior Manager Airline Industry
Accenture

More often than not, when people think of "digital" in the context of airlines, it's websites, customer apps, and e-commerce that spring to mind. But the reality goes much deeper. The evolution of digital technologies is starting to transform the way airlines fundamentally operate and organize their businesses. This development is irreversible and accelerating. In the next decade, winners and losers in the industry will be largely determined by their ability to understand and capitalize on digital opportunities.

Opportunity: Personalizing the Travel Journey

It today's world, the value of using customer data in analytics is undisputed. Customers expect consistent, relevant, and personal treatment.

The airline industry always had plenty of customer data, but most of it was used for operational reasons rather than to the customers' benefit.

The growth of digital customer interactions through websites and apps now provides additional data points on customer behavior.

With the cost of data storage continuously declining, airlines have an unprecedented opportunity to store and analyze vast amounts of customer data from internal as well as external sources and use these to create offers and personalize the customer experience. Leading airlines are working on exactly that, leaning heavily on their customer databases, with a prominent role for the frequent flyers.

However, for many carriers the overwhelming majority of their customers are actually infrequent flyers. Examination conducted by Accenture at one large European network carrier revealed that almost half of all frequent flyer program members appeared to be one-time flyers (or at least have less than one transaction in average over a three-year period). Outside the frequent flyer population, these statistics are even more dramatic. Recently, American Airlines revealed that 87 percent of customers travel one time per year or less on the airline, representing over half of its revenues (American Airlines 2015 Q3 Earnings Call transcript).

For these infrequent flyers, airlines have little or no customer data in their databases. And the situation is similar for other customer groups. With the economic outlook looking bright in emerging markets, the industry is anticipating more airline trips (Figure 10.12). As wealth distribution changes, we believe many of these trips will likely be taken by new passengers that were not able to afford air travel before. Research by Airbus and IHS Economics shows that wealth is becoming more evenly distributed globally. Twenty years ago, 70 percent of the World's population represented less than 10 percent of the global wealth. This has evolved to around 20 percent currently and is expected to reach more than 30 percent over the next 20 years (Airbus Global Market Forecast 2015).

In addition, we observe some major carriers, such as the big three in the Middle East, introducing newly created capacity at scale, deployed on new routes. This capacity, to a large extent, will be filled with first-time flyers that are initially unknown to the carriers involved.

In summary, we see that low customer interaction frequency and the advent of new (first-time) travelers presents a challenge for airlines in attaining a 360-degree view of each customer.

But is that really an issue? Not necessarily. Airlines have as many opportunities as those in other industries to provide every customer with a personalized experience. In addition to collecting and applying insights from the customer database, airlines can capitalize on the real-time insights they have in the travel process of all of their passengers, by constantly managing the customer dialogue. During the customer journey, the airline continuously has an opportunity to interact with customers on either commercial or operational matters. The type and timing of messages and offers can be determined by the airline's real-time insights into factors like: In what stage of the travel process is the passenger? Is he/she traveling alone or with others? On business or vacation? But also by situational factors such as disruptions. Sending a special offer to someone who is still waiting for a missing bag may be counterproductive.

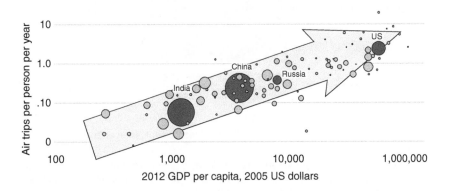

Figure 10.12 Propensity to Travel Increases with Income (source: Boeing Current Market Outlook 2015–2034).

Digital capabilities such as real-time analytics can help the airline continuously adapt the customer dialogue exactly to passengers' needs to maintain a high level of personalization and relevancy, all the time.

Opportunity: Improving the Physical Product and Service

In the last decade, a new generation of "disrupting" companies has emerged, powered by digital capabilities. It seems they are particularly attracted to the travel industry, with players like Airbnb and Uber as the most prominent examples. To the frustration of airlines, they do not carry the legacy of industry standards nor the cost of assets, which better enables them to really design their services around the customer.

Thanks to new players such as Expedia, Priceline, Hipmunk, and Google Flights, most customers no longer need a travel professional to find and compare the best air fares and schedules. The passenger airline markets have become extremely transparent.

There is no doubt that, together with global economic developments, increased transparency has contributed to the customer's focus on price as the deciding factor for airline choice more than ever before. As an example, 59 percent of international travelers in the United States cite low price as an important factor when selecting an airline (research conducted by Kelton, commissioned by Norwegian Air Shuttle – see Figure 10.13). We even observed this trend in the traditionally less price-sensitive business travel market. As Mary Bastrentaz, Managing Director, Global Travel & Events at

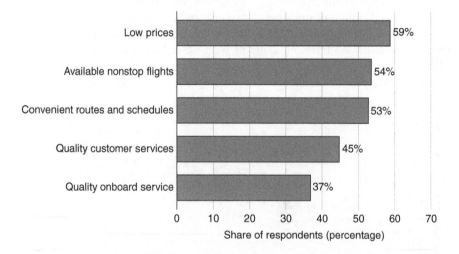

Figure 10.13 Most Important Factors when Selecting an Airline Among International Travelers in the United States (source: research conducted by Kelton, commissioned by Norwegian Air Shuttle).

Note
1,006 respondents, aged 18 years and over.

Accenture points out, "many companies are working to reduce the significant costs they incur supporting employee travel."

Aggressive price competition is a reality, with airlines following each other closely. Especially on short-haul routes, competition between low-cost carriers (LCCs) and network carriers became fierce and their products started to converge, with full-service carriers dropping service elements in order to be able to be more competitive. This reinforced the idea that air travel is a commodity.

Over time, many markets seem to be heading toward a turning point, starting with short haul. Absolute differences in fares between carriers are becoming increasingly insignificant. As a result, schedule, service, and the physical product will gain importance again as competitive factors. In these situations, price effectively becomes the new commodity factor. Some leading LCCs already recognize this trend and are investing heavily to improve the customer experience. In such a context, customers' brand preference will be key.

To help create brand preference, airlines have an opportunity that new digital and disruptive industry players do not. Airlines control the physical product and service experience and can turn what seems like a comparative burden in terms of overheads to their competitive advantage. They can create a lasting impression and make up for mistakes or irritations through personal and digital interaction with the customers – to some extent at the airport, but certainly also in the air. Airlines should maximize this opportunity by focusing on improving the physical product and providing seamless service.

Connecting with different parties to deliver a seamless handover of services will be key. Unfortunately, customers do not make sharp distinctions among all of the service providers enabling their journey; they tend to regard entities such as airports and feeders (other airlines or other forms of transportation) as being part of their overall airline experience. Better integration among partners could help to ease this problem. Airlines can use digital capabilities to improve the customer experience, from booking a flight, all the way through the day of departure and onboard. They will need to act in real time and at scale to deliver what is promised to (and expected by) the customer and thus need to bi-directionally connect with ecosystem partners.

Opportunity: Creating Open Platforms

Many LCCs around the globe have proven that airlines can stimulate demand for air travel and create markets where they did not exist before. However, most airline customers base their travel plans on a possible destination and reason for traveling. They are not flying just for the sake of flying, they are traveling because they want to go somewhere. And an airline is just a link in the chain.

As mentioned before, most customers are not very intimate with airlines. Companies like Google, Facebook, Apple, Microsoft, and Amazon – significant brands in customers' day-to-day lives – know much more about them than airlines could. Based on their analytics, they are able to figure out the airline customers' travel intentions long before the airline does. In addition, where in the past customers relied on a limited number of travel arrangers, today they have access to a fragmented array of specialized communities that suggest travel options, ranging from religious groups to sports communities and professional associations.

These developments make it a bigger challenge than ever for airlines to reach potential customers in time to secure their business. To face this challenge, airlines need to be an active partner in the new travel ecosystem. They need to be where the customer is: at the online travel agencies (OTAs), in the domain of mega-companies like Google and Apple, and in specialized communities such as networks for diving and golf. This is where customers should be able to see the personalized offers and bundles that airlines want them to see.

The only way for airlines to do this is to open up their platforms and look for connections to others who are also serving their customers. Especially in the "inspire" and "search" steps of the travel process, we see a mix of competition and partnership with these mega-companies and communities that individual airlines will not be able to fully control.

By joining others in the travel ecosystem with interfaces that are opened up to the public environment (open APIs) and other digital developments, airlines can continue to play a meaningful role and indeed benefit from the opportunities offered by new business models, rather than trying to fight them.

Opportunity: Breaking Down Silos for the Benefit of the Customer

Airlines talk about customer experience design and come up with excellent, creative ideas to please the customer. While much appreciated, it is important to remember passengers' priorities. What is the value of receiving your favorite welcome cocktail, mixed exactly to your liking, while your bag is not on the flight with you, or the plane is delayed because line maintenance was informed late of a defect?

Today's world is real-time, and passengers are digitally connected, sometimes more so than the airlines. If a flight is delayed, they will find out about it. In many cases they have discovered the delay before the staff, which is simply unacceptable for everyone. An aircraft incident in 2015 highlights the issue: Pictures and videos of the aircraft involved were all over Facebook and Twitter, where the airline itself was still promoting new services without any mention of the incident.

Even with digital tools at hand, an airline needs to put in place the right structure and processes to make the collaboration across the company work. It is the collaboration between all airline functions that truly shapes the customer experience. Traditionally, most airlines have had trouble aligning the activities between organizational silos. Digital technology offers solutions that did not exist before. By exchanging information, comparing data, and real-time interactions and analytics, the whole airline can work together in the interest of the customer and stay in sync. Flight operations, ground operations, maintenance, marketing, sales, customer service, and loyalty are looking at the same information and working collaboratively towards the same goals. Because finally, they can.

The latest digital tools are great and can certainly transform the customer experience, but becoming a digital airline involves taking a more comprehensive view of digital: improving communications throughout the ecosystem and integrating business processes with technology. If done well, airlines can attain the much needed agility. Going forward, digital will be an absolute necessity to keep complexity (and thus cost) under control.

In reality, this approach requires much more than only open APIs; it requires a robust but flexible platform to hook up customers, crews and staff, agents and partners.

Opportunity: Introducing New Business Models, Technology Models, and Operating Models

Becoming a digital airline requires more than equipping ground staff with iPads, striving for "Likes" on Facebook, putting more of the organization's data in the cloud, or providing mobile access to electronic versions of paper documents. Even though these kinds of moves can be crucial steps on the road to becoming truly digital, airlines tend to hold on to their existing ways of working, by automating some processes still supported by paper documents or their electronic equivalents. A good example is the e-ticket that in its essence is a non-printed version of the flight ticket document that it succeeded.

A digital airline is not shaped solely by the next wave of automation. It delivers growth and results by creating unique customer experiences through new combinations of information, business resources, and digital technologies. They produce innovative outcomes designed to meet the new expectations of the digital world. Digitizing business processes results in more significant efficiency and productivity gains by rethinking processes, changing them or even removing them entirely. To achieve this, not just the technology model, but also the business model and operating model need to change.

Imagine that a customer's seat cannot recline anymore due to a technical malfunction: by using digital devices and technology, empowered crew could offer on-the-spot compensation for the inconvenience, thus saving the customer the trouble of filing a complaint that needs to be processed in the back office later. This directly impacts the customer experience and satisfaction. At the same time, the customer record is updated with incident details and the type of compensation received. Customer-facing staff at all passenger touchpoints will be able to retrieve details of the incident as needed.

While the crew makes the entry through their mobile device, the relevant information about the incident also feeds into the maintenance planning and scheduling system, sending a notification to an engineer's digital device with an update of his daily plan. Being able to repair the seat during turnaround saves the engineer precious minutes, contributing to on-time performance, the most important key performance indicator for any airline.

Airlines can even take this a step further. Tapping into the Internet of Things, the seat itself could identify that its recline function does not work according to specification and so trigger an alert. Predictive analytics could even flag a possible issue with this specific seat before it occurs, based on variables like usage patterns. The engineer can 3D-print the parts where and when needed. All of this would directly impact the nature of the work and cooperation for the crew, the back office and the service engineers. The crew and engineers would be able to use the same digital devices to access other functions, such as their self-service HR environment, again helping to reduce the (administrative) workload at head office.

As airlines become digital businesses, the readiness of the workforce must become a priority. From new roles, different ways of organizing work and changing work practices there are significant opportunities to humanize work. Some employees' jobs would change from managing a process (checking in bags behind a desk) to managing a customer's experience (helping passengers in the terminal), affecting the employee experience too. Digital devices and technologies can enable better collaboration across the organization, where information is shared in real time.

This development will require airlines to re-evaluate the types of skills they are likely to need, and be ready to reskill and retool their existing workforce. As some jobs might be eliminated by changes in business process or sourcing, there will be new opportunities to transfer employees to more value-adding activities or support them in finding a new job.

There is no aspect in an airline that will not be directly or indirectly touched by digital innovation. Airlines will have no choice but to reinvent themselves. Where "digital" as such is a topic today, this will change. Digital strategy will eventually disappear and become airline strategy. For airline executives, this is a fantastic opportunity to finally start breaking down some of the legacy that this industry has been carrying around for too long.

WHAT CAN AN INDUSTRY, LIKE AIR TRAVEL, DO TO EMBRACE CHANGE AND TRANSFORM ITSELF?

Eric Leopold
Director, Transformation, Financial & Distribution Services
International Air Transport Association

In June 2004 leaders of many of the world's leading airlines joined together at the Annual General Meeting of the International Air Transport Association (IATA). Gathered in the ballroom of the Shangri-La hotel in Singapore, the members of IATA contemplated the need to make some radical changes across the industry. It would have to be a collective initiative owing to the interconnected networks that this industry had developed over the past 60-some years. When a change would affect approximately 500 airlines, 100,000 travel agents and 2,000 airports around the globe, only a coordinated effort could be successful, based on globally accepted standards and a partnership approach with other stakeholders.

In June 2004 those airline leaders decided to launch a global change program focused on improving the customer experience and reducing industry costs. Called Simplifying the Business (StB), the program has resulted in dramatic efficiency improvements and cost savings for the industry and less-complicated processes for air travelers and other stakeholders. This contribution describes the lessons learned after ten years of StB and ends by asking you, a freshly appointed airline leader attending the IATA AGM for the first time, what changes you would expect in 2016 and beyond.

2004–9, Wave 1: The Electronic Wave, Automating Complexity

The StB program kicked-off in 2004. At that time, the burning platform for change was:

- growing low-cost competition
- rising fuel prices
- post-9/11 crisis
- online sales/e-commerce

Low-cost carriers (LCCs) were created more recently than legacy flag carriers and have several cost advantages related to their business models. To highlight only one difference relevant to the StB program, LCCs are usually ticketless, meaning that once a reservation is made and paid, they don't issue a ticket. Legacy carriers issue tickets for various reasons: interlining, ground handling, revenue accounting, etc. Remember when an agent at the gate used to check that you had a paper coupon inside your boarding pass? Most LCCs don't do interline and never issued any tickets, which saves them money and reduces complexity.

Fuel prices in 2004 were roughly $45[1] per barrel. Fuel prices impact airline profitability because they represented up to 17 percent of an airline's costs. Their volatility is a challenge and requires airlines to have hedging strategies. High fuel costs drive necessary attention to ways to reduce non-fuel costs and the development of a program like StB.

The 9/11 attacks and subsequent terrorist plots had a major impact on air travel. One effect, for example, was the increase in security measures at the airport which resulted in long queues at security, new restrictions on carry-on items such as liquids and the emergence of the "hassle factor" as a disincentive to air travel. Short-haul traffic in particular took a beating as ground transportation became an attractive alternative in view of the time and unpredictability of the airport security process. As security requirements continued to expand with each new threat or plot, it became clear that the system would not be able to cope with rising traffic numbers absent a change to how security was managed,

The early 2000s also saw the rise of online sales and e-commerce. As the internet became a major channel for ticket sales, the customer experience became more self-service. Especially in markets with a high-cost workforce, simple tasks like issuing a boarding pass were transferred to kiosks.

In this context the StB program was kicked-off with the following key projects:[2]

- e-ticket (from paper ticket)
- 2D boarding pass (from mag-stripe boarding passes)
- common-use kiosks (from check-in desks)
- RFID bag tags (from barcoded bag tags)
- EMD[3] (from paper miscellaneous documents)

E-tickets already existed in 2004. IATA had a standard in the books since 1996. However, only 10 percent of all tickets were electronic at the industry level. Going to 100 percent e-tickets had benefits for passengers, who no longer needed to bother with carrying a paper document, and for airlines, which could avoid the costs of printing, storing, securing and handling paper documents. For the first time, at the direction of our membership, IATA set a deadline by when the industry would fully comply with a standard: by May 2008[4] IATA would only process e-tickets in its Billing and Settlement Plans (BSP).[5] The project was indeed successfully completed on June 1, 2008.

Online boarding passes already existed in 2004 as some airlines enabled customers to check-in online and print their boarding pass containing a barcode. At the time the standard for boarding passes required data to be encoded in a magnetic stripe, which meant dedicated paper stock, printing and reading equipment, which eliminated the possibility of home printing. The barcode is simply the technology to make a paper document machine-readable, which increases the throughput and reduces reading errors. With an industry-agreed deadline of 100 percent barcoded boarding passes by the end of 2010, the next five years were spent developing a standard and working with airports and airlines to upgrade systems and hardware for the change.

Common-use self-service (CUSS) kiosks were introduced to simplify passengers' access to airline services and to reduce industry costs. With the proliferation of airline-specific kiosks in shared terminals passengers ended-up going from one kiosk to another until they found the one serving the right airline, which made no sense. At the same time every airline had to bear the maintenance and support cost for their respective kiosks. The industry standard enabled airlines to run their respective check-in applications on shared kiosks. Passengers could find any airline on any kiosk and maintenance and support costs went down. After four years 135 airports had CUSS kiosks; this achievement was considered a satisfactory critical mass.

When the RFID project was launched the first step was, as with other projects, to assess the cost benefits at industry level. Unlike for the other projects, the numbers did not add up. The investment in new infrastructure across the network of global airports could not be justified, or offset, by the savings in operations or by the increased efficiencies in baggage tracking. Eventually the project was re-launched as the Baggage Improvement Program, which focused on reducing baggage mishandling by 50 percent compared to 2008, regardless of the technology used.

When the e-ticket project was launched, airlines knew that there were other paper documents in the passenger process, for miscellaneous purchases, like excess baggage fees. During the e-ticket project a new standard was developed to support all miscellaneous orders in one electronic document, called EMD. At the end of the e-ticket project the EMD project was launched. The deadline for 100 percent EMD was the end of 2013. This project was successfully completed and in 2014 all the paper documents, tickets or miscellaneous orders were removed from industry systems.

From this first wave of projects we learned a few lessons about:

- leadership from the top
- setting 100 percent targets
- driving industry change

Leadership from the top means that the IATA Board of Governors proposed targets and deadlines and that the Annual General Meeting endorsed them. Of course this endorsement requires serious stakeholder engagement. But once the approval is given, the implementation can take place in a very structured way, almost like in the closed environment of an individual company. Many obstacles can be overcome through the creation of globally accepted standards, developed with industry expertise and know-how, although ultimately every investment and implementation is up to each individual airline or partner.

Setting 100 percent targets gave more than a direction to the industry: it gave it a pace and a momentum. In the absence of 100 percent targets the risk is always that some airlines will wait and see, some vendors will delay investments until a critical mass is reached, some will notice the "chicken and egg" dilemma and the new standard does not get traction. The power of 100 percent combined with an agreed-upon deadline gives a sense of urgency and enables business cases to be approved based on a reasonable forecast that the standard will be implemented across the industry.

In 2010 IATA considered the achievements so far and the need to continue driving change through the StB program. Figure 10.14 shows a summary of the Waves of Change.

2010–15, Wave 2: The Digital Transformation Wave

In 2010 the burning platform had evolved, although with some similarities with 2004:

- low-cost competition (again)
- even higher fuel prices
- Global Financial Crisis of 2008–9.

In 2010 full-service carriers had made progress with cost efficiencies, but the gap with the LCCs remained. Some full-service carriers tried to run both operations (low-cost and full-service) in parallel with only limited success. Besides operational costs, LCCs had lower distribution costs, owing to having the majority of sales come through their own websites.

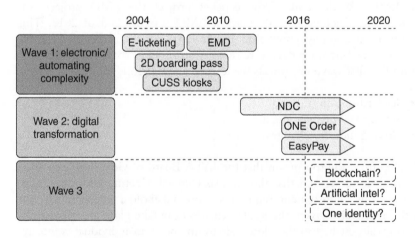

Figure 10.14 Waves of Change.

Fuel prices had doubled, and in 2010 represented 28 percent of operating expenses. Although the industry had returned to profit, margins remained thin.

The gap with LCCs and the pressure on costs remained the priority; the StB program resumed with a series of new projects[6] focused on distribution and payment:

- new distribution capability (NDC)
- enhanced order delivery and accounting (ONE Order)
- new payment method (EasyPay[7]).

NDC is a new standard enabling the distribution of airline content to travel agents and aggregators. NDC is similar to other StB projects in the sense that a standard was developed and implemented across the industry. This standard enables doing something consistently and cost-effectively among many players. Before NDC was developed, many airlines (full-service and low-cost) had their own connectivity to travel agents using XML[8] or had established an XML-connectivity with a GDS.[9] However, each airline or GDS had its own version or format. NDC provided a technical standard for a common interface that all airlines, regardless of their business model, could use to sell all their products through travel agents.

ONE Order leverages the concept of Order created by NDC. Once an order is created, who needs three separate documents (ticket, EMD and PNR) to fulfill the order effectively? ONE Order proposes to store all the relevant data in one document with the relevant controls in place. This concept has the potential to streamline airline financial back-office processes and airport handling systems.

EasyPay, a part of the NewGen ISS initiative, aims to update the ways in which travel agents can participate in the industry settlement systems managed by IATA by implementing an electronic wallet facility for air travel purchases. Travel agents will be able to use the wallet to pay and confirm the orders made. As such EasyPay will represent a third method of payment after cash (bank transfer) and credit cards.

Those three streams, referred to as "shop–order–pay" converge into the modernization of the air travel retailing capability.

This second wave offers some additional lessons:

- driving business transformation
- involving the entire value chain
- defining a vision that challenges the status quo (things that existed for 50 years).

Driving business transformation requires engaging experts who understand the business in various domains. The teams leading the transformation projects are multi-disciplinary by nature and design: business expertise, IT knowledge, standard development, communications, legal, advocacy and program management.

Involving the entire value chain is critical when the transformation has such a major impact on other stakeholders whose processes and systems may also change. Those initiatives led to the creation of new stakeholder forums that did not exist before and that will be essential in successfully driving future initiatives.

Defining a vision that challenges the status quo is the catalyst for transformational change, as opposed to evolution. Where backward compatibility guarantees stability in the evolution of systems, disruptive change enables leaps in cost efficiency.

As we're progressing with this second phase, or wave, of change, and look back at what we've learned in the first two phases, we are asking ourselves whether a third phase, or wave, is needed and, if so, what success could look like in 2020.

2016–20: A Wave 3?

What does the burning platform look like in 2016?

- Fuel prices are at an 11-year low, back at the 2005 level. Airline profitability is at an all-time high, although just covering the cost of capital. This performance highlights the better health of the industry achieved over 12 years, for similar fuel prices.
- The worst of the financial crisis in the eurozone was avoided. China's growth is slowing but still robust. The economic factors are not the key drivers of change.
- Legacy carriers are embracing the methods of low cost carriers to some extent.
- The old drivers of the first two waves are not relevant in 2016.
- Disruptions may come from outside the industry, e.g. Uber in ground transport, Airbnb in hotels, Blockchain in payment. Silicon Valley may be where change is coming from.

What key projects are relevant in this new wave?

- First, of course, we need to complete the delivery of the previous wave.
- Then we should rethink how standards are developed and implemented. Think "agile," "developer portal," "innovation fund," "ecosystem." The next standards will not take ten years from inception to full implementation – maybe one year, maybe one month. Hackathons show us that it is possible to increase speed by an order of magnitude.
- Eventually we need to rethink how the industry can cooperate to transform itself and how IATA can add value in driving transformation, beyond standards, through data, tools and infrastructure.

What will be the key success factors in this new wave?

- We've learned the lessons of the first two waves. They will apply in this third wave.
- Transform the way we set standards so that the industry can further transform itself.
- The industry needs to embrace the digital transformation mindset – "ship fast, fail fast, iterate."

The Next Disruptive Change

In this case study, imagine that you are an airline leader contemplating the track record of change in your industry, the game changers happening in other industries, the obvious challenges of driving change in your own organization and the obvious need to stay ahead of competition and to improve your results. You are sitting in an IATA meeting where the presentation of the next disruptive change is about to start. You are asking yourself what should be your contribution to the next decade of changes in the airline industry.

Vision: 2016 ideas for the perfect trip – from inspiration in search to home bag delivery:

- inspiration search using natural language;
- artificial intelligence suggesting trip plans before you actually start searching;
- mobile travel adviser or partner offering guidance during the trip;
- last-minute delivery of personal items by drone before take-off;
- all identity checks performed seamlessly using a sensor in the traveler's watch and associated biometrics;
- virtual reality experience during the flight;
- multiple services completed online during the flight, e.g. confirmation of ground transport, completion of immigration forms;
- ancillary services provided onboard and consumption updated in real time on the traveler's watch, e.g. deluxe meal served;
- arrival services by drone leading to a self-driving electric car parked outside the terminal.

Note: this list is not complete. The "Simplifying the Business think tank" captures ideas and transforms them into change programs.

Moreover, there are illustrations of digital transformation in other industries.

- Express shipping: how e-commerce boosted the need for express shipping or delivery, how 3D printing may reduce the need for shipping, how shipping centers may become 3D printing centers.

- Cars: how connected car networks (Uber, Lyft) reduce the need for car ownership in cities, how self-driving cars remove the need for drivers.
- Tennis: how a connected racquet and its mobile app become a coach.
- Hospitality: how connected homeowner networks (Airbnb) compete with established hotels and vacation rentals.
- Music: how digital music on CDs replaced vinyl, how digital music downloads replaced music stores, how streamed digital music replaced downloads.
- Publishing: how online news on tablets replaced print newspapers.

Notes

1 IATA website: fuel price analysis.
2 StB originally included a cargo project called "IATA e-freight." StB eventually focused on passengers and "IATA e-freight" became a program for cargo, with "e-AirWay Bill" its key project.
3 Electronic Miscellaneous Documents (EMD) followed the e-ticket project and was not part of the initial projects of 2004.
4 Originally the deadline was December 2007. It was delayed by five months to accommodate a smooth transition by all IATA members.
5 BSP is where IATA calculates the ticket sales of travel agents, sends them the bills, collects the money and settles the funds with the participating airlines.
6 Note that StB included other projects: Automated Baggage Rules, Fast Travel, Security Access and Egress, Checkpoint of the Future (became Smart Security). For a full list please refer to www.iata.org/stb.
7 Technically EasyPay is an IATA project that is not part of the StB program; however, it is presented in this case study because it matches the context and is relevant to the objective.
8 XML is a format to exchange data over the internet.
9 Global distribution system, like Amadeus, Sabre and Travelport. For example, since 2007 easyJet was selling through travel agents using an XML connection to Amadeus.

SMART AIRLINES GET CONNECTED: THE CASE FOR ON-BOARD CONNECTIVITY

Leo Mondale
President, Aviation
Inmarsat

A revolution is taking place in the airline industry.

This revolution concerns carriers and customers alike and is made possible by in-flight, high-speed internet connections. As airlines get connected, the customer has the full flexibility of the internet at his or her fingertips. Connectivity revolutionizes duty-free retail and consigns the traditional in-flight purchasing experience to the trash can. And for carriers, it is about getting one over the competition. Any way you look at it, broadband connectivity is seriously impacting air travel.

This revolution is made possible both by strong demand and much better supply. Passengers have a clear preference to remain connected during flight, having little understanding of why "in-flight" still often equals "offline." On the supply side, technology for onboard internet has made great strides over the last years, with increasing bandwidth, higher reliability and lower prices.

A few carriers have understood the signs of the times and have committed to broadband connectivity onboard their planes. These *"smart airlines"* have built their decision on a clear business case with significant revenue and cost benefits. They are developing a range of new services and products, drawing on cutting-edge technology. And they are adjusting their organization and processes to ensure a change of mindset.

The Case for Connectivity

In recent years the aviation industry has rather brashly talked up connectivity as the new standard. All major US airlines offer live TV and onboard internet, as do many major European and Asian airlines on their long-haul fleet. However, most current technology is anything but smart, utilizing slower air-to-ground connections or older-generation satellite technology.

The good news is that state-of-the-art satellite technology in combination with next-generation ground networks is now being introduced that seriously ups the ante and is proving truly disruptive to the airline industry. Connectivity speeds are on the increase, while the cost of bandwidth continues to fall. Those benefiting from innovative new products utilizing the new technology include first and foremost, as highlighted above, passengers, but obviously this will include aircrew and ground operations staff as well.

There are three areas where smart airlines will benefit from connectivity.

1 Ancillary Revenues

Most airlines depend on the sale of ancillary products to make a profit, with a wide range of goods in their portfolios. Many have gone on to de-bundle the travel experience to better target passengers' individual requirements, selling onboard catering or checked-in baggage separately from the ticket. Also, many airlines introduce new product ranges or sell travel services, hotels and rental cars on their online channels.

Onboard connectivity will open the floodgates to a whole new range of ancillary products. Based on management consulting research conducted in 2016 by industry experts and commissioned by Inmarsat, smart airlines will generate further profit from *ancillary revenues of 2–4 euros per passenger*, depending on their business model. This compares favorably to the 10–15 euro already generated by airlines selling other ancillary products, e.g. frequent traveler miles, onboard catering or checked-in baggage.

The 2–4 euro per passenger can be broken down into three distinct product groups. For starters, smart airlines will spotlight passengers based on their frequent flyer profile, destination or travel purpose. Via internet connection, passengers will have online access to promoted products during the flight, thus ensuring higher conversion of ancillary sales. Non-specific advertising, such as banners or exclusive sponsorship deals across the entire web portal lends itself well to this environment. Next in the pipeline is a range of destination services and products, such as excursions, tour guides or musicals and theater tickets. Many low-cost carriers (LCCs) already sell tickets for shuttle trains or buses onboard, but in-flight high-speed internet will allow a much wider offer, with immediate booking confirmation and real-time updates to prices and availability. But not least, airlines may of course want to continue to sell internet sessions, allowing passengers to access the internet from their own devices.

2 Cost Savings

Despite demonstrating sustainable growth, the airline business is characterized by volatile demand, fierce price competition and unstable, often low or negative margins. Many legacy carriers have undertaken large-scale cost reduction or restructuring programs. As a knock-on effect of oil prices peaking in 2008, many airlines have invested in new fuel-efficient aircraft and thoroughly reviewed their flight operations to reduce fuel burn.

In this environment onboard connectivity is one of the few significant levers left to airlines to further reduce operating costs. We believe smart airlines can save up to *2 percent of fuel costs* and *1 percent of maintenance costs*, simply by installing a range of new applications utilizing onboard internet. This is similar in effect to installing fuel-saving winglets.

This whole new dimension in connectivity will enable the use of future-generation electronic flight bags (EFBs) to process real-time weather and traffic updates during the flight, allowing pilots to calculate routing and speed more tactically than ever before. Based on airline estimates, this may reduce fuel costs by up to 2 percent. Aircraft condition monitoring systems (ACMS) can in future send more data on monitored systems, flight conditions and equipment in real time during the flight. This could reduce maintenance costs by at least 1 percent, by identifying potential technical issues in advance. This allows better pre-planning of maintenance down-time, the prevention of unexpected break-downs and the reduction of irregularity costs such as passenger re-bookings or compensation. Also, we expect hub carriers to reduce the size of their transfer centers, as they move information on connecting flights and self-service re-booking facilities into the aircraft.

3 Product Differentiation

Numerous travel websites, including Google Flights, allow easy comparison of flights, thus guaranteeing full transparency for airlines' prices and schedules. While this transparency puts pressure on yields, it is also a platform for airlines to differentiate themselves from their competitors in a more determined manner. In addition to pricing and scheduling, we believe that in-flight internet will become another highly significant differentiator for smart airlines.

Currently, *two-thirds of US and European travelers* consider onboard internet as a prerequisite of their making a booking. The improvement in the quality of onboard internet will lead to greater understanding and acceptance of the benefits. Correspondingly, we expect the availability of high-quality internet to become a key influencing factor on passengers' booking decisions.

Success Factors for Smart Airlines

The prize for smart airlines is there for the taking. Our research has demonstrated that airlines can generate significant revenues, save costs and set themselves apart from their competitors. The tools to do so are ready and waiting. The key question for airlines is hence how to make best use of these tools and make the connection.

We have learned from working with our most successful partners that best practice involves focusing on three specific areas.

First, most successful digital players in the airline industry have given connectivity a central and prominent place in their *organizational set-up*. Connectivity is new for most airlines both from a product and technology point of view, even for those with a strong engineering and product quality focus. To generate the required drive and foster a new connectivity mindset, smart airlines have set up dedicated connectivity departments that span all the functions involved: product development, in-flight service, flight operations and ground processes. The danger otherwise is that individual teams may go it alone, introducing single connectivity solutions, which fail to reap the full revenue and cost potentials across the company.

Second, the same successful players have also adjusted their *processes* to facilitate state-of-the-art on-board connectivity. Flight operations have digitalized all documentation, including for example electronic flight plans, thus enabling real-time exchange with pilots during flight. Cabin-side, airlines are preparing their catering and service processes to make use of "connected galleys," allowing to free-up cabin crew and reduce galley weight by remote controlling galleys, for example, from across the cabin or from the ground. Ground stations have automated key passenger handling processes, enabling passengers to be re-booked automatically in case of irregularities. These self-service options can be brought onto the aircraft, allowing passengers to re-book themselves during flight. Also, the airlines' engineering and maintenance operations are adapting to the latest generation of airliners such as the B787 and A350, which produce considerably more operational data than earlier types. Currently, most of these data are downloaded on the ground post-flight and then used for maintenance planning. Some airlines are already preparing for the transfer of data in real time during flight, which will necessitate fitting high-speed internet.

Finally, the most successful airlines have seen fit to select a strong *partner* to introduce and run connectivity products and services. Given that the industry for airline connectivity is fragmented, spanning the large satellite communication providers, value-added resellers and numerous developers of services and applications, even those airlines equipped with dedicated connectivity departments have selected partners. Their task is to coordinate the different stakeholders and select the most suitable products. Given that a revolution is going on in the market, these partners need to be innovators themselves, ready to evolve and to push forward the technology and service, in line with airline requirements and changes in customer demand.

Conclusion

It's the smart airlines that make the connection. Broadband connectivity on aircraft is that rare thing in business, representing in outward terms a significant and very welcome addition to an airline's "arsenal" of revenue tools and inwardly a highly adept way to manage cost. There is clear demand by passengers, pilots and ground staff. The benefits to be derived by the smartest players in this competitive industry are considerable. It is not surprising that many leading carriers are committing to high-speed connectivity.

ON THE QUESTION OF AIRLINE DISRUPTION

Barry Parsons
Cii Holdings

How have airlines been disrupted and what is the remaining scope for disruption?

"Disruption" to date has essentially been from within the airline industry, so how does this differ from innovation? True external disruptors still want to get between airlines and their passengers/customers, which will continue to impact the demand side of airline business models, which are rapidly changing anyway through a combination of: the scale and complexity of industry-driven supply-side disruption; market liberalization and the resulting market consolidation; and technological change.

What Constitutes Disruption for Airlines?

The airline industry fully understands the risks involved in commercial aviation and airline shareholders and executives are acutely aware that the airline element of the air transport value chain has a severely distorted risk/reward equation. Airline investment is high-risk, both labor and capital intensive and delivers historical revenue margins of 2–3 percent and a return on capital (ROC) well below its cost of capital.

The airline industry is also subject to periodic external shocks (e.g. epidemics, volcanic ash clouds, extremes in oil price, civil unrest, terrorism, etc.), although the best airlines usually find a way to weather these shocks. This is essentially through the strength of their business model, including customer value proposition (CVP), its ability to deliver positive returns between these shocks and build balance sheet strength and adapt to new market conditions. However, the effect of these shocks on some airlines overtake even well-regarded airline executive teams; recent examples are Egypt Air with the civil unrest from the Arab Spring, and Kenya Airways with the collapse of home-market in-bound tourism due to terrorism.

These shocks are not disruption, but part of the inherent cyclically realized risk in operating an airline. What is also generally considered by many airlines and industry commentators as industry disruption – such as low-cost carriers (LCCs); the rapid growth of (sixth freedom) Middle Eastern network carriers; open markets; the increasing role of airline joint-ventures with anti-trust immunity; etc. – primarily come from within the industry and although disruptive could also collectively be termed "innovation," which has led to a new market reality for airlines and their customers.

A harsh view of our industry would also conclude that it is simply innovation in a market that has, until relatively recently, been very highly regulated, with various forms of protection remaining from cases of irrational state ownership of airlines (and their often inefficient capacity not being allowed to exit the market by their government shareholders) to bankruptcy protection laws and is still relatively highly regulated when compared to other markets, such as automotive, telecoms, and pharmaceuticals. This view has some merit but is both harsh and unfair, as despite this the changes to the industry in the last 15 years that have directly benefited consumers has been significant and the current generation of airline executives cannot apologize for the history of an industry that has undergone now radical change in both developed and many emerging[1] markets.

Airline business models and revenue streams face external disruption from a usual list of candidates, including Google, which is no different to most other industries. Disruptors, typically using new technologies and/or business models, will focus on any industry with the $727 billion annual revenue stream of airlines.[2] Despite potential airline disruptors not looking at an industry in a similar state, as Uber would have observed with the taxi industry which had undergone very little innovation in a century, they have no regard for whether an industry has undergone recent (or even extensive) disruption. They are only interested in the potential for disruption from today and its challenges and rewards.

That said, airlines and the air transport value chain have a very specific disruption profile after a recent period of major disruption (i.e. change) and this will heavily inform future disruption.

Has the Airline Industry Already Been Disrupted?

When I was first asked to consider writing this thought leadership piece, I had the view there was tremendous scope for further disruption and the barriers to disruption were quite different to the way the industry thinks of barriers to entry e.g. regulatory and high start-up costs. The more I considered disruption in the air transport value chain and the differences to innovation, the greater the clarity with which I saw that airlines have already been significantly disrupted.

A 2013 IATA study, *Profitability and the Air Transport Value Chain*, concluded that airlines, within the air transport value chain, had already suffered the ultimate disruption as investors in all sectors other than airlines earned a higher ROC than airlines and most earn more than or close to their weighted average cost of capital (WACC) (see Table 10.3).

In some instances, airlines are the victims of monopoly/regulated market supply, such as with air navigation services and (often) airports. Otherwise, airlines have (perhaps ironically) busily outsourced "non-core" functions such as aircraft maintenance, ground handling, and catering that are all far better businesses to invest in than airlines themselves, which the outsourcing had a base intention of allowing them to focus on. This may only worsen, as the profitability of these non-airline sectors is being driven by an increase in

Table 10.3 Supplier ROC-WACC Deltas in the Air Transport Value Chain

Sector	Average ROC (%)	WACC (%)
Travel agents	44	8–11
Computer reservation systems (CRS)	20	10–11
Freight forwarders	15	7–8
All services (maintenance, catering, ground handling and fuel)	11	7–9
Aircraft lessors	9	9–11
Air navigation services	9	6–8
Original equipment manufacturers	7	9–11
Airports	6	6–8
Airlines	4	7–10

Source: Supplier ROC-WACC Deltas in the Air Transport Value Chain.[3]

airline operating activity, represented by fleet numbers, capacity production, and passenger numbers.

IATA quite correctly concluded that "airlines are surrounded by 'stronger business partners'" and it is clear that the smarter investors with an appetite for aviation investment and monopoly service providers have progressively surrounded airlines in the air transport value chain, or airlines have invited them into the value chain through a long period of heavy outsourcing. So what remains to disrupt in airlines if they are capital and labor intensive with poor revenue margins and are not recovering their cost of capital?

The IATA study points toward a particular concern, in that the highest returns on capital are earned by the two distribution-related sectors: travel agents and the CRS supplied by the major global distribution system (GDS) operators,[4] who achieve returns that double to quadruple their cost of capital. Unfortunately for airlines, the high ROC to cost of capital delta already being achieved in their distribution channels makes this very attractive for potential disruptors who will focus on taking a further share of airline revenue by finding innovative ways to embed themselves between airlines and their customers. Technology-driven solutions are ideal instruments for disruption, with mobile solutions now dominant; legacy airline IT infrastructure is a particular weak point for many airlines and the industry generally.

Supply-Side Versus Demand-Side Disruption

Historically airline disruption has either been supply-side or demand-side.

Supply-side disruption has a primarily long-term incubation and at first does not necessarily seem like disruption. While LCCs have revolutionized the aviation market, the concept had a long incubation period arguably from 1949 with Pacific Southwest Airlines, through the 1970s with Laker Airways, America West and Southwest and into the early twenty-first century with Ryanair, AirAsia, and others. Many did not survive and the more recent

LCCs have offered unbundled products/services, then rebundled and emulated full-service airlines without the legacy cost base and inefficiencies. The disruption was in the simplicity, lower unit cost and ability to translate this into consistently lower fares – but it took time.

The growth of Middle Eastern network carriers has also been a long-term disruption, gaining critical mass a decade ago. It has been facilitated by the convergence of geography, capital availability and newer engine/airframe combinations; once a scale inflection point is reached (e.g. as Emirates Airline found), economies of scale-driven schedules and pricing could be focused into end-point markets, and good business acumen and network geometry have allowed the disruption to reach a high threshold in markets such as Australia, Europe, and Africa. The advent of the Airbus A380, operated on frequency-based bilateral rights, has further amplified this effect and some industry analysts now consider Emirates to be another form of LCC.

Although less prominent than supply-side disruption, there has been more recent *demand-side disruption*, which typically has a short-term incubation (with a reduced time to market). The next phase of airline alliance development is airlines (typically with one to three of its alliance partners) forming joint-ventures with anti-trust immunity – such as Atlantic++ between United/Continental and Lufthansa and the trans-Pacific alliance between American Airlines and JAL – to trade in specific markets such as EU–US, US–Japan and Middle East–Australia/New Zealand. This is disrupting the premium traffic flows and revenue base of alliance members and airlines not participating in the joint-venture, in some cases severely. This is another example of the airline industry disrupting from within.

An external example of demand-side disruption is online travel agencies (OTAs) such as Expedia, Orbitz, and Priceline, and any form of online travel fare aggregator or metasearch engine. In the previous section I discussed the very attractive ratio of ROC to cost of capital being achieved by travel agents and CRS; OTAs have already disrupted airline distribution on a material scale and this likely points the way for future disruptors as the way to embed themselves between an airline and its customers and is discussed further below. They will mainly be (new) technology based; the success of OTAs also demonstrates there is still much to disrupt even in an industry with such poor investment fundamentals. Anecdotally, it is apparent that highly skilled individuals who understand the travel business and airlines, and who cut their teeth in building OTAs, are moving into sharing economy/disruption start-ups and this would suggest the opportunity for further disruption in airline distribution and the potential ROC is very well understood.

A final example of demand-side disruption is how airlines became almost completely disconnected from their cargo customers, with the relationship being replaced by a range of forwarders, consolidators, integrators, asset-based operators such as Cargolux and parcel/express heavyweights like Fedex and UPS. How this happened should be a lesson to the industry; the precise reason is subject to debate. My personal view is that not enough airlines understood the significance of air cargo to their businesses; having worked for or consulted with a wide range of airlines in both developed and emerging markets I witnessed many airline business case discussions where cargo was initially presented as an afterthought to major decisions on fleet and network, and even excellent air cargo professionals failed to have their voices heard in airline board rooms. The very best airlines understood the true potential of air cargo and have been relatively insulated from the disruption; however, many have lost the direct connection with the air cargo customers they once had.

Were Code-Share Agreements an Early Form of the Sharing Economy?

With the current focus on the sharing economy, airlines could be considered early pioneers of this for air transport in the form of code-share agreements that, like LCCs, had a long period of development with origins in the late 1960s but gained greater significance from the 1990s (see Figure 10.15). While the earlier block space agreements have given way to free-flow and capped variants, the fundamental of two or more airlines' passengers travelling in an aircraft operated by one of the airlines has some of the attributes of what is now termed the sharing or access economy or collaborative consumption.

While Airbnb and Uber are the pin-ups of this economy, are they truly peer to peer? With Airbnb, is a property owner necessarily a peer of someone who is seeking accommodation and is not a property owner (and possibly will never be or aspire to be)? With Uber, is a vehicle owner necessarily a peer of someone seeking three 20-minute vehicle trips per week? Decades ago airlines took their fixed capital cost base (the aircraft), found like-minded commercial partners and effectively shared the fixed capital cost of their productive capacity and made it far easier for the consumer to fly, as airlines

Figure 10.15 Fukuoka Airport Code-Share Flights.[5]

(often a consumer's preferred airline, which had significant impact on loyalty programs) created a network reach and schedule far beyond their operating networks.

Airline code-share agreements certainly share capacity, therefore limiting excess capacity and information is shared in an online marketplace and has also increased value for the airlines themselves. Despite this being progressively disrupted by the travel agent and CRS sectors, as discussed above, without having pioneered code-share agreements airlines and the industry would be in far worse financial shape than now and far riper for disruption.

Nuances in Disruption between Developed and Emerging Markets

Although there are some inescapable rules of aviation economics, not all markets are the same and certainly developed and emerging markets have some differences. Disruption therefore has some nuances and most are technology related.

While considering that Africa still accounts for less than 3 percent of passenger air transport,[6] it has also had a different disruption experience to most developed markets. The level of supply-side disruption varies, with African LCC penetration outside of South Africa less than 5 percent.[7] In regard to the growth of Middle Eastern carriers, 16 years after the Yamoussoukro Declaration resolved that African states would open their markets to each other they have essentially opened them to non-African states, with the Middle Eastern network carriers (including Turkish Airlines) and to a lesser extent European carriers, the major beneficiaries. On the demand-side, taking almost all of the 54 African Union member states and comparing airline distribution requirements at African points of sale (POS) with, say, Japan and Finland, these differences point toward a different distribution solution path and therefore the future for airline disruption.

LCCs in Africa require innovative distribution and, given the low internet connectivity, poor broadband quality (and its high cost), high mobile telephony penetration, low credit card penetration, and the high incidence of credit card fraud, African POS distribution disruption likely needs a different solution path to Milwaukee or Munich.

Airline customers in these markets have been faced with higher-cost indirect distribution models, with buying tickets directly from an airline at an airport or city office the primary direct channel, with often poor websites compounding the connectivity and payment challenges highlighted above. Many emerging markets have effectively skipped a generation of technology without computers and laptops and are fully engaged with mobile devices (many with smartphones), with mobile cellular telephone penetration rates in many cases much higher than internet penetration, as is the case with the selected sample of Algeria, Nigeria, and Tanzania (Table 10.4). Rising disposable incomes in emerging markets will make air travel increasingly affordable

Table 10.4 Select Comparison of African and Development Countries' Internet Penetration and Mobile Cellular Telephone Subscription Rates

Country	Internet Penetration (%)	Mobile Cellular Telephone Subscriptions (%)
Algeria	18.1	96
Nigeria	51.0	78
Tanzania	14.9	62
Japan	90.6	120
Finland	97.0	140

Source: Select Comparison of African and Developed Countries' Internet Penetration & Mobile Cellular Telephone Subscription Rates.[8]

and airlines have both the ability to innovate and be disrupted in these markets, and innovative distribution and payment method combinations could gradually solve the key issue of accessibility to air services as well as assisting with their affordability.

Future Airline Disruption

So with airlines already significantly disrupted and their distribution channels containing annual revenue streams of $727 billion and the highest ROC to cost of capital delta in the air transport value chain, disruptors will definitely continue to focus on airlines. The rewards are great and the start-up capital required for the often technology-based disruption is relatively modest, and disruption will be further facilitated by the continued evolution of airlines and the industry. There are already deeply entrenched disruptors, such as Google and the OTAs with a tremendous base from which to drive further disruption.

The major forces already driving change in airlines, such as market liberalization leading to accelerated market consolidation and LCC growth, will continue to play a key role in facilitating disruption, and many airlines also have a level of preoccupation/distraction with themselves and their industry while competition continues to increase. While the very best airlines have clear strategies that consider this (and are good at implementing these strategies) and are striving to be customer-centric, most are not and by any definition the world has far too many airlines and is only really commencing the consolidation phase that other industries like financial services and automotive have spent decades moving through.

State ownership of airlines, while not a problem in itself if done well and with the right objectives, does in many instances lead to irrational investor behavior and inefficient capacity not being allowed to exit the market as competitive forces are increasingly applied. Inherently, the revenue streams of weaker airlines should be more easily disrupted, they should be slower to respond and have less means at their disposal or expertise to both identify the cause and respond. Stronger individual airlines, larger airline groups sometimes bound by equity relationships and airline alliances (particularly the newer joint-venture form with anti-trust immunity) will find it easier to prey on weaker airlines through supply-side and demand-side disruption, and this should lead to an ever-accelerating level of competition.

As discussed, there is a thin line between disruption from within the industry (primarily supply-side) and innovation and it should be taken as given that airlines will continue to develop innovative ways to both collaborate and drive efficiencies that will steadily change the industry. What is certain is that:

1 *The stronger airlines will gravitate to each other* and the opportunities created by liberalizing markets will be fully exploited in the form of equity and/or commercially based consolidation by the airline market participants. This is more about human behavior than airline/aviation economics.

2 Technology will continue to develop and be the basis for innovation by both airlines and other suppliers in the air transport value chain. An example is *new engine/airframe combinations* being developed by OEMs, such as Boeing's 777X project and a potential 757 replacement and Airbus' A321Neo. While definitely innovative, they have significant development lead-time and then the industry has to have the means to acquire significant units to impact cost bases, networks and schedules.

These forms of disruption from within are now the "new normal" and the market reality for *all* airlines, so the remainder of this thought leadership piece will focus on the scope and opportunities for "pure" disruption from non-airline sources.

The Potential Sources of Future Disruption and Their Medium-Term Likelihood

As discussed, the primary disruption opportunity based on the current air transport value chain is in *airline distribution* and the candidate disruptors are those we currently know and who have already had some level of success, i.e. Google, Facebook, Expedia, Priceline, etc. They have considerable innovation and financial resources, industry knowledge and airlines still have no effective strategic or tactical response apart from working with them, which is frankly the right response as ignoring them is not an option, and trying to be them would be absurd given the outsourcing of services such as aircraft maintenance and catering which are better investments than airlines themselves. Any enhancements in current technology and new technology, particularly on mobile platforms, are the obvious source of disruption to airline distribution and OTAs have led the way to this point.

The distribution disruption will likely be incremental, with some step changes becoming apparent only with 6–18 months of hindsight. The disruptors will require innovative technical solutions for mobile platforms, as the rapid shift to mobile is resulting in shorter "sessions" and search is also concurrently moving into the paid world and search engine optimization is losing its power. Having a good website and mobile solution, such as Expedia or Priceline, can look great one day and ordinary the next as disruptors move; if the disruptor also controls the most popular search engine, as Google does, then as a disruptor it is best placed of any of the current known innovative technology companies in the air transport vertical.

Although in its early phase of effective deployment in the market,[9] Google Flights is the strongest candidate to further disrupt airline distribution and at face value to the consumer it simply seems a better experience and the next level of flight-booking experience. However, with Google's market power and user analytics behind it, Google Flights has a huge advantage over incumbent and any aspiring new disruptors; if successful it may itself provide a strong barrier to further disruption. Combined with Google Hotels and eventually Google Pay under a Google Destinations umbrella it is quite easy to see the potential disruptive future although there will no doubt be anti-trust debate around search result listings/rankings.

It is already easy to see the Google strategy in the market, building Google Destinations with Google Flights as a key pillar. Rich content, mystery flights (I'm feeling lucky) based on what's popular plus your search history flight notifications, high response speed, low click count to optimize short sessions and other transport modes (e.g. German, French and Italian rail) for intermodal connections. While not yet having the lowest price capability across as many markets as, say, Expedia, Google Flights is quickly developing, but not without challenges.

Ryanair announced a European partnership with Google Flights in 2014, which by late 2015 appeared to be breaking down over Google allegedly redirecting (via a paid advert) searches to a travel site eDreams. Ryanair litigated, against both Google and eDreams, over alleged deceptive conduct with consumers believing they were booking direct with Ryanair, paying 30–100 percent more than booking directly with Ryanair and leading to a range of customer service issues. In late 2015, Lufthansa announced a deal with Google Flights for their US users to link directly to lufthansa.com on desktop and mobile without changing websites. Lufthansa (as did Ryanair) clearly decided to work with the disruptor and it is part of a broader strategy of "direct connect" deals to bypass GDSs.

Lufthansa simply need to get a lower cost of sale with Google Flights than via the GDS to make it an attractive option as long as they are reaching their target market, and it is hard to see how a GDS will be a superior customer experience to Google Flights for a customer wanting to search and book via a direct channel. This points the way to how airlines will work with disruptors; airlines should have learned all the lessons required from the last round of disruption by OTAs and how they lost control of the customer relationship with their freight customers. Airlines that retain control of their customer relationship management (CRM), while effectively partnering with disruptors such as

Google and Expedia and closely managing their cost of sale line (underpinned by highly effective channel and payment method strategy and deployment) will survive disruption and likely thrive at the expense of airlines who do not. Retaining control of the CRM is key for an airline's long-term survival and the strongest airline brands with highly nimble and effective strategic and commercial management will thrive if they do this. Airlines who lose control of the CRM will either cease to exist or become increasingly marginalized by the disruptors who gained control of their CRM that could be easily and stealthily "switched." While Ryanair have litigated, they understand they must take a position with the disruptors and they will resolve their differences and move on as isolation is unlikely to work for even the strongest airline brand with the best CVP (in their case price).

The *replacement of the need for air travel* has been misread before, particularly in relation to the early days of videoconferencing, which some suggested would significantly reduce the need for business travel. After an initial novelty phase, it has taken well over a decade for videoconferencing technology and broadband bandwidth to develop sufficiently to make videoconferencing a consistently pain-free experience. However, the early predictions on its impact on business travel did not really come to pass or at least are not accurately measured. The human need for contact and engagement in business meant that videoconferencing simply became an additional means of engagement in business.

In regard to leisure travel, more recent developments in virtual reality (VR) now allow almost any travel experience to be had virtually, although again there is a deep human need for the real experience that will not be easily overcome even if it was desirable to do so. Advancements in VR hardware mean that good-quality VR experiences can be easily had and the travel industry, content creators and advertisers are quickly moving into this space. Two examples are Marriott and Thomas Cook. Marriot have a VR travel experience from inside a hotel in London, to Hawaii; Thomas Cook have VR travel experiences from inside select UK branch locations. Perhaps, like videoconferencing, VR will become a supplement to the travel experience and may become an integral part of planning leisure travel, much like we use a travel guide like Lonely Planet for today.

Despite the potential for further "pure" disruption, I doubt whether disruption to airlines can take the form of true peer-to-peer sharing (as is claimed with Airbnb or Uber) with current aircraft technology, as the barriers to peer-to-peer disruption are too high. Two immediate reasons are that the capital cost of an aircraft far outweighs a home, apartment or automobile, and far more training and skill are required to operate an aircraft. Then there is the very solid existing base of code-share agreements and airline alliances, which provide consumers with considerable choice on network, schedule and price. The final barrier is that aviation is highly regulated and high risk.

Airbnb essentially operate in an unregulated market, while Uber are taking years in some cities to break down regulatory barriers in an industry with only a few relatively simple regulations in place, such as taxi operator licenses and the employment status and taxation requirements of drivers. So true peer-to-peer sharing is unlikely to materially penetrate airline operations in even the long term.

The Connectivity Paradox and the Outcomes of Disruption

In 2010, Northwestern University Associate Professor Paul Leonardi and colleagues considered a teleworker connectivity paradox where IT and communication advances created an expectation of constant connectivity that negated the original benefits of distributed work arrangements.[10] In regard to advances in communication and connectivity potentially adversely impacting the demand for air transport, there are no reliable data.

We know that, except for the 2008–9 Global Financial Crisis, the demand for air transport steadily grows each year, as (online) connectivity particularly through social media platforms does now despite repeated forecasts since 2011 that Facebook growth had peaked. It may well be that increasing technology-based connectivity is one factor driving the increased demand for air transport, as the more people connect online and the more (in the case of leisure travel) they can see and dream of destinations the more they want to physically interact and travel. However, it may also be that the demand for air transport would have grown at a higher rate than it has if connectivity was not steadily increasing, based on factors such as population growth, globalization, LCC growth, etc. This is one of the great unknowns of disruption and of change generally, although intuitively I hold the former view.

With data from various industries mixed, the effects of disruption over time are often glossed over or misunderstood. As discussed, videoconferencing was expected to reduce the need for business travel and the opposite happened. The introduction of home video recorders/players was meant to significantly impact or even kill-off movie theaters, which simply moved to another business model of multiplexes – US movie ticket sales in 2015 are at a similar level to 1995. Sounds acceptable? Maybe, except that over the same period the US population increased by 20 percent, content streaming is now widespread and the DVD market is dying off. Spotify was at the forefront of what the music industry thought were illegal attempts to kill it off and it is now seen by some to be what will be the streaming-led saving of the industry. But it has helped change the market and put more power in the hands of the performers and their live performances at the expense of traditional record companies. Streaming pricing, mobile download capability, the general improved efficiency of the market, etc. has also fundamentally changed the market.

So concurrent changes in an industry's key variables and structure, over a long period and after several significant disruptions, leave it impossible to conclude on the *precise* causes of change or what would have happened to an industry with only incremental innovation. Similarly in the air transport value chain, without videoconferencing, LCCs, increased connectivity, changes to corporate travel policies, the scale growth and maturity in airline loyalty programs and the closure of many corporate branch offices (to name a few changes), what would business travel have looked like today? Impossible to tell, but certainly far less interesting to the consumer and with far less pressure on airlines to compete, innovate and improve their CVPs.

In the case of LCCs, we have seen the outcome of airline supply-side disruption in many markets. LCCs entered markets with half the unit cost and direct selling models that created a steady wave of cash to fund the acquisition of additional fleet units. They quickly grew the market, as low fares were consistently taken up by an "un-flown" market and they enticed existing air travelers to fly more often and trade-down from full-service airlines. So a larger market, often with the pre-LCC entry full-service participants carrying the same or slightly reduced number of passengers and the LCCs capturing most or all of the growth. On demand-side disruption, given the CRS supplier ROC to WACC delta it would be reasonable to conclude that the GDS adapted to both LCC entry and the full-service airlines shifting sales into direct channels to reduce their cost of sale and direct sales into channels that customers (certainly in developed markets) wanted to transact in.

It is quite possible that disruption leads to opportunity and this may well take place with VR and leisure travel, and may already have taken place in both business and leisure travel with rapidly growing connectivity. Disruption is concerning and airlines have already been significantly disrupted; however, it is not something to inherently fear and how airlines respond to further disruption is the key question for airline shareholders and executives.

How Will Airlines Respond to Further Disruption?

The historic airline reactions to disruption have been ineffective, although it is easy to construct an argument that airlines self-disrupting the air transport value chain and outsourcing business functions that were better investments than their core business was an inevitable outcome of increased competition. So the reaction to something self-inflicted is a nebulous discussion. That said, airlines need to be vigilant on what remains to disrupt, and I have great confidence that the best airlines will do so and are looking hard at how to turn disruption into opportunity.

As the market consolidates, airlines are also better organized to withstand disruption. They have better information, time to market for disruption responses/their own innovation should be reducing and the greater concentration of market power should also strengthen barriers to disruption.

As a general principle, lessons from other industries would suggest that fighting disruptors is not the correct response, primarily because the customers of many airlines will welcome the disruption, so an airline being customer-centric and strengthening their CVP now is the best basic defense. Doing nothing is not an option if an airline wants to stay in business for the long term, so working with disruptors and strengthening that basic defense (as Lufthansa decided to do with Google Flights) is the best way to respond.

Conclusion

The airline industry has seen great change in the last 15 years, with high levels of innovation being blended with and leading to a seemingly endless cycle of disruption from within and from elsewhere in the air transport value chain. This has been good for the consumer; however, the weakness of the general airline investment case is a long-term and apparently intractable problem and with the most likely point of future disruption airline distribution only making this problem worse.

Airlines face challenges from existing disruptors making further in-roads into their revenue streams, as well as new disruptors on their demand side. I am optimistic that the very best airlines will find a way to work with disruptors and to the benefit of their customers while retaining control of their relationship with customers, and disruption will have a positive impact on the demand for air transport. This will have major consequences for the competitive position of weaker airlines and should contribute to the already accelerating market consolidation.

Our industry is going to be disrupted and will change, but that is what we should have all come to expect.

Notes

1 For the purposes of this thought leadership piece, "emerging markets" includes "developing markets" based on the definitions in Chapter 5.
2 2015 IATA forecast.
3 *Profitability and the Air Transport Value Chain* (McKinsey & Co. for IATA). Data for 2004–11, with goodwill valuations excluded.
4 The world's major GDSs were also started and eventually outsourced by airlines, but this much earlier phase of outsourcing has been largely forgotten.
5 Photograph by Chihaya Sta and licensed under CC BY-SA 3.0 via Commons.
6 IATA data: 2.3 percent of annual global revenue passenger kilometers, September 2015.
7 CAPA data: 30 October 2015.
8 2014 ITU and World Bank Data.
9 Even though technically launched in late 2011.
10 Leonardi, Paul M., Treem, Jeffrey W., and Jackson, Michele H., "The connectivity paradox: using technology to both decrease and increase perceptions of distance in distributed work arrangements." *Journal of Applied Communication Research* 38, 1, 2010, pp. 85–105.

LESSONS LEARNED AND ISSUES THAT LINGER

Robert L. Solomon
Co-Chairman
International Airline Symposium (IAS) Planning Committee

Over the past decade, I have served as co-chair of the planning committee for the IAS. In our candid and collegial meetings around the world with senior airline industry colleagues and business leaders from many other industries, we have explored and debated high-level issues of strategy, business model innovation, technology, transformation and disruption. What follows are some personal conclusions and observation on both lessons learned and issues still ahead.

Twenty Years Later: It's the Big Bang not a Black Hole

Back in 1996, when I took over marketing for Outrigger Resorts, we had one of the first bookable websites in the hotel industry. Although we still depended on fax machines, call centers and the airline global distribution system (GDS), it was obvious that change was inevitable and irreversible. However, it was not clear at all whether the internet would create a collapsing universe and disrupt, disintermediate and destroy margins (the Black Hole), or whether it would lead to a Big Bang of expanding global demand enabled by greater accessibility of content and transparency in pricing.

In the short term, with adoption uneven, execution in its infancy and analytics haphazard, we saw instances of both.

In the midterm, wild swings were amplified by the business cycle. On the downswing, margins were crushed. On the upswings, servers crashed, and the verdict remained in doubt. Technology leaders saw induced demand and honed in on profit zones. Laggards bemoaned the unfairness of it all as customers defected. Expense soared as travel providers hedged and technology suppliers introduced newer and more powerful versions even while barely keeping up with demand for their own services. Costs of going to market were driven up even further as new media entered the scene.

There was a genuine sense of excitement, but underneath it all it was chaotic. There was no choice but to invest, because consumers were flocking to the internet, yet the physics of the new cosmos of travel was not clear.

Now, in retrospect, evidence is conclusive: the Big Bang prevails. Black Holes still lurk here and there, but travel is a robust and expanding category. Expansion is driven not just by enabling technology, but also by demographic, economic and geographic factors that make fundamental conditions for air travel more positive and dynamic than most analysts expected, especially when the cumulative profit picture was suffering.

In the Big Bang universe, not every enterprise will succeed. Missing or mis-reading the dynamics will still lead to failure or collapse if strategy or execution does not stay ahead of the curve. These are significant challenges because in many ways, the expanding universe means tougher, not easier choices for management. In the Black Hole scenario, cost cutters reign, restructuring and consolidation rule. In the Big Bang universe, one must take a much wider view of opportunity and think differently about where, why, how, when and with whom to play. Innovation, as opposed to incremental-ism, requires a broader view as well of benchmarks, best practices, competi-tors, supplier community, geography and market segments.

Marketplace Winners Embrace or Displace Distribution, Whiners Complain About It

Distribution has always been a controversial cost center for low-margin busi-nesses, and airlines are no exception. The advent of the internet and spin-offs of the GDS systems intensified the love–hate relationships between airlines and their various classes of distributors, including online travel agents (OTAs) and search engines. At the end of the day, the market clears, the money issues are settled and the emotion is forgotten. In such a large and diverse industry, systems and technology are not always in sync and more technical issues can arise. Many of the same factors are at work in the hotel and ground transportation industries.

Two decades of observation and listening have led me to some basic con-clusions. The best way to think about distribution is that the enterprise must manage its portfolio of market segments and customers with a consistent strategy, supported by allocation of resources (including technology infra-structure and marketing investment) appropriate to the target business mix and financial results.

Simply put, marketplace winners put the necessary resources behind the strategy. If I mainly want direct business, then I must configure for that, keep the assets up to date and keep investing until we reach the point where it is more efficient to let another channel do the work. If I control my product, pricing, content and inventory, then I cannot complain if some channel is taking too much (or accuse the channel partners of "stealing" it), unless I can produce the incremental business at lower cost. Am I really entitled to com-plain if my distributor updates technology *every six months*, or even continu-ously, and I update mine *every six years*? Of course not. It just means I have chosen to put my resources elsewhere, or that I value the class of customers provided less. If I am just looking for inventory fill, market share or billboard effect, and I'm not willing to spend more to make it come direct, I manage it up or down as needed, but I cannot blame the business partners.

To take one example in the USA, Southwest Airlines has both the scale and the commitment to pursue a direct strategy. Their business model, advertising, promotion and online and human resources infrastructure effect-ively support that approach to the market. A smaller competitor might find a similar approach appropriate in their backyard, but they might find it to be less efficient at a certain stage of development in other geographic areas or market segments.

It all sounds simple and logical, and it is. That's why I have no sympathy when I hear hoteliers or airline executives whining about their distribution costs and partners. It just means that they have not worked out how to align their business goals, market segments and customer strategies with appropriate resource allocation and execution. Competitors that get too far behind the curve or lack the capability to manage customer portfolios successfully are candidates for reorganization or consolidation.

I have also observed that a lot of this confusion results from a mis-reading and underestimation of the importance of leisure travel and discretionary travel in general. Major hotel chains and many airlines and car rental companies focused for so long on the profitable business traveler that they failed to recognize the growth and importance of the leisure segment, which eclipsed business travel in volume more than a decade ago. This blunder fueled the opportunity for new competitors and more effective distributors with a sharper focus, newer technology and better understanding of consumer preferences that drive discretionary spend.

There Are Many Right Answers (No One Size Fits All) But Not if You Ask the Wrong Questions

The global airline industry is so large, varied and dynamic that there are few if any one-size-fits-all answers. Even the most successful business models may be inappropriate and fail in other environments, while some of the best new ideas evolve in the most unlikely places.

There are some key corollaries to this that may be particularly important to industry leaders of seasoned companies in more mature markets. There is an asymmetry at work here: it is natural for new entries to look to global leaders for examples and insight as well as affiliation in alliances or buying groups. But how likely is this to work in reverse? Are the high-level delegations from the leading companies going to emerging markets to listen and learn about both their unique challenges and novel solutions? Are they dispatching rising stars to embed in start-ups or taking risk positions to stretch, test and learn, or are they stuck in the bunker back home?

If growth is organic, incremental or achieved through consolidation in mature markets, shouldn't more management attention and learning be taking hold in more rapidly growing markets that are outside of or remote from the comfort zone?

In a world where consumer expectations and preferences are formed more readily in other categories where they shop and buy more frequently than they do for travel in general and air travel in particular, shouldn't the boundaries of inquiry and attention be much wider than benchmarking competitors doing essentially the same things in the same ways and the same places?

Leadership Is Everything, and It's a Lot Harder in Many of the Leading Business Cases (e.g. Legacy, Post-Merger, Statist, and Two-Tier)

Over the last decade, we have reviewed dozens of airline business cases and looked at extensive data from thought leaders and analysts from all around the world. Business models, scope and scale, operating environment, business cycle and life stage have varied across the board. Whether one believes that execution trumps strategy or vice versa, by far the single greatest factor for success has been *leadership*, followed by a strong organizational culture. In principle one would expect the two to go together, but this is not always the case, primarily because of the difficulties that may be encountered when the enterprise is a consolidated business that may need to meld different corporate cultures and practices, or where multiple brands and operating units serve a variety of different customer segments.

The point here is not to admonish industry chiefs to be better leaders, but to emphasize the criticality and the challenges involved. If the corporate governance structure, stakeholder impetus, business model and organizational culture add up to a perpetual series of distractions and crises, the odds for leadership success are unfavorable before the business day even begins.

In large enterprises, like the auto manufacturers and some airlines, even capable and well-intended management can become so isolated from the business, the product, the customers and the workforce that the result is complete failure. Fourteenth-floor leaders at General Motors had no clue about how unappealing and lackluster their products were until it was far too late. As Steve Ballmer of Microsoft would have put it, they failed to eat their own dog food. Strong-willed CEOs despised by frontline and middle management at major US carriers oversaw the corporate equivalent of "controlled flight into terrain." One week playing "undercover boss" would have made the extent of the problem undeniable.

The success cases are equally if not more dramatic. They demonstrate that any and all negative factors that become excuses or explanations for failure can just as well be viewed as challenges to overcome where leadership supports the right priorities. AirAsia, Azul, Southwest, Westjet and many others have found ways to overcome the same obstacles. Sometimes it takes an outsider to look at things differently, but that's certainly not a prerequisite for being able to challenge conventional wisdom and align the entire organization around better solutions.

All this has nothing to do with how smart, accomplished, charismatic or expert the leader may be. It might be helpful to think of the leadership challenge as another form of risk analysis. That discipline is well developed, learns systematically from failure and relies on informed and unrestrained imagination. Solid leadership risk assessment is like confronting brand truth – it requires relentless objectivity, good listening skills including voice of the customer, and a disciplined checklist.

Customer-Centricity and Workforce Engagement Are No Less Important, if Leadership Is in a Position to Focus Meaningfully on These Areas

One of the takeaways from the discussion on leadership is that top management must be able to pay real attention to customers and workforce. While we hear a lot about customer engagement, and there are now many more and effective ways to measure that, we hear much less about how deeply airline management is engaged with the customer base and how effectively they drive that approach through the organization. When that situation changes, it becomes headline news.

The travel industry, broadly defined, is a service business that relies primarily on discretionary consumer spend. Yes, there is a B2B component, but at the end of the day, all travelers are consumers. Having spent a decade or more working in and studying each of the hospitality, auto rental, automobile and airline industries, I can state with confidence that the hotel brands do an inherently better job when it comes to customer (guest) and employee engagement than the others. Airlines routinely advertise how friendly and welcoming they are and may share and reinforce these messages with the internal audience but there is often a big gap between the messaging and the reality *as perceived by their guests*.

Granted that large, mature, unionized companies may have a more difficult course, good employee relations and positive employee engagement are just as achievable in unionized as in union-free businesses (even if at higher cost). The responsibility lies with management to make that possible. Oscar Munoz, recently appointed CEO of United, interjected from sick leave (while recuperating from a heart transplant) on the importance of employee engagement in delivering customer satisfaction. This takes real commitment, and will require much more than the annual employee climate survey in any organization.

Customer Focus is Like Practicing Medicine: The Physician That Cares for the Patient, Cares for the Patient; the Airline Management That Cares for the Customer, Will Care for the Customer

The tools and instruments for execution are available to everyone with a license or operating certificate, but the standard of care is all over the map. For those inclined to bother, the right data are available. Travel is a high-emotion category. Air travel for most consumers is a low-frequency discretionary purchase. The probability of things going wrong for the customer is, statistically speaking, relatively low, but consequences can be high. Results vary widely. Why is this? Leadership sets the tone for the standard of customer care. Highly engaged leadership takes a broader view of customer satisfaction and embraces the fact that the overall impression of the brand is the result of all aspects of the customer experience, not just those measured or surveyed. From a customer point of view the list is longer and includes all of the following and more:

- Pricing: Was the fare reasonable and did I get good value for the money I paid?
- Policy: The fact that I may accept bag fees and other nuisance charges doesn't mean I am happy about it and today, only Alaska and Delta offer a service guarantee for checked bags. Does anyone else care?
- Problem solving: is service recovery satisfactory from the customer point of view? How do the airline and its people respond? Are the systems in place so people *can* respond?

Decades of observation convince me that in this area, the job is never done. The good news is that by and large, there has been continuous improvement. Unfortunately, that has not always kept pace with rising consumer expectations set in other categories. To be frank, improvements in operating efficiency, such as capacity discipline and resultant higher load factors, and policies designed to boost ancillary revenue, can exacerbate problem situations if the airline or alliance group does not take additional steps to mitigate the downside. Bringing back the peanuts won't close the gap. Earning customer preference is a much larger challenge than paying for their "loyalty" with frequent flyer miles.

In the Big Bang Expanding Universe, Opportunity for Growth and Incidence of Innovation Have Been and Will Be Greater in the Emerging Economies Than in Traditional Markets

Enterprises that fail to raise their game and learn from these areas risk falling behind. In mature markets, technology-based entries like Uber and Airbnb have disrupted large sectors of the travel business. In emerging markets, a long list of entries and innovations have re-defined best practices. These stories are well known, but there is a back-story in the global business cycle that has been less appreciated. During the long period of losses, failures, reorganization, restructuring and consolidation among airlines in the mature economies, there was a period of extraordinary growth and innovation in other parts of the world. It is not surprising that the large established firms were inwardly focused during this time. With consolidation mostly completed and apart from the collapse of fuel prices, future improvements may be mostly incremental.

The takeaway is that tomorrow's leaders need to look beyond the enterprise and its traditional competitors, beyond the boundaries of current operations, and beyond the airline category itself for opportunity, new and different thinking, and re-defined customer expectations.

Thanks to Enabling Technology and Changing Mindset, the Tempo of Experimentation and Change and Willingness to Take Risk Have Improved: Organizational Culture Remains the Main Impediment to Reach Full Potential

Leadership and organizational agility are more important than ever because along with expanding opportunity, the Big Bang brings increasing volatility.

When I began my career in the original think tank at the RAND Corporation (which itself began as on offshoot of the US Air Force), the first lesson I learned from the most sophisticated strategic planners of the time was that "You always miss the Big Ones." Along with the sense of humility that comes from this realization, is the comfort that asking the right questions about what may happen tomorrow is more important than having the right answer for yesterday.

"GOOGLE IT?"

Dan Wacksman
Senior Vice President, Global Distribution
Outrigger Resorts

In his 2011 book *The Filter Bubble: What the Internet is Hiding from You* and in his well-viewed TED talk, Eli Parser talks about "a world where all the news you see is defined by your salary, where you live, and who your friends are … a world where you never discover new ideas." His premise was that in the world of "curated" content, search engines and advertisers learn enough about you that they only serve you information that their algorithms indicate you are "interested" in, whether it be news with your particular slant or products based on previous search patterns or purchases, limiting you from discovering new ideas or products. In fact some have already begun to muse that these algorithms are a form of social control and have even gone as far as stating that it is a potential "threat to our democratic system." While this might be an extreme opinion, search has clearly changed the way we get information. This is acutely felt by marketers who are trying to reach out to customers who are more and more getting their information from the internet and more specifically starting with search engines. Travel is the ultimate product for the internet as every step in the process, with the exception of actually taking the trip, can be accomplished easily through one's screen: dreaming, searching, booking and sharing. Each touchpoint can be accomplished easily and effectively on a screen and at each touchpoint there is an opportunity to monetize the "eyeballs" looking at the screen.

In most markets Google has become the default search engine; in fact it has become the default library and fount of information. The expression "Google it" has come to mean easily searching up and getting an accurate answer to a question. In 2006 the verb "Google" was added as a new word in the *Oxford Dictionary*.

Google It

- How tall is Tom Cruise? 5 foot, 7 inches according to the first search result.
- How old is Hillary Clinton? Sixty-eight according to the first search result.
- What is the best hotel in New York? Hotels.com first search result (paid ad).
- Quickest flight from New York to Tokyo? Expedia.com first search result (paid ad); next set of responses taking up a third of the page is Google Flights.

Net-neutrality advocate Tim Wu recently published a study that concluded "Google is reducing 'social welfare' by biasing the best search results in favor of those that are best for the company." This is not news to anyone who advertises with Google or other search engines (including MetaSearch). One could argue that the Google mission statement has pivoted from "*organize*" to "*monetize*" the world's information.

In the early days of the internet, paid search and organic search (SEO) lived side by side, allowing searchers to clearly identify advertisers who are paying for their search results and sites that come up due to relevancy. Over the past several years, in areas where money is to be made, organic search has become buried below the fold and it may not be long before it is pushed off the first page altogether, which has already occurred on mobile. Paul Hennessy, CEO of Priceline, was recently quoted by Skift as saying "As far as SEO, my view on that is it's more of a desktop thought because as the devices get smaller and smaller and smaller, the number of choices from an SEO perspective on mobile decline dramatically. And so I believe it is a paid world."

An early shot across the bow of net neutrality came in 2013 when Google changed its trademark policy, which now states "Google will not investigate or restrict the use of trademark terms in key words, even if a trademark complaint is received." This policy is highly lucrative for Google, very expensive for advertisers and in many cases may be misleading to consumers. As Google pushes further and further down the purchase funnel, testing ways to keep customers on its site and enable them to fulfill their needs, from a supplier perspective it may feel as though this is pushing customers through Google before they can find the supplier. The next obvious step may be to actually conduct the transaction directly on Google, as TripAdvisor has done with its instant book product in the hotel space. Google Flights and Google Hotel Finder have gone through numerous iterations and Google is still searching for that sweet spot, and with the acquiescence of many suppliers they are sure to find it.

The issue with Google and other search companies is not that they have created an amazing money-making machine, it is that they control the largest source of information, and in some markets (especially the EU) they have been alleged to have a monopoly position.

Google is a source that many people believe to be unbiased; however, as a business, like most marketplaces, its sort order is affected by margins and commercial relationships. I will leave the implications of this on society to the sociologists and academics; my focus is its effect on companies, including airlines, who are trying to get the attention of customers who are searching for them.

Content-based media sites like TripAdvisor and Google are evolving toward the transactional side in addition to a pay-for-play environment (where in order to get in front of customers, even if they are specifically looking for you, you have to pay a "toll"). Even if your airline has the best connection and best prices to a destination there is a good chance, if you do not pay the toll, that you will not show. Suppliers need to be mindful about how much control they give up as they seek to get in front of their customers. Larger suppliers, for example the global hospitality brands, may have the scale to negotiate acceptable commercial terms. Smaller players face greater challenges, especially on mobile.

While Google is the most visible, any "search" company or marketplace that is perceived to be an unbiased third party but is actually behaving as a "pay to play" model is putting consumers' trust at risk. With rising costs there is increasing pressure to monetize site traffic. As a supplier and as an advertiser, one has to be careful how to work with these "partners." On one hand they have built incredible machines that consumers trust, but on the other they are putting up virtual toll booths in front of your customers. When considering how to work with them one has to take a strategic view and not just a tactical one. The easy answer may be to utilize the tools offered to the full extent to drive immediate revenue, but long term if you don't adequately invest in building and fulfilling your own traffic, your partners will slowly but surely commoditize your brand.

Footnote: Video Killed the Radio Star – Google in a World of Mobile Apps

While Google is clearly the leader to watch in this space, the growth of mobile is a clear threat to Google. Once a person finds a good-quality app that they trust for a particular vertical it is likely that more and more people will go to those apps instead of search. While one might search the news on Google, they are more likely to go to their news app; while one might search for flights on Google, they are also more likely to go to a trusted app on their mobile device – which could be anything from a specialty site to a mega-site like Facebook. Clearly Google sees this and is working on ways to stay competitive. This is the next wave that suppliers need to be ready for and will be very interesting to watch unfold as the world moves more and more to mobile and next-generation platforms.

INSIGHTS FROM THE AIR CARGO SECTOR

Guo Xianqin
Senior Vice President, Revenue Management and Network Planning
MASKargo

As consumer travel demand increases globally, the airline industry has been on a healthy path over the past several years, and the growth trajectory on the passenger side looks quite encouraging. However, for the majority of these passenger airlines, the story for cargo has been quite different and many are struggling to maintain the status quo, let alone see business growth year on year.

Historically, cargo might not be the first priority for passenger airlines, especially the ones without freighters. The top line revenues generated from cargo were not significant enough for company top leaders to pay close attention to cargo. However, as competition intensifies and there are increasing pressures to improve company profits, leaders are taking another look at cargo and trying to figure out how to better utilize its network capacity to enhance companies' overall performance.

For airlines with freighter capacity, cargo had been performing well until the Great Recession in 2008. After the recession, freighters have had strong headwinds over the past several years in both volume and revenue as a result of significant belly capacity increases and transportation mode shifting from air freight to ocean freight. In addition to these market challenges, the current cargo business model restricts airline carriers' capability to proactively pursue growth opportunities. This contribution will address these challenges by further examining the structure of the current business model, analyzing its impact and providing observations/recommendations. In addition, it will discuss the implication of potential 4PLs emerging on the passenger side, if IT companies such as Google, Amazon, Facebook and the alike attempt to enter the industry by creating a new business model.

Let's start with how cargo moves throughout the entire cycle and its key stakeholders (Figure 10.16).

There are numerous touchpoints throughout the entire cycle of the shipment and a number of stakeholders are involved. Errors in any part of the cycle can impact the overall shipment flow and create issues for downstream activities. The errors could be anything from data entry to loading freight in the wrong container. With multiple stakeholders involved – shipper, consignee, forwarder, customs broker, carrier and sometimes distributors, things are getting more complicated and extremely challenging to coordinate and execute.

As shippers and consignees are increasingly focusing on better managing their supply chains, and investing more in technologies to stay competitive, they demand to have total visibility of their shipments, timely information sharing, ready IT support, and service exception management solutions. In

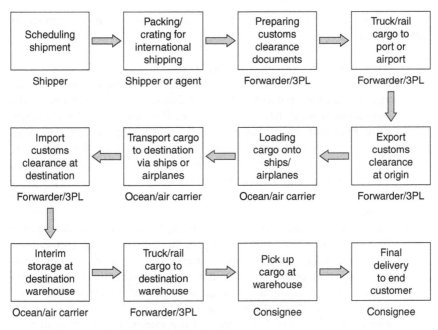

Figure 10.16 Touchpoints in the Cargo Cycle.

doing so, they can proactively manage their businesses with reduced costs, and communicate with their customers more effectively and enhance business performance. It also helps them create a competitive advantage in the global marketplace. However, with increased complexity of the global supply chain and constantly changing regulations, things are more often likely to go wrong. When things do go wrong with the scenario shown in Figure 10.16, it is not difficult to see how challenging it can be just to pinpoint the issues and their root causes, let alone resolve the problems.

Now, let's take a closer look at the current business model. The challenges are twofold. On one hand, airline carriers primarily participate in the transportation part of the supply chain due to their network configuration and regulatory requirements. This by itself limits airlines' capability of playing a bigger role in the global supply chain and puts pressure on commoditizing their own services. On the other hand, the airline carriers, who own the assets and the network capacity, don't interact with the customers directly. Shippers or consignees go through freight forwarders when they need to move freight. These freight forwarders then purchase capacity from the carriers and resell the capacity to shippers/consignees together with other value-added services such as customs brokerage, consolidation, deconsolidation, warehousing and distribution, pick and pack, etc. Airline carriers just watch their capacity being increasingly commoditized as competition increases and overcapacity worsens.

This current business model hurts airline carriers in a number of different ways:

- *There is no brand recognition and brand equity for carriers.*
  When customers use the services from the forwarders, they interact and transact with the forwarders, and they don't oftentimes know who the carrier is until they have a copy of the airway bill. This is drastically different from the passenger side as carriers are focusing on creating brand awareness and brand equity as part of their effort to differentiate and enhance customers' experiences. Carriers' brand equity is completely lost on the cargo side.
- *Multiple hurdles to achieving service reliability, and perception challenges make it even worse.*
  Again, due to the fact that carriers don't interact and do business directly with end customers (shipper or consignee), all communications take place with forwarders instead. Imagine a situation of incorrect data entry on the airway bill by the customer, the error skips the forwarder, and is caught by the ground agent of the carrier. The communication will have to go back to the forwarder, who contacts the customer, who then comes back to the carrier. By the time all these activities have taken place, the booked flight may have already left. As a result, there is a service failure. In addition, when forwarders consolidate the freight, if there is inaccurate information of weight/dimensions, this will cause them to either over-book or under-book the capacity they need. Therefore, when they actually tender the freight, this could cause another service failure due to under-booking or over-tendering. Third, the regulatory requirement changes put additional pressure on service reliabilities as new requirements are being implemented by government entities around the world. Finally, when forwarders purchase capacity from multiple carriers, the result of a service failure of one carrier may impact the overall perception of carriers negatively as customers do not form such perceptions directly with carriers; instead they perceive service reliability via forwarders.
- *Mis-alignment/disconnect of product offerings creates additional challenges.*
  When forwarders market their air freight services, they generally offer three categories – express, standard, and deferred services. They also market their services based on customers' transit time requirements. For *express*, it is a guaranteed service with a premium price. It has the shortest transit time, normally for time-sensitive and high-value goods. If the forwarders fail to deliver the freight at the specified transit time, forwarders pay a penalty to the customers. For *standard*, it is offered at a lower price with a longer transit time than *express*. Oftentimes, standard is not a guaranteed service and there is no penalty if the forwarder did not deliver the service within the required transit time. *Deferred* is the most cost-effective service for customers who want to

move the freight faster than other transportation modes, but can afford a longer transit time for a cheaper price. It is often a consolidated service too. However, when forwarders purchase capacity from the carriers, oftentimes they book standard freight with requests that "freight move as booked," which implies that carriers need to move the freight as express shipments although it was booked as standard; carriers also need to move the freight on a specific booked flight. Under such a circumstance, there is no transit time alignment between forwarders and carriers, and this also indirectly dictates how carriers manage their network capacity. If standard freight did not move as booked, then it will fall into service failure based on the forwarder's definition. This misalignment not only creates service execution challenges for carriers, but also puts additional pressure on carriers' bottom line because carriers cannot sell their capacity at a premium due to the fact that everything is "move as booked." Since everything should move as booked, there is no motivation for forwarders to purchase premium service.

- *Network capacity has been increasingly commoditized.*
  Due to the fact that carriers in general just offer point A to point B transportation services, and as a result of capacity increase in the market place for the past several years, carriers' capacity has been commoditized and the pressure keeps increasing. On some occasions, carriers are trying to offer value-added services such as warehousing, limited pickup and delivery, and dedicated staff on site at forwarders' facilities to provide timely support. However, all these offerings are being offered to the forwarders, and have little to no effect at all in order to stimulate growth demand from the shippers/consignees. In addition, the exponential increase of belly capacity in the past five years and air freight growth being at a much lower pace have created fierce competition among carriers. As a result, carriers are "grabbing" volumes from each other through the same group of forwarders by offering them lower rates. All these have further exacerbated the situation of carrier capacity commoditization.

- *The current business model has impacted carriers' capacity and desire to invest in IT.*
  Due to this current model, carriers have relied on forwarders to communicate with customers because carriers do not interact with shippers/consignees directly. As a result, carriers have not invested in IT capabilities in the same fashion as forwarders or integrators have done, and they oftentimes do not have the required IT capabilities to provide complete shipment visibility. In today's digital world, customers need to have end-to-end visibility simultaneously and information flows instantaneously to all parties around the world. They demand shipment-level visibility as well as single-piece visibility information. Due to the structure of the current business model,

carriers' investments in IT on the cargo side have not kept pace with market demand. The IT system functionalities are lagging other industries, even significantly behind the IT capabilities on the passenger side. It would be unimaginable for the passenger side not to have a robust and user-friendly portal and mobile apps for consumers to book online, receive confirmation and proactive communications at any time, anywhere. It is all-digital and consumers have a number of options regarding how they want to receive the information. In contrast, cargo booking can be done online, and everything else is still pretty much manual and significantly lagging other industries.

Despite all the challenges this model creates for carriers, forwarders feel pained in this model and are being impacted while acting as a middle man. They are being constantly pressured by shippers and consignees to reduce shipping cost, and feel that they have been squeezed hard in the middle.

Given all the above challenges, it is obvious that cargo as an industry needs to be reinvented and transformed. It needs innovation to make it better and sustainable. The question is: What can carriers do in order to transform the industry and manage their cargo business more effectively? Or is the industry better served if IT companies such as Google, Amazon, Facebook and the like seize the opportunity to transform the industry by providing disruptive service offerings?

To begin with, airline carriers need to clearly understand the position of their cargo business, and the role cargo plays in the overall organization. If cargo is not the main focus of the belly carriers, then these carriers need to manage their network capacity more efficiently so that it can offer its capacity at a lower rate without taking a significant hit to its margins and bottom line. The downside of this is further erosion of margins when additional capacity comes into the marketplace. If the belly carriers and carriers with freighters determine cargo as an integral part of the company's growth and as critically important to create a sustainable model going forward, below are some observations/recommendations:

- Transform the business model by going customer-direct or at least partially customer-direct at the initial stage. This will alleviate a number of pain points identified previously. It will help strengthen the brand equity on both passenger and cargo side, improve service reliability and streamline customer communications. In the end, it will stimulate growth demand and give carriers more control over their own assets and increase network utilization.
- Enhance service reliability by focusing on execution processes and investing in IT infrastructure and capabilities. Now that carriers can directly communicate and transact with customers, they have a better understanding of customers' needs and challenges. In turn, they can use their resources in the most impactful areas to make a difference in

service execution, and ultimately change the customers' perception of service reliability. This will also help carriers differentiate themselves in the marketplace and help position their services at a premium rate.

- Explore e-commerce opportunities by either investing in in-house IT or partnering with an e-commerce company. In recent years, e-commerce has been growing rapidly worldwide; e-commerce giants such as Amazon and Alibaba are constantly looking into new ways of better managing their logistics and supply chains. If carriers are committed to improving their IT capabilities or partnering with other IT companies, this could provide an opportunity for carriers to better align their services with end customers.

However, if carriers do not take serious actions to transform their businesses, the chances are that an IT company, a 4PL (integrator) or even a risk insurer could enter the industry and change the cargo world. As a matter of fact, Uber has been piloting a new service offering called Uber Cargo in Hong Kong. It is true that currently Uber only offers cargo services for short-distance movement needs, but this could be the start of a string of innovative service offerings. In addition, Bloomberg News recently reported that "a 2013 report to Amazon's senior management team proposed an aggressive global expansion of the company's Fulfillment By Amazon service, which provides storage, packing and shipping for independent merchants selling products on the company's website." The report also "envisioned a global delivery network that controls the flow of goods from factories ... to customer doorsteps. *Merchants will be able to book cargo space online or via mobile devices, creating what Amazon described as a 'one click-ship for seamless international trade and shipping.' It will also create a 'revolutionary system that will automate the entire international supply chain and eliminate much of the legacy waste associated with document handling and freight booking.'*" As this happens, the result of the revolutionary system remains to be seen in the near future, but the immediate impact on all the players in the cargo industry is huge, especially for carriers and forwarders. The fact that the cargo industry has been stagnant for the past several decades increases its vulnerability to disruptive innovations and provides opportunities for companies such as Amazon.

Another note worth sharing is the impact of internet connectivity and how it has disrupted certain industries. Airbnb has significantly disrupted the established hoteliers, and so has Uber the taxi services by connecting the users directly with the asset owners. It is not hard to imagine an innovator such as Amazon who can connect all the dots through the combination of IT capabilities and industry know how to revolutionize cargo shipping and global supply chain. At that point, carriers will be just a source for capacity, which will be completely commoditized and purchased with just a few clicks.

Finally, what's happening on the cargo side would be a good reminder for passenger businesses to continue innovative services in order to avoid similar situations. Otherwise, online travel agents, Google, Facebook and Amazon could potentially become the 4PL-type service providers on the passenger side. They would be able to provide all the services a traveler needs – from rental cars, to air tickets, to hotel selections, and could disconnect carriers from their customers with just a few clicks. Passenger carriers will lose their brand in the marketplace and will be facing similar challenges to those cargo carriers are facing today.

INDEX

Taylor & Francis eBooks

Helping you to choose the right eBooks for your Library

Add Routledge titles to your library's digital collection today. Taylor and Francis ebooks contains over 50,000 titles in the Humanities, Social Sciences, Behavioural Sciences, Built Environment and Law.

Choose from a range of subject packages or create your own!

Benefits for you

- » Free MARC records
- » COUNTER-compliant usage statistics
- » Flexible purchase and pricing options
- » All titles DRM-free.

Benefits for your user

- » Off-site, anytime access via Athens or referring URL
- » Print or copy pages or chapters
- » Full content search
- » Bookmark, highlight and annotate text
- » Access to thousands of pages of quality research at the click of a button.

REQUEST YOUR **FREE** INSTITUTIONAL TRIAL TODAY

Free Trials Available
We offer free trials to qualifying academic, corporate and government customers.

eCollections – Choose from over 30 subject eCollections, including:

Archaeology	Language Learning
Architecture	Law
Asian Studies	Literature
Business & Management	Media & Communication
Classical Studies	Middle East Studies
Construction	Music
Creative & Media Arts	Philosophy
Criminology & Criminal Justice	Planning
Economics	Politics
Education	Psychology & Mental Health
Energy	Religion
Engineering	Security
English Language & Linguistics	Social Work
Environment & Sustainability	Sociology
Geography	Sport
Health Studies	Theatre & Performance
History	Tourism, Hospitality & Events

For more information, pricing enquiries or to order a free trial, please contact your local sales team: www.tandfebooks.com/page/sales

Routledge
Taylor & Francis Group

The home of
Routledge books

www.tandfebooks.com